RUSSIA
AT THE
BARRICADES

RUSSIA
AT THE
BARRICADES

EYEWITNESS ACCOUNTS
OF THE AUGUST 1991 COUP

EDITED BY
VICTORIA E. BONNELL,
ANN COOPER, AND GREGORY FREIDIN

M.E. Sharpe
Armonk, New York
London, England

Library of Congress Cataloging-in-Publication Data

Russia at the barricades : eyewitness accounts of the August 1991 coup /
edited by Victoria E. Bonnell, Ann Cooper, and Gregory Freidin.
p. cm.
Includes index.
ISBN 1–56324–271–0 (cloth)   ISBN 1-56324-272-9 (pbk.)
1. Soviet Union—History—Attempted coup. 1991—Personal narratives.
2. Soviet Union—History—Attempted coup. 1991—Sources.
I. Bonnell, Victoria, E.
II. Cooper, Ann.
III. Freidin, Gregory.
DK292.R86 1991
947.085'4'0922—dc20 93–27944
CIP

Printed in the United States of America

The paper used in this publication meets the minimum requirements of
American National Standard for Information Sciences—
Permanence of Paper for Printed Library Materials,
ANSI Z 39.48-1984.

∞

BM (c)   10   9   8   7   6   5   4   3   2   1
BM (p)   10   9   8   7   6   5   4   3   2   1

To our children, Anna Freidin and Tom Keller

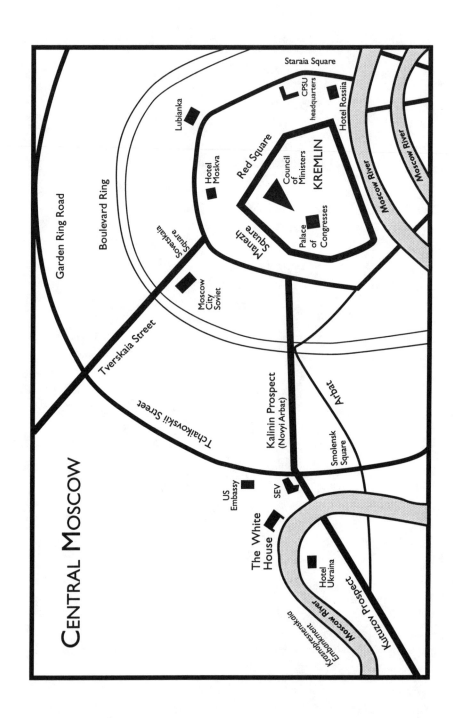

CENTRAL MOSCOW

Contents

List of Photographs

Preface

On August 19, 1991, eight high-ranking Soviet officials took over the government of the USSR by force and proclaimed themselves the country's new rulers. Less than seventy-two hours later, their attempt to seize power had collapsed. Though short-lived, the coup produced consequences few could have foreseen. Soon afterward, the Communist Party that had ruled Russia since 1917 was suspended and dispossessed. Five months after the coup, the Soviet Union itself had ceased to exist.

The editors of this volume had the good fortune to witness at close range the monumental events that shook Russia and the world in August 1991. Ann Cooper, the National Public Radio bureau chief in Moscow since 1986, was covering a story in Vilnius, Lithuania, when the coup began. By the end of the day she was back in Moscow. Victoria E. Bonnell, a sociologist at the University of California, Berkeley, and Gregory Freidin, a former Muscovite who teaches Russian literature at Stanford University, arrived in Moscow on August 15 to do research and visit friends and family.

Experienced though we all were in observing and writing about Soviet affairs, we found ourselves overwhelmed and astonished by the tremendous power of the events. With millions of others in Moscow, St. Petersburg, and throughout the Soviet Union and the world, we watched with horror and fascination as the junta sought to turn back the clock to a time—a mere six years earlier!—when a corrupt and brutal Communist party-state had ruled Russia.

Several months after the event, the three editors reunited in Berkeley, California. Despite the time that had passed, we still felt the magnetism of the August days, when democratic reforms were suddenly in jeopardy, and the whole country teetered precariously on the brink of a civil war.

To do honor to the events and their participants and to preserve the vibrancy of the moment, we decided to put together this collection of eyewitness accounts of the three fateful days in August. We wanted to show the events from a variety of points of view—those of the plotters, the leaders of the democratic resistance, foreign and Russian journalists, visiting émigrés and scholars, military officers and ordinary citizens of diverse occupations. Our accounts concentrate on Moscow, where most of the key events were played out. St. Petersburg (then still called Leningrad), the provincial city of Saratov, and the Tajik capital of Dushanbe are represented as well. We have included some documents, such as the major declarations and decrees issued by the Emergency Committee and by Russian President Boris Yeltsin, to provide the context for the August events.

Above all, we have tried to give a sense of what it was like to be there and to see with one's own eyes how the people of Russia, as George Kennan put it, "turned their back on the manner in which they've been ruled—not just in the Soviet period but in the centuries before. . . . Even 1917 had nothing quite like this" (*New York Times*, August 24, 1991).

Acknowledgments

The editors would like to thank George Breslauer, who gave us the idea for this volume. Gail Lapidus provided valuable and timely support for the project through the Berkeley-Stanford Program on Soviet and Post-Soviet Studies. Without research assistance, the volume would have been far longer in the making.

When we began work on the volume, we placed a notice in the newsletter of the American Association for the Advancement of Slavic Studies inviting contributions. We received quite a number of responses, and some of them have been included here. We regret that we could not publish all of them, and we thank those contributors whose work did not fit the final format of the book. Dorothy Atkinson was especially helpful in alerting us to material and potential authors for the volume.

The project benefited greatly from the assistance of several Berkeley graduate students. Special thanks to Howard Allen, Jeffrey Rossman, and especially Veljko Vujacic. George Breslauer, Victor Zaslavsky, and Veljko Vujacic gave us valuable comments and suggestions on the introduction. We also appreciate the help we received from Donald J. Raleigh, David Hartsough, and Irina Mikhaleva and Marianna Freidina in Moscow.

Most of the translations from Russian that appear in this volume are by Gregory Freidin. We have found it necessary, in many instances, to retranslate well-known documents and speeches because of inadequacies in wire-service and newspaper translations. Howard Allen, Jeffrey Rossman, and Veljko Vujacic also contributed to the translations.

At M.E. Sharpe, Patricia Kolb's enthusiasm for the project gave us the burst of energy we needed to finish it. She provided excellent assistance, and we thank her and her colleagues for bringing out the book so expeditiously. Leona Schecter also provided valuable advice along the way.

Some of the selections in this volume originally appeared elsewhere, mostly in Russian newspapers and journals. The editors would like to thank these publications for permission to reprint the following articles:

Gregory Freidin, "To the Barricades: A Street-Level View of Moscow, August 19," *The New Republic*, September 30, 1991.
Vladimir Petrik, "Moscow's M.V. Khrunichev Machine-Building Factory Reacts to the August Coup," *Literaturnaia gazeta*, January 1, 1992.
Nikolai Vorontsov, "Minutes of the Council of Ministers Meeting, August 19, 1991," *Komsomolskaia pravda*, August 24, 1991.
Interview with Yevgenii Shaposhnikov, "The Coup and the Armed Forces," *Nezavisimaia gazeta*, September 12, 1991.
Interview with Anatolii Sobchak, "The Breakthrough: The Coup in St. Petersburg," *Moscow News*, August 26, 1991.
Interview with Aleksandr Yakovlev, "Our Children Were on the Barricades," *Ogonëk*, no. 36 (August 31–September 7, 1991).
Interview with Aleksandr Prokhanov, "Defenders of the White House," *Komsomolskaia pravda*, September 3, 1991.
Michael Hetzer, "Death on the Streets," *Guardian*, August 23, 1991.
"A Man in the Crowd," *Ogonëk*, no. 41 (October 5–12, 1991).
Iain Elliot, "Three Days in August: On-the-Spot Impressions," RFE/RL Research Institute, *Report on the USSR*, vol. 3, no. 36 (September 6, 1991).
Interview with Tatiana Malkina, "The August 19 Press Conference," *Ogonëk*, no. 41 (October 5–12, 1991).

Photo Credits

Cover illustration and photographs on pages 80, 87, 89, 96, 97, 103, 174, and 250 courtesy of the PhotoGroup of the White House Defenders (PhotoArt, Moscow).
Photographs on pages 73, 75, 76, 82, 94, 99, 102, and 105 by Gregory Freidin.
Photographs on pages 90, 91, 92, and 98 by Victoria E. Bonnell and Sandor Szabo.
Photograph on page 140 by Donald J. Raleigh.
Photographs on pages 150, 152, and 156 courtesy of Vladimir Zavorotnyi.

Note on Transliteration and Interpolations

We follow the Library of Congress system for transliterating Russian words into English, but have made some exceptions in the interest of readability. Throughout, we have omitted soft signs, and we use a "Y" to begin such names as Yakovlev, Yevtushenko, and Yurii. More generally, we have adopted the *New York Times* usage for well-known names, titles, and places.

The reader will also note that we have used two different conventions for interpolations into the text. If the interpolation is by the author or interviewee, it appears in parentheses. If it was made by the editors for the purpose of clarification or identification, it appears in square brackets.

The explanatory footnotes that appear in the volume were supplied by the editors.

Guide to the Print Media

The following Russian media are mentioned in the book under their Russian names. English translations of these titles are as follows:

Periodicals

Argumenty i fakty (Arguments and Facts)
Den (Day)
Izvestiia (Information)
Kommersant (Man of Commerce)
Kommunist (Communist)
Komsomolskaia pravda (Komsomol Truth)
Kuranty (Chimes)
Literaturnaia gazeta (Literary Gazette)
Literaturnaia Rossiia (Literary Russia)
Magnitogorskii rabochii (Magnitogorsk Worker)
Moskovskii komsomolets (Moscow Komsomol Member)
Moskovskie novosti (Moscow News)
Moskovskaia pravda (Moscow Truth)
Nevskoe vremia (Neva Times)
Nezavisimaia gazeta (Independent Gazette)
Obshchaia gazeta (Joint Gazette)
Ogonëk (Flicker)
Pravda (Truth)
Rossiia (Russia)
Rossiiskaia gazeta (Russian Gazette)
Rossiiskie vesti (Russian News)
Smena (New Generation)
Stolitsa (The Capital)
Vecherniaia Moskva (Evening Moscow)

News Agencies

TASS (Telegrafnoe agenstvo Sovetskogo Soiuza): the official news agency of the Soviet Union

ITAR-TASS (Informatsionnoe telegrafnoe agenstvo Rossii–TASS): the Russian wire service–TASS

RIA (Rossisskoe informatsionnoe agenstvo, or Russian Information Agency): the official news agency of the RSFSR

Novosti: semi-official news agency of the USSR

Interfax: an independent news agency

Postfactum: an independent news agency

RUSSIA
AT THE
BARRICADES

VICTORIA E. BONNELL AND GREGORY FREIDIN

Introduction

The events of August 1991 can best be understood as a consequence of the reform program put into motion by Mikhail Gorbachev and his closest allies, Aleksandr Yakovlev and Eduard Shevardnadze, following Gorbachev's appointment as General Secretary of the Communist Party of the Soviet Union in March 1985. Recognizing that the country faced severe and intractable economic and social problems that had long been neglected, Gorbachev and his team embarked on a series of fundamental reforms of the Soviet system. In a December 1988 meeting with U.S. President George Bush, Gorbachev described his intentions:

> You'll see soon enough that I'm not doing this for show and I'm not doing this to undermine you or to surprise you or to take advantage of you. I'm playing real politics. I'm doing this because I need to. I'm doing this because there's a revolution taking place in my country. I started it. And they all applauded me when I started it in 1986 and now they don't like it so much, but it's going to be a revolution, nonetheless.[1]

Experts disagree as to how much of Gorbachev's revolutionary program should be attributed to his team's original plans and how much to the unanticipated consequences of the initial reforms.[2] But few would deny that the changes that took place were significant and far-reaching. The introduction of *glasnost*—a policy of increasing openness in the mass media—irrevocably transformed the political culture of the country. Beginning in November 1987, Gorbachev relinquished the Communist Party's monopoly on truth. Encouraged from above, intellectuals and political activists saw to it that a pluralism of ideas quickly replaced the Leninist idea of a single truth defined by a single party, disseminated by propagandists, and backed up by censorship. By 1990, with the revision of Article 6 of the Soviet Constitution, which had guaranteed the Communist Party's "leading role" in political and social life, there was virtually no subject that could not be discussed openly in the media or other public forums. Society was now able to challenge the Party's preeminence on all fronts, and the Party, as was becoming increasingly clear, was not up to the challenge.

In the political sphere, the Gorbachev reforms led to a restructuring —*perestroika*—of the system of government, which since 1917 had been firmly controlled by the Communist Party. Representative bodies, from local soviets to the Supreme Soviet of the USSR, were staffed in single-candidate elections and functioned as rubber stamps for decisions taken at the higher echelons of the Communist Party apparatus. Gorbachev revamped these pseudo-democratic institutions. His first major innovation was the creation of the USSR Congress of People's Deputies as a national assembly that would select the standing legislature—the Supreme Soviet—from among its members. Two-thirds of the deputies to the new Congress were chosen in elections in the spring of 1989, and—in a radical break with the Communist past— many of these were free elections with competing candidates. The remainder of the deputies were selected by so-called "public organizations," including such stalwarts of the old regime as the "official" trade unions and, of course, the Communist Party. (Gorbachev himself chose to become a deputy not by election, which he could easily have won, but through the Communist Party quota—a decision that deprived him of any popular mandate, with fateful consequences for his future in politics.) Similar legislative institutions were then created at the republic level (elections for Russia's Congress of People's Deputies took place in 1990), and, for the first time, genuine elections for local soviets were held in cities throughout the country.

Though often dominated by old-guard elements (including Party bureaucrats, industrial managers, and military officers), the new legislatures provided a powerful forum for discussion of a wide range of political opinion. Most important, they made it possible for *democratic* politicians, like Andrei Sakharov and Boris Yeltsin, to speak directly to the Soviet public. Incessant television coverage of parliamentary debates and political commentary practically took over the air waves and the print media. The secretive or largely ceremonial politicking of the Soviet era gave way to full-blown political theater, open to all. For a while it seemed that the whole country was glued to television sets, watching the thrust and parry between Gorbachev and Sakharov and clashes between the liberal deputies of the Interregional Group and the conservatives of the "Soiuz" (Union) faction. In the process, the political horizons of the attentive public expanded so much that what seemed only yesterday a daring political move appeared today as an exercise in timid half-measures—and would be seen tomorrow as a betrayal of democracy.

The heady atmosphere of those days was propitious for the creation of voluntary associations, and they quickly proliferated during the Gorbachev era, evolving into a multitude of political parties and movements with diverse aims. These opportunities for open expression and political involvement helped to draw people into new forms of activism in the public sphere. At first encouraged, protected, indeed nurtured by glasnost and perestroika, the new political activists eventually began to chafe under the restrictions implicit in these policies. Little by little, they distanced themselves from Gorbachev, whose position (or, some would say, convictions) did not allow him to stray too far from the center of the Soviet political spectrum.

Nowhere was this process more evident than in the Baltic republics, where the first advocates of glasnost and perestroika soon emerged as champions of national independence. In a matter of months after the first free elections, this phenomenon spread throughout the Soviet Union, not excluding its heartland, the largest republic of them all— the Russian Federation.

At the republic level, the new legislative bodies, in which former dissidents sat side by side with old-style Soviet bosses, did not take long to develop their own political dynamic. The "democrats," who were gaining in authority at the expense of the Party but still had little power, and Party apparatchiks, who held on to the levers of power but were losing their mantle of authority, found common ground on issues of nationalism—the ideological heir of communism in the modern world. Across the Soviet Union they formed powerful coalitions to challenge the authority of "the center," namely, the top Soviet political elite presided over by Gorbachev. By the summer of 1991, many republics, acting through the newly elected legislatures, had declared their sovereignty. Among them was the Russian Soviet Federated Socialist Republic, led by its newly elected President, Boris Yeltsin.

For the first time since the revolution of 1917, the integrity of the empire was threatened from within. Whether they sought disintegration or opposed it, most responsible and foresighted politicians, among them Gorbachev and Yeltsin, understood that the old Union structure had to be replaced by a new arrangement that would transfer much of the center's power to the republics. This became especially clear after Moscow's attempt to overthrow the nationalist government in Lithuania in January 1991 ended in bloodshed and failure. In an effort to institutionalize the new *status quo* in relations with the center, Gorbachev and the heads of nine republics (the Baltic states, Moldova, Georgia, and Armenia did not participate) drafted a new Union Treaty, initialed the final version of it, and agreed to have it signed on August 20, 1991. It was to prevent this from coming to pass that opponents of change attempted their coup d'état on August 18.[3]

Another important aspect of perestroika was the program of economic restructuring. Although the Gorbachev government failed to move decisively in the direction of a market economy, it did create opportunities for certain types of private enterprise, known by the catch-all term *kooperativy*, or cooperatives. This easing of central controls over economic activity made it possible for people to leave employment in the state sector for the first time since the 1920s, and by August 1991, new groups of private entrepreneurs had proliferated throughout the country.

* * *

It should not be surprising that the policies of glasnost and perestroika found some of their most ardent supporters among urban, educated, "middle-class" citizens who appreciated—and took advantage of—the new opportunities for individual and collective activity in the economy and in politics. This group emerged as a critically important new force in the country during the Gorbachev era.

At the same time, three pillars of the old system still clung to the resources and power, if not the authority, that they had enjoyed throughout the Soviet era: the military-industrial complex, which included a large part of the heavy industrial sector of the command economy; the all-pervasive Committee for State Security, the KGB; and above it all, the Communist Party of the Soviet Union, or more precisely its central apparatus, which controlled virtually all top government appointments from the revolution of 1917 until August 1991. Whether for lack of will or lack of power, out of tactical considerations or out of conviction, and most likely for all of these reasons at once, Gorbachev did not break with the Communist Party. Yet his policies continuously undermined the position and authority of the Party apparatus and fostered the emergence of reform groups within the Party at all levels as well as rival political movements outside the Party.

Until its suspension on August 24, 1991, the Communist Party was the sole political organization spanning the entire Soviet Union. Using the art of political maneuver of which he was a consummate practitioner, Gorbachev tried to enlist the Party in the cause of reform and to use its organizational resources as a counterweight to the centrifugal forces that were pulling the country apart. This paradox lies at the heart of Gorbachev's achievement, but it was the cause of his failure as well. In the year preceding the coup, grassroots political forces that Gorbachev himself had helped to unleash were becoming increasingly radicalized in frustration over the seemingly slow pace of change. At the same time, conservative elements within the Party were stiffening their resistance to reform. To placate them, Gorbachev retained key conservative figures in his government even as he was preparing to sign the new Union Treaty that would have dealt a fatal blow to their power.

As political forces polarized, Gorbachev moved first in one direction and then the other. The result was that Gorbachev appeared timid and indecisive as he repeatedly drew back from the bold strategies proposed by some of his more radical economic advisers. At the top, there was a gradual attrition among liberal politicians, including those most intimately associated with the post-1985 reforms—Aleksandr Yakovlev, Eduard Shevardnadze, and Vadim Bakatin. Foreign Minister Shevardnadze's resignation from his post drew world attention; yet his dramatic warning of an impending coup d'état—"Dictatorship is coming!"—spoken from the high rostrum of the Congress of People's Deputies in December 1990, seemed to fall on deaf ears. Gorbachev's apparent acquiescence in the use of brute force to suppress the nationalist movements in the Baltic republics, and, especially, the bloody attack on Lithuania's parliament building in January 1991, cost him support among the democrats while not winning him many friends among the conservatives, who had grown to mistrust him personally as much as they mistrusted his policy of reform.

In the months preceding the coup there were many signs that conservative forces—a coalition of leading officials in the RSFSR Communist Party and key members of the KGB, the Ministry of Internal Affairs (MVD), and the armed forces, along with some well-known ultra-nationalist Russian writers—were coalescing in opposition to reformist policies.[4]

In mid-June, critics of perestroika in the government leadership—including future putschists Valentin Pavlov, Dmitrii Yazov, Boris Pugo, and Vladimir Kriuchkov—attempted to carry out a "constitutional coup d'état" by expanding the powers of Prime Minister Pavlov, an outspoken opponent of the new Union Treaty which was then being negotiated. Their efforts failed.

On July 23, 1991, twelve Soviet leaders, including high-ranking army officers, published a dramatic appeal in the conservative newspaper *Sovetskaia Rossiia* which called on "citizens of the Soviet Union" to resist the breakup of the country, allegedly being engineered by greedy capitalists, foreign-directed elements, and cunning apostates. Hitherto such charges predictably had issued from the lunatic fringe of the conservative opposition. Not so this time: the signatories included such powerful figures as Colonel General Boris Gromov, the Deputy Minister of Internal Affairs and a hero of the Afghan War. This appeal, published under the title "A Word to the People," prefigured many of the arguments put forward by the putschists less than a month later. With its special reference to the role of the armed forces in preserving "Holy Russia," this statement brought into the open the possibility of a military seizure of power.

Both former Foreign Minister Shevardnadze and Aleksandr Yakovlev felt sufficiently alarmed by the course of events to issue repeated warnings of an impending coup.[5] In June 1991, Secretary of State James Baker conveyed to Gorbachev, through secure channels, a report that Pavlov, Yazov, and Kriuchkov were plotting his overthrow. But Gorbachev refused to follow up these and other alarm bells with decisive action.[6] In an interview conducted in August 1991, only a few days after the attempted coup, Shevardnadze was asked why Gorbachev had failed to take action to prevent a seizure of power by high-ranking officials, most of whom he had appointed. Shevardnadze replied:

Most likely, he did not understand; probably he did not want to understand. Therein lies the whole tragedy, the whole trouble. This feature is characteristic of many leaders. There are numerous examples throughout history where a person does not want to believe that terrible things are going on. In my opinion, this is what happened with Mikhail Sergeevich. And this grieves me tremendously. It has cost the country dearly.[7]

The immediate circumstance that precipitated the coup was the signing ceremony for the new Union Treaty, scheduled for August 20. The treaty would have granted supremacy to the laws of the republics in many areas and permanently curtailed the power of the central government—and with it, Communist Party rule. Conservatives, among others, were especially indignant when Gorbachev did not make public the text of the new Union Treaty. Even cabinet ministers had no access to the text until a draft version fell into the hands of the editors of *Moscow News*, who published it a few days before the coup.[8] There was also suspicion that Gorbachev may have struck a secret deal with the G7 leaders with whom he had met in London in July, leaving Prime Minister Valentin Pavlov out of the negotiations.[9]

Although the impending Union Treaty was the galvanizing event, there were other factors that aroused the plotters to action.[10] Gorbachev's skill at maneuvering between the opposite ends of the political spectrum had been making conservatives seasick for a number of years. From their point of view, the worst turn had come in April 1991. From September 1990 to April 1991 it had seemed that Gorbachev had thrown in his lot with the old guard. How outraged they must have been when Gorbachev suddenly struck an alliance with Boris Yeltsin (who had publicly resigned from the Communist Party the previous July) and embraced a number of important economic and political reforms in the months preceding the coup. One item high on the conservatives' bill of particulars was Yeltsin's ban on the workplace activities of political parties in the Russian Federation, issued on July 20, not long after his election as President of Russia. Clearly directed against the Communist Party, since it spelled an end to the Party's grassroot system of control, the ban caused great consternation among conservatives. Worse yet, their failure to force Yeltsin to rescind this decree demonstrated unmistakably that the Party, the erstwhile colossus, had lost its iron grip.

All of these developments, moreover, took place against the background of a deteriorating economic situation. By mid-summer, there were strong indications of impending shortages of fuel and food, as the command system collapsed and republics and even localities set up protectionist barriers to guard local supplies.

Feeling increasingly irrelevant, afraid that Gorbachev's next maneuver would throw them overboard, the plotters resolved to take action. The decisive meeting of the conspirators took place on August 16 at a KGB resort on the outskirts of Moscow.[11]

* * *

When the coup began on Sunday, August 18, 1991, Gorbachev was vacationing with his family in Foros, on the Crimean peninsula. The plotters' first act was to send a delegation to Foros—led by Valerii Boldin, the President's Chief of Staff, along with Yurii Plekhanov, Chief of the Security Directorate of the KGB—to seek Gorbachev's own sanction for the takeover. Some of the plotters, it appears, believed that, although he might offer resistance at first, Gorbachev would in the end cooperate with them by declaring a state of emergency in the country. After all, he had yielded to pressure from conservatives in the past. Gorbachev, however, refused to play any part in the scheme, calling the instigators "adventurists" and using (in the words of one of the plotters) other "non-parliamentary expressions." Held under house arrest and with no means of communication with the outside world, Gorbachev and his family would remain in complete isolation, unsure of their fate, until the afternoon of Wednesday, August 21.

Gorbachev's refusal to play along with their plans disoriented the conspirators, but they decided to proceed with the takeover, in the hope that the country would welcome their move as heralding a respite from disruptive change and mounting disorder.

* * *

In the early morning of Monday, August 19, troops were mobilized in the vicinity of Moscow and large numbers of tanks and armored personnel carriers (APCs) began moving toward the city. Beginning at 6:00 A.M. Moscow time, the country awoke to television and radio broadcasts announcing the formation of the State Committee for the

State of Emergency.[12] The junta consisted of eight men, seven of them high-ranking members of the government and all of them identified with the top echelon of the party-state: Vice President Gennadii Yanaev; KGB chief Vladimir Kriuchkov; Defense Minister Dmitrii Yazov; Minister of Internal Affairs Boris Pugo; Prime Minister Valentin Pavlov; Oleg Baklanov, First Deputy Chairman of the National Defense Council and leader of the military-industrial complex; Vasilii Starodubtsev, Chairman of the Peasants' Union; and Aleksandr Tiziakov, President of the Association of State Enterprises and Industrial Groups in Production, Construction, Transportation, and Communications and member of the Council of Ministers.

The Committee's first public statements announced the imposition of a state of emergency in the country to rescue "our great Motherland" from the "mortal danger" that loomed over it. The form as much as the content of these statements indicated clearly that the Emergency Committee wished to turn back the clock to an earlier era, to restore the law and order once commanded by an all-powerful Communist Party, and to preserve the Soviet Union as a unitary state.

Yet it was also obvious that the conspirators wanted to give a constitutional gloss to their actions, for the benefit of the Soviet population as much as the rest of the world. Although in clear violation of the Law on the State of Emergency,[13] they claimed to be acting in accordance with certain articles of the USSR Constitution (adopted in 1977, but much amended since 1988). Article 127(7) of the Constitution provided for a transfer of power to the Vice President of the USSR if the President was for any reason "unable to continue to execute his duties." (Throughout the coup, the Committee would maintain the pretext that Gorbachev was incapacitated by health problems.) Ironically, this effort to formulate a constitutional justification for the seizure of power suggests that, as one commentator observed, "the reform process begun by Gorbachev ha[d] been effective in introducing some semblance of the rule of law in the USSR."[14]

By mid-morning on Monday, large numbers of tanks and APCs and truckloads of soldiers had begun to enter the city of Moscow. Later that day, both Moscow and Leningrad (now St. Petersburg) were placed under martial law. Although martial law was not formally imposed in the Baltic republics, troops began moving there, too, and the commander of the Baltic Military District declared that he was assuming control of the region.[15]

Popular resistance to the takeover did not appear immediately. The galvanizing force was Boris Yeltsin, the newly elected President of the Russian Federation. On Monday morning Yeltsin issued an "Appeal to the Citizens of Russia," denouncing the takeover as illegal and calling for popular resistance, including a general strike. At midday Yeltsin mounted a tank near the building known as the White House (the House of Soviets, which housed the Russian government) and made an appeal to soldiers and officers, exhorting them to give their allegiance to the government of the Russian Federation.

In the late afternoon, at around 5:00 P.M. the Emergency Committee held a televised press conference, open to Soviet and foreign press. Speaking in a booming, authoritative voice, but with his hands visibly trembling, Vice President Yanaev, ostensibly the leader of the coup, offered the junta's case for the takeover. Without producing any evidence for his assertion, Yanaev repeatedly declared that Gorbachev was ill and would eventually, Yanaev hoped, resume his duties.

That same evening, in one of those odd twists that abounded during the coup, the image of Yeltsin on a tank, captured by a CNN camera, was beamed to millions of Soviet viewers on the news program "Vremia." This icon of defiance was part of a remarkable five-minute segment on "Vremia" about the appearance of a democratic resistance to the coup in the country's capital. Put together by television journalist Sergei Medvedev, the short segment conveyed a vast amount of information: the tanks rolling down the streets of Moscow, Yeltsin's "Appeal to the Citizens of Russia," the building of barricades, and the massing of people determined to defend the White House from attack. Medvedev's report on the evening news, following a taped rebroadcast of the Emergency Committee's press conference, helped to turn the tide against the coup d'état.[16]

As motorized armor converged on the streets of Moscow—over six hundred pieces, not counting the trucks carrying soldiers in full battle gear—people began erecting barricades, some in Manezh Square (a large plaza near Red Square where big rallies are held) and many more outside the White House. In some cases, people stopped the movement of tanks and APCs by forming a human chain.

Many among the first barricade-builders understood that the putschists were using a tried-and-true Soviet technique, one that had been used successfully all over Eastern Europe in the years after World War II: while tanks surround the government headquarters, a junta offers the alternative of "national salvation" through Party-imposed order. Most recently the scenario had been employed in Vilnius, Lithuania, in January 1991. This time, however—unlike Hungary in 1956, Czechoslovakia in 1968, and Poland in 1981, where coups d'état had been carried out under the cover of the Cold War and with totalitarian controls—Lithuania stood firm. Indeed, the Lithuanians enjoyed broad and vocal public support among Russia's intelligentsia and democratic politicians, and the "Committee for National Salvation" failed to take power.

Thanks to the Vilnius example, and to Sergei Medvedev's brief but incisive "Vremia" report about the barricade-building in Moscow, Russian citizens knew what they had to do: defend the White House, the seat of their freely elected government. That the putschists expected to succeed in Moscow (where close to 80 percent had voted to elect Yeltsin President)[17] with a plan that had not worked in Vilnius speaks volumes about the plotters' general competence, political imagination, and horizons.

A major change in the alignment of forces occurred as early as 10:00 P.M. on Monday night, when several tanks from the Taman Division, stationed in the vicinity of the White House, declared their loyalty to Russia and moved to defend the building, cheered on by a large crowd that had been gathering since the early afternoon. An hour later, eight armored scout vehicles flying the Russian tricolor arrived to protect the White House; they were led by Major General Aleksandr Lebed, under orders from the commander of the airborne paratroop forces, Colonel General Pavel Grachev.[18] These were the first indications of divided loyalties within the military.

Meanwhile, in Leningrad, Mayor Anatolii Sobchak had hastily returned from Moscow to take charge of the democratic resistance. One of his first acts was to reach an agreement with local military officers to keep tanks and APCs out of the city. In the evening he delivered a rousing televised speech, calling for resistance and urging people to attend a protest rally the following day. From that time on, the Leningrad television station transmitted information in support of the democratic resistance.

On August 20, the second day of the coup, large rallies were held in Leningrad and Moscow. The Leningrad rally, attended by an estimated 130,000 to 300,000 people, took place in Palace Square. The Moscow rally, variously estimated at 70,000 to 150,000 people, was held at noon in front of the White House.[19] Yeltsin and other major political figures from the democratic resistance addressed the Moscow rally and appealed to citizens to defend the White House against an imminent military attack.[20] As many as 70,000 people—among them students and young people, middle-class Muscovites in their thirties and forties, and a large contingent of veterans of the war in Afghanistan—responded to Yeltsin's call. They streamed to the White House and, despite the curfew declared by the Military Commandant of Moscow, they stayed there through the night, forming self-defense units.

An attack on the White House was expected in the early hours of Wednesday morning. Shortly after midnight, shots rang out about half a mile away: a column of APCs had found itself trapped by the barricades blocking an underpass a couple of blocks from the U.S. Embassy. As the APCs tried to ram through a row of trolleycars, a mêlée ensued in which three young men died defending the barricade. This incident notwithstanding, evidence indicates that there was no concerted attack mounted on the seat of Russia's government, although an attack—a brutal one—had been planned and ordered. Soon afterward, tanks and APCs began to depart from the city. At 9:25 A.M., Marshal Yazov, one of the plotters, resigned his post, and the coup leadership, or what remained of it, rapidly collapsed.

On Wednesday morning an emergency session of the Supreme Soviet of Russia convened at the White House. A high-level delegation from the Russian government was dispatched to the Crimea to rescue Gorbachev and his family, who would return to Moscow shortly after midnight. Meanwhile, most of the plotters were arrested.

The following day, Thursday, August 22, was officially proclaimed the Day of Freedom. Banned newspapers began to publish again, and television and radio programs resumed their regular schedules. Yeltsin made an appearance before the Russian parliament where he thanked Muscovites for having defended the White House so courageously.

At noon, tens of thousands of Muscovites gathered at the White House for a victory rally and a march to Red Square. The speeches by Yeltsin, Ivan Silaev of the Russian Council of Ministers, Russian Vice President Aleksandr Rutskoi, Aleksandr Yakovlev, Eduard Shevardnadze, and other leading figures in the democratic movement attributed the victory over the junta to the "people of Moscow," who heroically mobilized to defend freedom against "totalitarianism." The potent admixture of local patriotism and Russian nationalism brought the crowd to a frenzy of delight, with much flag waving and cheering. The speeches continued when the crowds reached Red Square, but Gorbachev was conspicuously absent.

The symbols of victory were everywhere. Many people carried small tricolor flags which had become the symbol of democratic Russia. Later that day, the tricolor was made the official flag of the Russian Republic. The square adjoining the White House was renamed Freedom Square.

On Thursday evening a massive display of fireworks had been arranged to mark the culmination of the day's events. Perhaps the organizers of the festivities conceived of victory day as a Russian version of the Fourth of July or Bastille Day. But these were not the only fireworks. In Dzerzhinskii Square—named for the head of the infamous revolutionary-era Cheka, precursor of the KGB—an angry crowd had gathered in the late afternoon. Some called for an attack on the KGB building, the Lubianka. It was the first time in four days that popular indignation appeared ready to spill over into spontaneous violence. Soon a delegation came from the White House to calm the crowd and dissuade them from rash actions. Some hours later, a mammoth yellow crane, bearing the logo "Krupp," arrived in the square and began dismantling the imposing statue of "Iron Feliks" Dzerzhinskii which stood on a tall pedestal in the center of the square.

Gorbachev conducted a press conference on Thursday evening, his first extended appearance since the conspiracy had begun. Many were surprised that the President had chosen as his first audience the press corps and not the Soviet public at large or the people of Moscow, who had risked their lives to, among other things, secure his freedom. At the press conference, Gorbachev appeared shaken by the events, even contrite, yet still unable to grasp (as his critics put it) that he had returned to a different country. In response to a question about the possible complicity of the CPSU leadership in the attempted coup d'état, Gorbachev equivocated. The impression was further amplified when, in response to another question, Gorbachev launched into his all-too-familiar defense of the "socialist idea." Still the General Secretary of the CPSU, he failed to take advantage of what was, perhaps, the last opportunity to dissociate himself publicly from a party whose leadership had betrayed him and the country by remaining silent during the coup.

The action on Friday, August 23, took place in the sphere of high politics and on television rather than on the streets. For the first time since Monday, Muscovites became spectators rather than actors as the drama of retribution went forward in the chambers of the Russian parliament. Gorbachev and Yeltsin played the leading roles that day as they came face to face for the first time since the crisis began.

Standing like a deposed leader before an angry crowd, Gorbachev was heckled, criticized, interrogated, and disgraced by Yeltsin and other deputies. After Gorbachev finished his address, expressing gratitude to the "Russians" for their role in defeating the plot, Yeltsin walked up to him and insisted that Gorbachev now read aloud the minutes of a meeting of the USSR Council of Ministers held on the first day of the coup, in which Gorbachev's own cabinet betrayed him. Gorbachev hesitated because the authenticity and accuracy of the minutes had not been established, but Yeltsin went on bullying him, and Gorbachev submitted, reading what turned out to be an inaccurate transcript. Then Gorbachev took questions from the deputies.

From time to time, Yeltsin interrupted the proceedings, declaring with a broad grin that "in order to relieve accumulated tension" he would now sign a decree with far-reaching implications for the future of the country. In this way he made public decrees ordering the Communist Party to cease activities in the armed forces serving on the territory of the RSFSR; suspending publication of newspapers that had cooperated with the junta; confiscating Communist Party publishing houses and printing plants and placing them under the Russian government's control; and sealing the headquarters of the Central Committee and suspending the activities of the Communist Party in the Russian Republic, pending an investigation into its role in the coup. This last move had momentous consequences, for it signaled the end of the Party's legal existence in Russia.

On Saturday morning, a massive funeral was held for the three men who had died at the barricades early Wednesday morning. A crowd of tens of thousands of people gathered in Manezh Square to hear speeches made by major political figures, including Gorbachev. Somber and emotional, Gorbachev paid tribute to the three men and announced that he had signed a decree posthumously awarding them the title of Hero of the Soviet Union. The crowd then proceeded to Kalinin Prospect and on to the White House, pausing to hear Yeltsin's funeral oration, perhaps the most powerful speech of his public career. Marching in the funeral procession were Afghan War veterans, Russian Orthodox priests, rabbis, colorfully bedecked Cossacks, and, of course, defenders of the White House carrying a large tricolor flag. Later that day, Gorbachev resigned as General Secretary of the Communist Party of the Soviet Union and suspended the Party's activities, extending to the entire country Yeltsin's decree banning the Party on the territory of the Russian Republic.

* * *

How can we account for the rapid and ignominious defeat of the "gang of eight"? Among the important factors were the ineptitude of the plotters, the general decrepitude of the centralized system of control, and, perhaps most critical at that moment, the Emergency Committee's inability to command authority among the top brass in the military and the KGB. Their orders to arrest Yeltsin and other key political figures were disobeyed (in fact, only four people were arrested during the coup, all of them People's Deputies). The conspirators then failed to cut off communications with the White House even after it became the headquarters of the resistance.[21]

The spokesmen of the Emergency Committee did not make a convincing case for themselves at their one and only press conference, where they were openly ridiculed by members of the Soviet press—all of this broadcast live for the benefit of the entire country. More surprising is the fact that they could not even control the content of the one and only television news program, "Vremia," or the government newspaper *Izvestiia*.[22]

When rumors of a coup had circulated some months earlier, Gorbachev reportedly dismissed the possibility on the grounds that people like Yanaev were incapable of masterminding a takeover. He was wrong about that, but the plot did in fact unfold like a comedy of errors. By the time it was over, two of the conspirators had landed in the hospital (Pavlov and Yazov); one had committed suicide (Pugo);[23] and another lay unconscious in an alcoholic stupor (Yanaev).

But ineptness does not preclude brutality and may even facilitate it. A few days before the coup began, the plotters had placed an order for 250,000 handcuffs, and the Moscow police commandant had 300,000 arrest forms printed in advance. The plotters prepared a list of sixty-nine people, most of them public figures, who were to be arrested. Some of the men involved in the coup gave orders to arrest Yeltsin and shoot civilians at the White House. These orders were not obeyed, as we know now, because commanders such as Colonel General Grachev (subsequently appointed Russia's Minister of Defense), Major General Lebed (subsequently the Commander of the Fourteenth Army), and Major General Viktor Karpukhin (at the time, Commander of the KGB's anti-terrorist "Alpha" brigade, and under pressure from his subordinates) refused to shed the blood of their compatriots.

The internal security forces provide a particularly telling example of the plotters' failure to mobilize key segments of the military behind their effort. Moscow policemen provided the nucleus of Yeltsin's security forces during the coup. The staff and cadets at the Riazan Higher Police Academy and a Moscow platoon of the elite Specialized Designation Police Detachment—known by the Russian acronym OMON—threw their support behind Yeltsin.

Even more critical for the defeat of the putsch was the equivocation and noncooperation within the KGB. An interview with Major General Karpukhin later disclosed the extent of insubordination. According to Karpukhin, he first disobeyed orders on the morning of August 19 when he was instructed to arrest Yeltsin at his country house. Although he was in a position to make the arrest ("My vehicles were staked out around the entire settlement. All roads were blocked . . ."), Karpukhin nonetheless allowed Yeltsin to depart.

On the evening of August 19, Karpukhin participated in a secret meeting of commanding officers at the USSR Ministry of Defense. At that point, Karpukhin had operational command over elite forces numbering about 15,000 men. He described the plan of attack as follows:

> At 3:00 A.M. the OMON divisions would clear the square [around the White House] and disperse the crowd with gas and water cannons. Our divisions were to follow them. On the ground and from the air, using helicopters with grenade launchers and other special equipment, we would take the building.
>
> My boys were practically invulnerable. All this would have lasted fifteen minutes. Everything depended on me in this situation. Thank God, I did not lift a hand. Had there been a battle, there would have been a bloody mess. I refused.[24]

Karpukhin was not alone among top KGB officers who resisted the plan for attack. Other Alpha commanders shared Karpukhin's view that the White House could easily be seized, but only at the cost of many casualties among the defenders. To be sure, some KGB officers were initially attracted by the putschists' appeal. But by Monday evening, following the press conference of the Emergency Committee, they concluded (in the words of a KGB major general) that "this was a simple adventure, and the perplexing questions [about Gorbachev's health] multiplied."[25] A number of them viewed the coup as "unlawful and unconstitutional."[26]

Insubordination in the police, the army, and the KGB, and especially in the elite units, prevented the putschists from carrying out their plans.[27]

The number of Muscovites who participated publicly in some aspect of the popular resistance during the three days of the coup has been estimated at as many as 500,000 (many more joined the victory rally on Thursday and the funeral on Saturday). Even this high figure represents only a small proportion of the city's total population of eight or nine million.

Yet, within hours of the coup d'état, the junta's claim to govern had been reduced to one issue: who would control the White House? In this context, a relatively small number of people—but enough to fill to overflowing the vast space around the structure—made a tremendous difference. They stopped the movement of tanks with barricades and with their own bodies. They fraternized with soldiers and officers. They protested in the Tuesday mass rally. They organized self-defense units around the White House on Monday and Tuesday nights.

By these acts, ordinary people helped to demoralize soldiers and their officers and to dissuade them from carrying out the junta's orders. The attack on the White House ordered by the Emergency Committee never took place. Just as in the February Revolution of 1917, when the defection of the Cossacks sealed the fate of the "old regime," so in this case defections among army, police, and KGB officers prevented the junta—the last holdover of the Communist old regime—from imposing its will on the country.

Although evidence on the situation in the provinces during these events is incomplete, we know that local governments supported Yeltsin in a number of key cities in the Russian Republic including Sverdlovsk, Voronezh, Khabarovsk, Tula, Novosibirsk, Rostov on Don, Arkhangelsk, and Yaroslavl. The fact is that opposition was considerable—enough to prevent the tanks from even entering Leningrad and to send signals to the plotters that compliance throughout the country could not easily be achieved.

The preceding years of glasnost and perestroika, with unprecedented opportunities for public activism, had prepared the ground for
resistance to the coup. First, there was no longer only one center of
power and authority in the country. Apart from the central state structure —the government of the USSR—there was now an elected government of the Russian Federation, and other republic-level
governments as well. The government of Russia had become identified
with the new social forces in the country struggling to liberate themselves from the Communist system. It stood for constitutionalism and
democracy, headed as it was by a President chosen in an open and
competitive election (the only Soviet leader on Russian territory to
govern by a truly popular mandate). The junta, by contrast, was identified with the old regime seeking to perpetuate the hegemony, if not of
communism, then of its self-selecting political elite, the Communist
Party *nomenklatura.*

The August Revolution provided a major test of popular allegiance
in Russia: would the people, including the officers and soldiers of the
armed forces, side with Russia against the central authorities of the
Soviet party-state? A potent mixture of democratic sentiments, Russian
nationalism, and hatred for the Communist Party drove thousands of
people into the resistance movement against the junta. In the words of
a Leningrad protester, people "knew what could happen, they knew
what this might lead to. They felt that they were people, human beings.
They had stopped being afraid."[28]

* * *

It is surely one of history's great paradoxes that the August 1991
coup produced results diametrically opposed to the aims of the putschists. The coup was intended to prevent the signing of a new Union
Treaty and decentralization of the Soviet Union. But in the aftermath
of the coup, negotiations over the treaty faltered and, barely four
months later, the USSR had ceased to exist.

The plotters, all of them high-ranking Communist officials, also
sought to preserve the Party's unique position in the country's political
and economic life. Their ill-conceived and poorly executed plan had
precisely the opposite effect. The most immediate consequence was
the dissolution of the Communist Party, whose activities were sus-

pended in the Russian Republic on August 23 and in the entire Soviet Union on August 24. Though Party officials and organizations remained important actors in the months and years following the coup, the Communist Party of the Soviet Union—the country's ruling party for more than seven decades—ceased to exit.

The coup was led by people who had come to oppose many of the political, economic, and cultural reforms inaugurated by Gorbachev. Again paradoxically, when the coup failed, it elevated one of the boldest and most outspoken of the reformers, Boris Yeltsin, to an unprecedented position of power and authority. He emerged as the hero of the August crisis—the David who smote the Communist Party Goliath once and for all. In the months following the coup, Yeltsin carried forward with renewed vigor many of the reforms that had been stalled under Gorbachev's equivocating leadership. The progress of these reforms has been far from easy, and Yeltsin's own popularity has sometimes plunged very low. Nevertheless, when a legitimation crisis was precipitated in the spring of 1993 by the conservative opposition in Russia's Congress of People's Deputies, Yeltsin and his reform strategy once again won substantial popular support in a national referendum.

The seven surviving members of the Emergency Committee, together with five other high-ranking officials considered complicit in the Committee's actions, were arrested and imprisoned following the abortive coup.[29] They were charged with "betraying the Motherland," a crime punishable by death. After remaining in jail for eighteen months, they were released on bail. Since that time, many of them have given interviews, addressed public gatherings, and participated in public rallies, including a May Day demonstration in 1993 that ended in a bloody confrontation with police. Meanwhile, the prosecution prepared a case against them.

After some delays, the trial finally began on April 14, 1993, but was suspended almost immediately when one of the defendants (Tiziakov) suddenly became ill. The defense team raised a number of objections to continuation of the trial and sought dismissal of the charges. It argued that the court had no jurisdiction to try the defendants on charges of betraying a country (the Soviet Union) that no longer exists. The court rejected these arguments.

On May 18, 1993, the three military judges hearing the case accepted a defense motion to suspend the proceedings indefinitely. The

court had been persuaded by defense arguments about the alleged bias
of the prosecution team, citing the fact that Russia's Chief Prosecutor,
Valentin Stepankov, and his deputy, Yevgenii Lisov, had used the
materials from the pretrial investigation in their book *The Kremlin
Conspiracy*, published in late 1992.[30] Since the authors of the book
were unequivocal in their indictment of the alleged conspirators (went
the argument of the defense), and the prosecution team was subordinate to the country's Chief Prosecutor, its members could not be im-
partial in presenting to the court the results of their investigation. The
judges referred the case to the Supreme Soviet to determine how "real
independence" of the prosecution team could be guaranteed.[31] The
Supreme Soviet subsequently rejected the appeal as unfounded and
the trial resumed yet again on July 7, 1993, only to be postponed
due to the illness of one of the codefendants.[32] In September 1993,
the court ruled against a motion for postponement by the prosecution and thereby removed the last procedural hurdle to the resumption of the trial.

Popular attitudes toward the case are deeply divided, mirroring different retrospective evaluations of the coup itself. For some, the three
days in August remain inscribed as a courageous victory for the forces
of democracy and reform. For others, the takeover was a well-meaning
but bungled effort to rescue the Soviet Union from chaos and disintegration. Still others view the events of August 1991 as signifying little
more than a shift in power from one segment of the *nomenklatura* to
another. A public opinion poll conducted in August 1993 showed the
general public to be deeply divided about the coup and the criminality
of the plotters. A survey of 1,600 people conducted by the "Mnenie"
opinion research service disclosed that 48 percent thought the coup
plotters should get "no punishment" or be formally pardoned (in the
fall of 1991, only 30 percent had felt that way). The proportion of
those who believed their lives would have been better had the coup
succeeded rose from 4 percent in the fall of 1991 to 14 percent in
August 1993.[33]

Given such ambivalent popular attitudes about the events of August
1991, it is hardly surprising that the first two anniversaries of the coup
were commemorated in a low key. The celebration has been deeply
compromised by an inversion of some of the symbols of the democratic resistance to the August coup. The White House and the plaza
behind it, renamed Freedom Square, were once symbolically associ-

ated with Yeltsin, the Russian parliament's resistance to the putschists, and the crowds of Muscovites who turned out to defend freedom against resurgent totalitarianism. Between August 1991 and August 1993, those symbols—the White House, Freedom Square, and the Russian parliament itself—became transformed into their opposites through association with the anti-Yeltsin opposition in the Supreme Soviet and its motley collection of supporters, including ultranationalists, pro-Communists, neo-Stalinists, neo-Nazis, anti-Semites, and others. The dismal economic conditions and political disarray at the highest levels of the Russian government put a further damper on the celebration of a victory that promised far more than it has delivered to ordinary people.

On the first anniversary of the putsch, Yeltsin delivered a major address to the nation praising those who, a year earlier, had been "motivated by a noble patriotic impulse from the heart and by a sense of civic duty to defend freedom and democracy." He castigated those who wanted to "erase [this heroic deed] from the people's memory."[34]

Moscow Mayor Gavriil Popov marked the first anniversary with an extensive and highly reflective statement about the coup and its aftermath. Popov argued that the democrats' "main mistake [was] that they imagined they had taken power in Russia after the coup. Unfortunately, the people believed this, too." Instead, argued Popov, the democrats' victory "finally forced the reformist Party apparatchiks and *nomenklatura* to do what they had not done [under Gorbachev]—to organize themselves, unite, cleanse themselves of ideological garbage, remove the conservatives and start making reforms." Reforms were under way, but there was still much work to be done to strengthen democratic principles.[35]

By August 1993, nearly all vestiges of the celebratory aspect of the anniversary had been extinguished. An angry confrontation of groups demonstrating for and against the putschists took place near the White House, with strong overtones of latent violence. The once hallowed ground near the White House, stained by the blood of three victims, had become identified with a coalition of forces calling for the ouster of Yeltsin and the reformers and advocating some of the very measures that the plotters had tried to impose on the country. The anniversary had been transformed into another contested symbolic terrain for Russia's political leaders and the public.

In early October 1993, the contest escalated into an armed conflict, with the White House once again becoming the focal point of Russia's post-communist politics. In reaction to Yeltsin's September 21 decree disbanding the parliament and calling a new election for December, Ruslan Khasbulatov and other parliamentary leaders, the renegade Vice President Aleksandr Rutskoi, and several thousands of their supporters mounted an armed uprising, including lethal assaults on the nearby Moscow Mayor's office and the Gosteleradio building at Ostankino. This bloody outburst forced Yeltsin to declare a state of emergency in Moscow and to call in the army under Defense Minister Pavel Grachev, who two years earlier had refused to carry out a similar order. Stormed by paratroopers on Yeltsin's orders, the White House burned through the night of October 4–5, 1993.

Ironically, by the spring of 1994, the cause of the August 1991 putschists had become conflated with that of the leaders of the October 1993 uprising—Yeltsin's erstwhile allies. In late February 1994 Russia's newly elected State Duma passed an amnesty covering those charged with crimes in connection with both events. The trial of the coup plotters was terminated, and Rutskoi and Khasbulatov were released from prison. Then, in mid-March, the case took another strange twist. Ruling in favor of the prosecutor's appeal, to the effect that amnesty could not be granted to anyone who had not been tried and convicted, the Supreme Court ordered a resumption of the trial of the August 1991 putschists. Matters were at this impasse as this book was being sent to press.

* * *

The accounts that follow have been divided into five sections, each focusing on a particular group or aspect of the events of August 19–21, 1991. In selecting from a wide range of letters, reports, interviews, transcripts, and documents, the editors have attempted to include in the volume accounts by men and women, Russians and non-Russians, who personally took part in the August days. Since we wanted to show the events from many different angles, depending on the location and orientation of the individual, we have tried to incorporate material from a wide spectrum of people from many walks of life, but there are some gaps. We were unable to find an account by a veteran of the Afghan War who helped to defend the White House or from a businessman who provided supplies for the democratic resistance. The actions of these groups are recounted by others.

Part I, "Saving the Old Country," is devoted to the putschists. This section includes the major decrees, proclamations, and pronouncements of the State Committee for the State of Emergency as well as the full transcript of the press conference conducted by members of the Committee on August 19. Soon after the coup, the putschists were interrogated by government investigators preparing the legal case against them. We have included excerpts from the transcripts of interrogations of Yazov, Pavlov, and Kriuchkov. These selections show the motivations and outlook of the men who directed the putsch.

In Part II, "The Public Reacts," eight Russians and Americans of diverse backgrounds give their personal impressions of the coup. Their accounts are based on observations of and participation in events that took place in Moscow, Leningrad, and the provincial city of Saratov. Three of the selections are by Russian citizens (the anonymous author of the "Letter from Moscow," Vladimir Petrik, and Valerii Zavorotnyi); one author is an émigré (Gregory Freidin) and another the son of émigrés (Serge P. Petroff); and three more accounts are by American scholars (Victoria E. Bonnell, Lauren G. Leighton, and Donald J. Raleigh).

Part III, "In High Places," shifts to the centers of power and influence among the opponents of the coup. Here we see how some of the most powerful men in the country responded to the putsch. This part begins with Gorbachev's lengthy personal statement about what happened to him between the afternoon of Sunday, August 18, and Wednesday, August 21, when the putschists held him incommunicado at his summer residence in Foros. Gorbachev's account is followed by the appeal "To the Citizens of Russia" issued by Yeltsin, Silaev, and Khasbulatov, and other appeals and decrees issued by Yeltsin during the first day of the coup. We have also included Yeltsin's speech to the Russian parliament on Wednesday, August 21, when victory over the plotters seemed assured. Here Yeltsin gives his own version of the events.

Part III also contains reports and interviews from six other leading political figures in Moscow, Leningrad, and Dushanbe. These authors are generally quite well known and influential figures in Russian political life. Among them are Nikolai Vorontsov, Minister of the Environment under Gorbachev; Yevgenii Shaposhnikov, head of the Soviet Air Force at the time of the August coup; Vladimir Shcherbakov, a Deputy Prime Minister in the Gorbachev government; Davlat Khudonazarov, a filmmaker from Tajikistan who rose to political prominence under Gorbachev, serving as People's Deputy in the USSR Supreme Soviet and a member of the Central Committee of the Communist

Party; Anatolii Sobchak, the Mayor of Leningrad; and Aleksandr Yakovlev, a former CPSU Politburo member and a leading architect of perestroika.

Part IV focuses on an event—the defense of the White House against military assault by the putschists. In this section we have included accounts of the activities both inside and outside the White House, with particular attention to the night of August 20–21, when three young men died defending the barricades. Here we hope to show the character and composition of the public opposition that gathered at the White House and the extraordinary atmosphere among those who risked their lives on the barricades. The reports, letters, and interviews are from an American student, Theresa Sabonis-Chafee; a well-known Russian ultranationalist writer, Aleksandr Prokhanov; an American journalist, Michael Hetzer; an anonymous Russian man; a Russian scholar, Aleksei Kozhevnikov; a People's Deputy to the Russian parliament and democratic political activist, Viktor Sheinis, and his wife, the sociologist Alla Nazimova.

Part V of the volume, "Getting the News In and Out," is devoted to the role played by the media. The mass media—both Soviet and foreign —were critically important during the putsch. Despite heavy censorship, the shutdown of most newspapers and radio stations, and the suspension of regular television programming, the media continued to function outside official control during the three days of the coup. As these accounts show, adverse conditions did not prevent television, radio, and newspaper journalists from transmitting critical information to the Soviet people and abroad. The foreign press is represented here by Iain Elliot of Radio Liberty and Ann Cooper of National Public Radio. The television journalist Sergei Medvedev recounts his experiences reporting for "Vremia"; Valerii Kucher describes the efforts of journalists to publish a collective underground newspaper; and Tatiana Malkina reports on her participation in the August 19 press conference.

* * *

A Chronology of Events has been provided at the conclusion of the volume with a timetable of developments during the coup, day by day, hour by hour, sometimes minute by minute. This will help to guide the reader who is interested in sequential coverage of the events of the three days and will serve as a point of ready reference.[36]

Notes

1. Quoted in Michael R. Beschloss's review of *The Turn from the Cold War to a New Era: The United States and the Soviet Union, 1983–1990* by Don Oberdorfer, in *The New York Times Book Review*, October 27, 1991, p. 11.

2. For analyses of Gorbachev's reforms, see the essays in Alexander Dallin and Gail Lapidus, eds., *The Soviet System in Crisis: A Reader of Western and Soviet Views* (Boulder, San Francisco, Oxford, 1991); and George Breslauer, ed., *Will Gorbachev's Reforms Succeed?* (Berkeley, 1990).

3. Valentin Stepankov and Yevgenii Lisov report that it was Gorbachev who insisted on August 20 as the signing date for the Treaty; other cosigners had wanted to wait until the end of the vacation season. See Stepankov and Lisov, *Kremlevskii zagovor: versiia sledstviia* (Moscow, 1992), p. 83.

4. A close observer of the Soviet scene noted that in June and July 1991, "the army–KGB–MVD troika undertook a well-orchestrated effort to weaken Gorbachev domestically and to humiliate him internationally. . . . [It] seems evident that the coup leaders were laying groundwork for a move against Gorbachev [and] the anti-Gorbachev alliance was gaining experience in working together." See Scott R. McMichael, "Moscow Prelude: Warning Signs Ignored," RFE/RL Research Institute, *Report on the USSR*, vol. 3, no. 36 (1991), pp. 10–11. The account that follows draws upon McMichael's article.

5. Yakovlev's last warning came in an "open letter," dated August 16, 1991, that was published in *Nezavisimaia gazeta* on August 18. Among other things, Yakovlev wrote that "shadow structures" had already been established and were "waiting for the right moment to carry out a takeover."

6. Foreign Minister Aleksandr Bessmertnykh and the U.S. Ambassador in Moscow, Jack Matlock, served as intermediaries (David Remnick, *Lenin's Tomb: The Last Days of the Soviet Empire* [New York, 1993], pp. 436–37). According to Bessmertnykh's testimony, when he conveyed Baker's warning to Gorbachev (after Ambassador Matlock had done the same), Gorbachev responded that he had already had a "talk with these *statesmen,* a *tough* talk" (Stepankov and Lisov, *Kremlevskii zagovor*, p. 79).

7. The interview, published under the title "Nachinaetsia revoliutsiia snizu," appeared in *Literaturnaia gazeta*, August 28, 1991. The text may be found in English translation in *Russian Politics and Law: A Journal of Translations*, vol. 31, no. 1 (Summer 1992), pp. 21–26.

8. The official text of the Treaty was made public on August 15. Under the provisions of the Treaty the office of USSR Vice President was to be abolished, a fact that throws some light on Gennadii Yanaev's participation in the plot.

9. Gorbachev chose Vladimir Shcherbakov, Pavlov's deputy, to accompany him to the G7 meeting of leaders of the top industrial nations.

10. A comprehensive discussion of these factors can be found in Dawn Mann, "The Circumstances Surrounding the Conservative Putsch," in RFE/RL Research Institute, *Report on the USSR*, vol. 3, no. 36 (1991), pp. 1–5.

11. Stepankov and Lisov, *Kremlevskii zagovor*, p. 85.

12. The Committee's name was officially abbreviated as GKChP (pronounced Geh-Keh-Cheh-Peh), which not only sounds awkward but is suspiciously reminis-

cent of the well-known and much disliked acronyms for the secret police—KGB, GPU, and Cheka.

13. The law stipulated that a state of emergency could be declared only in the event of "natural and man-made disasters, epidemics, and large-scale public disorders," either by the Supreme Soviet of a constituent republic of the USSR or by the USSR President, "following the petition or consent of the Presidium of the Supreme Soviet of the USSR or constituent republic, or the supreme organ of the constituent republic." If the President decided to declare a state of emergency on his own, he had to "immediately seek the approval of the Supreme Soviet."

14. Carla Thorson, "Constitutional Issues Surrounding the Coup," in RFL/RL Research Institute, *Report on the USSR*, vol. 3, no. 36 (1991), p. 22.

15. Ibid., p. 21.

16. See Victoria E. Bonnell and Gregory Freidin, "*Televorot:* The Role of Television Coverage in Russia's August 1991 Coup," *Slavic Review*, vol. 52, no. 4 (Winter 1993), pp. 810–38.

17. In the Russian Federation as a whole, Yeltsin received 58 percent of the vote.

18. According to General Lebed's recently released memoirs (published in the Transnistrian Republic), the paratrooper division under his command had been ordered by General Grachev to be battle ready on August 17. Neither Grachev nor his staff disclosed to Lebed the nature of his mission. The order for Lebed to move his division into Moscow came at around 4:00 A.M. on August 19. Still in the dark about his mission, Lebed (who had not listened to state radio while on the march) reached the outskirts of Moscow at 10:30 A.M. He was soon contacted by Grachev's staff officer, who conveyed to him another order from Grachev: Lebed was "personally," and without using any communications equipment, to lead the 2nd Batallion to the White House and there, after contacting the head of White House security, to assume the defense of the building. Still unaware of the coup d'état, Lebed arrived at the White House at 1:30 P.M. He tried to follow Grachev's order but was chased out of the building by an irate crowd of about 200 defenders who assumed that he was on the side of the Emergency Committee (at one point in the ensuing fracas, Lebed practically had to run for his life). As a result of the confusion, Lebed was able to carry out his order to defend the White House only late in the evening of the 19th. See Aleksandr Lebed, *Spektakl nazyvalsia putch* (Tiraspol, 1993); also excerpted in the right-wing nationalist newspaper *Literaturnaia Rossiia*, September 24, 1993.

19. The crowd estimates come from the Russian Information Agency. See *Khronika putcha: chas za chasom. Sobytiia 19–22 avgusta 1991 v svodkakh Rossiiskogo informatsionnogo agenstva* (Leningrad, 1991), p. 43.

20. Throughout Tuesday, specially organized groups of People's Deputies of Russia were dispatched to the city's military garrisons; using their parliamentary immunity to gain access, they endeavored to explain to army officers the unconstitutional nature of the Declaration of the State of Emergency. See the interview with Viktor Sheinis and Alla Nazimova in part IV, below.

21. In the confrontation of September–October 1993, Yeltsin did not hesitate to cut off all White House communications, as well as water and electricity.

22. On "Vremia," see the account of Sergei Medvedev's film report, above, and the interview with Medvedev in part V. For an analysis of television's role in defeating the coup, see Bonnell and Freidin, "*Televorot.*" The government newspaper *Izvestiia* also eluded control by the putschists. Due to internal conflicts on the paper's

staff, no issue of *Izvestiia* appeared on August 19. The issue published on the morning of August 20 carried statements from the Emergency Committee on page one and Yeltsin's "Appeal to the Citizens of Russia" on page two. The afternoon edition on August 20 had two photographs which showed a vast crowd carrying the Russian tricolor flag at the Moscow rally and civilians fraternizing with soldiers in tanks. Again, Yeltsin learned his lesson well. After issuing his decree disbanding the Russian parliament in September 1993, he took firm control of news programming on Russian television and briefly invoked press censorship in the wake of the October military confrontation.

23. Two other notable figures associated with the plotters (Marshal of the Soviet Union Sergei Akhromeev, and Nikolai Kruchina, Chief of the CPSU Central Committee's Administrative Office) committed suicide soon afterward.

24. The interview with Karpukhin appeared in *Literaturnaia gazeta* under the title "Oni otkazalis shturmovat Belyi dom," August 28, 1991, p. 5. An English translation may be found in *Russian Politics and Law: A Journal of Translations*, vol. 31, no. 1 (Summer 1992), pp. 8–11.

25. See the interview with Major General Aleksandr Korsak, "Nam byl otdan prikaz arestovat Popova," in *Literaturnaia gazeta*, September 11, 1991. An English translation appears in *Russian Politics and Law: A Journal of Translations*, vol. 31, no. 1 (Summer 1992), pp. 16–20.

26. Lieutenant colonels Mikhail Golovatov and Sergei Goncharov of the Alpha unit made these statements in the interview with *Literaturnaia gazeta* cited in note 24.

27. According to the account by the head of the investigative team, the Russian Federation's Prosecutor General Valentin Stepankov and his deputy, Yevgenii Lisov, the plans for the attack on the White House and the decision to proceed were made in the middle of the day on August 20. The attack itself was to commence at 3:00 A.M. on the 21st and was to be carried out by a combined force of the Airborne Paratroopers, the Special Forces of the Ministry of Internal Affairs, and three special units of the KGB—"Alpha," "Group B," and the "Wave." However, commanders of the operation soon began to develop doubts about its wisdom, partly under the pressure of the lower ranks; partly for fear of losing up to half of their force (according to one estimate) in storming what had already become a well-fortified and well-defended building; and partly from the conviction that it would be wrong to spill their compatriots' blood. According to the plan, code-named "Operation Thunder," the paratroopers were to be the first to take up their position. Their commander, Pavel Grachev, refused to order them to advance. After talking to Grachev, Viktor Karpukhin, the commander of the "Alpha" unit and the man in charge of "Operation Thunder," followed Grachev's example, as did most other commanders. When in the early hours of the morning Yazov was informed about the first instance of bloodshed and the possibility of thousands of victims if an attack were to take place, his order was to "halt" the entire operation. See Stepankov and Lisov, *Kremlevskii zagovor*.

28. Felicity Barringer, "Chronicle of the Resistance: 48 Tense Hours in Leningrad," *New York Times*, September 10, 1991, p. A4.

29. The others were: Anatolii Lukianov, Chairman of the USSR Supreme Soviet; Oleg Shenin, Secretary of the CPSU Central Committee; Valentin Varennikov, Commander-in-Chief of Ground Forces and Deputy Minister of Defense; Yurii Plekhanov, Director of the Security Directorate of the KGB; and Viacheslav Generalov, Director of the KGB's Specialized Operational-Technical Administration.

30. We have cited the book several times in this account (Stepankov and Lisov, *Kremlevskii zagovor*). To date, it is available only in Russian.

31. See Steven Erlanger, "Russia Suspends Coup Trial, Citing Bias by the Prosecutor," *New York Times*, May 19, 1993, p. A6.

32. See the issues of *Radio Free Europe/Radio Liberty Daily Report* for January 27, April 15–16, May 18–19, May 27, and July 7, 1993.

33. "Growing Minority in Russia Wish '91 Coup Hadn't Failed" (Associated Press), *San Francisco Chronicle*, August 19, 1993, p. A13.

34. Foreign Broadcast Information Service, *Daily Report: Central Eurasia*, FBIS-SOV–92–162, August 20, 1992, p. 17.

35. Popov's remarks appeared in *Izvestiia* on August 21, 24, 25, 26, 1992. For an English translation see *Current Digest of the Post-Soviet Press*, vol. 44, no. 34 (September 23, 1992), pp. 1–6.

36. Accounts of the coup and its aftermath may be found in the following English-language sources: James H. Billington, *Russia Transformed: Breakthrough to Hope, Moscow, August 1991* (New York, 1992); Victoria E. Bonnell and Gregory Freidin, "*Televorot*: The Role of Television Coverage in Russia's August 1991 Coup," *Slavic Review*, vol. 52, no. 4 (Winter 1993); George W. Breslauer, "Bursting the Dams: Politics and Society in the USSR Since the Coup," *Problems of Communism*, November/December 1991; John B. Dunlop, *The Rise of Russia and the Fall of the Soviet Empire* (Princeton, 1993); Mikhail Gorbachev, *The August Coup: The Truth and the Lessons* (New York, 1991); Amy Knight, "The Coup That Never Was: Gorbachev and the Forces of Reaction," *Problems of Communism*, November/December 1991; Michael Mandelbaum, "Coup de Grace: The End of the Soviet Union," *Foreign Affairs*, vol. 71, no. 1 (1991/2); William E. Odom, "Alternative Perspectives on the August Coup," *Problems of Communism*, November/December 1991; Lilia Shevtsova, "The August Coup and the Soviet Collapse," *Survival*, vol. 34, no. 1 (Spring 1992); Anatole Shub, "The Fourth Russian Revolution: Historical Perspectives," *Problems of Communism*, November/December 1991; Hedrick Smith, *The New Russians*, Part Seven: The Second Russian Revolution (New York, 1991); Melor Sturua, "The Real Coup," *Foreign Policy*, no. 85 (Winter 1991–2); and David Remnick, *Lenin's Tomb: The Last Days of the Soviet Empire* (New York, 1993).

Russian-language sources on the coup are as follows: *Avgust–91* (Moscow, 1991); . . . *Deviatnadtsatoe, dvadtsatoe, dvadtsat pervoe . . . : svobodnoe radio dlia svobodnykh liudei* (Moscow, 1991); Leonid Ivashov, *Marshal Iazov: Rokovoi avgust 19-go* (Moscow: Muzhestvo, 1992); *Krasnoe ili beloe? Drama Avgusta–91: Fakty, gipotezy, stolknovenie mnenii* (Moscow, 1991); *Korichnevyi putch krasnykh avgust '91: Khronika, svidetelstva pressy, fotodokumenty* (Moscow, 1991); Iu. Kazarin and Boris Iakovlev, eds., *Smert zagovora: Belaia kniga* (Moscow, 1992); *Khronika putcha: chas za chasom. Sobytiia 19–22 avgusta 1991 v svodkakh Rossiiskogo informatsionnogo agentstva* (Leningrad, n.d.); Valentin Pavlov, *Gorbachev-Putch: Avgust iznutri* (Moscow, 1993); *Putch: Khronika trevozhnykh dnei* (Moscow, 1991); Iu.S. Sidorenko, *Tri dnia, kotorye oprokinuli bolshevizm: Ispoved svidetelia, pokazaniia ochevodsta* (Rostov-on-Don, 1991); V. Stepankov and E. Lisov, *Kremlevskii zagovor: versiia sledstviia* (Moscow, 1992).

I

Saving the Old Country

In the early morning of August 19, 1991, eight high-ranking Soviet officials made an announcement that stunned the country and the world: President Mikhail Gorbachev had resigned due to illness, and his government had been taken over by a State Committee for the State of Emergency (GKChP). The committee included Vice President Gennadii Yanaev (who was named Acting President); KGB head Vladimir Kriuchkov; Defense Minister Dmitrii Yazov; Minister of Internal Affairs Boris Pugo; Prime Minister Valentin Pavlov; Oleg Baklanov, First Deputy Chairman of the National Defense Council and leader of the military-industrial complex; Vasilii Starodubtsev, chairman of the Peasants' Union; and Aleksandr Tiziakov, President of the USSR Association of State Enterprises and Industrial Groups in Production, Construction, Transportation, and Communications.

Through their proclamations and appeals, their one and only press conference, and their subsequent interviews with interrogators, the members of the Emergency Committee articulated their version of the events leading up to and during the August crisis.

1 | Proclamations and Decrees of the State Committee for the State of Emergency, August 19, 1991

On the first day of the coup, the members of the State Committee for the State of Emergency issued several documents justifying their actions and explaining their policies. The following texts were transmitted by the TASS news agency and read repeatedly over the Soviet Union's central broadcast facilities beginning the morning of August 19.

Document 1: Decree of the Vice President of the USSR

In connection with Mikhail Sergeevich Gorbachev's inability, for health reasons, to carry out the responsibilities of the President of the USSR, and in accordance with Article 127(7) of the USSR Constitution, responsibilities of the USSR President have been transferred to the USSR Vice President, Gennadii Yanaev, beginning August 19, 1991.

Vice President of the USSR, Gennadii Yanaev
August 18, 1991

Document 2: Appeal to the Soviet People

Compatriots,
Citizens of the Soviet Union,

We are addressing you at a grave, critical hour for the destinies of our Fatherland and our peoples. A mortal danger looms large over our great Motherland.

The policy of reforms, launched at Mikhail S. Gorbachev's initiative and designed to ensure the country's dynamic development and the democratization of social life, has, for a number of reasons, run into a dead end. Lack of faith, apathy, and despair have replaced the original enthusiasm and hopes. Authorities at all levels have lost the population's trust. In public life, political games have replaced concern for the fate of the Fatherland and the citizen. An attitude of malicious contempt toward all state institutions is being imposed. The country has in effect become ungovernable.

Taking advantage of the liberties that have been granted, and trampling on the first shoots of democracy, extremist forces have emerged, embarking on a course toward liquidating the Soviet Union, ruining the state, and seizing power at any cost. They trampled on the results of the nationwide referendum on the unity of the Fatherland.* The cynical exploitation of national feelings serves merely as a cover for satisfying personal ambition. Political adventurers are worried neither by the misfortunes that their peoples are experiencing today nor by those in the future. Creating an atmosphere of moral and political terror, and seeking to hide behind the shield of the people's trust, they forget that the ties being condemned and severed by them were established on the basis of far broader popular support, which, furthermore, has stood the test of many centuries of history. Today, those who are working toward the overthrow of the constitutional system should be brought to account before mothers and fathers for the deaths of the hundreds of victims of interethnic conflicts. The broken destinies of more than half a million refugees are on their conscience. They are to blame for the loss of tranquility and joy of tens of millions of Soviet people, who only yesterday lived in a united family, but today find themselves living as outcasts in their own home.

People must decide what kind of social system should be established, but attempts are being made to deprive the people of this choice.

Instead of showing concern for the security and well-being of every citizen and all society, persons who have come to positions of power frequently use it for interests alien to the people, as a means for unscrupulous self-assertion. Torrents of words and piles of declarations and promises only underline the scanty and meager nature of their

---

*On March 17, 1991, a nationwide referendum was held on the future of the Union. The majority of citizens voted for the preservation of the USSR.

practical deeds. The inflation of authority, which is the most terrifying type of inflation, is destroying our state and society. Every citizen is feeling increasing uncertainty about tomorrow and deep concern about the future of his or her children.

The crisis of power has had a catastrophic effect on the economy. The chaotic, elemental descent along the slippery slope toward a market economy has led to an explosion of egotism at all levels—regional, institutional, collective, and personal. The war of laws* and the promotion of centrifugal forces have caused the disintegration of a unified economic system that it has taken decades to create. The result is a sharp decline in the standard of living for the majority of the Soviet people and the spread of speculation and black marketeering. It is high time people were told the truth: if urgent and decisive measures are not adopted to stabilize the economy, hunger and another spiral of impoverishment are imminent in the near future, and from there it is but a single step to mass manifestations of elemental discontent, with devastating consequences. Only irresponsible people can put their hopes in some kind of aid from abroad. No handouts can solve our problems. Our rescue is in our own hands. The time has come to measure the influence of each individual or organization by its real contribution to the development of our economy.

For many years, we have been hearing incantations from all sides about this or that politician's commitment to the interests of the individual, his rights, and his social protection. In fact, what has happened is that the individual has been humiliated, his actual rights and opportunities have been constrained, and he has been driven to despair. Right before our eyes, all the democratic institutions, created on the basis of the will of the people, are losing their authority. All of this is the result of the systematic activity of those who, in gross violation of the Fundamental Law of [the Constitution] the USSR, are, in fact, carrying out an unconstitutional coup d'état, pursuing the goal of unrestrained personal dictatorship. The prefectures, mayoralties, and other unlawful structures have been increasingly usurping the power of the popularly elected soviets.

---

*"War of laws" is the phrase used to characterize the jurisdictional disputes that followed upon unilateral declarations by some republics and even lower political units that in the event of a conflict between Union legislation and local law, the latter should prevail.

An offensive is under way against the rights of working people. The rights to work, education, health, housing, and leisure are in jeopardy.

Even the elementary personal security of people is increasingly under threat. Crime is rising fast, becoming organized and politicized. The country is sinking into an abyss of violence and lawlessness. Never before in the nation's history has the propaganda of sex and violence assumed such a scale, threatening the health and lives of future generations. Millions of people are demanding measures against the octopus of crime and flagrant immorality.

The increasing destabilization of the political and economic situation in the Soviet Union is undercutting our position in the world. Revanchist notes are to be heard in some places, and demands are being made for a review of our borders. Voices can even be heard speaking of dismembering the Soviet Union and of the possibility of establishing an international protectorate over certain facilities and regions of the country. Such is the bitter reality. Only yesterday a Soviet person finding himself abroad felt himself a worthy citizen of an influential and respected state. Now he is often a second-class foreigner, whose treatment bears the imprint of disdain or pity.

The pride and honor of Soviet people must be restored in full measure.

The State Committee for the State of Emergency in the USSR is fully aware of the depth of the crisis that has afflicted the country. It takes responsibility for the fate of the country and is fully determined to take the most serious measures to pull the state and society out of the crisis as soon as possible.

We promise to hold a nationwide discussion of the new draft Union treaty. Each individual will have the right and opportunity to think over this important act and determine his attitude toward it, because the fate of the numerous peoples of our great Motherland will depend on what the Soviet Union will be like.

We intend, without delay, to restore law and order, end bloodshed, declare a merciless war against the criminal world, and eradicate the shameful phenomena that discredit our society and degrade Soviet citizens. We shall clean our cities' streets of criminal elements and put an end to the tyranny of those who pillage the people's wealth.

We stand for truly democratic processes and for a consistent policy of reforms, which should lead to a renewal in our Motherland and to an economic and social efflorescence that will enable her to take her rightful place in the world community of nations.

A nation's development must not be based on a drop in the living standards of its citizens. In a healthy society, constant improvement of the living standards shall become the norm.

Without slackening in our devotion to the strengthening and protection of the rights of individuals, we shall concentrate our attention on protecting the rights of the population at large, those who have been hurt the most by inflation, disorganization of production, corruption, and crime.

Developing the multitiered character of the national economy, we shall support private enterprise, granting it the necessary opportunities for developing production and services.

Our prime concern shall be solving the food and housing problems. All available forces will be mobilized to meet these, the most essential needs of the people.

We are calling on workers, peasants, the working intelligentsia, and all Soviet people, within the shortest period of time, to restore labor discipline and order and to raise the level of production, in order to march forward resolutely. Our life and the future of our children and grandchildren, as well as the fate of the Fatherland, depend on this.

We are a peace-loving country, and we shall steadfastly honor all our commitments. We make no claims against anyone. We wish to live with all in peace and friendship. But we firmly declare that no one will ever be allowed to encroach upon our sovereignty, independence, or territorial integrity. All attempts to speak the language of *diktat* to our country, no matter where they originate, will be resolutely repelled.

Our multinational people has lived for centuries in pride of their Motherland. We have never been ashamed of our patriotic feelings, and we hold it to be natural and right to raise the present and future generations of citizens of this great power in this spirit.

To remain inactive at this hour of crisis for the fate of the Motherland means to take upon oneself heavy responsibility for tragic, truly unpredictable consequences. Each individual who holds our Motherland dear, who wants to live and work in peace and confidence, who does not acquiesce in the continuation of bloody interethnic conflicts, who sees his Fatherland independent and prospering in the future, must make the only correct choice. We call on all true patriots and people of good will to put an end to the present time of troubles.

We appeal to all citizens of the Soviet Union to recognize their duty before the Motherland and extend all possible support to the State Committee for the State of Emergency and its efforts to lead the country out of the crisis.

Constructive proposals of public and political organizations, work collectives, and individuals will be gratefully accepted as an expression of their patriotic readiness to take an active part in the restoration of the age-old friendship in the unified family of fraternal peoples and the revival of the Fatherland.

The State Committee for the State of Emergency
August 18, 1991

Document 3: Resolution No. 1 of the USSR State Committee for the State of Emergency

In order to secure the vital interest of the peoples and citizens of the Union of Soviet Socialist Republics, the independence and territorial integrity of the country, the restoration of law and order, the stabilization of the situation, to overcome the most acute crisis and prevent chaos, anarchy, and fratricidal civil war, the State Committee for the State of Emergency has resolved as follows:

1. All political and administrative organs of the Union of Soviet Socialist Republics and of union and autonomous republics, territories, regions, cities, districts, towns, and villages must follow without deviation the regime of the state of emergency in accordance with the USSR Law "On the Legal Regime of the State of Emergency" and resolutions of the USSR State Committee for the State of Emergency. In those cases where the specified organs prove unable to conform to this regime, their powers are suspended and the implementation of their function is entrusted to persons specially appointed by the USSR State Committee for the State of Emergency.

2. To disband without delay those power and administrative structures and paramilitary units acting contrary to the USSR Constitution and the laws of the USSR.

3. Immediately to render invalid all laws and decisions adopted by organs of power that contradict the USSR Constitution and the laws of the USSR.

4. To suspend the activities of political parties, public organiza-

tions, and mass movements that interfere with the normalization of the situation.

5. Due to the temporary assumption by the USSR State Committee for the State of Emergency of the functions of the USSR Security Council, the activity of the latter is suspended.

6. Citizens, institutions, and organizations must without delay give up all illegally held firearms of all types, ammunition, explosive materials, military equipment and materiel. The Ministry of Internal Affairs, the KGB, and the USSR Ministry of Defense are to provide strict enforcement of this requirement. In case of resistance, the above items must be confiscated by force and the violators prosecuted by the criminal and administrative justice systems.

7. The Prosecutor's Office, the Ministry of Internal Affairs, the KGB, and the USSR Ministry of Defense are to organize efficient coordination of the organs of law and order with the Armed Forces in their effort to establish public order and maintain the security of the state, society, and citizens in accordance with the USSR law "On the Legal Regime of the State of Emergency" and the resolutions of the USSR State Committee for the State of Emergency.

Public rallies, marches, and demonstrations as well as strikes are prohibited.

When necessary, a curfew is to be introduced as well as patrols, inspections, and a strengthening of measures to enforce the border and customs regime.

To assume control of, and when necessary to defend, the most important state and economic organizations as well as essential life-supporting facilities.

To curb decisively the spread of all destabilizing rumors, actions provoking the violation of law and order and contributing to interethnic strife, and insubordination in dealing with the official persons responsible for the maintenance of the state of emergency regime.

8. To establish control over the mass media, this control function to be assumed by a special arm of the USSR State Committee for the State of Emergency which is being set up for this purpose.

9. Organs of power and administration and the heads of institutions and enterprises must undertake measures to increase coordination, order, and discipline in all spheres of our society. They must secure conditions for the normal functioning of enterprises in all branches of the economy; strict observance of the measures directed at strengthen-

ing horizontal and vertical links among all economic subjects through-out the entire territory of the USSR; and unflagging fulfillment of designated quotas in production and deliveries of raw materials, prod-ucts, and spare parts.

To establish a regime of strict economy of technical, material, and hard currency resources, to design and carry out concrete measures against squandering of people's wealth.

To struggle decisively with the shadow economy, to prosecute as-siduously instances of corruption, theft, speculation, hoarding, squan-dering, and other violations in the economic sphere.

To create favorable conditions for the expansion of the contribution to the country's economy and the vital needs of its citizens made by all types of private enterprise operating within the laws of the USSR.

10. To make holding a full-time government post incompatible with private enterprise activity.

11. The USSR Council of Ministers is to carry out in a period of seven days a complete inventory of all available foodstuffs and basic consumer goods; report to the people what the country has at its dis-posal; and assume the strictest control over the storage and distribution of these resources.

To remove all obstacles to the movement throughout the territory of the USSR of foodstuffs, consumer goods, and material necessary for their manufacture; to assume strict control over this sphere.

Special attention must be paid and first priority assigned to sup-plying preschool children's establishments, orphanages, schools, intermediary-, specialized-intermediary, and higher-educational insti-tutions, and hospitals as well as pensioners and the disabled.

In the period of one week to prepare proposals for stabilizing, freez-ing, and lowering prices for certain types of industrial and food prod-ucts, first and foremost those that are meant for children, consumer services, and public food services, and for increasing salaries, pen-sions, subsidies, and compensations for various categories of citizens.

Within two weeks to design measures for streamlining the salary structure for the top-management personnel at all levels of state, public, cooperative, and other establishments, organizations, and enter-prises.

12. Taking into account the critical situation with the harvest and the threat of hunger, to take extraordinary measures to organize supply, storage, and processing of agricultural products. To help the rural toil-

ers as much as possible by providing them with equipment, spare parts, lubricating materials, fuels, etc. To organize without delay the dispatching, in requisite numbers, of blue- and white-collar workers, students, and servicemen to rural areas [to help with the harvest].

13. Within one week, the Council of Ministers is to prepare a resolution making it possible to provide in the course of 1991–1992 all willing city dwellers with gardening plots of 0.15 hectare.

14. Within two weeks, the USSR Council of Ministers is to complete plans for solving the crisis in the country's energy industry and preparing for the winter.

15. Within one month, it is to prepare concrete measures for radically improving the housing situation in the country and report to the people about them.

In the course of six months, to develop a concrete program for accelerated development of state, cooperative, and individual housing construction for a five-year period.

16. To make it a duty of the organs of power in the center and in localities to give first priority to the basic needs of the population. To locate additional resources for improving free medical care and free education.

[*Pravda,* August 20, 1991]

**Document 4: Resolution of the Chairman
of the Supreme Soviet of the USSR on
the Convening of an Extraordinary Session
of the Supreme Soviet of the USSR**

In connection with the petition directed to the USSR Supreme Soviet to confirm the decision to introduce a state of emergency in certain localities in the USSR, it is resolved to convene an extraordinary session of the Supreme Soviet of the Union of Soviet Socialist Republics in the city of Moscow on August 26, 1991.

Chairman of the Supreme Soviet of the USSR A. Lukianov
Moscow, the Kremlin, August 19, 1991

2 | The Press Conference of the State Committee for the State of Emergency, August 19, 1991

On the evening of Monday, August 19, five of the eight plotters (Yanaev, Baklanov, Pugo, Starodubtsev, and Tiziakov) held their first and only press conference at the Foreign Ministry's press center in central Moscow. Millions of people gathered by their televisions and radios to learn more about the fate of their country. With visibly trembling hands and evident confusion, Gennadii Yanaev came forward as spokesman for the Emergency State Committee and Acting President. Below is a slightly abridged translation of the transcript of the press conference.

Yanaev: Ladies and gentlemen, friends and comrades: As you already know from media reports, because Mikhail Sergeevich Gorbachev is unable, owing to the state of his health, to discharge the duties of President of the USSR, the USSR Vice President has temporarily taken over the performance of the duties of the President on the basis of Article 127(7) of the USSR Constitution.

I address you today, ladies and gentlemen, at a moment that is crucial for the destinies of the Soviet Union and the international situation throughout the world.

Having embarked on the path of profound reforms and having gone a considerable way in this direction, the Soviet Union has now reached a point at which it finds itself faced with a deep crisis, the further development of which could both place in question the course of reforms itself and lead to serious cataclysms in international life.

It is of course no secret to you that a sharp drop in the country's output, which has so far not been compensated for by the activity of the alternative industrial and agricultural structures, is creating a real threat to the further existence and development of the peoples of the Soviet Union. A situation of ungovernability and multiple authority has arisen in the country. All of this cannot fail to arouse extensive dissatisfaction among the people. A real threat to the country's integrity has also arisen, with a consequent collapse of the unified economic space, the unified space for civil rights, a unified defense, and a unified foreign policy.

Under such conditions normal life is impossible. In many regions of the USSR, as a result of interethnic clashes, blood is being spilled, and the collapse of the USSR would have the most serious consequences, not only internally, but also internationally. In such conditions we have no alternative but to take decisive steps to stop the country from sliding into disaster.

As you know, in order to govern the country and to realize most effectively the regime of the state of emergency, a decision has been made to set up the State Committee for the State of Emergency in the USSR, consisting of the following members: Comrade Baklanov, First Deputy Chairman of the USSR Defense Council; Comrade Kriuchkov, Chairman of the USSR KGB; Comrade Pavlov, the USSR Prime Minister; Comrade Pugo, Minister of Internal Affairs of the USSR; Comrade Starodubtsev, Chairman of the USSR Peasants' Union; Comrade Tiziakov, President of the USSR Association of State Enterprises and Industrial Groups in Production, Construction, Transportation, and Communications; Comrade Yazov, the USSR Minister of Defense; and Acting President of the USSR Yanaev.

I would like to make a statement today that the Emergency Committee is fully aware of the depth of the crisis that has struck our country. It assumes responsibility for the fate of the Motherland and is full of resolve to undertake the strongest measures in order to enable the country and the state to overcome the crisis in the shortest time possible.

We promise to conduct a broad-based popular discussion of the draft of the new Union Treaty. Each citizen of the USSR will have the right and the opportunity to analyze this most important document in circumstances of tranquillity and to define his own position, for it is on the future shape of the Union that the fate of the multitude of peoples of our great Motherland shall depend.

[Yanaev then repeats verbatim many of the points contained in the Emergency Committee's Appeal to the Soviet People.]

Newsweek correspondent Carroll Bogert: Where is Mikhail Sergeevich Gorbachev? What is he sick with? Specifically and concretely, what disease does he have? And against whom are the tanks that we see on the streets of Moscow directed? What is the purpose of those tanks? Thank you.

Yanaev: I have to say that Mikhail Sergeevich Gorbachev presently is on vacation and undergoing treatment in the Crimea. He has, indeed, grown very tired over these past years, and he will need some time to put his health in order. I would like to say that we hope that when he is recovered, Mikhail Sergeevich will return to carrying out his duties. And at any rate, we will continue to follow the course begun by Mikhail Sergeevich Gorbachev in 1985.

As for the state of emergency, it goes without saying that the state of emergency is being introduced, as I have already said, at a very difficult time, and to avoid excesses of any kind, we have been forced to take some measures for the safety of our citizens.

Correspondent from *Pravda:* I have two questions. Perestroika has not produced tangible results for many reasons, primarily because it possessed no precise tactical and strategic plan for its realization. Do you have at present a concrete plan for reviving the country's economy? More specifically, will the previously adopted laws continue to function? Will the movement to a market economy continue?

My second question: The Russian Information Agency has broadcast today an appeal to the people of Russia from Yeltsin, Silaev, and Khasbulatov. In it, the events of the past night are defined as a right-wing, reactionary, anticonstitutional coup d'état. What is your reaction to this statement?

And the second part of that same question: This appeal contained a call for a general strike. In my opinion, such statements can lead to the most tragic consequences. Are you planning to take any concrete measures in this regard?

Yanaev: I'll answer the second question, and Comrade Tiziakov will answer the first.

Tiziakov: Indeed, the policy of perestroika, announced in 1985, has not, as you know, yielded the results we had expected. Our economy today is in a most difficult state. The decline in production is continuing because of a whole series of factors. Of course, we have got to take into account the fact that restructuring on such a scale was being carried out by us for the first time.

Of course, we are and have been seeking the right way, and any search involves some mistakes or omissions. This situation which has come about is what constitutes the main reason for the introduction of the state of emergency.

You know that the horizontal links among enterprises have been badly damaged. Many of those who are present here probably know that at the end of 1990, there was a conference of enterprise directors which focused precisely on the issue of creating a network covering enterprises of all the regions. We have managed to move this matter forward in a serious way. By the beginning of January, we already had 85 percent [of the enterprises] sign agreements, and those are agreements that actually yield products. It would seem this should create the proper conditions.

But as time went on, because of a whole slew of measures that had been carried out with regard to the so-called sovereignty matter, a number of borders between republics were closed. In particular, such republics as Ukraine, Belorussia, and the Baltic republics blocked the cross-border flow of products from their enterprises.

This has created an extremely difficult situation for our enterprises. Our enterprises started spinning their wheels in their work. This led to production stoppages, creating an atmosphere of uncertainty in work collectives.

What are our actions? First of all, we will direct our efforts at stabilizing the economy, and, naturally, we are not rejecting our reforms, which are to effect our transition to a market economy. We believe that this is the right way, but we must study it in greater detail and organize it at a higher level, taking into account all our activities.

Yanaev: I will now answer the second question. Indeed, today, when the Soviet people were being informed about the creation of the Emergency Committee, I, along with some of the other members, had contact with the leaders of all nine republics that had expressed their readiness to become members of the new Union Federation. We have had contact with the leadership of many regions and territories of the Soviet Union. And I can state that, on the whole, they support the creation of the Emergency Committee and the Committee's attempts to enable the country to overcome the crisis we find ourselves in.

I have talked today to Boris Nikolaevich Yeltsin. I am aware of the statement made by Boris Nikolaevich, Comrade Khasbulatov, and Comrade Silaev, and I would like to emphasize today that the Emergency Committee is ready to cooperate with the leadership of the republics, regions, and territories in accordance with our desire to find such adequate forms of development of our democracy, our economic growth, development of culture, and guarantees of human rights that could make it possible for us to solve most effectively those problems we are now confronting. I believe that if the leadership of Russia is ready to cooperate with us on such a basis, we will be able to find ways of effecting such cooperation. I consider the call for an indefinite general strike an irresponsible statement, and we probably cannot afford such a luxury now that the country is in chaos, the luxury of some kind of political games. Ultimately, these political games hurt our long-suffering people. If we are not indifferent to the fate of the Fatherland, the fate of Russia, we must seek out real forms of cooperation.

Correspondent from the Italian newspaper *La Stampa:* Two questions for Mr. Yanaev. The first question: Can you tell us, what is the state of your health?* The second question: According to the Constitution, a state of emergency can be introduced by the President of the country, or by the USSR Supreme Soviet Presidium, with mandatory agreement from the republics. Which of these three parties participated in this decision? And are there plans to set up some national salvation committee?† Do you intend to convene a meeting of the USSR Supreme Soviet immediately?

Yanaev: As for my health, I think it is all right, it allows me to work 16–17 hours a day, and as you can see, I am alive, sitting here before you. I do not look too bad, despite the fact that we really did have a sleepless night last night.

---

*This was a *double entendre* question, referring not only to the alleged illness of Gorbachev, but also to the answer Yanaev gave when he was asked about his health at the USSR Supreme Soviet at the time he was being considered for the post of Vice President. "My health is all right," he responded, "My wife ain't complaining."

†The National Salvation Committee of Lithuania was a shadow organization in whose name die-hard Communists, aided by the Soviet Army, were planning to take over Lithuania in January 1991.

As for the introduction of the state of emergency, we took as our premise and do proceed from this fact, that there can be critical situations requiring immediate actions, and we intend to ask the USSR Supreme Soviet, which will be convened on August 27, to confirm our mandate to introduce the state of emergency.

Soviet Television: I have a question for Gennadii Ivanovich Yanaev. In its address to the people, the Emergency Committee has stated that it would, first of all, take care of the interests of the public at large and would seek to solve the food and housing problems. Could you please tell us what concrete measures you are planning to undertake in this regard, and what are the resources at the disposal of the Emergency Committee?

Yanaev: You know, this is really a very interesting, very important question. The first step we are planning to undertake is to do everything possible to save the harvest. Probably tomorrow, we will issue an appropriate document, which will be oriented toward undertaking emergency measures to save the harvest. Further, we intend to utilize all the resources of the state in order, first, to carry out a special inventory of everything that we have in the country and, as you recall from our statement, after we have completed this inventory, we will tell the people what we have at our disposal. This will include the material resources which we will be able to mobilize in order to solve the housing problem.

In the last three years, we have not done a good job building housing, and many citizens who expected that we would carry out the program that we had announced at the outset of perestroika [have been disappointed]. Unfortunately, as it turned out, we were not up to the job, which is why I think we are now confronted with three major tasks. The first is food; the second is housing; and the third is transportation and energy, because we are moving toward winter. The situation in the energy industry is now very tense, and there, too, we need extraordinary measures if we are to avoid plunging the country into a difficult situation because of the winter.

Argumenty i fakty: Apart from his post as President, M.S. Gorbachev also holds the post of General Secretary of the Central Committee of the CPSU. Who will be discharging the duties of the General Secretary of the Central Committee? And my second question: As we have learned today, a series of newspapers, including *Argumenty i fakty*, *Moskovskie novosti*, *Kuranty*, *Stolitsa*, and a few others have been declared closed. For how long are they to remain closed, and when will they be opened? Thank you.

Yanaev: I think that since we are introducing the regime of a state of emergency, we will have to re-register some of our mass-circulation publications. Re-register. We are not talking about closing down newspapers; we are talking about re-registration, because this chaos that has overtaken the country is due, in part, to some of the mass-circulation organs. As to the post of the General Secretary, I would not like to comment on that. We have a Deputy General Secretary. He is fully capable of functioning, he is working, and I think that the plenary session of the Central Committee or a Party Congress can resolve this issue. I am now discharging the duties of the Acting President of the country, and I would not like to use my authority, or lack thereof, in order to influence the decision making of party organs.

Question: Mr. Yanaev, sir, what response did you get to your appeals to the heads of state and the Secretary General of the United Nations?

Yanaev: I must state that we are analyzing very carefully the statements of foreign statesmen and politicians, and I must state that their reaction is rather restrained, because, apparently, there are very few facts available at this point to take a definitive stand. I am familiar with the last statement by President Bush, where he expresses his hope that those foreign policy commitments that the Soviet Union had made would be adhered to in the future, which is what I have confirmed today, speaking before this audience, which is what we affirmed in our statement right after the Emergency Committee had been set up.

Novosti Information Agency: I have two questions to Boris Karlovich Pugo and to Comrade Starodubtsev. A lot has been written and said lately about the war on crime. Boris Karlovich, what new measures are you planning to undertake in this regard? And the question for Comrade Starodubtsev: Do you have the support of the mass of the peasantry, and do you think that the mass of the peasantry will support the Emergency Committee?

Pugo: In answer to your question, I would say that it is unlikely that we will be able to find any new, entirely new ways for combating crime that have not been used before. I believe that first of all, the organs of law and order, all of them, must improve their work. We must be more demanding with law-and-order personnel. They must improve their work to a considerable degree. We must create the conditions so that professionals can be more effective. I especially stress professionalism—this is my *credo*. Working in the Ministry of Internal Affairs, I believe that we can do a lot following this precept. As to concrete measures, I think that such methods as joint [militia–military] patrols of city streets have brought substantial results, as evidenced by the experience of over fifty cities. You may recall that at first, this measure was met with some sort of suspicion, but it has demonstrated its effectiveness. Indeed, recently even the Mayor of Leningrad, Sobchak, has resorted to this method of policing.

We must restore our ties to the community, but, above all, in my opinion, we must work with the leadership of law-and-order organs in such a way that all the potential of our personnel can be realized.

Starodubtsev: The greatest losses during the period of perestroika have, of course, been sustained by the peasantry; especially this year, the blow has been most crushing. The majority of the collective and state farms, along with the nascent individual farms, are today on the brink of disaster. The price equilibrium between the city and the countryside has been undermined. Lack of fuel and spare parts and a sharp reduction in other technical supplies have created a very difficult situation for the peasantry.

I think that the peasants, driven to despair, hope that, at long last, order will be restored, and that our society will turn its gaze to the peasantry and will help peasants to find a firm footing, to experience revival.

Nezavisimaia gazeta correspondent Tatiana Malkina: Could you please say whether or not you understand that last night you carried out a coup d'état? Which comparison seems more apt to you—the comparison with 1917 or with 1964?* This is the first question.

The second question concerns newspapers. First, how long will it take to re-register newspapers, and what criteria will decide whether or not a particular publication should be re-registered? Who will deal

---

*Reference is to the abrupt removal of Soviet leader Nikita Khrushchev from power in 1964.

with this? Will political censorship be introduced in the re-registered publications? Thank you.

Yanaev: With regard to the re-registration of newspapers, we will try not to drag out this process. I would not like to comment now on the criteria that will be used as the basis for this re-registration.

As for your allegation that a coup d'état was staged last night, I would beg to disagree with you, inasmuch as we are following constitutional norms. And I assume that confirmation by the USSR Supreme Soviet of the decisions we have made will enable us to state that absolutely all the juridical and, so to speak, constitutional norms have been observed.

It does not seem to me correct to draw a comparison with either 1917 or 1964. I believe any analogy here is simply dangerous.

Correspondent from the Italian newspaper *Corriere della Sera:* A question about Mikhail Sergeevich Gorbachev. Did you discuss with the President your takeover of power? Did he agree with you? Why is there no medical report on the state of his health? And a second question: Bearing in mind the wording of your communiqué, did you ask for advice from General Pinochet?* Thank you.

[Laughter in the audience.]

[Yurii Gremitskikh, an official of the Press Center: "Please refrain from displaying emotion. This is a press conference."]

Yanaev: I imagine that at some time we will publish the medical findings on Mikhail Sergeevich Gorbachev's state of health. As concerns your assertion that we took power from President Gorbachev, I would like to express disagreement with that, too, because what we are talking about is a temporary inability on the part of the President to fulfill his duties by virtue of the state of his health. And in accordance with the Constitution, the duties of the President pass temporarily to the Vice President or the Chairman of the Supreme Soviet.

ADN [German News Agency]: Will the introduction of the state of emergency affect the agreements with Germany; specifically, the timetable for the withdrawal of Soviet troops from Germany? Has Chancellor Kohl reacted in any way?

---

*A military junta led by General Augusto Pinochet overthrew Chilean President Salvador Allende in 1973.

Yanaev: I have already stated this in my opening statement, and the Emergency Committee has made its statement on this matter: We affirm all the commitments which the Soviet Union has assumed in the sphere of foreign policy, including our obligations with respect to Germany.

[...]

Soviet Television: Gennadii Ivanovich [Yanaev], could you please elaborate on the statement that "in certain areas, a state of emergency has been introduced"? What does "in certain areas" mean, and what is the geographical location? And the second question: When will reporters be able to meet with Mikhail Sergeevich Gorbachev?

Yanaev: You know, as soon as Mikhail Sergeevich's health improves, I am sure he will be happy to meet with reporters and representatives of the mass media. As to the state of emergency, I believe we have no need to introduce it throughout the entire country. There are regions which have such problems that cannot be solved without the introduction of the state of emergency. At the same time, I see that neither Kazakhstan nor Uzbekistan requires a state of emergency, because the situation there is stable enough.

So far, I cannot put a number on all such places. I believe that Moscow is one, and beginning today a state of emergency will be introduced in Moscow.

[...]

Question: Honorable Comrade Yanaev [. . .], I have the following question: Are you prepared to undertake some form of legal, constitutional measures against Yeltsin's decree aimed at removing the Party not only from society but also from the trade union structures?*

Yanaev: I believe that all the decrees and orders that are issued will be screened from the point of view of the state of emergency that we are introducing in the country. But taking advantage of this question of yours, I would like to emphasize: what the Russian Federation leadership is doing now—building barricades, calling for disobedience—is a very dangerous policy.

---

*Earlier in the summer of 1991, Russian President Boris Yeltsin had issued a decree prohibiting all political parties, including the Communist Party, from locating their chapters at workplaces anywhere on the territory of the Russian Federation.

This policy may lead to some form of military provocation so that later the blame for this tension, for this excess which may take place, can be put on the Emergency Committee. Soviet citizens should be forewarned, especially the inhabitants of Moscow, where a state of emergency has been introduced. We hope that peace and order will be guaranteed.

[. . .]

Correspondent from *Al-Ittihad*, United Arab Emirates: Mr. Yanaev, this is now the first news conference given by the interim President of the USSR, and your obligations include many things. At this time can you give us a guarantee—or your word, an oath to the public—that everything will be all right with the health of Mikhail Sergeevich Gorbachev?

Yanaev: I must tell you that Mikhail Sergeevich Gorbachev is completely safe. There is no danger to him. The only thing is that a certain amount of time is needed for him simply to recover his strength. Ladies and gentlemen, working in a regime like the one that President Gorbachev has been working in these past six years, the organism naturally . . . gets somewhat worn out. I hope that my friend President Gorbachev will return to the ranks and that we will work together again.

Interfax [news agency]: You have mentioned that every citizen of the USSR will have an opportunity to think over the new Union Treaty in peace and determine his position. In what way do you plan to find out what this position really is? Do you mean that you are planning to hold a referendum? And one more: What is the position of the Emergency Committee with regard to the Baltic republics and Georgia, Armenia, and Moldova, which do not intend to sign the new Union Treaty? And did Mikhail Sergeevich [Gorbachev] know that today a state of emergency is being introduced and the Emergency Committee has been formed? Thank you.

Yanaev: As to the formation of this Committee, as one of my colleagues has already noted, the Committee was set up today in the early hours of the morning. I believe that President Gorbachev understands and will understand that, indeed, at a moment when the country is in a critical situation, we will have to find some effective measures that would allow us to overcome this crisis.

With regard to the Baltic republics, Moldova, Georgia, and Armenia —that is, those republics that have stated they were not ready to sign the Union Treaty—our position is unaltered. President Gorbachev has stated it repeatedly. We will respect the will of the people. You know, I think we will find a way of finding out what the mood of the people is with regard to the Union Treaty. I do not know what form this will eventually take—whether a referendum or something else—but we will do our best to have the Union Treaty, on which the future development of our country depends, be discussed and accepted by our people in its entirety.

[. . .]

Novosti correspondent Vladimir Riabinnikov: My question is to Boris Karlovich Pugo. So, today, from approximately 15:00 in the afternoon, residents of Moscow are looking at the tanks standing around the Press Center. How do you technically see the organization of this emergency regime—as I understood from the reply given by Gennadii Ivanovich—in Moscow, given the situation that exists today? Hundreds, maybe thousands of people will start for the airports today and for places far away from the capital. How is this regime going to be put into effect?

Pugo: The introduction of military hardware, even including troops, onto the territory of Moscow—well, it is already completely evident that this is a measure wholly forced on us by the circumstances. It has been taken only to prevent any disturbance of order in Moscow, to prevent any casualties. That is our chief purpose. As for how things will be controlled, I see the development of events in the following way: Provided nobody forces us to extend it or to make it too long-term an arrangement, we would favor withdrawing all military units and hardware from Moscow as soon as possible.

Yanaev: We do not envisage a curfew.

Pugo: But that is something that comes within the jurisdiction of the Moscow commandant. If it should suddenly come about that this is necessary, well, that is within his jurisdiction. But we did not plan for this. We did not consider it necessary to do that today.

Postfactum [news agency]: Gennadii Ivanovich, your Committee consists of eight people. It's an even number, which makes voting difficult. How are you going to deal with this issue? Perhaps it would be a good idea to bring in another person, say Anatolii Ivanovich Lukianov [Chairman of the USSR Supreme Soviet]?

And the second question. Is it possible that the role of Mikhail Sergeevich Gorbachev in, say, the Tenghiz oil fields deal, will be investigated?

Yanaev: I believe we will be making our decisions in a consensus fashion. Your recommendation with regard to Comrade Lukianov is taken under advisement, but we believe that there must be a separation of functions, and the Chairman of the Supreme Soviet should be Chairman of the Supreme Soviet.

I can't tell you anything about the oil deal. I believe that Mikhail Sergeevich has made an immeasurable contribution to launching the democratic processes that were launched in 1985. This is a man who deserves all possible forms of respect, not an investigation.

You know I can't say anything about this oil. . . .

Question: But is an investigation of this type possible at all?

Yanaev: I believe that Mikhail Sergeevich has made an immeasurable contribution to the development of the democratic processes on a large scale throughout the country beginning in 1985. He is a man who deserves all respect, and not, pardon me, an investigation. He is not a state criminal. He is a man who has done everything so that we could embark on this democratic path. One last question?

Associated Press: Can you please tell us whether your committee is prepared to order the use of force against civilians? And under what conditions would force be used against civilians?

Yanaev: First, I would like to do everything to ensure that the use of force against civilians is not required. We must do everything to prevent any excesses. And what we are envisaging now—some extraordinary measures—they are not at all linked with any attack on human rights. On the contrary, we want to protect human rights as much as possible. And I would like to hope very much that we will not be compelled, we will not be provoked, into using some kind of force against the civilian population.

3 | Statements and Explanations by the Putschists After the Coup

Document 1: Interrogation of Defense Minister Dmitrii Yazov on August 22, 1991

In a post-coup interrogation held on August 22 by state investigators Leganov and Sychev, former Defense Minister Dmitrii Yazov confirmed that the coup attempt began when it did because the plotters wanted to prevent the signing of a new Union Treaty, a document that Yazov and his co-conspirators believed would bring the political death of the Soviet Union. Perhaps better than any other document, the interrogation shows the mentality of the people who brought the country to the brink of catastrophe. This transcript of the interrogation first appeared in Der Spiegel *and was subsequently reprinted in* Izvestiia *(October 10, 1991). It is reproduced here in English translation with only minor omissions.*

[. . .]

Investigator: You must understand that you are being interrogated in connection with your role in a crime that is defined as treason, conspiracy with the aim of seizing power, abuse of office. Now I would like to know how you respond to this accusation.

Yazov: I have a somewhat different view of what constitutes treason, and I don't want to hide this. Betrayal of the President, perhaps, but I did not betray my people or my country. I have known Gorbachev for a long time. We have worked together, solved many problems together.

Personally, I like Gorbachev very much. There must have been compelling reasons for me to go against the Commander-in-Chief of

our Armed Forces. Many, including myself, began developing a negative emotional attitude to Gorbachev. The reason for this was the
decline in the standard of living of our people, the collapse of our
economy, and the intensification of ethnic conflict and conflicts
among the republics. In certain Party leadership circles, people
began discussing [Gorbachev]. Gradually, the opinion emerged that
Gorbachev had run his course as an active statesman. Some felt that
he had either run out of steam or lost direction. His economic policy
consisted of begging for foreign credits, running up foreign debt,
but he did very little inside the country to repair the economy. We
talked about this with Mikhail Sergeevich in the [CPSU] Central
Committee and at [USSR] Supreme Soviet sessions. But he kept to
the same course: solving economic problems through foreign policy.
He and his government practically ignored economic problems inside the country. Our economic mechanism has grown threadbare,
and the country is on the verge of disintegration. On August 20, the
Union Treaty was supposed to be signed. . . . It became apparent to
me and many other comrades with whom I discussed this matter that
we were facing the disintegration of the country. Everybody had
been supporting the Union of Soviet Socialist Republics, and all of a
sudden we get the draft of a treaty of sovereign states!

We were convinced that this was not just a mistake but purposeful
activity aimed at doing away with the Union, substituting for it a
confederation of republics, each with its own president.

Investigator: [. . .] But why did you decide to remove the President
by unconstitutional means?

Yazov: I never thought that it was necessary to remove the President
from power. I am guilty of this crime to the extent that my participation in all of this made it possible. I could have prevented it all; I ought
to have informed the President about all of this. On Sunday, August
18, we decided that five people would fly to see him and to talk to
him about a voluntary resignation, with the proviso that Vice President Yanaev would assume the function of the President. Unfortunately, I did not know Yanaev. I just supported everything without
going into details. I regret all of this very much. This was, I believe, a
very grave mistake.

Investigator: This sounds pretty naive, coming from an experienced
statesman like you, the Minister of Defense.

Yazov: Discussions of this sort had taken place before, under different circumstances. More often than not, Comrades Kriuchkov, Baklanov, and Boldin were present at these discussions. We would talk about the situation in the country, about the disintegration of the Party, the economy, growing foreign debt, impoverishment of the people. Shouldn't someone be responsible for all that? Gradually, we came to the conclusion that the blame for all this lay with the President of the country because, as some said, he had put distance between himself and the Party, or as others said, he had betrayed the army. . . .

Investigator: Can you be specific about who was saying those things?

Yazov: Not really. These were just discussions. Of late, conversations tended to dwell on the fact that Gorbachev had been going on foreign tours too much in recent years, and that we often did not know what important matters he was discussing there. For example, what kind of speech did Gorbachev make in London at the G7 meeting [July 1991]? We did not have a good idea about what he was saying there. Until that time at least, we used to discuss these issues in the [CPSU] Politburo or in the Presidential Council or the Security Council.

Investigator: It was better when all these decisions were made in an open forum?

Yazov: Well, perhaps such an approach is not constructive, but all the decisions were made collectively. . . . Of course we were not ready to become even more dependent on the United States politically, economically, and militarily.

Investigator: So what decision did you come to?

Yazov: We had neither a plan nor a conspiracy. We just got together on Saturday. . . .

Investigator: Who called the meeting?

Yazov: Kriuchkov.

Investigator: Where?

Yazov: At one of the military installations in Moscow, at the end of Leninskii Prospect, close to the traffic police post, on a side street. Kriuchkov called at the end of the day and said: "There is something we must discuss." And I went there. After me, came Shenin and Baklanov. . . . That's when it all began. They were saying, "Well, maybe we should go and see Gorbachev, talk to him. . . ."

Investigator: Why were you in such a hurry? Is it because the Union Treaty was about to be signed?

Yazov: Of course, we were doing this because we were unhappy about the draft treaty, we did not want the state to fall apart. I said that I was ready to provide them with an airplane. The five people were to take off from Chkalovskoe [military airfield]: Shenin, Varennikov, Boldin, Plekhanov, and Baklanov. Plekhanov was the man who knew the entire security system there. I already understood that Kriuchkov had ordered Plekhanov to replace all the guards.

Investigator: What for?

Yazov: In order to persuade Gorbachev. . . . And if he refused, then we would have to take decisive measures.

Investigator: So whose idea was it—to fly there, to try and persuade Gorbachev, to break all communications, to switch the guards?

Yazov: I believe this was a collective decision. For my part, I had always been skeptical. I doubted whether we should undertake anything at all. I had my own doubts. When they came back, we were sitting in the Kremlin, in Pavlov's office. [. . .] Yanaev came at about 8:00 P.M. The five came at about nine. . . . The Committee was set up after the emissaries returned in a pretty gloomy mood from seeing Gorbachev. He had practically kicked them out. He said to them: "You must decide by yourself what you are going to do." So when they reported this to us, when they told us that they had shot their wad, that the original idea was unrealizable, then it became clear: Yanaev would have to sign the paper. Since Gorbachev was not sick, we were, first, to declare him sick. That's when we realized that our original plan had collapsed.

Investigator: How was the Emergency Committee formed?

Yazov: We were sitting in Pavlov's office. Yanaev arrived at around nine. Then came Lukianov. He arrived by plane, recalled from his vacation. Lukianov said that he could not become a member of some committee or other. He was the Chairman of the Supreme Soviet, the legislative organ that ruled supreme over everything. "The only thing I could do," he said, "is to make a statement about the unconstitutionality of the new Union Treaty." By that time Yanaev was quite drunk—that is, he had by that time had quite a bit of fun.

Investigator: Was Kriuchkov drunk, too?

Yazov: Pugo, myself, and Kriuchkov. We told Pugo that we had sent people to Gorbachev, but that Gorbachev would not receive them for a whole hour. He was, at the time, seeing some doctor who had with him some vaccine or other. And if Gorbachev agreed [to our terms], then Yanaev would for some time carry out his duties.

Investigator: And what if he did not agree?

Yazov: If you are talking about the complete removal, liquidation, or something like that . . . I assure you that was never discussed. Around eleven o'clock, we were joined by the Foreign Minister, Bess-mertnykh. He said: "If you put my name on this Committee, that will be the end of all foreign affairs." I was home at Bakovka about half past midnight. I got up at 5:30 and went to my office.

Investigator: Had you issued any orders before that?

Yazov: No, I did not give any orders in the evening until the documents were signed. The TV Center stopped functioning beginning at 6:00 A.M. We sent our own troops there.

[. . .]

Investigator: From a psychological point of view, the introduction of troops into the city was precisely what made people suspicious about the President's alleged illness.

Yazov: Our President—he is invincible, and the introduction of the troops, too, was probably a mistake. False rumors had been circulating: Gorbachev is abusing his office, there is someone behind him manipulating him. Possibly these rumors pushed us to undertake this action, this risky business.

[. . .]

Investigator: Then you saw that you had gotten too entangled in this caper, that it was time to get out.

Yazov: Yes, of course. I began taking certain steps early on. Things were going downhill, and fast. Those people at first agreed that the Committee would meet twice a day. But on the second day, it met only once. And the following day, I did not even attend the meeting.

Investigator: You mean the 21st of August?

Yazov: Yes, yesterday. I began withdrawing the troops.

Investigator: If you realized after the press conference that you had gone too far, that you had committed a crime, why did you go on with it? I have in mind the decision to bring the tanks in on the night of the 20th and early morning of the 21st, the introduction of the curfew, the appointment of the city's military commandant.

Yazov: It just happened that way. I'll speak frankly, and I always speak frankly. When the state of emergency was introduced, rumors begin to circulate that there would be a curfew, too. This Vice President, this Yanaev, introduced the state of emergency only on the second day.* And when the state of emergency was finally introduced, and I appointed General Kalinin to be the Moscow Military Commandant, he required very different means and forces, because a state of emergency and a curfew are two different things. And that's exactly how it happened. It was only on the evening of the 20th that he was able to issue his order introducing a curfew. That required additional forces—a difficult situation given the pouring rain and the politicization of the people.

Investigator: Who could have proposed to Yanaev to introduce a curfew in Moscow? After all, he could not have come up with the idea himself, he is not a military man.

Yazov: [. . .] Yanaev introduced the state of emergency in Moscow, and Commandant Kalinin ordered the curfew.

Investigator: Who suggested it?
Yazov: I did.

Investigator: Was it your recommendation to disperse the forces defending the White House? You would have had a formal excuse: by 11:00 P.M. everybody ought to have been at home.

Yazov: There were 70,000 people there.

Investigator: But there were tanks patrolling the city.
Yazov: Yes, they were, but I prohibited the use of fire power. All they were supposed to do was to block streets.

[. . .]

Investigator: Did you rotate the troops, for example those that were stationed near the White House? And was it because the men were

---

*According to Yanaev's statement at the press conference, the state of emergency was to be introduced in Moscow on August 19.

entering into contact with the people and were becoming politically unreliable?

Yazov: There was a battalion from the Tula Division there. Its commander was formerly the commander of the division, and he was Yeltsin's personal friend. Well, he withdrew his battalion—just to relieve the tension. [. . .] Then we sent in another unit, from the same division. After all, the men could not stay there all the time, they had to eat, sleep. That's why we had planned to rotate them. And when the second day began, I saw a whole busload of vodka being brought to them. That's how they tried to encourage the soldiers to betray their duty. Just imagine drunks in the armored personnel carriers! That's a whole different sort of danger.

Investigator: When did you realize that this putsch, this coup d'état . . .

Yazov: How can you call this a coup d'état? We said to Yanaev: "This is a joke, isn't it?" At the end of the press conference he presented everything as some kind of a joke. Didn't he say, "Mikhail Sergeevich is a friend of mine, and when he recovers, he will resume carrying out his duties"? That was done to calm people.

Investigator: It was then that you decided to withdraw the troops and, practically, embark on the road to repentance.

Yazov: For God's sake, very early in the morning* I issued the order to withdraw the troops and, along with that, to help with the dismantling of the barricades, so that we could put an end to this shameful business. It was in accordance with my own will, my own decision, that the troops began to withdraw. I knew that one must not play such jokes with the people.

Investigator: Now tell me honestly, when you planned this whole thing, you thought that people would swallow it without a peep?

Yazov: I think such an outcome would not have been possible. I am speaking frankly.

Investigator: Suppose people had swallowed it, what would you have done with Gorbachev then?

Yazov: I think we would have restored the communications then and would have returned Gorbachev to his duties, because those people who took over from him were incapable of governing.

---

*The order to withdraw was issued by Yazov on the morning of August 21.

Investigator: But a man whose honor had been violated, who had been arrested together with his whole family, how would he have been able to continue after that?

Yazov: This is a legitimate question. I am now torturing myself because of this.

Investigator: But you had to think things through, consider the options for the future.

Yazov: We thought about nothing, either in the short or the long run.

Investigator: But in case of your success, you had to have an idea of what to do with Gorbachev.

Yazov: Nobody thought about that. My position was that Gorbachev must be allowed to return.

Investigator: So that you could persuade him [to change his mind]?

Yazov: I did not plan for this, but I did count on it.

Investigator: How, then, were you planning to win over the people to your side?

Yazov: We counted on some goods, some reserves, some stocks hidden away somewhere. For this reason, we called in [Deputy Prime Minister] Shcherbakov. He said: "What you want does not exist. There may be some in the republics, but we have none of it. We don't have such-and-such. . . . Our requests for credits will be rejected, and in five days, we'll be baying like wolves from hunger."

Investigator: What was the cause of Pavlov's illness?

Yazov: I think it was alcohol abuse. I think he was doing this purposefully, to get out of the game. I saw him two or three times, and each time he was dead drunk. When he called me [for the first time], I realized this just from his voice. He said: "Arrest them all." This was after the meeting of the Cabinet on the evening of the 19th.

[. . .]

Investigator: What role do you now envision for yourself?

Yazov: The best thing for me now . . . I wish the earth could part and swallow me up. I am suffering terribly. I would like to beg Mikhail Sergeevich for forgiveness. I realize my guilt before the people.

[. . .]

Investigator: You have the opportunity now to send a message to President Gorbachev.

Yazov: In November, it will be fifty years since I joined the armed forces, and I, an old fool, took part in this . . . caper. Now I realize what a nightmare I caused you. I regret it very much. But it is probably too late after all I have done, bringing troops into the streets of Moscow. I know you as a man with a kind heart who shows so much understanding. I fought in the war, I was wounded twice. I would like to plead with you not to court-martial me, but instead simply to send me into retirement. I denounce this plot, and I will keep denouncing it until the end of my days, along with my complicity in doing harm to you, to our country and our people.

Document 2: Interrogation of Soviet Prime Minister Valentin Pavlov, August 30, 1991

In an August 30 interrogation, former Soviet Prime Minister Valentin Pavlov told an investigator "No," when asked whether he acknowledged his guilt in the coup. Pavlov insisted there had been no advance plotting. He sought to portray himself as an innocent dupe taken in by others closer to Gorbachev, who deceived him with tales of Gorbachev's illness and inability to rule the country. Pavlov insisted that he himself grew ill at an August 18 meeting, when the coup leaders agreed to form the Emergency Committee. The transcript was first published in Der Spiegel; *it was reprinted in* Izvestiia *(October 10, 1991).*

[. . .]

Pavlov: Yanaev also stated that he was assuming the functions of the President only until the meeting of the Supreme Soviet or the return of the President. On Sunday night [August 18], we were saying that we ought to call the Supreme Soviet into session on Tuesday. We—myself, Yanaev, and others—proposed this to Lukianov. He replied that it was not possible for purely technical reasons and that the session would probably convene on September 16, and then everything would be finalized. We responded: If it is not possible to convene the Supreme Soviet on Tuesday, then it should be done on Wednesday at the latest. What this means is that, as we were creating the Emergency

Committee, we thought we would need two or three days to convene the Supreme Soviet. Then, either power would then be vested in the Emergency Committee, or the Supreme Soviet would order other steps to be taken.

During the meeting at which the Committee was formed, I developed a powerful headache, my blood pressure shot up, and I had to take my pills. They are called "Valimeton" or something. I always carry them with me.

During those very sharp debates, they brought us more coffee, and some alcohol to go with it. After some time, I apparently lost consciousness. My guards told me that they carried me from the restroom, where I was lying on the sofa. So, to put it mildly, I couldn't move independently. They had to carry me to my car. I was simply incapable of taking part in discussions or debates. My only activity was on Monday night, when I was able, with the help of my doctors, to go to the Council of Ministers meeting. There, people were supposed to say what they wanted, but my condition was no better. This is the truth. And I would like to draw attention to the fact that I heard nothing about bringing in troops, about storming the White House or anything of the kind, or about depriving the Russian leadership of power. If there was such a discussion, I was in no condition to grasp it.

Investigator: When one listens to you, one comes to the conclusion that you fully deny your guilt.

Pavlov: It's possible that I already carry this guilt.

Investigator: Could you explain?

Pavlov: At the time of the meeting of the Council of Ministers, I said, "No confrontation should be allowed, no stoppage of an enterprise, no bloodshed, no thievery or looting on the streets and in the stores." I could and should have taken a more active position. I could have united with the other side, which was defending the White House.

Investigator: You mean you could have been among the defenders of the White House?

Pavlov: Probably. But I was very sick, and as my doctor told me, my blood pressure was 200 over 100. I am repeating once again: for me the only justification is the state of my health.

Investigator: Your earlier testimony suggests that you were aware that the President refused to yield to the pressure exerted on him.

Pavlov: The group that had come back from the Crimea reported: "The President is incapable of doing anything in the state he is in today. He refused to sign anything. He is incapacitated, and one cannot even have a conversation with him." That's what they said. Besides, they said that they had had to wait over an hour to be received by him, and that they saw his family, who were in a state of shock as if someone were gravely ill. He had doctors there. And only after the doctors had left. . . . He was in no shape. He threw out Plekhanov, the head of the Presidential Security Force. He would not even speak with him. He raged and raged, and Plekhanov was forced to leave the premises. It was simply impossible to have a conversation with him. He was out of shape, he wasn't a normal human being. Which is why he did not sign anything.

Investigator: How am I to interpret your testimony of last Friday when you said: "I was informed that the President had categorically refused to sign any papers that had anything to do with the state of emergency."
Pavlov: The people from that group said that it was not possible to have a conversation with him at all.

[. . .]

Investigator: One of the participants said: "So, we have completely exposed ourselves by that visit [to Gorbachev]. Everybody who is present here now is implicated in it. Now we must make a decision." In other words, you thought that since you had gone that far already, you would have to take the next step: to take over completely and transfer to Yanaev all the functions of the President.
Pavlov: Under those circumstances [. . .] I could not help believing Boldin that it was impossible to explain anything to the President.

[. . .]

Investigator: You didn't try to phone the President, did you?
Pavlov: I wasn't in any condition to do so, since in the middle of this meeting, I was already lying down and not participating. Physically, I simply could not have called.

Investigator: Did you have any alcohol or coffee in the afternoon?
Pavlov: No, no.

Investigator: Your bodyguards are testifying otherwise.

Pavlov: I mean we had coffee and a little alcohol. Now I know that it was whisky, because a bottle of whisky stood on the table. And I probably took a gulp.

[. . .]

Investigator: Was this all an attempt to seize power?

Pavlov: I am firmly convinced that no one intended to deprive the President of power. That was not the point. There was an attempt to convince the President that decisive steps ought to be taken. Nobody believed that Yanaev was trying to take power away from the President.

Document 3: Interrogation of the Head of the USSR KGB, Vladimir Kriuchkov

Arrested on Wednesday, August 21, Vladimir Kriuchkov was interrogated the following day. Below is an excerpt from the transcript of his interrogation. It appeared first in Der Spiegel, *and was subsequently reprinted in* Izvestiia *(October 10, 1991).*

Investigator: Describe, please, the circumstances under which you decided to fly to the Crimea to see the President.

Kriuchkov: We were planning to say it straight to Gorbachev that after his departure for a vacation we had come to a conclusion: the country is paralyzed. For example, take sugar beets. It was complete irresponsibility. All deliveries were off. And if we did not take immediate measures to stabilize our state, then we would have an imminent collapse of the state. We wanted to inform him about this. Besides, we were interested in hearing his position, and after that, in our opinion, we had to undertake stabilization measures. We were going to propose stern measures, but we saw no other way out. We wanted to do everything to have full employment, to reduce the number of factories that needed to be closed. The situation appeared to be so critical that it was not possible to drag things out until September or October. And we were planning to tell Gorbachev that it might be a good idea if he, for some period of time, would relieve himself of his duties and then, later, would assume them again.

Investigator: You wanted him to announce his own resignation?

Kriuchkov: We wanted him to delegate his duties to Vice President Yanaev, temporarily. But we knew that Gorbachev would soon. . . . According to Article 127, Paragraph 1, of the Constitution, he could have transferred his duties to somebody else.

Investigator: So it had nothing to do with some illness or other, but Gorbachev simply refused to delegate his authority to someone. Is that true?

Kriuchkov: He said: "You may try, but nothing will come of it." He also said that he was not feeling well. But today, of course, nobody can say that he is feeling well. We switched off the communications channels to maintain order, in our terms, and reinforced the security.

[. . .]

Investigator: Did you instruct Plekhanov to do this?

Kriuchkov: Yes, I did, personally.

[. . .]

Investigator: [. . .] You testified that at first the discussion [with Gorbachev] was very heated.

Kriuchkov: We proposed that he declare a state of emergency and transfer power to Yanaev, temporarily, so that he could return to his duties at some later date. His reaction to this proposal was very stormy. After a while, though, he calmed down, but he did not change his position: he would never give consent to this. So it had nothing to do with depriving the President of his powers. This is an important point: we did not breathe a word about it in any of the discussions.

Investigator: You mean physical liquidation?

Kriuchkov: What are you talking about?! We did not even discuss or think about what you are implying. Never. Gorbachev was to continue living. When we discussed Yanaev, we all understood very well that he could serve only for a very short period. We knew in advance that if it came to [armed] confrontation and the like, then we would have to resign right away, or take a completely different tack.

Investigator: Were there any written or verbal orders to storm the White House? Did you enter into negotiation with Yeltsin's people?

Kriuchkov: Our Emergency Committee did not undertake any actions that would in any way be directed against Russia or Russia's leadership. We were aware that no force would be sufficient [for that].

Investigator: Were there any attempts made to prevent Yeltsin from leaving his dacha for Moscow?

Kriuchkov: Nothing of the sort. We knew that he had left his dacha and was on his way. We were not watching him, though, we were simply aware of it.

Investigator: Did you activate your armed forces?

Kriuchkov: In Moscow, we strengthened the Kremlin security force. We did it on the 19th. We weren't prepared. And we issued no orders on the morning of the 19th. Everything was postponed till *mañana*. Of the things we planned for the 19th, nothing was realized. We took those measures later. You are saying now that the people were against us, etc. But the people reacted ambiguously. The first reaction resembled an expression of trust, emerging hopes. People did not respond to the calls to go on strike. Somewhere, four mines went on strike: one in the Komi Republic, the others in the Sverdlovsk region. But the country as a whole reacted far more calmly than one could have expected. However, the next day, the situation changed considerably. And yet, in industry, things did not go as far as strikes, just public rallies. The biggest rally was held in Leningrad, and there are reasons for that. But Moscow was much weaker; it had only 160,000 demonstrators. [. . .]

II

The Public Reacts

All over the Soviet Union, news of the coup caught people by surprise on Monday morning, August 19, 1991. Though many people remained watchfully on the sidelines during the crisis, others thrust themselves into the fray. The accounts in this section tell the stories of people who felt passionately about the coup and gravitated to the centers of action where they witnessed, and to some extent participated in, the momentous events.

1 | To the Barricades

When the August coup took place, Gregory Freidin, a professor of Russian literature at Stanford University, was making his fourth visit to Moscow since emigrating to the United States in 1971. He has written extensively about Soviet literature and culture as well as contemporary affairs. He produced this piece originally for The New Republic.

As she stuck her hand through a police barrier, a heavy-set middle-aged woman whispered to a pimply young sentry guarding a bevy of mean-looking armored personnel carriers (APCs) lined up near Red Square: "Sonny, hey sonny, here's a candy bar, go ahead, take it, please."

"Against regulations," he muttered, shaking his head, his hands gripping a Kalashnikov, and then added almost inaudibly, "Stick it in my pocket, fast."

The hand lunged forward—and a tiny chocolate bar disappeared into the pants pocket of the soldier's fatigues. Further on, more of the same: chocolates, cigarettes, sandwiches sliding into the pockets of the young soldiers standing guard before their APCs, as their officers looked the other way, both embarrassed by the soldiers' mendicancy and moved by the crowd's consideration and warmth. An occasional latecomer to the revolution, anxious to show his militant resolve, elbows his way to the barrier and begins to berate the soldiers, exhorting them to come over to the people's side, to join Yeltsin and Russia. The soldiers, mostly Slavic-looking, wink and smile at him indulgently from under their rain hoods.

On Monday morning, having deposed—and possibly disposed of—the country's President, the self-appointed Emergency Committee declared an all-out war on the opposition. It was hard to imagine at 8:30 A.M. that there was another power in the Soviet Union that could accept the challenge of those who had taken over the omnipotent central state. Yet the recently installed mechanism of the separation of powers was already working. By late morning, Yeltsin was climbing a tank—a big tank dispatched to bring this big man to his knees—to thunder away at the junta and to pronounce its actions illegal. A lone member of the Union Cabinet, Minister of the Environment Nikolai Vorontsov, a People's Deputy from Russia, joined Yeltsin on the tank to the cheers, as he told me later that day, of a hundred or so people. For a space the size of the Capitol steps, this was a sparse crowd.

No more than an hour earlier, on my way to the writers' enclave in Peredelkino, I asked my taxi driver to circle once around the White House, the seat of Russia's parliament. All was calm and ordinary as befits a government building on a sleepy Monday morning in August (inside, Yeltsin, Khasbulatov, and Silaev were denouncing the Committee as unconstitutional to the Moscow press corps). As we drove west through the outskirts of the city, a column of tanks, APCs, and trucks full of armed soldiers was rumbling in the opposite direction. By the time we turned off the main highway half an hour later, I had counted 150 tanks and APCs.

"This is my fourth coup d'état," confided the ninety-two-year-old writer I had gone to Peredelkino to visit. I inscribed for her a copy of my Russian translation of *The Federalist Papers*, published a few months earlier in the United States: "To Tamara Ivanova, on the day of her fourth coup d'état." Starved for news, we turned on the TV only to be treated to a splendiferous Bolshoi production of *Swan Lake*. The sole channel that was broadcasting over most of the country was teasing the viewers—at the brink of a civil war—with a well-preserved vestige of Russia's imperial adornment. The high-brow news blackout lasted pretty much throughout the coup, but on the second day an inventive soul in programming ran a concert hall production of *Boris Godunov*—an operatic blast at regicides, silent majorities, and pretenders. "Now, come to think of it, I have lived through six coups d'état," Ivanova corrected herself as we were parting. I amended my inscription accordingly. The book now seemed no more than a cruel reminder of yet another chance that Russia had missed.

Part of the tank column I had run into earlier was already parked in the center lane on the Kalinin Bridge just opposite the White House. A

Erecting a barricade near the White House

cop was blocking the traffic, but in such a dazed and half-hearted way that my taxi driver jumped the curb under his very nose and sped on without looking back to the other end of the bridge. There, something strange was going on. The column of tanks had stopped short of a flimsy barrier made of sections of wire-mesh fencing, behind which a dozen or so people were silently pushing an empty trolleybus. "It must've stalled," I said to myself, and wondered why they were pushing it at a right angle to the line of traffic. Next to the trolleybus, a small crowd, consisting of two respectable-looking women and several men in business suits carrying attaché cases, was pursuing a weaving milk truck. One of the men managed to jump onto the step of the cabin but was immediately pushed off by the irate and foulmouthed driver: "You fuckers, I'm the one who'll be paying for it, not you. . . ." They were trying to commandeer the truck. Only then did it dawn on me that what I was witnessing was the construction of a barricade.

Further up, where the bridge formed a thoroughfare with the road leading to the embankment and the White House, half a dozen tanks had already taken up positions, their gun barrels trained quizzically onto an empty patch of overcast sky between Russia's White House and the ghost tower of the new American Embassy building. The leading tank peaked out dinosaur-like from behind a barricade consisting solely of a ten-foot-long garden bench. Up close you could see the insignia of one of Moscow's two elite tank divisions. A helmeted soldier sitting on top of the gun turret displayed that intensely sullen and distant look that one readily associates with the actual Soviet man engaged in actual socialist construction. Before long, neighborhood kids were crawling all over the armor, their presence transforming the tank, if not into ploughshares, then into a heavy-duty tenement jungle gym. Taking in this scene, my eye paused to register a few inch-thick metal bars, used for reinforcing concrete, sticking out of the wheels of the tank treads. The bars disabled the vehicle, but the soldiers were in no hurry to take them out.

A young man in his twenties was now climbing on top of the tank. Leaning against the gun barrel and without any regard for the soldier, he began waving Russia's non-Communist tricolor flag. "Folks in the White House say you ought to stick another flag into the gun barrel," an unassuming elderly woman whispered loudly to the flag-waver. "Tell 'em I can't do it: the gun is sheathed," he hissed back, his face showing that he was at the limit of his pluck, and with added fervor went on making figure eights with his giant tricolor. Did the people holed up in the White House, for whose benefit the flag was being waved, find in this sight the needed encouragement?

The news spread that more tanks were coming along Kalinin Prospect from the direction of the city center. By 3:00 P.M. the crowd, which had swelled to a few hundred, rushed to the end of the avenue, which opened onto the White House. Men and women, mostly well-dressed types in their thirties and forties, scurried around in search of barricade-building debris. As barricade building goes, Moscow is Europe's most efficient city. You don't need to overturn cars or newspaper booths, or tear up roads for the sake of the archetypal cobblestones, because the city's construction bosses have unwittingly positioned stores of debris within everybody's easy reach. Unfinished buildings, torn-up roads, and mounds of fragments of reinforced concrete are as plentiful in Moscow as outdoor cafés in Paris. Past me marched a team of several men shouldering a heavy pipe, their shopping bags and attaché cases swaying in unison.

A column of light tanks and heavy APCs was rumbling along Kalinin Prospect. The fortification, intended to block their passage,

Civilians rush to form a human chain against approaching tanks on Kalinin Prospect

consisted of wire mesh screens strung across the street, held erect by some sort of telepathy or magic. To shield this contraption from the caterpillar treads, men and women joined hands to form a chain across the breadth of the avenue. The approaching column, headed by a tank-like thing without a turret, slowed to a crawl. It halted a few feet before the human chain, filling the air with the noise and stench of idling diesel engines. People rushed around the leading vehicle, some shouting heart-rending pleas not to shoot, others hurling insults at the helmeted head of the convoy commander which was sticking forlornly out of the vehicle's top hatch. "Shame!" "Don't shoot at your own people!" "Yeltsin is your President!" "Lackeys of the junta!" "Murderers!" "Be with the people!"

The commander climbed halfway out of the hatch. This exhausted wiry man of about forty was wearing a paratrooper's uniform with the two stars of a lieutenant colonel. Crouching behind him was a junior officer, a beefy young man with an anxious smile, cradling in his enormous arms a handy little automatic rifle. Red-eyed, his face the color of dust-covered asphalt, the commander had the tormented look of a rudely awakened man who was ordered to choose between his

A civilian appeals to a soldier near the White House

duty as an army officer and killing his own mother. The worst was still to come. Waving his half-empty string bag at the commander, a grizzled diminutive man—a lifetime of labor stamped indelibly into his demeanor—elbowed his way to the side of the tank. He was shaking with rage. Almost bursting to make himself heard over the engine noise, he shouted: "I've worked all my life, you see, all my life I've paid for this army, and now you've turned against me, you're shooting at me!" "Shame, shame!" the crowd was egging him on. Several people were pressing into the officer's hands photocopies of the Russian government's first appeal, issued at 9:00 A.M., calling the Emergency Committee "unconstitutional," its members "putschists," and declaring an "indefinite general strike." Many were yelling: "You did vote for Yeltsin, didn't you? You yourself voted for Yeltsin, and now you've got your guns pointing at him." The officer would not take the bait, but his gold-toothed smile made it clear that he did not mind being counted among Yeltsin's supporters.

A young man in blue jeans climbed on top of the tank, helping onto the armor two very good-looking, stylish young women. Like many in the crowds around the White House, all three had about them the air of people who "owned the place." Nonchalantly, they took surveys of the tank's top, located a comfortable spot, and without much ado settled down, park-bench style, for a chat and a smoke. But before their charm could begin to melt the armor, a corpulent matron, her graying hair in a tight bun, wrestled her way to the front of the tank and began to bellow at the officers. Gesticulating forcefully, as if unaware that her hands were ensnared by a brace of string bags, she pointed to her breast and roared: "I've nurtured you, bastards, and now you will be shooting me in this breast!" A vein on the commander's temple, which had been pulsating visibly throughout the encounter, swelled enormously; his dust-covered face grew ruddy, jaws clenched, but the eyes were clearly pleading to spare him this unbearable ordeal. His aide let go of the rifle, and it disappeared down the hatch. "Cut off the engine, commander, save your fuel for the crops!" The engine was stopped, and minutes later every vehicle in the convoy followed suit. No, he will not obey if ordered to shoot at the people, he said to a French reporter in reply to the question on everybody's mind.

The family reunion was now in full swing. The paratroopers had not eaten for twenty-four hours and had been on the march since leaving their base in Riazan two days ago. The contents of the barricade builders' shopping bags—those unprepossessing horns-of-plenty stuffed with sausage, bread, candy, cartons of milk—flowed freely into the open hatches of the paratroopers' tanks and APCs. An hour or so later, an order came for the convoy to leave. The street grew empty, exposing to all the vicissitudes of a revolution the still flimsy barricade and the wearied, vulnerable men and women who had the determination to build it. There were the people, there was their elected government, which the people had gathered to defend, and there was the enemy, epitomized by the old Communist state. There was a nation in the making.

2 | Letter from Moscow

At the time of the coup, the author of this letter was in Moscow with her daughter, Masha. Her son Artem was in Czechoslovakia, and her husband, Volodia, was on a concert trip in Nizhnii Tagil. She wrote this letter to a friend in Berkeley, California, and prefers to remain anonymous.

On the 19th, when our neighbor woke me up at 8:00 A.M. and said very rudely, "We have a military coup, and you're just lying around," it became clear that I had to act independently. On television they were broadcasting only Beethoven. Radio Russia and Moscow Echo were already silent, and the "voices" [Western radio broadcasts] were already jammed. I was frightened because it had happened so quickly and so easily. I telephoned Artem and told him not to come home, as I was afraid these bastards would announce a military draft. It turned out that the European countries had already closed the borders, and Artem asked me not to lose my head, that he would try to fly back.

I was surprised the entire time that the telephone kept working. I began to telephone around, and I learned that the tanks were already moving on Lenin and Kutuzov Prospects, and that they had long since surrounded our White House. I finally reached the people at *Nezavisimaia gazeta*, and there I heard the first consoling news: that Yeltsin had already written an appeal and that people were asked to gather on Manezh Square. I tried to phone anyone I could, just to tell them the news. I found a place for Masha to stay, and then, with the only (!) person who agreed to go with me, I headed for Manezh Square. It was 12:00 noon. Trolleybuses were still running along Tverskaia Street, and they were selling television sets and washing machines in the stores WITHOUT SPECIAL COUPONS (!). People were standing in huge lines for gasoline and food, and the rest of the city looked as though nothing were going on. There were people everywhere, and it seemed to me there was no alarm on their faces. We took a trolley to Manezh Square. . . .

There were not a lot of people on the square—more than the 150 that "Vremia" [the news program] mentioned, but no more than 500. Everyone felt lost, and some man was shouting into a loudspeaker that Yeltsin had not asked people to come to the square, and that it was just a provocation. I told him: "Don't get hysterical. People will come here anyway. Tell us what to do." No one knew anything. No one understood anything. Deputies of the Moscow City Council appeared, but although they were wearing their deputy pins, they somehow looked small in their beards and jeans. They didn't look serious. But they brought the text of Yeltsin's appeal and began to call us to go to the White House. Someone said that THIS was a provocation. I asked whether they couldn't find someone more serious to explain everything to us. At that moment we all heard a terrible noise and saw that on two sides—Manezh Square and Revolution Square—tanks were coming and trying to surround the square and us. It was terrible (one of the most terrible moments). I stood with my eyes closed and kept saying, "I'm frightened, I'm afraid!" An elderly Georgian who was holding me by the shoulder said, "Everything is okay."

Then the tanks coming from the side of Revolution Square stopped, and those from the side of Manezh Square continued to move and we ran there. When we ran up to them, the tanks that were surrounded by people had already stopped, and the people immediately began to climb on them. What the hell (I was wearing a skirt). One of the officers emerged from a tank and said that he gave his word as a Russian officer that they did not have weapons and their guns were not loaded. This was met with terrible shouts and whistles. He said the magazines of their guns were empty. I said, we already know about empty stores [Russian: *magaziny*]! In a word, there was a terrible ruckus, with everyone speaking at once.

Then a Deputy appeared again with a loudspeaker. We all followed him to the White House. Everyone was saying that the storming of the White House would begin at 16:00, and we should build barricades. It was really pouring rain. When we came to the embankment there were some people already there (very few!) and we learned that Yeltsin had

Tanks lined up on Kutuzov Prospect

already spoken, that he had read his appeal. We were all standing in the rain and there was a rumor that Yeltsin was already arrested. Later, he appeared on the balcony. Everyone shouted for him to leave because there might be snipers around.

Tanks appeared from the side of the bridge that connects Kutuzov and Kalinin Prospects. Everyone began to scream horribly and many, including myself, began to weep. Then we saw how people who were on the other side were weeping and sitting down on the bridge, blocking the path of the tanks. The tanks stopped and I heard some man in civilian clothes yelling hysterically into a radio transmitter that they couldn't move forward because people were lying down in front of the tanks, and that if the tanks all stayed on the bridge, it would collapse.

Then I saw something that made my hair stand on end. A Japanese man (!), carrying his child above his head, began to approach the tanks. I rushed to him and screamed like mad, in English: "You must come out!" I don't remember how many times I repeated this, seizing his elbow, before I heard him say, "Why?" I screamed again, pointing at the tanks: "This is our things!" At this moment, everyone screamed that the OMON [special police] had arrived, and everyone ran to them. The crowd carried me to the other side of the White House, the side by the Krasnopresnenskaia embankment.

I describe to you the most horrible, scary moments, though now I understand that the incident with the Japanese man was really funny. God only knows what he thought of me (I mean, what he thought of my English). In a calmer situation I probably would have said "This is our problem," not "This is our things." I'm afraid he probably thought that we didn't want to give him our tanks. . . .

There were indeed two cars full of OMON at the entrance. We surrounded them and began to rock them. They shouted back that they were Russian OMON, but no one believed them, and people said that decent people would never join OMON. Then Rutskoi came out and said that they did belong to the Russian OMON. Everyone shouted "Hurrah" and applauded, and said "Let the cars go."

Then we began to build barricades. Guess who was carrying the first logs and boxes? That's right, our women. Then the men joined us and began to carry logs from the park. Then we uprooted a telephone booth—and we were sorry that night, because we had to go to the metro station to make calls. It was five o'clock. After six, we all began to disperse. We all went home to put on something warmer for the night and to get food. I also went home to change clothes, to feed Masha, to find a place for her to spend the night, and to write a note to Volodia. My mood was terrible. I didn't want to listen to the radio, because at that time they were broadcasting the press conference of this new committee. Lenka called me from somewhere around the White House and said that everything was quiet so far. She came to see me, to leave her bags and to dry off. We cried together a little bit, got everything in order, and then went to the White House for the night with my sister and another man.

The crowd grew. To my surprise I saw many young people. They were setting up tents and making campfires. Tanks were standing at the White House under the Russian flag, and everyone was discussing the new heroes—the officers who took the side of Yeltsin. Three cars of soldiers arrived, and everyone hurried to give them food, tea, or coffee. The radio of the White House was working. There weren't really that many people, but we had a feeling of organization. There were persistent rumors that at four o'clock in the morning the storming would begin. So we began to strengthen the barricades.

Women hauling debris to build a barricade as tanks approach the White House

A barricaded street near the White House, mid-afternoon on August 19

Then an announcement was made on the radio that really scared me. They reported that in hospitals and clinics, toxicological and intensive care units were being freed up, and it was explained what one should do during a gas attack. And I didn't even have a handkerchief. People who had some supplies distributed bandages and rags. I said that I would not soak those rags in a rain puddle—it wasn't clean. The experienced people said that we should not soak the rags in water, but in urine! I should tell you that I was peeing in the bushes all the time, because I was really scared, and when you're scared, you have to. Everyone tried to get me to save this valuable liquid, or at least put it all in one bottle.

We were all waiting for four o'clock. The tension was so great that we could actually hear the hum of arriving tanks, though in reality, they weren't there. . . .

When it got lighter, everyone understood there would be no storming. I felt cold and bored. We were waiting for the metro to open, hoping that replacements would arrive to give us a rest. And I only went home when I saw that a thin stream and then a current of people was arriving.

As I was climbing over the barricade I looked back and saw people running to and fro. Suddenly I thought: "I love them all!" And I'm not afraid to say it; it was a moment of truth.

What came after that, I really don't have the strength to write. It was the end of the most terrible, nerve-racking day. The unknown was terrible. The night was sleepless. I was worried about Volodia. (He arrived on the morning of the 20th and went to the White House.) Desperation, hope, inhuman hatred. But there were already many of us.

Now I understand that we had many amusing moments. For example, on the 20th, the day of the storming, an army of taxis and gypsy cabs came to the barricades. The owners of the new cars were using them to form part of the barricades. Co-operators [private businessmen] in Volvos and Mercedes brought boxes of imported beer and American cigarettes. I can't describe it all. In short, life went on. As Berezhkov said, the last two days of communism were terribly rainy. . . .

We didn't go to the celebration meeting. We just turned off the telephone and finally had a good sleep. We didn't have a crumb of food in the house. We had eaten it all up or taken it to the barricades.

The shops were empty. My apartment was a mess. Thank God it's all over. However strange it may seem to you, I don't feel any joy. Things are very confused and unclear. I will never forget the fear and terror. Volodia went to Lubianka and cut a piece of granite off of Feliks.* We should have had a drink; then we would have felt better. Masha cries at night, and it makes me feel terribly guilty.

But all the same, God is with us.

---

*This is a reference to the toppling of the statue of Feliks Dzerzhinskii, founder of the secret police, on Thursday evening.

VICTORIA E. BONNELL

3 | **August 19 and 20 in Moscow**

Victoria E. Bonnell, a sociologist at the University of California, Berkeley, made her first visit to the Soviet Union in 1970. She has written extensively about the Russian labor movement on the eve of the 1917 revolution, but never imagined she would witness personally a major upheaval in Russia. At the time of the coup, she was in Moscow completing the research for a study of Soviet political art.

DAY ONE

"Wake up, there's been a coup," were the first words I heard that Monday. I was blissfully asleep when my husband rushed into the bedroom to announce the news.

"So what?" I said, still half asleep, "What do you mean, a coup?"

He was visibly agitated. "Gorbachev has been declared ill, and power is now in the hands of some emergency committee. Don't you understand, it's civil war now!"

The seriousness of the situation was beginning to sink in. Still, somehow the news did not quite fit with what I knew about the country. "Don't be so sure," I said, summoning what little remained of my American cool. "The Soviet Union is no banana republic."

He was not convinced.

My husband and I had met in Moscow in 1970, two years after Soviet tanks put an end to the Prague Spring. For the Russians of his generation and outlook (he was involved in the dissident movement), that was the harshest blow, and now, it seemed, he was destined to witness a replay of it all with a twenty-year delay.

We were visiting our in-laws in Moscow, and had brought our five-year-old daughter with us. Now the whole family gathered around the small white plastic radio with a single station. A Soviet announcer was reading the proclamations of the newly created Emergency Committee. His word-of-God style of delivery, seldom heard since the onset of glasnost, aroused unpleasant memories. Gorbachev, while on vacation at his dacha in the Crimea, had been taken ill, and was being replaced by Vice President Gennadii Yanaev. Yanaev and seven other top government officials had formed a State Committee for the State of Emergency to rescue the "great Motherland" from chaos.

My in-laws—Gita Samuilovna, a retired doctor, and Monos Grigorievich, a retired engineer, both in their mid-seventies—looked stricken by the news. Shaking their heads, they muttered again and again that it was *uzhasno* (frightful), really *uzhasno*, and shuffled around the apartment with bewildered expressions. And truly, the news was hard to assimilate. No one in our family believed for a moment that Gorbachev had stepped down because of illness. But what did it all mean? Our fears that first morning were almost too terrible to contemplate. Yet one thing seemed clear: the long expected right-wing coup, predicted by Shevardnadze and others, had finally taken place.

Soon the immensity of the events bore down on us. Gita Samuilovna turned on the television and found a test pattern instead of the usual morning programs. The mute television had a profoundly disturbing effect on my in-laws, who depend on it for a steady stream of information and entertainment throughout the day. Somewhat later, the blank screen yielded to films of opera and ballet, and that evening, the television carried the evening news and a broadcast of the junta's first and only press conference. Inexplicably, even children's programs were suspended on Monday and for the duration of the crisis. For seventy-two hours, the regular routine of television broadcasts on the four available stations almost entirely disappeared.

Monos Grigorievich quickly dressed and went to visit the local newspaper kiosk. He returned soon afterward with his lips tightly pursed and a frightened look in his eyes: the kiosks were closed and rumors had it that the non–Communist Party press had been shut down. As we later discovered, only Party-controlled papers such as *Pravda* continued to publish during the three days of the coup. The country's astonishingly successful independent newspapers—*Argumenty i fakty, Nezavisimaia gazeta, Kommersant,* and *Komsomolskaia pravda*—vanished for the duration of the crisis. The junta's appropriation of the media not only

Demonstrators marching from Manezh Square to the White House

disrupted the sense of normalcy but also aroused tremendous indignation among educated middle-class people, such as my in-laws, who
have come to cherish freedom of information and communication.

At about 2:00 P.M., I arrived in downtown Moscow. As I came out
of the Lenin Library metro station, I saw a crowd of people moving
through Manezh Square and up Kalinin Prospect in the direction of the
White House, headquarters for Yeltsin and the Supreme Soviet of the
Russian Federation. Manezh Square is an immense area extending the
length of several city blocks, adjacent to Red Square and the Kremlin,
and flanked by the Manezh (a large exhibition hall that had once been
a tsarist stable) on one end and the Hotel Moskva on the other. The
militia had closed off the entire square and nearby streets to traffic.
The demonstrators—numbering from one to two thousand people—
marched without interference. They were a somber and well-dressed
crowd; many of the men wore suits and carried briefcases. As subse-

quent events confirmed, the protest movement against the coup in Moscow was overwhelmingly a middle-class affair.

I stopped a tall man with a bushy beard—the kind of person I might encounter in my hometown of Berkeley, California—and asked what was going on. He told me that Yeltsin had called for a general strike against the junta. What did he think this was all about, I asked. He said with great conviction that Gorbachev had orchestrated the coup and was now pretending to be under arrest while watching to see if it succeeded. When I expressed some skepticism over this scenario, he insisted that Gorbachev was not a victim but a perpetrator of the plot against Yeltsin and the country's democratic forces. This conspiracy theory circulated rather widely until Thursday morning, when a haggard Gorbachev reappeared in Moscow, together with detailed reports of his incarceration and the illness of his wife.

Turning away from the demonstration, I crossed the street into Manezh Square, savoring the marvelous, almost illicit sensation of crossing aboveground on streets usually reserved for Ladas and Volgas, instead of in the underground passageways through which Muscovites are obliged to shuffle like moles. On this Monday afternoon, amid intermittent rain showers, the square was filled with demonstrators, strollers, curious bystanders, people fraternizing with soldiers, young couples holding hands, and people eating ice cream. The line at the popular joint-venture Penguin ice cream store, next to the Hotel Moskva, never slackened that afternoon. The atmosphere might have seemed almost festive had it not been for the presence of the tanks, armored personnel carriers (APCs), and military trucks that had moved in so suddenly that morning.

The sight of all the hardware was awesome. A long line of APCs extended from the Moscow River into Manezh Square. Besides the armed soldiers, equipped with Kalashnikov machine guns, several busloads of OMON special forces ("black berets") blocked the entrance to Red Square. APCs, rather than tanks, dominated the scene around the Manezh. I later learned that many tanks had been moved into Red Square. Similar concentrations of APCs and tanks—several hundred in all—could be found around the Central Telephone and Telegraph office on Tverskaia Street, in Sovetskaia Square, and in the vicinity of the White House.

The spectacle of so many military vehicles and soldiers reminded me of the monumental victory parades held in Red Square twice each year since 1918 on the occasions of May Day and November 7. Yet the

A civilian confronts an officer in Manezh Square

scene on this overcast afternoon of August 19 was dramatically different. The vehicles were going nowhere; the young soldiers who occupied them, though fully armed, appeared dazed and confused. As it
turned out, they were also hungry and had no bathrooms. The APCs
seemed oddly unprotected and even vulnerable.

Even more astonishing—almost surreal—was the lively fraternization between civilians and soldiers. By the time I arrived in Manezh
Square, fraternization was already well under way, leavened by cigarettes,
chocolates, and other goodies. Civilians, even some children, were
perched on APCs or circled around them. Most of the soldiers—very
young men with Central Asian or Ukrainian names imprinted on their
ammunition pouches—stood mute but not hostile. Since they had been
told that their presence in Moscow was needed to prevent a left-wing
coup against the government, they were understandably perplexed.

"Yeltsin Has Called for a General Strike"

"Outlaw the CPSU!" and "Put the Bolshevik Putschists on Trial!"

People gathered for a rally by the Hotel Moskva in Manezh Square

That day, neither the officers, nor soldiers, nor Moscow militiamen (generally sparse and aloof) interfered with the protesters or tried to protect the APCs from civilian intrusion. People took advantage of the situation and scrawled chalk slogans on APCs, such as "Shame on the CPSU" and "Yazov on Trial." Two young men stood on one APC holding placards with the message that Yeltsin had called for a general strike. Not far from them, someone had painted slogans on the pavement in large white letters: "Outlaw the CPSU" and "Put the Bolshevik Putschists on Trial." Officers must have had second thoughts about the fraternization because the next day the area around the APCs had been cordoned off. But on Monday civilians had easy access to the APCs, which were bedecked with flowers, protest signs, and offerings of food and cigarettes. The mighty defenders of the old regime of communism had already lost some of their aura of invincibility.

As I moved toward the far end of Manezh Square in front of the Hotel Moskva—a hotel reserved for members of the Supreme Soviet and other government dignitaries—a rally was in progress. An earlier rally organized here around 11:00 A.M. had already moved on to the White House, and new people, perhaps five hundred or more, were

Protest leaflets at a metro station on Kalinin Prospect

gathered around the platform. We strained to hear speeches by four men, including several members of the Moscow City Soviet, who exhorted people to support Yeltsin and defy the junta with a general strike. From time to time the crowd erupted into rhythmic chants: "Yeltsin, Russia, General Strike."

Behind the speakers stood a small but visible flag of the Russian Republic, a tricolor with horizontal bands of white, blue, and red. The flag has a long history in Russia, dating back to 1799, when it was introduced as the country's merchant flag. In 1883 it became an alternative civil flag, and in 1914 Tsar Nicholas II added to it a double-headed eagle, symbol of the monarchy. The flag, minus the eagle, served the Provisional Government but was abandoned after the Bolsheviks seized power. During Russia's August Revolution, the tricolor flag became a potent symbol of Russian democratic resistance.

A scruffy man appeared and began to hawk photocopies of Yeltsin's appeal, "To the Citizens of Russia," for fifty kopecks each. Some people grumbled and complained about paying for the proclamation, but there was no shortage of buyers. I later noticed identical photocopies of the proclamation posted on the walls of metro stations in central

Moscow, providing many people with their first information about Yeltsin's opposition to the coup. Only the most determined citizens could take advantage of this form of communication, since the type-script was extremely small and poorly spaced. During the next critical forty-eight hours, communications did not flow easily in this sprawling city of nearly nine million people. Word of mouth—at places of work and residence, in the streets, and over the telephone—probably trans-mitted more information than any other channels of communication.

As I returned home late that afternoon, I looked at Muscovite faces —weary, stolid, care-lined faces, eyes averted—and wondered: Will these people mobilize to resist the attack on their freedom and their fledgling democratic institutions? How will they overcome their dispersion in this enormous city, their poor communications, the apparent absence of net-works for organization? That first day, I did not see a single instance of leafleting or proselytizing in public places, except at the White House and around Manezh Square. My fears intensified when I got back to my in-laws' district of Sokol, about half an hour from the center of the city. There, people were going about their business as usual. The White House and the barricades suddenly seemed very remote.

When I put my daughter to bed, she asked about "the war" and whether we would be taken to prison. Unthinkingly, I assured her that foreigners would not be arrested, which she interpreted, quite logically, to mean that Muscovites might be. "Will they come and take *babushka* and *dedushka* away?" she asked with a grave look. No, I told her, certainly not your grandparents, for they are old and have done nothing but sit at home. "We're all safe," I said in my most reassuring voice, stifling my own alarm.

Later my husband and I talked about evacuation if things continued to deteriorate. We were relieved to learn earlier that air travel had not been interrupted. But we were not ready to leave yet. The situation seemed too ambiguous and our emotions—a mixture of caution and daring, hope and despair, exhilaration at being there and fear for our personal safety and that of our family—were too contradictory to guide us toward decisive action.

DAY TWO

On Tuesday morning the situation seemed unchanged except that a major public rally was scheduled to take place at the White House at noon. The announcement came over the Moscow Echo radio station

People carrying an enormous tricolor flag to the midday rally at the White House

and shortwave broadcasts. I saw notices of the meeting on the walls in some metro stations with instructions about which station to exit from. Since the junta had taken almost complete control over the mass media, communication networks remained extremely restricted and many Muscovites never found out about the rally.

Tuesday was sunny. Enormous crowds of people streamed toward the White House, covering the entire area of the parking lot behind it. They spread out on the lawn beyond the parking lot and into nearby streets. Some people perched on the pedestal of a huge sculpture of a woman waving a Soviet flag, flanked by a soldier with a rifle. Others stood on ledges of nearby buildings. People crowded onto the tanks that had gone over to Yeltsin the evening before, now decked with flowers and heaped with milk cartons, bread, potatoes, and canned food.

The sight of so many people—perhaps as many as one hundred thousand—gave me hope, for the first time since the coup began, that Muscovites would mount significant resistance to the junta. The size and determination of the crowd and the tone of the rally reminded me of civil rights and antiwar demonstrations I had participated in during the late 1960s and the 1970s. This was no random collection of ordinary

Muscovites. Judging by their faces, clothes, and deportment, the vast majority were people with higher education, solidly middle class intellectuals and white-collar workers. Apart from the Afghan vets who came to defend the White House, few of the demonstrators looked like factory workers. Although there were some young people, especially students, the vast majority of the participants in the demonstration were in their thirties and forties. Photographs we took at the time confirm this impression.

There were women in the crowd, but noticeably fewer than men. "They're probably standing in line somewhere," I thought to myself. Political figures and public speakers during the coup were nearly all male. At the Tuesday demonstration, only one woman spoke publicly: Yelena Bonner, the widow of Andrei Sakharov, a featured speaker at the rally.

People did not come in organized political groups, and there were few placards. The crowd consisted of individuals, brought there by a common opposition to the junta, their allegiance to Yeltsin, and Russian nationalism. Three chants that periodically rang out over the square conveyed the mood of the crowd: "Put the junta on trial," "Yeltsin, we support you," "Russia is alive" (the latter proclaimed at the rally by the poet Yevtushenko).

For three hours, speaker after speaker took the microphone to exhort people to resistance. They reminded the crowd of the long history of submission to unjust authority (mention was made of Czechoslovakia in 1968, the millions who had been arrested and sent to camps, and so on) and urged each citizen to take a stand against the coup. Others spoke about the illegality of the junta, its violation of Article 62 of the Constitution of the USSR and the criminal code, its unlawful introduction of martial law, and the necessity for proper legal proceedings against its members. One phrase was repeated over and over: "Put the junta on trial."

Speaker after speaker praised the people of Moscow and Russians more generally, giving the rally a strong nationalist tone. This was most vividly symbolized by the arrival of a gigantic tricolor flag, carried by several hundred people and hung along the balcony of the White House that served as the speakers' platform. A few smaller flags were also sprinkled throughout the crowd.

Eloquent and moving speeches, such as the one delivered by Bonner, aroused strong feelings of allegiance to Moscow and Russia. Bonner began with an anecdote from her days of exile in Gorky. She had asked a KGB officer: "Why do you write lies about my husband's activities?" "It is written not for 'us,' " he replied, but for 'the rabble' [*bydlo*—literally,

The Tuesday rally, with the tricolor flag draped over the White House balcony

cattle]." The junta is the same, Bonner continued. Everything they have said and written is for the "rabble." "They think we are rabble." All putsches and revolutions are decided in the capital, and Muscovites must demonstrate that they are not rabble and cannot be bought with a salami paid for with a Pavlov ruble—a reference to the terrible inflation that devalued the ruble following the appointment of Valentin Pavlov as Prime Minister in January 1991. This statement elicited tremendous applause.

Relentlessly, Bonner exhorted the crowd, calling on them to defend the Russian parliament, the Russian President, and the President of the USSR. For although he was sometimes mistaken, Gorbachev was, after all, "our President" (applause). We must not give over our country to a "gang of crooks"; we must resist as we did in 1941. She concluded with a paean to Moscow, so dear to Russian hearts, where she chose to live even though she could have moved anywhere (prolonged applause). She spoke with great authority and elegance.

Some speakers mentioned the general strike, but this was not a major theme at the rally. The timetable for the beginning of the general strike, vague on Monday, become even more uncertain on Tuesday. The tactical issue on Tuesday was not the general strike but the de-

The crowd listening to speeches at the Tuesday rally

fense of the White House against what many believed to be an imminent military attack. An extraordinary session of the RSFSR Supreme Soviet had been scheduled to begin there on the following day.

The mood of the departing crowd was tense, determined, and somber as it moved away from the White House in a disciplined manner. I was struck by the fact that there had been no disturbances or incidents, no hint of violence during the entire afternoon, despite the fact that policemen were conspicuously absent and no informal networks of civilians had been created to guide and regulate the crowd.

The junta had declared a curfew in effect from 11:00 P.M. to 5:00 A.M.. This, it seemed, was the prelude to an attack on the White House. Speakers had urged people to remain and defend the White House, and some five or ten thousand people heeded their call. Around five o'clock they began to form self-defense units. A group of some fifty or sixty Ukrainian men gathered in front of the White House to discuss procedures. Some political groups had units, such as the anarchists, and the supporters of Memorial, an organization devoted to the preservation of information about Stalin's terror. Other units consisted simply of volunteers without any common allegiance except their opposition to the junta. As night fell, small groups set up camp in the

Children on a pro-Yeltsin tank near the White House (Anna Freidin, the author's daughter, is at center)

area, making fires, eating food, listening to radios; some took naps.

Having collected my daughter at the American Embassy, where she was in daycare, and photographing her standing on a friendly tank, I departed for home. Everyone in my family was glued to the radio that evening. There was a feeling of intense apprehension and foreboding. We all expected a confrontation later that night. Around nine o'clock I put a call through to my father in California, my first since the coup began. He wept on the phone as he told me how frightened he had been for our safety. We were not in physical danger, I told him, but tonight would probably lead to violence. It was hard explaining to him that so far most of the city remained unaffected by the coup. Despite the high probability of violence around the White House, our neighborhood presented no dangers whatsoever.

My father's alarm gave me a sense of how ominous the situation must appear to the outside world. With memories still vivid of the government attacks in Lithuania and Latvia as well as the Tiananmen massacre, a major loss of life and even a civil war seemed likely. I went to sleep that night with a heavy heart.

Defenders of the White House set up camp

Men guarding the White House early Tuesday evening

LAUREN G. LEIGHTON

4 | **Moscow: The Morning of August 21**

Lauren G. Leighton, who teaches Russian literature at the University of Illinois at Chicago, is the author of many scholarly works, essays, and translations. He lived in Russia during most of the two years preceding the coup and in 1991–92 was a Fulbright Exchange Teacher at the Moscow Pedagogical University.

I was in the orchard taking a lukewarm shower in a cold rain at the dacha near Kharkov, in Ukraine, when the Emergency Committee made its now well-known statement that it had taken power. The voice over the radio sounded like it is supposed to sound at such a moment: spooky, without human quality, distanced, ominous. It had the Party Old Guard ring of a lie to it—not the words themselves, but the presumptive ease with which the Old Guard lies for its view of history. My wife, her father, and I immediately decided to return to Moscow, not out of any sense of apprehension, but because we knew that the future would be decided there and we wanted to see it.

When we arrived in Moscow we got a glimpse of tanks near the Kremlin and passed a standing column of armored troop carriers on our way home, but the city seemed calm and our taxi driver reported that most of the city had not reacted. Life also continued as usual in our neighborhood, and I saw no signs of military control when I walked down to look at the Ostankino television center. Radio Free Europe reported resistance, but the impression we received was that people had not reacted. So far as we could tell throughout the remainder of August 20, the putschists seemed to be in control; we had plenty of time to decide what, if anything, we could do.

In this we erred, of course, and it was only in the evening, with rain pouring down and public transportation halted, that we learned from friends that we had lost another day. We tried to make our way across the city on foot, but finally turned back, wet and feeling foolish. We spent the rest of the night listening to the reports of the confrontation on the Garden Ring Road near the American Embassy. I had spent most of the previous two years in Russia because, as a colleague once remarked, "History is happening there and it would be shameful to miss it." Now we were missing it.

The rain was still alternately drizzling and pouring on the morning of August 21. We were able to make our way by trolleybus to the Garden Ring Road at the junction with Tverskaia Street and then walked about a mile to the American Embassy. We had to make our way through two columns of light tanks, engines running, the air thick with diesel fumes. People surrounded the tanks, begging the soldiers to return to their barracks. ("Please go home, children," is the way one woman put it.) The street in front of the embassy was littered with the remnants of the confrontation. Further along the Ring stood the first outer barricade: smashed trucks and trolleybuses, huge blocks of cement, iron rods, boards, glass. We climbed with difficulty through the mass of junk, and were helped by irregularly dressed RSFSR soldiers, Afghanistan vets in their distinctive combat fatigues, and young men in pseudo-military dress of every description. Russians of all ages welcomed us. People stopped each other to exchange information. Further along, where the lane along the center of the Ring descends beneath an overpass at the junction with Kalinin Prospect, we came upon the now well-known site of the "Three Fallen," masses of flowers and candles, and people crossing themselves and kneeling in prayer.

A graduate student reported the first of many contradictory explanations of the clash: the tanks had been ordered to pull back, took the wrong direction, and descended into the underpass. When the soldiers realized they were trapped by the high walls, they panicked and tried to smash their way through the row of trolleybuses. The *"barrikadniki,"* assuming that this was the long-awaited attack, panicked in turn. Further along, another young Russian told us that eager young tankers, or their commanders, had acted on their own. Later that day we were assured that the incident was a last-minute provocation. One report was that it was a diversion to draw attention from an assault by a KGB team through the heating tunnels into the White House.

A makeshift memorial on the spot where a young man was killed in the early morning of August 21

The three young men who perished at the barricades (photo from the funeral procession, Saturday, August 24)

The mood within the perimeter was a mixture of defiance and anticipation, but not fear. The expectation was that the real attempt to storm the White House would occur after dark. Until then a lull. There was hope that a tank column approaching along the Leningrad Highway the night before had stopped not under orders of juntists experiencing second thoughts, but in outright refusal to confront the troops of the Russian Republic and crowds of unarmed citizens standing in the way. That hope became what I consider a litany of the three days: Russian soldiers must not fire on Russian people, Russian soldiers must not kill Russian soldiers. I am impressed by what we saw only later on television: People surrounded the tanks on Red Square and elsewhere in the city center for the whole three days, begged the soldiers not to obey the orders of the putschists, painted slogans on the tanks and covered them with flowers, and fed the soldiers when they realized they were not being supplied. For their part the soldiers—in most cases naive and provincial—were initially hostile, then sullen, then confused. Most had no idea why they had been called into the city. Only one soldier declared he was prepared to obey orders to shoot. Many showed as much interest in their legendary surroundings as any other tourist in Moscow for the first time. All clearly enjoyed the unexpected abundance of food, candy, cigarettes, and souvenirs given by one and all.

Among the first things we noticed as we approached the White House were the pun-slogans covering windows and barricade junk. "We are not afraid of Pugo-Pugach" (a pun on the surname of Minister of Internal Affairs Boris Pugo and the Russian word for a toy gun). "Put the putschists to a people's trial!" "Let's put the putschists a putsch in the tush." More than a few slogans were plays on the word *khunta* (junta) and *khui* (prick). Many slogans were straightforward: "Yazov is a piece of shit!" All were defiant: "Defend Russia!" "Russia! Lithuania is with you!" "They tried to drive us back into the barn, but we won't go!" "Traitors, out of Russia!" In several places garbage cans were marked with signs "Party cards here." During those three days and after, hundreds of Party membership cards were thrown at the front door of Party headquarters on Staraia (Old) Square. Interestingly, there were no anti-Gorbachev slogans, but as soon as the President was safe, a number of extremely bitter signs appeared, including one reminding Yeltsin that "the only cure for a hunchback [*gorbatyi*] is the grave."

We had to make our way through three barricades before reaching the huge marble White House standing back from the long curved

A trolleybus damaged by an armored vehicle in the early morning of August 21

embankment of the Moscow River about two miles to the northwest of the Kremlin. It can be approached from the Kremlin along Kalinin Prospect past the Garden Ring Road. Adjacent on a rise at its southwest corner stands the American Embassy, which obviously figured prominently in the defense. The juntist troops would have to forgo approaches along two streets from that direction, for fear of causing an international incident. Both streets were left open, as if daring the juntists to risk that approach. The bridge across the river was barricaded by large vehicles and heavy construction machinery of all kinds. The river itself was blocked by barges and ships. All other approaches on all sides were similarly barricaded three times: trucks, trolleybuses, construction machinery, beams and pipes, boards and beams, glass, blocks of cement, piles of bricks and cobblestones, anything and everything that could be piled up to halt and delay tanks. Many people remember the double and triple rows of public transportation vehicles that formed the strongest barriers; I remember the long concrete-reinforcement rods that stuck out in all directions like straws. Around the Soviet-style monument to the workers who barricaded this area in 1917, the straws had been arranged with pleasing grace, as if with artistic forethought.

Units of armed citizens, MVD militiamen and MVD special police troops (OMON), young men and women, and curious onlookers surrounded every area control post, each marked by a campfire for hot tea, tents, and sleeping quarters jerry-rigged in vehicles. Within the center stood ten tanks arranged at strategic points around the White House. Regular army soldiers, Afghanistaners and other veterans, students and young workers of both sexes—Muscovites of all ages—had come to defend this last and only and best defense of Russia's democracy. Many were obviously tired. They slept in groups under whatever shelter they could find or build, or nodded around the fires. The seats of some vehicles were filled with people sleeping in every possible uncomfortable position. One young couple had a trolleybus all to themselves. While he slept with his head on her shoulder, she smoked and frowned at the rain. Later, when my wife complimented a group of Afghanistaners surrounding a tank, they protested that they were only standing in for exhausted regular soldiers sleeping somewhere inside the White House.

Even as we arrived, so also did hundreds of others, and soon thousands began arriving. Everybody tried to bring along another piece of junk to throw on the barricades. The flow was down on the Ring Road and Kalinin Prospect, through the barricades, and directly through the center of the square behind the White House. People looked with wonder at the splendid chaos of the barricades, and turned to anyone who looked like an experienced barricader for inside news of what was happening or might happen. Sometime around ten o'clock, others began to arrive too. Loudspeakers welcomed them and people rushed to hug them: busloads of heavily armed militia units from other cities —Orel, Yaroslavl, Vladimir, Rostov, Novgorod, Smolensk. People clapped them on the shoulders and helped carry their equipment. Together with them throughout the rest of the day, groups of soldiers of the regular army strode self-consciously, embarrassed by shouts of praise, "to the side of Russia," against "the junta," "the putschists," "the Communists," "the traitors," as they were called by one and all. We should have known then that the outcome had been decided. By the end of the day over a half a million people were there, and in the city as a whole several million people had taken to the streets. People were also taking to the streets in other cities; the demonstration on St. Petersburg's Winter Palace Square was another impressive event.

But the general view at that moment was that several tank divisions were in Moscow, and even though most of the troops might refuse to fire on their own people, the plain damn size of the confrontation could lead to bloodshed. No one thought that ten tanks could stop a division. No one could be sure that the juntists would not muster the courage to solve their dilemma "Lenin-style." That did not seem likely—Yanaev's shaking hands at the press conference the day before revealed the true character of the putschists—but it did seem possible that they would issue fatal orders out of desperation. There was every expectation that when the time came, the army would come crashing through, with no regard for the civilians determined to stand in their way. If the tanks did come, there could be no way out of that mass of people and metal.

Rain, fog, the smoke of campfires. Women, children, old people, students, and street toughs. Earnest young men in suits and ties—the "new businessmen." Tents, ambulances, medical stations, tables of food free for all. Many people had brought their children, and fortified shelters had been built for them. The organization was impressive: people had been divided into sectors with command posts, complete with colored arm bands to mark position, function, and authority. Weapons had been given only to civilians who clearly knew how to carry them. Vodka was conspicuous only by its absence. And the rain came down.

The long, high balcony on the side of the White House facing away from the river was lined with people. Someone was speaking over the loudspeakers, but we could see no one speaking from the balcony. Resolutions were being proposed and voted on, and the crowd on the square voted eagerly and unanimously. It took us some time to realize we were listening to the proceedings of the Supreme Soviet of the RSFSR inside, and people on the square were voting along with their deputies! There is no denying that this was the world center of democracy at that moment in our time.

We walked around, and I took lots of pictures. As an obvious foreigner I was recognized wherever we went, even given the special favor of climbing up on a tank to pose for a photo. I was gladly shown the interior, and the armament was explained to me. *Newsweek* later reported that a few tanks near the White House had turned their guns symbolically in the other direction, and that they were not armed. In fact, the tanks had gone early on to the side of Russia, and now they were inside, not outside, the barricades. People wanted to know who I was and how an American came to be there. But no one was particularly talkative: there was too much tension, and though people knew the world sympathized with them, they also understood that they were alone. It cannot be said that spirits were high. Even as people jeered and cheered, argued and orated, they were solemn and serious.

I tried an experiment. When I smiled at someone, that person smiled back. If I held out my hand, someone shook it. When I made a V sign, the sign was immediately returned with a smile. Wherever I pointed my camera, people assumed whatever pose they thought seemed appropriate to the day. People readily answered questions, and took a moment to tell us who they were and why they were there. Most of us were spectators that day—there was clearly a difference between experienced barricaders and those who had arrived too late to be given a job to do—but solidarity is still the best word in any language to describe the morale that day. The barricaders at one post immediately made room for me to sit with them while I changed film. The young men in charge of areas helped me reach a better vantage point, and showed by their polite manner that they wanted Russia and Russians to be seen in their best light by foreigners.

So, on the morning of August 21 the tanks in the center of Moscow would have to pass through massive crowds of people before reaching the White House. Troops had moved away from the Moscow City Soviet, where Mayor Gavriil Popov and his government had also barricaded themselves. Tank columns had halted on the roads into Moscow, and those on Red Square showed no indications of leaving or acting. The army had refused orders to advance on Leningrad. Several cities remained under the control of the still strong Party rule, but crowds had taken to the streets in many cities. By this time anyone who was anyone had arrived to support the Yeltsin government: Gorbachev's former political adviser Aleksandr Yakovlev, Vadim Bakatin (one of Yeltsin's opponents in the spring election campaign), Eduard Shevardnadze, Andrei Sakharov's widow Yelena Bonner, and poet Yevgenii Yevtushtenko.

Mstislav Rostropovich flew in from Paris the moment he received word of the coup. Later that day he walked through crowds of adoring Russians.

Some things never change. Russians only half joke when they say that the worst scourge of the Soviet period was not Stalin, but the little old ladies who appointed themselves guardians of Socialist Morality in every neighborhood. Nowadays they are called keepers of social or civil propriety. While we watched a tank maneuver its way through a barricade, it knocked over a tree. The usual band of little old ladies came running forth to scold the soldiers, who made a hasty retreat.

As in any country, where the action is, there the little boys are. Some had fashioned for themselves the most impressive military wear. All were everywhere and into everything. Their appointed duty was to hand out sandwiches from trays, and perhaps a sign of the patriotism of those days was that they seemed not to have found a way to sell what they were supposed to give. Those who were there on their own were of course envied by those who had to endure accompanying parents.

Old people were there too, many of them wearing the medals of their World War II generation. They helped make tea around the camp-fires, carried signs, stopped barricaders to offer words of encouragement. One well-known TV clip shows an elderly woman determinedly carrying cobblestones to the construction of a barricade.

The end came so swiftly and in such unlikely fashion that no one really believed it, neither then nor later. Ruslan Khasbulatov, acting presiding officer of the Supreme Soviet of the RSFSR, simply announced that the putschists had made a run for Vnukovo Airport. There were loud cheers, and then the Supreme Soviet began issuing orders: The MVD and KGB were to arrest the putschists. The army was to submit immediately to the government of the RSFSR, and troops were to return to their barracks. A delegation formed under the leadership of RSFSR Vice President Aleksandr Rutskoi was to go to the Crimea and free Gorbachev. Another delegation was sent to take control of the Kremlin. All local soviets that supported the junta were to be dismissed immediately. The headquarters of the Central Committee of the Communist Party of the Soviet Union was seized. All press, radio, and television personnel were immediately to resume control of their reporting facilities. A delegation was sent to KGB headquarters on Lubianka to take control. The Black Berets in Lithuania were told to cease and desist.

When we left the White House that evening, the sun was shining. I do not remember when the rain stopped. On Novyi Arbat, people stood as if frozen to the sidewalks, listening to the proceedings of the Supreme Soviet of the RSFSR being broadcast from loudspeakers every hundred feet or so along the promenade. Every face showed the same expression. I have tried ever since to find a word to describe that expression. Thoughtful is the one that fits the best.

5 | Moscow's M.V. Khrunichev Machine-Building Factory Reacts to the August Coup

At the time of the coup, Vladimir Petrik was chief of the assembly division at the M.V. Khrunichev Machine-Building Factory. Petrik's division of the factory built the Mir space station and assembled the Proton rocket launcher. What follows is his story of the coup as it was recorded by a staff writer at Literaturnaia gazeta. *It was published on January 1, 1992.*

"I began my career thirty years ago in this factory," says Petrik. "Back then, the factory was devoted to aviation and was simply called 'P.O. Box 222.'* A little later, after the introduction of an 'open,' consumer goods section, they gave it a second, parallel name [. . .]. And so it was also known as the M.V. Khrunichev Moscow Machine-Building Factory."

THE MORNING OF THE TWENTIETH

August 20, 9:00 A.M. The second day of the coup. An executive meeting of the factory administration. Seventy people in attendance. All are from upper management. The bosses. The elite. Kiselev, the director of the factory, rises. He has a copy of *Pravda* in his hands.
[Here is Petrik's account of what occurred at the meeting:]

"Have you had a chance yet to familiarize yourselves with Resolution No. 1 of the GKChP?" [asked Kiselev]. Silence in the hall.

---

*As a rule, military enterprises were referred to by post office addresses.

"Now then. Some events have transpired. Our job is not to get involved in politics. On the 26th, the Supreme Soviet will convene and reach a decision on the legality of everything that has occurred. Until then, we must not give way to panic! Everything is functioning normally. Our task is to make sure that the factory continues to operate."

Everything he said was correct. The factory must continue to operate. But there seemed to be some sort of misunderstanding. The President—who after all is the head of the entire state apparatus —was just discharged from his duties in a very peculiar manner, and the director of the factory—who is the highest-ranking state authority in this small sliver of our country's territory—calmly declares that nothing special has happened.

The instructions continue on how we are to behave. Special duties are assigned. Deputy chiefs of each division are to remain at their posts until eight in the evening; division heads stay on until midnight. Security is to be doubled across the factory. The chemical depots are to be specially protected.

Similar measures were taken in all factories at this time. One got the feeling that not even a tiny group of officials were angered by events, but rather that all of them were expecting some sort of major military attack by international imperialism or world Zionism—or perhaps by Arab terrorism.

Finally, at three o'clock came the director's speech—a general discussion and lament about how difficult the times are now and how unfortunate the factory's lot. All around us there is nothing but anarchy, everything is a mess. There's no program for conversion. There are no supplies. Each republic is trying to pull the blanket to its own side. All contracts are violated. Supplies of metal are stalled.

"All of you here—chiefs of the divisions and departments— think about how you can get your divisions out of this mess. Create small-scale [private] enterprises. Perhaps it would be worthwhile to set up a concern. . . ."

The speech ended. Any questions? The director's mouth was already open and about to utter the concluding phrase: "That's all, the executive meeting is over."

Petrik raised his hand. "I have one question."

SUICIDE

"I don't remember exactly what I said," recalls Petrik, "but it was something like this: 'Of course, we have supply problems, staff turnover, and we need to think about the creation of small enterprises and concerns—these are all very important questions. But the most important question today is, what will the factory do now that anticonstitutional actions have been carried out—essentially a coup d'état?' "

What??? What is this???

"I understand, Anatolii Ivanovich," continued Petrik, "that you are expressing your personal opinion. . . ." Kiselev was known to have been one of the signatories to the unforgettable Letter of 53, which called upon Gorbachev to tighten the screws on democracy.

At this point Kiselev interrupted: "This is not my personal position. I am a servant of the state. My responsibility is the factory. We must not allow any panic here."

"Sure, but didn't we vote for Yeltsin in June? Didn't we elect him President? I introduce a concrete proposal: Let's continue our meeting for another fifteen minutes and work out the position of the factory leadership. And there is only one stand we can take: support Yeltsin, the legally elected President, and declare a symbolic two-hour strike without interrupting any of the operations that require a continuous cycle of production. In short, make it clear whose side we're on. After all, we are widely viewed as one of the pillars of the military-industrial complex."

The director leaned back in his armchair. The initial shock had passed. He was even interested in finding out what the reaction of the audience would be. One of the division chiefs rose.

"This is demagoguery! He's for Yeltsin. . . . And what are we to do? We are on military duty. What does it mean to declare a strike? Leave the country without missiles, without the nuclear shield?"

Another person stood up, from the consumer goods division. He had other arguments. They employ "guest workers" there. If they declare a strike for just two hours, those guys won't get back to work for two weeks.

Two more spoke out. No support.

The director, calm by now, brought the meeting to a close. "Has everyone had a chance to speak? Everything is understood. The situation is clear. Everyone to his post."

After executive meetings people usually swarm around Petrik. The chief of the assembly division is an important person. In a sense, everyone works for him. If in a conference he asks someone an unpleasant question or tells a person to hasten a delivery—it's like a reprimand or a signal that the factory might be facing an emergency. Such matters are always better discussed and settled beforehand.

This time as he left . . . there was a vacuum around him. A complete void. People averted their gaze. They turned away. He was now an outcast. A death-row inmate. A goner. It was then that fear began to set in.

"I was standing there, smoking. Do people really have this much fear? It's been six years now. Was it all for nothing?"

True, one person did approach and congratulate him. "Well, you're quite a fellow!" They stood for a moment and chatted. Then, once more, Petrik was alone.

Now the director was leaving. As he did so, he mockingly slapped Petrik on the back: "For today's speech and the call for a strike, you've already earned five years in prison. The material just has to be turned over to the prosecutor's office."

Petrik wanted to respond: "Better five years in prison than seventy-four consecutive years of slavery." But the director had already descended the stairs. He was off to a meeting with some Americans.

"An Individual Strike of Protest"

Petrik returned to his division and sat in his office. To hell with work! He had received no support, none. What would he do now? He grabbed a sheet of thick draftsman's paper and with a magic marker wrote in large print: "As a sign of protest against the anti-constitutional coup d'état carried out on 19.08.91 by the so-called GKChP (CC CPSU) . . ." ("I understood intuitively even then that the Central Committee of the CPSU stood behind the GKChP," says Petrik), ". . . I declare an *individual* strike on 20 August beginning at 11:30 A.M." He underlined the word "individual" twice. He signed his name, and then he glued the announcement to his door, firmly, so that it could not be removed.

He then sat down and addressed a statement to the director:

"I bring it to your attention that on account of the anti-constitutional, anti-state coup d'état carried out by the GKChP (CC CPSU), an individual strike is hereby declared by myself beginning on 20 August at 11:30 A.M. My demands: (1) the members of the so-called and self-appointed GKChP must be brought to justice; (2) the legally elected President of the USSR, M.S. Gorbachev, must be restored to power."

I summoned my secretary. She was thoroughly frightened; the rumors had already reached her. According to procedure, I listed the declaration in her registry to make everything official. I did not want to wait for interoffice mail and so I sent her off at a trot to the administration headquarters.

After a while chief engineer Gorodnichev placed a call to me by direct line, via the factory line: "I have your declaration in my hand. Have you lost your mind?"

"Yurii Petrovich, how did you get hold of it? It was addressed to the director. How arbitrary, how out of bounds!"

He was a little embarrassed. "Well, the secretary brought it to me . . . before putting it on the director's desk." A "friendly" admonition ensued: "I have my doubts, too, you understand. This . . . well, this Yanaev. Let's just say, his hands were shaking as if he had just made off with a neighbor's hen. . . ."

"So, this means that you . . . What exactly is your position?"

He didn't answer that. "All the same, you would be better off taking back this declaration."

"Excuse me, but what do you take me for, a little boy? This is my clear and conscious choice, and I will not back down from it."

Fifteen minutes later, I received a more ominous call—from the local KGB officer, the deputy director for security procedures. "They gave me an order, here . . . ," he said. "To take measures with regard to you."

"Well, if they gave you orders, you'd better carry them out."

"None of this seems very serious now," says Petrik, "but at the time I was certain they were going to arrest me. After all, it is a military enterprise. A 'P.O. Box' factory. I thought to myself: They will carry out the order immediately. They will call for a black Maria [KGB car] and shove me in—only I don't know whether they'll be using handcuffs. To the 'Sailors' Peace' [detention center], or somewhere closer."

The [deputy director's] voice dropped a half-tone. "Is your division bringing operations to a halt?"

Well, how could a work stoppage be permitted in our division? That would be tantamount to closing down the entire factory! Holes would immediately appear in our nuclear shield. There would be gaps in our program of space exploration.

"No, the division has not brought operations to a halt," Petrik reassured the KGB officer. "The division is at work. The strike I declared is an individual one."

Let the Circus Show Begin

Then the stream of visitors began. Lengthy excursions to the office of the chief of the twenty-second division.

At least factory efficiency was dented somewhat: people were distracted from their work. They read the declaration. Some laughed, some cried. . . . That's how it was. Two women looked into my office in tears: "What have you done? They will crush and destroy you!"

"Well, listen," responded Petrik, "sometimes you have to get up off your knees! Or are we supposed to remain this way forever?" But most of the time, of course, they just laughed. One could hear everything through the door. How odd! Never before had they seen anything like this in the factory.

At that point, some interesting things were taking place in the factory headquarters. Once the declaration was read, orders went out to the legal department to prepare a case for Petrik's dismissal. The documents were to be conveyed immediately to the prosecutor's office. At this stage, however, a small problem arose: the legal department refused to go along and would not budge.

I had known this young woman, Olia Pobedinskaia—she was the entire legal department—for about a year. I always thought . . . how should I put it? . . . that she was your standard-issue factory lawyer: they tell her to do something, she does it. The bow-and-scrape type. But now, if you can imagine, she displayed her true character.

"There are no grounds for dismissal," she told them. "And even less for contacting the prosecutor's office."

Undoubtedly, the administration was shocked by her response: well, well, what in the world are we to do?!

It is well known, however, that there are no obstacles that Bolsheviks cannot overcome. So they turned the task over to the personnel department. And this time there was no problem. The order was greeted with a salute. The papers were drawn up. Later, the director showed them to Petrik.

> . . . Working hours were drawing to a close. Vitalii Lukich Tverskoi, the chairman of the factory trade union committee and a respected man in the factory, came to my office.
>
> "The director telephoned me. Go, he said, and explain everything to him. I cannot speak with him myself. This was with regard to you, Petrik."
>
> Oh, God, how well I know this overbearing, paternalistic, excessively familiar, lord-of-the-manor intonation of Soviet bosses. The embodiment of higher wisdom, inaccessible to mere mortals.
>
> We talked for a while. "Well now, you're in favor of Yeltsin? Or is it Gorbachev?"
>
> "It's not the names that are important to me now," I said, "but the process—the process of achieving freedom as such. I mean complete emancipation, not one that hides behind some sort of socialism—whether with a human face, without a face, or with a behind. . . . This is a unique chance, and we have only to make sure that it doesn't slip through our fingers."
>
> We discussed everything and understood one another very clearly. The trade union man then went to see the director —to persuade him not to issue the order. As they say, trade union officials must defend the workers.

. . . Vladimir spent the night of 20–21 August in the vicinity of the White House, where he worked alongside one of the groups of students.

THE PLODDING GAIT OF THE DINOSAURS

Vladimir Petrik is no politician. He's not on the left or the right, and he's neither a democrat nor a conservative. He reached his decision by

using common sense. As he himself puts it, common sense and prag-
matism are his most salient traits.

"My evolution took place beginning in 1986 with the publication of
information on what has taken place in our country, our history. I had
not yet lost my analytical abilities. I was never a dogmatic thinker. I
never idolized this sacred cow—the CPSU."

Shortly before the events of August, Petrik visited France. It was his
first trip abroad. In the old days, of course, this was unheard of; only
the top bosses could travel beyond the border. But now the door was
open. A full-scale model of the Mir space rocket was being put on
display at La Bourger Exhibition.

"We had a good time" [Petrik recalls]. "At first, of course, you feel
like a complete ass, but then . . . you feel as though you'd been born
prematurely. Of course, I had always assumed that life would be completely different there. That much was clear from the newspapers and
television. But to see it with your own eyes—that's a different matter
altogether. When you look into one of those Algerian shops and see an
array of goods that you would never dream of seeing in GUM or
TsUM [Moscow's main department stores]. . . . Obviously, this had an
impact. I felt then that I would no longer be able to live as before."

It is more or less clear why Petrik spoke out at the executive meeting. But what made him leave the factory after August? After all, no
one drove him out. (The order to sack him was quickly withdrawn.)
Was the director to blame?

"It wasn't just the director. It was the feeling of being in a 'dead
zone,' a vacuum, when I left the executive meeting after my speech,
and the belated approval, when everything was over: 'Well now, that
was really great! . . .' Worst of all, however, was when someone set
out to make a hero out of me for the sole purpose of using me as a
battering ram in the battle of one clique against another. All of this was
disgusting to me."

I don't know whether the 1:70 ratio—remember, there were about
seventy people at the executive meeting—accurately reflects the actual
level of support for the GKChP within the military-industrial complex.
I have no doubt, however, that the balance was entirely in favor of
Yanaev and Company—or more precisely, in favor of the "ideals" that
inspired them to act (nobody gives a damn about Yanaev). What is
especially disturbing is that this level of support continues to grow
with each and every passing week. This was certainly evident from

Rutskoi's recent trip to Siberia and the Altai region. (Incidentally, notice the paradox: the erstwhile opponent of the GKChP, it seems, has virtually been transformed into a vehicle for a new confrontation—or something like that. We certainly have our luck with vice presidents!)

I fear that the number of people possessing Petrik's frame of mind is not much greater in the organizations of the military-industrial complex than it is in the Army. Some, like Petrik, leave of their own accord; others are asked to leave, one way or another.

Vladimir has now set up his own small business.

"My goal is not to run one of those 'Russian businesses' that buys goods at one price and sells them at another. I want to make things."

6 | The Congress of Compatriots: Witness to a Democratic Counter-Revolution

Serge P. Petroff was born in Harbin, China, into a family of Russian émigrés who fled Russia in 1922. He grew up in Japan and the United States and has had a career as a business executive and historian. The author of a book about the late Communist Party ideologist Mikhail Suslov, he is currently completing research on the Russian Civil War. Petroff has visited Russia many times and is promoting U.S.-Russian business contacts.

I

By bizarre coincidence, the August 1991 coup in Moscow occurred on the same day as the opening of the First Congress of Compatriots—Monday, August 19. Convened with President Yeltsin's blessing, the Congress of Compatriots was organized by the Supreme Soviet of the Russian Federation to serve two objectives: to establish a communication channel for overseas Russians, and to create for the Russian government a supporting network of foreign businessmen and professionals of Russian origin.

Eight hundred men and women came from twenty-seven different countries, representing all three waves of Russian emigration since 1917. By far the largest number came from the United States and France, and more than half were descendants of the first wave of émigrés who fled communism in the wake of the October Revolution and the ensuing civil war. "Heaven from all creatures hides the book of fate," Shakespeare wrote, and so it seemed to many of the congress delegates—especially to those whose family backgrounds embraced a history of fierce anticommunism. They came to Moscow to reestablish long-severed contacts, but found themselves instead in the midst of a coup that triggered the end of Communist rule in Russia.

From the very beginning, the organization of the congress was steeped in controversy. The advance publicity and the program agenda had a decidedly nationalist-patriotic tenor. Some émigrés encouraged this; others felt that the organizing committee was placing too much emphasis on national rebirth. A number of prominent émigrés were convinced that it was mostly a public relations gesture, and therefore chose not to attend at all. I, too, had serious reservations. As a liberal democrat not unmindful of Russian nationalism, I was not sure that I would be comfortable in the company of flag-waving émigrés and their ultrapatriotic Russian hosts. But as a Russian-American vitally interested in the future of Russia, I felt a powerful pull to attend the congress. I had traveled to the Soviet Union regularly since 1983, and I was trying to make sense out of perestroika's tortuous course. I had watched Boris Yeltsin's gradual rise to power and was anxious to find out for myself who Yeltsin actually was. Was he a democrat, a populist, a Westernizer, or a Russian nationalist? In August 1991 there were still no reliable answers to this question, and the Congress of Compatriots seemed a perfect point of reference, particularly since many of Yeltsin's supporters were scheduled to participate in the program.

The Congress of Compatriots was planned as an important and gala political milestone. The Russian government allocated eighteen million rubles for it. Another twelve million rubles were raised by various new Russian business organizations, the Russian branch of the Union of USSR Leaseholders and Entrepreneurs coming through with the largest contribution. Giant banners with the inscription "Welcome, Compatriots" were hung along many of Moscow's main thoroughfares. To mark the event and maximize publicity, President Yeltsin was to open the congress, and it was rumored that he would use the occasion to acknowledge Communist oppression and offer a public apology for all the indignities thrust upon the Russian nation during nearly seventy-five years of Communist rule.

II

The official opening of the Congress of Compatriots was scheduled for 7:00 P.M. at Tchaikovsky Concert Hall. But the day's events cast a dark shadow over the planned festivities. Due to heavy traffic and crowds along Tverskaia Street, the congress did not open until 8:30 P.M. President Yeltsin, who had escaped arrest and was now directing the opposition from the White House, obviously could not attend. In his place, USSR Supreme Soviet Deputy Mikhail Tolstoi, grandnephew of the Russian writer Aleksei Tolstoi, opened the meeting with a reading of President Yeltsin's bold proclamation about the unlawful and unconstitutional seizure of power by the self-appointed Emergency Committee and a brief comment on the events of the day. The organizing committee had put together an ambitious cultural program of music, dance, and theatrical performances featuring a variety of artists from the multiethnic Russian Federation. The hall was packed with officials, delegates, guests, members of the Leaseholders and Entrepreneurs Union, and representatives of the Russian press, many of whom had come to Moscow from such faraway places as Perm, Yekaterinburg, and Novosibirsk to find out what their overseas compatriots looked like and what they had to say about the changing face of Russia.

Without Yeltsin's presence, the opening ceremony would have been of little consequence, despite the quality and richness of the cultural program. But an incident that took place early in the program made an enormous difference. A Russian-American delegate–I found out later that he was the New York avant-garde artist Smorchevskii-Butterbrod–arrived at the concert hall from the barricades outside the White House and asked to be recognized. His moving remarks electrified the audience: "Democracy has been slain, and Gorbachev, too, may be dead—killed in the Crimea," he announced, alleging that he had heard the news about Gorbachev from a reputable source only an hour before.

Throughout the day rumors about Gorbachev were flying, but nothing as drastic as this had been suggested. There were also informal discussions on how the congress should officially react to the coup. Should it go on record with a declaration in support of Yeltsin or should it and its delegates—most of whom were not Soviet citizens—refrain from participation in Soviet internal affairs? Despite a general feeling of support for Yeltsin, genuine consensus was hard to come by.

Congress officials were on the whole pro-Yeltsin, but did not want to take a firm position without further deliberation. Five years of glasnost and embryonic democracy had not yet erased completely the long-nurtured habit of caution and equivocation. Delegates also found it difficult to reach a conclusion. Although their sympathies were with

Yeltsin, they hesitated to take a decisive position, fearing that the Party and the KGB could easily defeat the opposition. The most resolute response came from the unofficial hosts of the congress—the new Russian businessmen. As former technocrats and Party apparatchiks who only recently had exchanged their Party privileges for the promise of unrestricted wealth and personal independence, they knew how far the central Soviet apparatus had already disintegrated. They had strong doubts that the gray men of the Emergency Committee were capable of accomplishing anything, let alone governing a tired and raucous nation. They also had a great deal to lose if the old "command-administrative system" were put in force again. Many of them had spoken in the early hours of the coup to their home bases, and had satisfied themselves that their employees were also supporting Yeltsin. It was not surprising therefore that they favored a strong statement of support for Yeltsin. Some were certain that the "putsch would ultimately misfire," but the best forecast came from a construction company owner from Tver who gave the junta "a maximum of one week before they would destroy themselves."

The staging of the congress in the midst of a coup presented formidable problems. In many ways, the congress was a *"pir vo vremia chumy"* (a feast during a pestilence), as one of the Russian businessmen called it, using the title of a short play by Pushkin. On the first day of the coup it was still very difficult to be unequivocal, and no sensible response to the artist's statement—explicit or implicit—seemed appropriate. Trying to relieve the built-up tension, Mikhail Tolstoi asked the audience to stand up and observe a moment of silence. Most did, but a number of prominent Soviet leaders and intellectuals in the audience declined to follow his call. If there ever was a moment of truth during the entire congress, this was it.

I don't know what prompted me to speak out and break the silence. It may have been a sudden flash of emotion in protest against those who refused to stand up. It may have had something to do with the distressing defeatism of the artist's comments and Mikhail Tolstoi's indecisive reaction. Or it may have been influenced by more rational thinking about what I had witnessed and assimilated during the day.

I had spent most of the day walking the streets and squares of Moscow trying to ascertain for myself the extent of support for Yeltsin, and I came to the conclusion that the odds were in his favor. The attitude of the troops, the vitality of the crowds supporting Yeltsin, the rapidity and thoroughness with which Moscow had mobilized its anti-putsch forces, the continuing transmission of clandestine radio stations, the dissemination of anti-putsch literature, and the favorable reports from the provinces all pointed to the conclusion that there was in Russia a large enough critical mass to sustain pressure against the junta. In the words of one "sidewalk philosopher" who knew his Lermontov, "Yeltsin as still 'the hero of his time,' despite the yelping of the drunks for the good old days."

Whatever it was, the moment of silence did not satisfy me. I felt that a more affirmative statement was called for, and I stood up to demand one. "There is no sane reason for a requiem," I cried out. "It's too early to bury Gorbachev and write off Yeltsin. What is needed is a declaration of solidarity with them." The hall exploded in a sudden rumble of voices. Some felt that my statement was too confrontational, others agreed with me, and still others did not hear what I had said. In the end, no positive action was taken that evening, although at an 8:00 P.M. meeting on August 20, after a heated discussion of who should receive the letter of protest, the congress did send one to the USSR Supreme Soviet with a copy to the United Nations.

My demonstrative response to the incident did not pass without consequences. On the positive side, I had suddenly become a celebrity for whom doors were now open where they had been closed before, giving me an opportunity in the aftermath of the failed coup to come in contact with people whose views and opinions gave me a much better understanding of what had actually happened during the three days. On the negative side, I found that I was being hounded by the Russian press and a profusion of new Russian social organizations and charities. But there was also a more encompassing element to the experience. I suddenly realized that, despite the resolution of the coup in favor of democracy, there were still deep divisions in Russia, especially among the elite.

III

The morning of August 20 arrived without any climactic developments during the night. At the morning news briefing at the Hotel Rossiia, where the congress staff had its headquarters, I found out that Gorbachev was under house arrest at his dacha in the Crimea. I also overheard someone say that the "Soiuz" group of rightist parliamentary deputies had backed the Emergency Committee, as did the rightist nationalist organization "Edinstvo." The defense of the White House was almost completed and pro-Yeltsin units of the Taman Division were now guarding it. There was also confirmation that the Social Democratic Party, the Republican Party of Russia, the Democratic Party of Russia, and the Constitutional Democrats had all issued strong statements of protest against the usurpation of constitutional powers by the junta.

I had agreed to participate in the Economic Round Table of the Union of Leaseholders and Entrepreneurs that morning. Organized in February 1990 under the leadership of economist Pavel G. Bunich, First Deputy Chairman of the Economic Reform Commission of the USSR Supreme Soviet, the Union of USSR Leaseholders and Entrepreneurs (since renamed the Union of Managers and Entrepreneurs) was established to protect and promote the interests of individual Soviet businessmen. According to General Director I.M. Baskin, in August 1991 it represented 14,000 members and 6,500,000 employees. The membership figure was probably accurate, but the number of employees was greatly exaggerated. Encompassing the whole spectrum of business activity from small mom-and-pop contractors to large enterprises, such as Dr. Fedorov's Eye Microsurgery Clinic in Moscow, and including trade, construction, agriculture, transportation, and services, the Union of Leaseholders and Entrepreneurs was at the time of the coup the undisputed domain of the new Russian capitalist elite. Some members, straight out of the pages of Soviet satirists Ilf and Petrov, had been hawking wares and repairing flats for many years. But a larger and more urbane contingent came directly out of the *nomenklatura*, aroused to business activity by the new Law on Individual Enterprises. Conservative, hard-working, zealously patriotic, and strongly anti-Communist, they were representatives of the newly emerging bourgeoisie in Russia. Carefully groomed and projecting paramount confidence, they could easily have been mistaken for positive-thinking American salesmen attending their first Dale Carnegie convention.

The round table was to begin at 10:00 A.M. at SEV,* one of Moscow's new modern buildings only a stone's throw from the White

---

*This building, the Moscow headquarters of the Council for Mutual Economic Assistance (Russian acronym SEV), would later house the Moscow mayoralty offices.

House. Because of overturned tram cars, barricades, and huge crowds, it took our specially dispatched bus more than one hour to travel the two-mile distance from the Hotel Rossiia to SEV. The conversation on the bus centered on the coup, but I did not sense any undue anxiety or vacillation about Yeltsin and his ability to resist the coup. Except for a San Francisco businessman, a Swedish agricultural specialist who was the grandnephew of Leo Tolstoi, and me, everyone on the bus was a native Russian.

The round table had an extensive agenda. There were a number of formal presentations, including Dr. Tolstoi's and mine. There were also reports from committee chairmen, but the most amazing aspect of the entire meeting was the confidence and unruffled composure of nearly four hundred Leaseholders and Entrepreneurs. It was as if nothing of consequence was happening outside. Most of the members had apparently already concluded that the putsch would undoubtedly be derailed and that President Yeltsin would emerge as the undisputed new leader. The auditorium came alive only during the vote on the declaration in support of Yeltsin. A strong statement had been prepared in advance, and it carried unanimously and boisterously. The Union of Leaseholders and Entrepreneurs was the first business organization to come out with such a statement; other business associations followed. By late evening, the Union of Co-operators, the Association of Small Entrepreneurs, the Association of Commercial Banks of the USSR, the All-Russian Commodity Exchange, and most of the Moscow business clubs, including the All-Russian Club of Young Millionaires, joined the Leaseholders and Entrepreneurs in declaring their solidarity with the Yeltsin government.

IV

From the sixteenth floor of the SEV building we could look diagonally at the White House. No other place in Moscow offered the same unobstructed view, except perhaps the roof of the unoccupied new American Embassy building. A giant Russian tricolor wrapped around the front and sides of the White House would have made even Christo proud of the handiwork, while a medium-sized blimp flying above the building with an inscription in Russian—"Welcome, Compatriots"—made the vista look almost surrealistic. Below, on the ground, a large mosaic made up of people, rubble, overturned trolleys, stalled cars, and lines of barricades and military equipment rendered an unforgettable tableau of a rebellion in progress.

I left SEV a few minutes before 3:00 P.M., maneuvering toward the White House through clusters of excitedly talking people and the unsightly debris of the barricades. The barricades had been substantially improved since I saw them last, but gangs of four or five young men, carrying railroad ties, twisted rails, large cement blocks, and other objects of obstruction continued to reinforce them. The tanks and armored personnel carriers were still deployed on the left flank of the White House, but they had turned their gun barrels away from the building. With flowers stuck in their barrels and teenagers clambering over them, they no longer looked menacing.

The noon meeting in front of the White House that I had been watching from the SEV building was coming to an end. At three o'clock, President Yeltsin came out to say a few words, followed by Eduard Shevardnadze, who received an equally warm ovation. More people were still arriving, even though the square in front of the White House was already packed to its limits.

The array of people and political groupings was beyond description. There were young and old, men and women, Cossacks and bearded Caucasians, Great Russians, Ukrainians, and Belorussians, Muscovites and people from the provinces, businessmen, professionals, and academics, Russian Orthodox priests and Seventh Day Adventist ministers, students, Afghan veterans in soiled fatigues, and military officers in uniform, monarchists and anarcho-syndicalists, groups from the new democratic political parties, and Moscow punks and drifters who came to see the spectacle. Many of these people had voted for Yeltsin in the June election and now came out to show their continued support for him. By no stretch of the imagination were all of them democratically thinking liberals. They were ordinary patriotic citizens who were fed up with communism and, like their East European neighbors, wanted to free themselves from its abuse. Nor were they backers or benefactors of a "Second Russian Revolution," as some commentators later classified the events of August 19–21. Like the declaration of the Leaseholders and Entrepreneurs, their presence on the barricades was a counter-revolutionary statement. They came to bear witness not only to the abandonment of Stalinism, as Gorbachev had been championing, but to a complete break with the revolutionary tradition of October 1917.

There was both good news and bad news that afternoon. A great cheer went up from the crowd when it was announced that USSR Prime Minister and junta member Valentin Pavlov was resigning on grounds of disability. It was a sure sign that the leadership of the coup was beginning to falter. News was also received that the USSR Constitutional Oversight Committee had issued a cautious condemnation of the coup,* and that the All-Union Confederation of Trade Unions had also denounced the action of the Emergency Committee. But reports of a possible storming of the White House by the special Alpha forces were also spreading, as was the news that an 11:00 P.M. curfew had been announced. At about 6:00 P.M., these reports were officially confirmed by the White House. At around 7:00 P.M., the White House command issued new instructions to the crowd. To provide more room for maneuvering, the crowd was asked to move farther away from the front of the building. Several months later, a participant in the defense of the White House told me that the credit for the successful defense of the White House should go to Russian Vice President Aleksandr Rutskoi. According to my friend, it was Rutskoi who established a military headquarters that coordinated the work of the volunteers with the pro-Yeltsin elements of the Army and the KGB. Yeltsin generated the meaning and spirit of the rebellion while Rutskoi organized the defense of it. If this was indeed the case, then, ironically, it was a symbiotic relationship not unlike that of Lenin and Trotskii in 1917.

A light rain had been falling throughout the day, but at 6:00 P.M. it began raining harder. People were getting thoroughly soaked, and the large crowd was slowly dwindling. It was also time for me to go home. At 8:30 P.M. I arrived at the hotel, tired and hungry, only to find that I had missed the regular dinner hour and now had to scrounge for something to eat.

V

The atmosphere in the hotel press room on Wednesday morning was tense. Word had gotten out that there were casualties during the night. Mikhail Tolstoi, who had taken charge of the morning briefing, confirmed that there had been three fatalities near Smolensk Square,

---

*According to S. Alekseev, the head of the committee, the version of the report as it appeared in *Izvestiia* had been heavily amended by the censor.

where a confrontation had taken place between pickets defending the outer barricades of the White House and the armored personnel carriers of the 27th Brigade. The White House itself had not been stormed, however, and the Taman and Kantemir Tank Divisions were moving out of Moscow. The night's official *khronika* (chronicle of events), a copy of which I was able to obtain, testified to the defenders' courage, but its salient message was more poignant. During that night, one Soviet organization after another—government, civilian, and religious —had fallen in line in support of Yeltsin. Even if the dull-witted "gang of eight" had given the order to storm the White House, it is doubtful that it would have been followed. By midnight of August 20–21, the rank and file of the KGB and the military had declared for Yeltsin, refusing to support the Emergency Committee.

The final resolution of the coup took place five or six hours later. At the barricades—as everyone by now referred to the area around the White House—a huge crowd had gathered in the afternoon. It was so large and so compact that it was physically impossible to move from one side of the square to the other. Along the embankment, a whole city of tents and makeshift shelters had sprung up during the night; a soup kitchen, organized by the Seventh Day Adventists, was dispensing food to a line of tired "defenders," while a first-aid station was administering to the old and the frail. Along the barrier facing the White House, young men and women—some with guitars and some singing—added color and gaiety to the excited crowd. The atmosphere was distinctly festive.

The climax came at around 3:00 P.M. Until then it was still hearsay, but a few minutes after three, President Yeltsin, surrounded by Gennadii Burbulis, Ruslan Khasbulatov, Aleksandr Rutskoi, and other loyalists, came out to announce that it was all over. Except for Boris Pugo (who, I discovered later, had committed suicide), the men who had tried to turn the clock back were all under arrest. A thunderous yell went up from the anxiously awaiting crowd. Some people laughed, others cried. I must admit that I had a difficult time controlling my emotions. My parents had been implacable foes of Bolshevism. In June 1918, my father, a career officer, had taken part in a similar demonstration of anti-Communist sentiment by backing the democratic anti-Bolshevik government organized by Socialist Revolutionaries in Samara. My mother, an army nurse, joined the anti-Bolshevik movement in the Urals six months later. Together, they spent nearly four years in the ranks of the White Army. They never regretted their decisions, even in times of great despair and privation. Nor did they ever give up hope that some day communism would be discredited. Standing transfixed in front of the Russian White House with the tricolor waving in the wind, I could not but think of them, wondering how they would have felt had they lived to see what I witnessed—the undeniable groundswell of a democratic counter-revolution.

DONALD J. RALEIGH

7 | A View from Saratov

Donald J. Raleigh is professor of Russian history at the University of North Carolina at Chapel Hill. He has written a history of the 1917 revolution in Saratov and was working on a sequel to that study at the time of the coup. After a fifteen-year battle to gain admission to that closed city, he visited Saratov for the first time in 1990 as a participant in an official academic exchange program. Raleigh returned to Saratov on the eve of the coup to edit a Russian translation of his book, Revolution on the Volga: 1917 in Saratov, *and to conduct research in local archives for his current project.*

The announcer's voice was cheerless, calm, soothing. Gorbachev was in "ill health." The measures "would be in force for only six months." Not meant as a rejection of reform, they were "necessary to save the economy from complete collapse." "Apathy, despair, and lack of faith" had seized hold of the population. "The country," in essence, "had become ungovernable." People demanded "law and order." Responding to popular pressures, the "temporary" leadership would assign top priority to assuring adequate food supplies and housing.

It was 9:00 A.M., Saratov time, Monday, August 19, 1991. Viktor Ivanovich, my host, about whom more will be said later, had just left with my passport and visa to register me with the police, a necessary ritual that could not be attended to the day before when I arrived in Saratov, a "closed" city, albeit one in the process of opening.

Viktor Ivanovich phoned twice from the police station, but both times my line went dead. I listened nervously to Resolution No. 1 of the cumbersomely named State Committee for the State of Emergency. I harbored no doubts about what I had just heard. Recalling Eduard Shevardnadze's resignation as Gorbachev's foreign affairs minister the previous December and his warning that "dictatorship is coming," I saw new meaning in the abrupt rejection of Stanislav Shatalin's plan to move to a market economy in five hundred days, in the violence in Lithuania back in January, and in reformer Aleksandr Yakovlev's sinister forecast a few days before that a conspiracy was in the air. But how could this gambit by (as would soon become evident) a group of blundering Party *apparatchiki* possibly work in a country whose entire belief system had been shattered by years of ferment and endless revelations about the tragedy of Soviet history? Although vulnerable, civil society had emerged upon the scene and had to be reckoned with. My thoughts then focused on my own predicament: I was a lone foreigner in Saratov; I was living in what I suspected was a KGB flat; I had no documents. Would I be forced to leave for Moscow? The broadcasts ended. Funeral music followed. Then the announcements and proclamations were repeated.

National radio broadcast four documents that morning: a decree of Vice President Gennadii I. Yanaev that he had assumed the duties of Acting President because of Mikhail Sergeevich Gorbachev's incapacity; a statement by the eight-person committee explaining why it had decided to introduce a six-month state of emergency; Resolution No. 1 of the committee, spelling out what specific measures it was taking to "normalize" the country; and a message from Yanaev to foreign leaders, emphasizing the temporary nature of the emergency measures, which would not affect the USSR's international commitments. I switched on the TV: ballet. The Saratov station was off the air.

The long-awaited ring at the door came. The police had registered me. "For now," Viktor Ivanovich cautioned. I then rushed to the nearby kiosks in the square adjacent to the large covered market, but there were no Saratov papers to be had. Proceeding to the central post office, accompanied by Viktor Ivanovich, I cabled my family that I had arrived safely and asked my wife to phone me from Chapel Hill, North Carolina. I wondered whether the ill-mannered and surly postal clerk had taken a dislike to me or whether the day's news had ruined her morning. People seemed tense and irritable.

At first glance nothing seemed to distinguish the outward appearance of the city from the previous, "normal day." But when I observed things more closely, I realized that people had clustered together in the parks and on street corners, absorbed in serious, and quiet, conversation. It was as if the volume control for street sounds and noises had been turned down. I took notice of the police, but had no way of knowing whether there were more of them than usual; what was different about today was that I was merely aware of their presence.

Feeling vulnerable, I did what most people did that day: I went to work. I dropped in at the publishing house that is putting out a Russian-language edition of my book *Revolution on the Volga*. There, staff members described their feeling as one of shock, dismay, sadness, numbness. No one seemed fearful. No one cared to work. An editor friend took me to meet a visiting Pole, not only in the hopes of getting served some exotic tea, but also because Gdansk-born Henryk knew about martial law firsthand. The water in Henryk's apartment had been turned off altogether, so instead of herbata, we drank in his prophetic words that the introduction of martial law would not last. But this was hard to believe, no matter how much we wanted to, as the only news came from national broadcasts which gave no hint of the opposition that had taken to the streets in Moscow. The Saratov Party organizations, at both the city and regional levels, failed to respond publicly to the events.

Lack of any news from the outside, other than the official broadcasts aired that morning, not only created an anxious atmosphere but also guaranteed the spread of rumors and relentless speculation. Where was Gorbachev? Had the very people he had selected to govern betrayed him? Or had he hatched the plot himself? Why were there only eight members of the State Committee instead of a ninth needed to break any tie votes if the Committee reached an impasse? Who had masterminded the plot? Anatolii Lukianov, Gorbachev's choice for Chairman of the Supreme Soviet? Or had he been invited to join the group but declined? Was Yeltsin dead? Gorbachev? Why hadn't the Central Committee of the Communist Party issued a statement? Whose side was the army on? Had the leaders of Saratov's democratic movement been arrested? Why were local leaders silent? Had the events taken them by surprise too?

Those with whom I shared my fears on August 19 expressed their outrage not only at the attempt by a group of mediocre personalities to derail Russia's unsteady new order, but also at the return to the old paradigms, the old language, the old lies. Although conversations, overheard in lines or on crowded buses, urged law and order, no one with whom I spoke that day—and I spent the entire day in conversation

—supported the action of the State Committee. But for Saratov, the reaction to the official decrees for now belonged to the private sphere, something shared with family and friends. People did not rush into the streets, as in Moscow, to defend any concrete symbol of Russia's shaky democracy, because that which needed their protection, for then, remained an abstraction.

I later learned that at 4:15 P.M. the local committee for radio and television had received a copy of President Yeltsin's decree, calling the activities of the State Committee unconstitutional, but apparently had little enthusiasm for publicizing it. When a small group of deputies from the city and regional soviets sought out the head of the local committee, A.P. Zotov, they found him deep in conversation with his assistant and with a representative of the KGB, who made a tasteful exit when the deputies announced themselves. In postponing his reaction to Yeltsin's decree, the unpopular Zotov further discredited himself in the eyes of Saratov's progressive elements, who during the local power struggle in the year preceding the coup had come to resent Zotov's conservatism and outright hostility toward glasnost and its consequences.

Saratov newspapers afterward revealed that at roughly the same time President Yeltsin's decree reached Saratov, the local department of health received a message from the Ministry of Health ordering officials to put two additional emergency medical crews on duty that night.

Although I learned little about the coup until that evening, I updated my knowledge of the course of perestroika in Saratov since my first visit the year before, in May–June 1990. Back then, my stay helped broaden my overall perspective on the reform movement by adding a sorely needed "provincial" corrective to the views articulated in Moscow. I had left Moscow for Saratov puzzled by the nonstop reference to imminent civil war. A month later I left Saratov for Moscow, cautiously optimistic about the country's future. Although Saratov lacked the frenetic political atmosphere of the capital cities, I realized how wrong it was to dismiss this as a fact of life in provincial Russia. Still in control of local politics, reactionary Party apparatchiki had repressed public demonstrations in February and May 1990, and they still ran the major newspaper, which was as dull as they come. Yet I could not help but wonder whether their remaining in power had something to do with the fact that local food supplies were significantly better than in Moscow. The country had already broken apart into local economic units, and city authorities had to attend to local needs first. Moreover, beneath the superficial calm agitated a civil society that measurably pushed the limits of the permissible. New faces had been elected to the Saratov Soviet—people who had campaigned to end the local Party apparatus's monopoly of power and to open the city to the outside world. While I was in town, the first issues of several independent newspapers appeared. Volga Germans and the local Tatar community pressed for reform and recognition. People exchanged views freely, and I found no forbidden topics of conversation. More important, local sentiments and broad social phenomena paralleled those in the capitals because they made sense in terms of local conditions. Saratov society suffered the familiar crisis in confidence as it searched desperately for something to believe in. As elsewhere, a nostalgic and uncritical interest in the tsarist past filled the spiritual vacuum, as did a revival of religious or other spiritual activity, which included a fascination with the occult. The political lineup among the local intelligentsia did not differ from that of Moscow (i.e., Sakharov was a hero, Yeltsin was popular, Gorbachev was neither). In other words, I sensed that the old guard still in charge felt more accountable than ever to its local constituency, whose passivity could no longer be taken for granted. Although the political mood in Saratov was far from uniform, I nonetheless detected broad public agreement on the most vital political and socioeconomic issue: systemic reform had to continue.

During the day's intense discussions on August 19, 1991, I realized the extent to which years of ferment and revelations about the country's tragic history had discredited Soviet power in many circles. Based in the city's Polytechnic Institute, the Democratic Russia movement had formed a caucus within the city soviet, which soon splintered. Battles over local rule had broken out in some of the neighborhood soviets as the formerly disenfranchised sought to exercise their rights. I heard and read about hunger strikes, anarchists, Hari Krishnas, the opening of soup kitchens and Sunday schools. The spring 1991 elections had given the "democratic forces" greater visibility and one of their spokesmen, V.G. Golovachev—soon to emerge as "Saratov's Yeltsin"—had been elected chairman of the soviet, to the dismay of the council's executive committee. The official paper,

Kommunist, maintained its conservative line, but *Saratov,* one of the several new publications debuting that year—a badly produced, officially reviled, and disrespectful biweekly—backed Golovachev and the *demokraty.*

It was unclear whether Golovachev, like many of the country's reformers, had been a Communist by conviction or by convenience. In either case, he had done well before perestroika, and seemed to know how to adapt himself now. Golovachev sided with the city's reformers on all issues that challenged the power of the entrenched apparatchiki. He and his supporters encountered bitter resistance from the chairman of the city soviet's executive committee, from the ruling cliques settled in some of the neighborhood soviets, from the regional soviet and its ruling organs, and from the local regional Party boss, K.D. Murenin, whose autocratic inclinations and egotism, so reminiscent of those of Romania's former leader, Ceausescu, earned him the nickname Murenescu. Murenin had actually been a favorite topic of conversation since June, when the granddaughter of Saratov-born Nikolai Chernyshevskii, who served as director of the local Chernyshevskii Museum that honored Saratov's revolutionary son, had committed suicide by plunging to her death from a window in Murenin's apartment. There was much speculation as to what had driven her to such desperation, the more so since her son died by his own hand three days later after poisoning himself. Now rumors circulated that the unsavory Murenin had left on a Volga cruise—and, in fact, he had.

That evening's nationally televised press conference organized by the ringleaders of the coup may mark one of the great historic moments in the history of the Soviet media. Reminiscent in many ways of the impact television had had in Romania the year before, when a dazed population heard resentful crowds demand the overthrow of the despised Ceausescu, the broadcast illustrates the extent to which the media had become an autonomous force both reflecting and shaping public opinion in the Soviet Union. No one could misread the Soviet media's disdain for the organizers of the coup. A sniffling Gennadii Yanaev, his face swollen by fatigue and alcohol, had a tough time fielding the combative questions. His trembling hands and quivering voice conveyed an image of impotence, mediocrity, and falsehood; he appeared as a caricature of the quintessential, boozed-up Party functionary from the Brezhnev era. Minister of Internal Affairs Boris Pugo, who normally seemed steely cold, tough, and loathsome, seemed merely loathsome when stripped of his usual confidence. Vasilii Starodubtsev, the head of Russia's unimportant Peasants' Union, didn't seem to know what all the disagreement was about. If the stunning spectacle exposed these mediocrities to public scrutiny, then the news program following the press conference cleared up any remaining uncertainty viewers may have nursed: it showed tanks rumbling through the streets of Moscow and it reported on the forceful opposition of Boris Yeltsin and other members of the Russian parliament, who had declared the actions of the State Committee treasonous. My phone rang off the hook for the next hour or so; the significance of the moment was lost on no one. Although I could not reach Moscow or Leningrad by phone that evening, I went to bed with the sense that Yanaev and his associates had seized not power, but merely its illusion.

The vivid image of tanks in Moscow convinced me that I would be departing into uncertainty if I left Saratov. Phoning from Chapel Hill, North Carolina, at 3:00 A.M. Saratov time, my wife, Karen, urged me to stay put, informed me of the reaction to the coup in Leningrad and some of the republics, and updated me on the response at home. Anxious telephone conversations with friends in Moscow served as a sort of spiritual breakfast that got me through the next morning. They reconfirmed what I had heard from my wife, and informed me of the valiant opposition of the well-informed Muscovites, some of whom followed events by watching CNN. I spent the next hour calling people in Saratov and receiving calls from those who had additional word from other cities. There was something complicitous and sweetly defiant in registering our indignation over the telephone. Despite the strain the technologically impoverished Soviet telephone system was under, it held up remarkably well: it enabled people to reach out to friends and family following the historic press conference. To a certain extent, opposition to the putsch spread by telephone, and, as I later learned, with the help of teletype and fax machines as well.

On Tuesday, August 20, the coup began to unfold locally. Saratovites who went to the newspaper kiosks that morning could no longer remain indifferent to the attempt to set the political clock back, for the official newspaper, *Kommunist*, and the "progressive" organ, *Saratov*, had hit the newsstands. *Kommunist* published all of the previous day's documents issued by the State Committee as well as a statement by Lukianov that further discussion of the new Union Treaty, scheduled to be voted on that week, had to be postponed. Popular suspicions that conservative elements saw the new Union Treaty as equivalent to the breakup of the Party's centralized power, and thus had decided to act before it was voted on, now seemed validated. The paper carried no statements whatsoever from the local Party organization or from the city council, and I suspect that only a handful of apparatchiki had been in the know beforehand. My eyes fixed upon the one photograph in the issue, which depicted the main agronomist and tractor driver from the Chapaev Collective Farm. In contrast, *Saratov* published portraits of Yeltsin and Gorbachev, as well as statements by Yeltsin, Acting Chairman of the Russian Supreme Soviet Ruslan Khasbulatov, and Chairman of the Council of Ministers of the Russian Republic Ivan Silaev. President Yeltsin's historic decree calling the actions of the State Committee for the State of Emergency illegal and unconstitutional declared unambiguously that those who supported this crime against the state would be prosecuted. A headline made reference to Khrushchev's ouster in 1964. The cartoon depicted the USSR inside a cage. An editorial queried: "Can it really be that the hunk of sausage they toss at us from their reserves will prompt us, the people, to deceive ourselves and sink back into the swamp once again. . . ?" "A dark cloud hangs over the entire country," flashed the headline.

As on Monday, I spent the day in heated, relentless, collective speculation and discussion, as well as eating, and consuming large amounts of alcohol. The comfort of being with kindred souls was dissipated by their reports that my visit to Saratov the year before, after a seventeen-year campaign to get there, had aroused deep suspicions on the part of the KGB, who insisted I was "no mere historian." For this reason, the coup attempt seemed directed as much against me; I had a personal stake in how it unfolded.

That evening the coup began to play itself out in Saratov. Meeting that afternoon, regional authorities could do no more than to issue a bland appeal to the local population to remain calm. As one of them, Yu.G. Slepov, so ironically put it, "Taking a position only complicates the situation." People with whom I came into contact understood this restraint for what it was: a sign of divisiveness, and an indication that a local power struggle had begun in earnest. In fact, having learned the reaction of Boris Yeltsin, leaders of the Kirov neighborhood soviet expressed their support for the popular Russian President, although they opposed his call for a general strike without the sanction of the Supreme Soviet. Such respect for the rule of law and constitutional order reassured me.

By 7:00 P.M. a crowd, eventually estimated to be ten to twelve thousand strong, began to assemble on Revolution Square, the largest square in Saratov, located in the heart of town, across the street from the splendid (tsarist) building that houses the Saratov City Soviet. Bordered on the north by Lenin Prospect, the city's major thoroughfare, which runs from the Volga River on the east to the railroad station and the hills that nestle up against the city on the west, the square is Saratov's equivalent of Moscow's Red Square. A tasteless, clunky Lenin monument towers over the large expanse. Lenin's slightly limp, outstretched right hand seemed to be pointing an accusing finger at those who fell under his stony gaze. As well it should. For in a few short days Lenin would no longer be standing in Revolution Square, but in Theater Square, as it was called before the revolution. The irreverent would be collecting signatures on a petition demanding his removal, while a few scandalized war veterans would try in vain to prevent vandals from defaming the icon by spraying in blood-red paint on the monument's pedestal, "Hangman of Russia."

Deputies from the city and oblast soviets, with the assistance of the emergency council of the local branch of the Democratic Russia movement, a broad caucus formed earlier in the year that brought together the numerous strands of the country's democratic opposition, organized the public meeting on the evening of August 20. The gathering turned into a public expression of support for President Yeltsin and popular rejection of the leadership of the regional soviet, which was synonymous with the local leadership of the Communist Party. A succession of emotional speakers read Yeltsin's decrees; demanded Gorbachev's return to Moscow and the arrest of his turncoat comrades; insisted that the leadership of the region clarify its attitude toward the events and lift the "information blockade" from Saratov; called for an immediate convocation of the regional and city soviets and for the dismissal of the executive committee of the city soviet, headed by V.S. Agapov, for supporting the putschists. Others thirsted for the blood of the overseer of the local radio and television channels, A.P. Zotov, and of the editor of *Kommunist*, N.F. Zorin, for setting up the information blockade. Golovachev urged approval of a resolution of support for the Russian President. The crowd endorsed the idea as well as calls to post

Revolution Square, Saratov: "Hangman of Russia"

guards over the local television and radio stations and the city soviet. Those who were unaware of the public meeting that night must have sensed a shift in the local balance of forces, nonetheless, for that evening Channel 5, the Saratov station, began broadcasting official communiqués from the Russian, that is, Yeltsin, government.

Several observations need to be made about the meeting on the evening of August 20. The KGB and police did not interfere at all. The crowd was heterogeneous, although members of the intelligentsia predominated. City soviet deputy V. Zhavoronskii, an activist in the Democratic Russia movement, and "mayor" Golovachev presided over the meeting. The former undoubtedly saw the public demonstration as a vehicle to strengthen the hand of democratic elements in town, a goal undoubtedly shared by Golovachev, who also had a personal stake in the matter, as he and Agapov and Co. had been sparring all year.

The herbal sleeping aid given to me by friends did not work. I welcomed morning because it ended my sustained dialogue with my subconscious and deepest fears, and despite the uneasiness I felt when I recalled that Victor Ivanovich was due to show up "to fix a broken kitchen faucet." No doubts remained in my mind that he worked for the KGB; consequently, the fact that he did not drop in or phone both relieved me and gave me something else to mull over. A call from Moscow informing me that three Muscovites had died the night before deepened my gloom, although it was reassuring to learn that the radio station Moscow Echo kept people there well informed. My efforts to place a call to friends in Leningrad once again failed.

Eager to learn if there had been any repercussions to the previous night's mass rally, I set out in search of fresh newspapers. *Kommunist* carried a spate of statements and announcements from the State Committee (referred to in Russian by its difficult-to-pronounce acronym, Geh-keh-cheh-peh), including hard-to-believe assertions that foreign powers understood the need for the adoption of extraordinary measures. Another announcement commented briefly on the opposition centered around Boris Yeltsin, Ivan Silaev, and Ruslan Khasbulatov, but insisted that the GKChP was patiently cooperating with these "confused patriots." I read as well that the Supreme Soviet was scheduled to meet on August 26 to discuss the measures taken by the GKChP. A sampling of local public opinion included remarks by only five individuals, four of whom supported the extraordinary measures. The fifth individual insisted the country's problems had to be solved on a legal basis. All of those canvassed stressed the need for law and order. Since the report on Monday evening's press conference did not at all accurately reflect what viewers had witnessed, I could readily dismiss the survey. *Kommunist* repeated the "temporary" ban on all but an approved list of newspapers. Among the short articles on health, beauty tips, and how-to-fix-it columns was tucked away a modest notice that Soviet citizens could no longer buy foreign currency. This, in effect, would prevent most people from being able to travel abroad. I saw no mention of the events in Moscow or elsewhere. The day's obligatory photo portrayed F. Alimov, a machine operator at the Banner of the Red October Collective Farm, who for four summers now had stacked fodder in an exemplary manner.

Despite the ban on non-Party newspapers, *Saratov* put out a special edition that morning as well. The tone reflected Boris Yeltsin's spirited defiance. Demanding that an international team of doctors examine Gorbachev, Yeltsin volunteered to have the Russian Republic pay the medical bill from its depleted hard-currency reserves. Once again emphasizing the unconstitutional nature of the attempted coup, Saratov's Golovachev called upon Saratovites to uphold all of Yeltsin's decrees, and upon city, regional, and neighborhood soviet leaders to back Yeltsin. Golovachev also prophetically stated that the coup would fail. Other articles assessed public opinion in the capitals as well as in Saratov. A roving reporter who took the First Secretary of the City Committee of the Communist Party, S. Slepov, by surprise, let Slepov's cautious and insipid remarks about the legality of the extraordinary measures speak for themselves.

A probing article analyzed the putsch itself and why it was failing. Posing questions that were on many people's minds about the ineptness of the coup's organizers, the author observed that their last chance to save themselves was a two-thirds vote of support within the Supreme Soviet, scheduled to meet on the 26th, or a decision to resort to force. A related piece decried the cheap populism of the coup's organizers as expressed in their vague promises to improve food supplies and housing, and lower prices. No happy workers adorned *Saratov*, but instead a cartoon of a jowly Party apparatchik with the caption, "The measures that I want to propose are unpopular, but, believe me, comrades, they're necessary."

In reading the paper, I could not help but think that Soviet society had been as closed to those who constitute it, including its leaders, as it had been to me. How else can we account for the colossal ineptitude of Russia's "Pinochets," as the newspaper *Saratov* began calling Gennadii Yanaev and his accomplices? Back in 1917 Lenin actually had a much better appreciation of the public mood out in the provinces than did those who had calculated on overthrowing M.S. Gorbachev. Had they taken the pulse of the Russian heartland beforehand, they probably would have reconsidered their plans or abandoned them altogether. It seemed to me that the putschists had been deluded by the widespread view that, apart from a few exceptions, the provinces represented a bulwark of conservatism, and by illusions of a yet sound centralized power that had the clout to compel the provinces to comply with the center's wishes. Failing to see that the old guard's ability to survive contrived elections in many provincial centers told us virtually nothing about prevailing attitudes in these settings, the putschists became victims of their own self-deception.

Emboldened by the tone of *Saratov*, I decided to drop in unannounced at the Saratov Regional Party Archive, located a short distance from my apartment. A month or so before my departure for the Soviet Union, I had written to the director of the archive, requesting permission to use its holdings during my forthcoming visit. Although laws forbade non-Communists from working in Party archives, several American and European scholars had been granted access to central Party archives in Moscow during the previous months. As I was about to begin writing a book on the Civil War in Saratov Region (1918–22), I wished to take advantage of the lifting of restrictions regarding access to vital materials that heretofore were off-limits, in the hope of obtaining access to Party archives, which, in effect, remained the only sources I had not yet examined.

Unable to tell from looking at the gray brick building how to find the entrance, let alone the director, I deliberately whisked past the armed guard without making eye contact. As I expected, he collared me, briefly questioned me, and pointed me to the correct passage. Once inside, I located the director's office and assured his perplexed secretary that I was willing to wait as long as necessary in order to see him. "Where did you say you were from?" she prodded. My answer sent her scurrying, and momentarily I was introducing myself to Mr. Lobanov.

Lobanov's sweaty outstretched hand made a hesitant handshake. I smelled fear. Yes, I told him, I knew that it was illegal for me to use Party archives, but he and I both realized that current practice had changed all that. And, yes, I had been told that Lobanov had assumed his post just a short while ago.

"Too bad your letter took so long in getting here and too bad your university colleagues sent us written support of your request just yesterday. We in Saratov look quite favorably upon your appeal, but we can't let you work here without the permission of the Central Committee. Unfortunately, I doubt that we will receive a reply to the letter I sent to Moscow before you leave Saratov."

"Excuse me," I pressed. "There's a telephone on your desk. Let's call Moscow. I'll be happy to argue my case."

"I'll call Moscow myself," Lobanov replied with some hostility.

"Should I come back tomorrow?" I asked, knowing full well what his answer would be.

"Don't bother. You can call me."

I left frustrated by my meeting with the soft-spoken, timid Lobanov, who to me epitomized the bland, morally neutral type that used to make a career within the Party establishment by being disagreeably agreeable. On my way to the state archive to report on my visit with Lobanov, I stopped in at the Volga Publishing House to leave some materials with my editor. There I had a chance encounter with an eccentric old man who had published a book on local medicinal herbs—a particularly timely subject, owing not only to the keen public interest in anything not given its due in the past, but also to the lack of pharmaceuticals. Genuine, sincere, and unpretentious, this veterinarian-turned-herbalist had dreamed for years of meeting a real American with flashy white teeth, and I walked into his dream the moment I entered my editor's basement office, which served as work station, reception area, trade center, and diner. My new self-proclaimed friend had one useless eye (he had been kicked by a horse), and the other twinkled at me impishly from behind smudged spectacles. His spontaneous display of emotion and affection lightened my heart, and once again directed my thoughts to the many fine qualities of the Soviet people I find so disarmingly endearing. They deserved better than Yanaev and his ilk, I thought to myself. Even Lobanov.

These qualities were just as evident at the state archive on Kutiakov Street, where archivists put a desk at my disposal in a room they occupied on the second floor. They invited me to work there, rather than in the Lilliputian public reading room, so that casual acquaintances would not bother me, as they had during my first visit to Saratov the year before. The archivists, four women, joked that the desk available to me was a parting present from one of their coworkers who had recently emigrated to Israel. They served me tea, pastries, and fruit and vegetables from the plots they worked on weekends. And they shared their food and drink with me not just that day, but during the coming weeks as well. For now, we worked together, listened to radio broadcasts together, and discussed local and national politics together. We got to know about each other's families and illnesses. In today's idiom, we bonded. From things they said, and from the way they said them, I came to understand the meaning of the coup from this provincial perspective.

In the early afternoon I met friends for lunch at the Volga Hotel Restaurant, considered the best restaurant in town. Service is horrible and the menu limited. While dining, one can observe the waitresses and waiters peddling or swapping rationed (and expensive) hard liquor for who knows what favors. The Volga's attraction is that the high prices keep it off-limits to most. As this was our first visit together, my friends and I sought to catch up on each other's lives and families, but no matter how hard we tried, talk reverted again and again to the political situation and to speculating about how long this frightful setback could last.

Shortly after I returned to my cozy corner in the archive, an agitated archivist burst into the room to announce that some of the organizers of the coup had been arrested. We broke into spontaneous applause. There were tears and phone calls. We turned up the volume of the radio, congratulating ourselves for suggesting earlier that the coup could not last. Experiencing boundless relief and yearning for more concrete news, we left for home to listen to the latest information. I heard the 6:00 P.M. broadcast at the Volga Publishing House, where the unrestrained goodwill and lightheartedness reigning there infected me. Later I was to find out that a block away from my publisher's at the very same time, eighty-three deputies of the city soviet, about twenty shy of a quorum, had convened. Golovachev read a statement about the arrests and about Yeltsin's authority to deal with the coup's consequences. All but four or five of the deputies demonstrated their pleasure with the outcome of the coup by standing when congratulatory telegrams were read. The deputies resolved to hold an emergency session that evening and to issue an official announcement to the people of Saratov.

A much welcomed change on the evening of Wednesday, August 21, was that conversation now centered on family, friends, and other personal matters, rather than on politics and the country's precarious future. We switched the TV off, not wishing to have the congenial ambience destroyed by any unexpected announcements. It was hard to believe that all we had lived through had been compressed into a few days.

8 | Letter from St. Petersburg

Born and raised in Leningrad (now St. Petersburg), where he was
trained as a computer scientist, Valerii Zavorotnyi has been actively
involved in the city's democratic movement since 1988 as a
participant, political observer, and commentator. Over the years he
has tried his hand at various professions—filmmaker, computer
scientist, sculptor, writer—before turning to public life. His writings
on public affairs appeared in numerous Leningrad publications
during the Gorbachev years.

I woke up on the 19th when my phone rang and a voice informed me:
"Everything is going to hell. Gorbachev was arrested, emergency rule
has been introduced." I mumbled something into the receiver and hung
up. Let me tell you, it is a horrible thing to be awakened by a phone
call like that.

What to do? I had to get up and turn on the TV. All I learned was
that the same symphony orchestra was playing the same piece on all
three channels. For a Soviet being, this represents a clear signal that a
sharp turn in policy in the beloved country is in the offing. Ten minutes later, an announcer began to read with a stony face, first, Lukianov's statement, then the Appeal to the Soviet People, and Decree
No. 1 of the Emergency Committee. . . . I had no more questions.

Now, hard as I try, I cannot recall what I felt in those moments. I
guess it was some kind of temporary numbness of feeling. I washed, I
dressed, I drank coffee, I tried to collect thoughts that I did not have.
But this state did not last long. Gradually, my brain regained its agility.
Under these circumstances I did not expect any more news, and, sure
enough, the TV merely repeated the earlier statement, followed by
more music.

That morning I had a date with two French historians who had been invited by the Memorial Society.* They had just come from Novosibirsk, and I had promised to show them the city. What a day for an excursion! I gave the matter some thought and decided to go to their place, pick them up, and take a walk with them to the Mariinskii Palace [the Leningrad City Soviet]. If anything at all were to happen, it was most likely to happen there.

I left home expecting to be greeted if not by tanks, then by heavy police patrols. There was nothing of the sort, nothing at all that would distinguish this morning from any other workday morning. People were rushing to their jobs, city buses came and went, and the owners of co-op businesses were opening up their stalls outside the subway station. . . .

It was then that, for the first time that morning, my mood really soured. "It looks like we are going to swallow this one, too," I said to myself.

I took the subway to Vasilevskii Island, where the French couple was staying. The first thing they asked me when they opened the door was, "Do you think we can stay here longer?" It would have been more appropriate for them to ask me whether they would be able to get out of here. We chatted a little over a cup of coffee in the kitchen and I began looking at my watch, angling to get out of their apartment as soon as possible. At the same time I felt badly about leaving two foreigners in that kind of a situation. "What do you think will happen next?" asked Alain (his wife's name was Sonya). I wished I knew someone who could answer this question. "Do you think the West will be able to help?" he continued. I wanted very much to assume a proud pose and answer, "No, we'll take care of it ourselves." However, I immediately thought of the scene on the street, where everybody was going about their business as if nothing had happened. Perhaps the West is our only hope, I said to myself, and mumbled in response to Alain's question something like, "We've gotten ourselves into this mess, and we'll have to take care of it ourselves." I remember this conversation very well and remember also that I was entirely disingenuous. What I was saying to myself ran differently: "What nonsense! *They* have all the power—the army, the KGB—which means they will be entrenched for years. Once again, the only free speech will be in the

---

*Memorial is a voluntary association dedicated to the history and rehabilitation of the victims of repression.

kitchen; once again, we'll have to hand copy the *samizdat*; once again we'll have to fear police searches and worry while reading clandestine literature. . . ."

We decided to take a walk in the city together. I thought I would take them to St. Isaac's Cathedral and while there I would take a peak at the Mariinskii Palace Square to see if anything was afoot.

Nevskii Prospect was busy as usual: there was traffic, retail kiosks were doing a brisk business, shops were open. . . . Alain, though, noted that people were gloomier than usual. I disagreed, saying that Leningraders are quite gloomy as rule. We walked all the way to Herzen Street without encountering anything unusual. Only after turning the corner did we come across a small band of young people, marching together, holding hands and displaying a handmade placard: "Down with Dictatorship!" An old woman hissed: "Damn you all! You made a mess and now you'll pay for it." About a dozen pedestrians crossed to the other side of the street. Others tried to avert their eyes and walked past as quickly as possible. Alain got out his camera and took a picture of the marchers, trying to be as inconspicuous as possible. Here we go again, I thought to myself, back to "you ought to be ashamed in front of the foreigner"; "foreign spies"; "clandestine CIA operations"; "the Iron Curtain."

Finally we reached St. Isaac's, I took them inside, showed the way to the top, and told them that I would be waiting for them in front of the Mariinskii Palace, on the Senate Square.

I expected the Mariinskii to be surrounded by soldiers or OMON special militia troops—the way they did it in Vilnius back in January— but there was nothing of the sort. What I saw was about a hundred people milling about under the columns with Russia's tricolor flag and a few placards. It was then that I saw for the first time the mention of the junta and a call for a general strike. One column was decorated with a big portrait of Yeltsin, the other sported a sign: "No to Red Fascism." A few militiamen were among the crowd. The palace doors were open and people kept going in and out. Finally, I spotted a few guys in gray OMON uniforms, but they were unarmed. I walked up to one of them. "What's up, officer?"

He did not answer me. We stood for a while, in silence. "There is something amiss here," I said to myself. "Things are a mess everywhere. Still, this is a coup d'état, after all. Could it be that they don't have the brains to pull this off either?"

At the Mariinskii Palace, St. Petersburg: "No to Red Fascism!" "Join the Indefinite Political Strike!" "No to the CPSU Dictatorship!"

Soon after Alain and Sonya rejoined me, I spotted a Deputy I knew from the days when we worked together for the Popular Front.* He was exactly what I needed then. I quickly said good-bye to my French friends, promised to call them later that evening, and ran off to catch the Deputy. Ten minutes later, I was inside the palace, climbing the marble staircase to the second floor, having no idea whatsoever that I would not leave this building until three days later. Thus began the most exciting and perhaps the best three days of my life in the last several years.

I was not lucky enough to find a job right away, though everyone there had plenty to do. At first, we were busy duplicating leaflets (we were afraid that newspapers would be closed down). TV and radio were closed tight, and our only hope was the photocopy machines at the palace. News came over two telephone lines and was written down longhand. We had only two fax machines. Yeltsin's first decrees and

---

*This was a grassroots, Gorbachev-encouraged democratic movement of the early years of perestroika.

addresses came over them from Moscow. Later in the day, two newspapers, *Smena* and *Nevskoe vremia*, managed to come out by some miracle (the deputies had to "muscle in" on the censors). Day and night during these days we kept getting leaflets, statements, and decrees from Moscow, kept duplicating them and distributing them all throughout the city.

On the evening of the 19th we found out that two columns of troops and equipment were moving toward the city from the direction of Pskov. At the same time, we learned that a Special Forces storm trooper unit of six hundred men had entered the city and was quartered at a military college on Voinov Street. Other military units regularly stationed around Leningrad were put on alert but were staying put for the time being. Several groups, headed by deputies from the city soviet, went to those bases as well as to the military colleges and to the navy bases. Many of those who came to the square later, especially former soldiers, organized themselves into groups and also went to speak to the military.

The staff headquarters organized at the palace was recruiting reserve officers from among those who came to the square (by that time, over a thousand people had already gathered there). Pretending to be one of those brave reserve officers (though I never got beyond the rank of sergeant), I managed to get myself admitted into one of these groups. I adapted to the role so well that three hours later I was promoted to group commander. They even issued me a very powerful mandate. I am sorry I will not have any grandchildren, for this piece of paper is exactly what one would like to frame and put on the wall for the sake of one's descendants.

What happened during the following two nights and two days is a long story. On the morning of the 19th, deputies and all those who had helped them to get elected began to stream into the palace. All of this resembled [the election campaign of] 1989, when people were only beginning to come out of hibernation, feel like actual human beings, and realize that they could make a difference. Many were simply those "men in the street" who had once made it possible for the deputies to be elected. As in 1989, the division between those who were voting and those who were being voted into office became blurred. This was all the more remarkable because just a few days ago it looked as if all factional infighting among the newly elected deputies would lead to a dead end. The attitude toward the "democrats" had been changing, and,

Rally in Palace Square, August 19

sad to say, not in their favor. And, God knows, this was understandable, just as it was clear that the deputies had not had any prior experience of democratic government, no political culture, and, saddest of all, were not always aware of their deficiencies. Who can blame them, though. One could not ask history to slow down.

I had never been enthusiastic about politics. It is interesting to study and analyze politics as a form of the relation between the government and society, but to be an actor in it was not for me. In any case, politics is not a clean business, it never is. However, at certain moments, many things become different; otherwise, we would not have had Sakharov or many other men and women I have encountered whose integrity I never doubted.

Our great politicians who thought up this coup d'état (oh, these wise men!) had made all the correct calculations, including the public's growing disappointment in the "democrats." But once again, they failed to take into account the "minutiae." They forgot that people had already had a taste of freedom and that they might not wish to go back. They might elect a bad government. But, having obtained the right to choose *their own* government, even if they subsequently damn it with four-letter words, they would not wish to part with this right. For the first time in decades, indeed, centuries, this *was* their government—a flawed government to be sure ("this fucking government!"), but the government that *they themselves* elected. And those people came out to safeguard this government, that is to say, to safeguard *themselves*. . . .

I can also tell you that despite the almost complete information blackout, with the radio and TV continuously spreading lies, we managed to set up the production, duplication, and distribution throughout the city of thousands of leaflets and news summaries. In many offices, where the authorities had not yet shut down duplicating equipment, dozens of different people did their best to produce a few hundred, a few thousand copies. . . . Dozens drove their cars to the palace to pick up stacks of leaflets and then distributed them in their neighborhoods or at military bases.

At a certain point, after we had learned about the troops moving toward Leningrad along the Tallinn Highway but did not know anything about the other approaches to the city, a taxi drove right up to the palace. A strapping fellow got out of it and, cutting through the crowd and the volunteer chain surrounding the palace, addressed me: "Listen, commander, here is what's happening outside the city. . . ." When I asked him how he had found about what was going on, he told me that a few dozen taxi drivers had gotten together and went scouting in the suburbs, communicating with each other on their taxi radios. These were our taxi drivers—the same guys who will not budge unless you wave a few large-denomination bills or a pack of Marlboros in front of their noses!

On the first evening, a group of doctors came to the palace, equipped with all the first-aid stuff—medicines, bandages, and so on—and they stayed to the end, ready to minister to the wounded. People brought food. Among them there were not only older women who had managed to scrape together a couple of sandwiches made with rationed sausage and the last packet of tea, but also the "new *biznesmeny*," who hauled in cartons and cartons of delicacies we had forgotten even existed. Outside the palace, people who knew each other got together and set up little improvised cafés, treating the demonstrators to hot tea and coffee—gratis.

Throughout the crisis, we kept receiving calls from "co-operators" (this is the term for small businessmen here), who would offer and then deliver copying equipment, paper, computers. . . . In recent times, this category of people on the whole, though with some exceptions, has not enjoyed great respect among the population. Indeed, a savage market economy is not a pretty sight. The crazy inflation destroying the value of money, and the opportunity to grab this same money in large quantities from an inept state, has been correctly described by one Western observer as a gang rape of the state by its citizens. I might add, though, that this state has done plenty of raping of its citizens and cannot expect to be treated properly by them; consider also the decades of inexcusable lying, thievery, and corruption by the state, and you will understand why people do not put much stock in business ethics and common decency. And of course, it is the common man who must foot the bill. Still, there was nothing we could expect. Alas, a civilized market economy always evolves from a savage one.

Be that as it may, these co-op owners had already separated themselves from the *system*, though they tended to duplicate some of its traits, unlike, for example, the dissidents, the so-called "sixties people," who did not want to have anything in common with the system or to accept any of the rules by which it played its game. The dissidents were guided exclusively by the idea of moral resistance against the system, while those co-op owners had already developed a taste for having their own autonomous businesses. They understood well that what was happening now might affect their right to continue to run their own lives. And the stand they took during those days made a significant contribution.

I recall one of those guys, who had been supplying us with paper for leaflets, saying to me: "Hang in there, boys. We know that if you keel over, we will, too."

Of course, this is not to say that they formed the majority of those who came to the square. The majority were common folk, ordinary people of different generations. Many of them had probably never thought they would ever wind up in such a crowd. And still, they came.

On the evening of the 19th, a bunch of very young people organized work teams and began building barricades. They, too, had their own commanders, even their own "boot camp." A young man of twenty, Maksim Poliakov, presided over this whole enterprise. He and I had a lot of dealings together, and I remember him well. Two strands curiously intertwined in his life: the August crisis in Petersburg and the

January one in Vilnius. Back in February, he and a few other young men formed a Petersburg detachment and went to Vilnius to guard the Lithuanian parliament building. He came back to Petersburg on August 18 for a brief vacation, and on the 19th he was already organizing people at the square. For all those three days, he walked around the square in his Lithuanian "uniform" of the "Regional Protection Forces." I had the opportunity to observe Maksim as he was teaching the guys how to build barricades according to the design he had learned while erecting barricades on the roof of the Lithuanian parliament building to guard against a paratrooper landing. And they followed his instructions, setting up the "antiparatroop" contraptions and then the ordinary kind—at first funny and awkward-looking and in the end, solid ones, made of blocks of concrete and loaded trucks.

The militia and the OMON troops did joint guard duty. Here in Leningrad, both of them took our side from the beginning. Maksim was shaking his head, saying that only a crazy man could have predicted that he would be drinking tea with the OMON troopers on the same barricade. The guys from OMON told us what to do if we were gassed (they were sure that gas would be used in case of an attack). We had never given this a thought. But while we were scratching our heads, trying to figure out what to do, a truck belonging to some "small business" began unloading gas masks. This was living proof of mental telepathy, and nobody doubted at that moment that the science of extrasensory phenomena was no less true to nature than Marxism.

On the evening of the 19th, a whole caravan of water trucks blocked the approaches to the square. The drivers came to see us and said: "Well, folks, you'll be safe for now—we parked them in such a way that a tank will bust before it moves them. We're going to turn in for the night: tomorrow is another workday for us." This self-generated organized activity was a common occurrence at the square. There were dozens of such grassroots organizations, uniting very different people, and they acted without waiting for anyone to tell them what to do. As hours went by, it was becoming increasingly clear that even if *those others* were to win, they would not be able to clamp down on us as before, to take back the past six years.

The people did not have fear in their eyes. They were anxious and tense, yes, but they were not frightened. At a certain point, as I was standing guard, Deputy Sale walked out onto the square. Right away a circle formed around her. It did not look like she was prepared to make

Rally in Palace Square, August 20

a speech, and a bit awkwardly, she said: "Well, my fellow citizens of Petersburg, have we gotten ourselves into trouble!" There was uproarious laughter. She told me later that that was the moment she realized the putsch had failed. Just think: a few years ago many of those who were laughing would not have dared to leave their homes at a time of such crisis. And there they were now, standing in the middle of a square that might soon be attacked by tanks, laughing.

I am not one to idealize what happened, and I am aware that changes have touched only a segment of our society, the most active segment, but a segment nonetheless. Yet in moments of such great stress, it is the most active part of society that plays the decisive role.

There were many military men on the square. On the first day they came wearing their civilian clothes, but on the second day they had put on their uniforms. They joined the staff headquarters and paid visits to the military bases. The Afghan veterans stood guard in the square and in a few other strategic locations in the city. One of them said to me: "When I returned from Afghanistan back then and saw what was going on in our society, I said to myself that there would soon come a time when I would be setting tanks on fire in the streets of our city." Those were his exact words.

I was fortunate enough to meet there, near the palace, many remarkable people and to experience things I would never have experienced had it not been for those three days. I am aware that some of my recollections might seem romantic. But I want to convey the atmosphere of those days with all possible authenticity. I want you to be able to see the faces of those people who, after all is said and done, were responsible for the outcome.

When we began receiving the news from Moscow that the tanks were leaving the White House, and realized that this might be the last night of the coup d'état, a new type of rumor started circulating at the square: "Yazov shot himself, the Emergency Committee has been arrested, the Baltic Fleet has struck against the putsch." (All the Baltic fleet had actually done at the time was declare its neutrality in the conflict.) That is when the public address system at the Mariinskii Palace, its windows wide open, began to play Glier's "Hymn to the Great City." I cannot begin to convey to you what it was like to be in the square during those moments. . . . Whatever happens in the next few years—and anything *can* happen—the memory of that last night in the square—ringed by the barricades, illuminated by the yellow street lamps, with the black silhouette of the cathedral in the background, the dark sky above, and the Glier hymn floating through the air—the memory of that night will stay with people for a long time. Many will remember it forever.

III

In High Places

Between August 19 and 21, the barricades erected on the streets of Moscow and Leningrad came to signify the great divide that separated advocates of democratic reform from defenders of the old Communist order. In no group was this great divide more visible and wrenching than in the political elite—among those at the apex of the country's government institutions, the Communist Party, and the military. For them, the coup was a moment of reckoning. Part III reveals how some of the leading figures in the Soviet political elite faced this challenge.

MIKHAIL S. GORBACHEV

1 | What Happened in Foros

After returning from his summer residence in the Crimea, where he was held incommunicado for three days, Gorbachev held his first press conference on Thursday, August 22. He devoted most of his long opening statement to an account of his and his family's isolation at the Presidential compound in Foros, his dealings with the conspirators, and his attempts to resist their will. He spoke without notes and without pausing, ignoring the occasional gentle tugs of his press aide, Vitalii Ignatenko. It is this account, extracted from the opening statement, that we reproduce in its entirety.

[. . .] On August 18, at 4:50 P.M., I was informed by the head of [Presidential] security that a group of persons had come down to the compound and demanded to meet with me. I said that I was expecting no one, that I had not invited anyone, and that nobody had told me to expect anyone. The head of security, too, told me that he did not know anything about it either. "Then why did you let them in?" "Because," was his answer, "they had the head of the Security Directorate of the KGB, [Yurii] Plekhanov, with them." Otherwise the security people would not have let them pass into the President's residence. Such are the rules; they are tough but necessary.

I decided to find out who might have sent them here. Nothing could be simpler, since I have at my disposal all means of communication: the ordinary [telephone] line, the government network, the strategic network, the satellite links, etc. . . . I picked up one of the telephones— I was working in my office just then—and it was dead. I picked up another phone, a third, a fourth, a fifth; they were all dead. I picked up the internal telephone—disconnected. That was it. I was isolated.

I realized that this mission was not going to be the kind of mission we deal with ordinarily. I asked my wife [Raisa Maksimovna], daughter [Irina], and son-in-law [Anatolii] to gather together and said to them: "Here is what has just happened. . . . I don't need any additional information. I can see that something very serious is going on. Evidently they are going to try and blackmail me into something, or they will try to arrest me, or kidnap me, or something else. In other words, anything can happen."

I told Raisa Maksimovna, Irina, and Anatolii that if it was a question of the most important matter—of policies, of [our political] course—I would stand my ground to the end. I would not give in to any blackmail, any threats, or any pressure, and I would not make any other decisions.

I considered it necessary to say this, and you understand why: anything at all could happen next . . . and especially, considering the consequences for the members of my family. . . . We understood that, too.

The whole family said that the decision was up to me: they were ready to share with me whatever might happen, right to the end. That was the end of our [family] council.

I walked out to invite the visitors in, but they, led by [Valerii] Boldin, the President's chief of staff, had already gone up to the office on their own—an unprecedented breach of protocol.

The President was given an ultimatum to hand over his powers to the Vice President. I said: "Before I start answering questions, I would like to ask you: Who sent you?"

The answer was : "The committee."

"What committee?"

"Well, the committee to deal with the emergency situation in the country."

"Who created this committee? I didn't create it, the Supreme Soviet didn't create it, so who created it?"

I was told that people [in the leadership] had already joined together, and that now a decree from the President was needed. The matter was formulated like this: "Either you issue a decree [establishing the state of emergency] and remain here, or else you hand over your powers to the Vice President."

"Why is the issue formulated in this manner?"

"The situation in the country is such—the country is sliding toward a catastrophe—that it is necessary to take measures, a state of emergency is needed. Other measures can no longer save the situation; we can no longer indulge ourselves in illusions. . . ."

And so it went, on and on.

In reply I said to them that I knew better than all of them the political, economic, and social situation in the country, the conditions of people's lives, all the cares that burden them now. Further, [I said] that we had approached the phase when all that is necessary to improve life must be done faster and with more decisiveness. But I am a determined opponent—and not only for political and moral reasons—of those methods of dealing with problems, methods that have always led to the deaths of hundreds, thousands, millions of people. We must reject [those methods] once and for all. Otherwise, we would have to betray and bury everything that we have started to implement and resign ourselves to launching another round of bloodshed.

That's why I said: "Both you and those who sent you are adventurists. You will destroy yourselves—but the hell with you, that's your own business—most important, you will destroy the country, everything we have worked for. We have now reached the point when it is possible to sign the [Union] Treaty. After the signing—and we have worked on [this agenda] for a whole month—major decisions will be taken regarding the problems with fuel, food, and finances so that we can quickly stabilize the political and economic situation, speed up the transition to a market economy, and create opportunities for our people to apply themselves freely in all walks of life. And [you have come up with] all this just as we are about to reach agreement!* True enough, it is not a perfect agreement, and we have not yet gotten rid of our suspicions—on either side. We see it in the relations between the Union [government] and the republics, and between political and social movements. All that is true. But the only way to deal with this is to seek accord. Accord is emerging, and we have begun to move forward. Only those bent on suicide can propose at this point the introduction of a totalitarian regime in our country."

There was a demand: "Resign!"

I said: "You'll never see me do either one. Tell this to all those who sent you here. There won't be any more conversations between us. You may say that the President is ready to put his signature under any telegram, at once. And we have a reason: on the 20th, we are signing a new Union Treaty."

---

*That is, among the prospective cosigners of the Union Treaty.

(By the way, this was the end of Sunday, and I was finishing work on my speech for this solemn occasion; as late as four o'clock, [Georgii] Shakhnazarov and I were exchanging opinions about it in the presence of my other aide, Anatolii Cherniaev, who was not at this meeting.)

"So, there we can meet with many leaders; and for the 21st, we have scheduled a meeting of the Federation Council—that's where we will discuss all of these questions. [There] we will seek agreements [on the issues] that have eluded us on the government level.*

"Here they are for you, the central issues," I said. "That's where we must hammer out solutions, and not the way you propose. So, tomorrow you want to declare a state of emergency, do you? And then what? Why don't you try to predict one day ahead, four moves ahead. What then? The country will reject it, it won't support these measures. You are trying to exploit the difficulties, the fact that people are tired, that they might support any dictator. . . ."

(Incidentally, during the past few days I had been working with Comrade Cherniaev on a very long article—it was shaping up to be thirty-two pages. There was a scenario of this sort in it, and now its cast of characters had shown up in person. My argument concerning this scenario was that it spelled ruin for society, it was a dead end, it would throw society backward and bury everything that we now have.)

[I said:] "I am ready to convene the Congress of People's Deputies and the Supreme Soviet, if some in the leadership have doubts. Let's meet, let's discuss things. The Deputies are all in their districts, they know what's going on there, let's adopt an emergency resolution, take other measures. I will defend the path of concord, the path toward deepening the reforms and cooperating with the West—these are the three main areas, and now they need to be synchronized and coordinated. Especially since there is a corresponding desire on the part of other nations to cooperate with us at this decisive stage."

But it was a conversation with deaf-mutes. Evidently they had already prepared. The machinery had been set in motion—that's clear now.

I said: "That's it, there can be nothing more for us to talk about. Report that I am categorically opposed, and that you will be defeated. But I am concerned for the people and for what we have accomplished over these years. . . ." And that's how it ended.

---

*That is, in the old Union government.

But after their ultimatum had been answered by my categorical demand that they report my conclusions, everything started to develop according to the logic of conflict. Total isolation by sea and land. I still had thirty-two of my guards with me. They decided to stand firm to the end. They divided up all the areas of defense, including my family, and assigned all the different posts. When I found out that it had been stated at the coup committee's press conference that I was seriously ill and unlikely to return to a normal life, it became clear to me that the next thing would be to make reality correspond to this statement. The guards realized this as well. A decision was made not to order any food from outside and to live on what we had on hand. I was absolutely composed, although I was deeply shaken and angered by the political blindness and irresponsibility of these criminals. I was sure, I was convinced, that all of this couldn't last long, that they wouldn't get away with it.

Seventy-two hours of complete isolation, of struggle. I think that it was all done in order to break the President psychologically. It was hard. What more can I say?

Every day, morning and evening, I made and transmitted demands that communications be restored and that an airplane be sent immediately to fly me back to Moscow, back to my job. After the press conference, I added the demand that a retraction of the false report about the state of my health be published—the report made by those oh-so-healthy people whose hands were shaking as they faced you. [Laughter and applause from the reporters.] You raised good questions and mocked them. It was a farce.

Everything was cut off. But the resourceful lads found some old radio receivers in the service quarters, rigged up antennas, and started to tune in whatever they could. The BBC and Radio Liberty broadcasts came in best of all. Then the Voice of America came in—at least, that is what I was told, what they reported to me. [. . .]

People took a civic, responsible position, and did not collaborate with the Emergency Committee. What happened was done by force. I know, I have already been told a lot about what went on.

I want to say here, before you, that I am really with you. We all have seen that it was not in vain that for the last six years, with such difficulties and so painfully, we have been looking for ways to move forward. Our society rejected the putschists. In the end, they were isolated . They did not succeed in turning the army against the people.

The army came into contact with the people, and after that no one could do anything. They [the putschists] realized that they had failed.

The republics adopted the right position. In this regard, I must give credit where credit is due—the most principled position was adopted by Russia's Parliament, Russia's deputies, Russia's government, and above all an outstanding role was played by Boris Nikolaevich Yeltsin.

I must say also that today we must give credit where credit is due— to the principled position of Muscovites, Leningraders, and inhabitants of many other regions. The [putschists'] attempt to create the impression that the country was virtually supporting them . . . Well, they did find some [support]. These days in our country, you can find anything.

But on the whole, the country rejected this road to bloodshed. I don't think it is possible to get a better argument, a better plebiscite, testifying to the true position of the people. [. . .]

When it became clear that uncompromising position had been adopted by Russia, her leadership, other republics, the people, and that the army had not moved against the people, they panicked and began to look for a way out.

I was informed that a group of conspirators had arrived in the Crimea on the Presidential plane in order to take the President to Moscow. When they came, I said [to my security people]: take them to another building, put them under guard, and convey to them my demand that I will not speak to any of them until the government communication line is restored. Their response was that this would take a long time. "Take your time," I replied, "at this point I am not rushing anywhere."

Communications were restored, and I began talking to the country. First thing, I talked to Boris Nikolaevich [Yeltsin]. I called [Nursultan] Nazarbaev, [Leonid] Kravchuk, [Nikolai] Dementei, and [Islam] Karimov.* I said to them: "I'm holding the fort here with my garrison." [Laughter in the audience.] But that was exactly what was going on: 72 hours of such terrible tension. The security people at a certain point feared that we might be overtaken from the sea. But, as we have learned, the sailors were giving the President a sign that they would rescue him. The Navy did not participate in the conspiracy.

After that, I went to work. I ordered [Mikhail] Moiseev [Chief of the General Staff] to take over the leadership at the Ministry of Defense (he had been earlier called away from the Crimea) and im-

---

*The leaders of, respectively, Kazakhstan, Ukraine, Belarus, and Uzbekistan.

mediately to have all the troops return to their barracks, to their bases, and to announce that [Dmitrii] Yazov was being removed from his post and would be arrested.

All of this has been carried out. I found the Commandant of the Kremlin and asked him under whose command the [Kremlin] KGB regiment was, and I requested that the regiment's commander be summoned. He was summoned. I gave an order over the phone: "Submit to no one's authority except mine and that of the Kremlin Commandant."

He said: "Yes, sir."

In general, I started calling all the most important points, to block off everything all at once, because things were still dangerous. They could do away with me en route, or wherever they chose. I decided not to leave.

Then I was told that a plane was on its way with a delegation from the Russian Federation. I said I would receive them before doing anything else. I called [Civil Aviation] Minister Boris Paniukov and Moiseev and said that the plane should land not in Simferopol—or it would take them three hours to get to me—but at the military airfield. I gave a command that they be met and that transportation be arranged to bring them to me.

The delegation arrived, and we talked for a while and found we had a high degree of understanding. I think that what we have lived through has given us not only experience, but also greater understanding. This is what it means when democratic forces are united, and this is what it means when they are disunited. Just think, sometimes we have rammed our heads fighting over some issue and practically called each other enemies.

We started thinking about how to make our way out of there. Then I had to issue a lot more instructions. Ivashko and Lukianov arrived separately. They got there, even though no transportation had been provided for them. I received them. I did not receive the conspirators, did not see them, and do not want to see them. We divided among different planes and took them back to Moscow; and when they left the planes they were all arrested and incarcerated. I gave an order to the Kremlin Commandant not to admit anyone who had cooperated with them.

I have scheduled for tomorrow a meeting of the nine republic leaders who have worked out the Treaty and prepared it for signing. Tomorrow we shall be meeting and we must discuss everything.

These were painful lessons, and for me personally, very painful indeed. This is simply a most painful trauma for me.

I think that tomorrow we will start discussing, thinking over and working out positions on the issues involved in moving forward and on new steps to take. We need to see in this not only the misfortune that befell us, but also the immense opportunity that these events have revealed. They have revealed the true position of our people. In my conversations with the leaders of foreign states, they all focused attention specifically on the fact that the position of the people and the position of the army showed that irreversible changes have taken place in the Union. Therefore, they are hoping that we will take advantage of all these opportunities. They all said that they would cooperate, and they believe that this cooperation should take more active, more decisive forms. Today I received twelve ambassadors from the EEC countries. They declared their solidarity and support.

What decisions have been made? I've issued a decree . . .

Oh, by the way, you know, at the time, it looked as if they might do away with me, with my family, with everybody who was there with me, and then issue a lie that the President had taken such and such position and, moreover, that they were acting on his behalf. This is why I saw through all this treachery during their press conference, however primitive and crude. As one comrade from the Russian Federation said, they are just as incapable of doing this right as anything else.*

I decided to make a video recording right away. I made four recordings. The kids, Irina and Anatolii, cut up the tape into four pieces, and we started looking for channels, someone we could trust, to send this tape out.

Here is one of them. I'm turning it over to [Vitalii] Ignatenko, let him have a look. The other tapes may turn up, because they did go out despite the obstacles. My physician wrote out several copies of his medical opinion, and we gave them out and distributed them so that everyone would know the true state of the President's health. And finally, I put forward four points in written form and added something by hand so it would be clear that I had written it (the four points had been typed on a typewriter), and I signed my own statement.

---

*Gorbachev is echoing comedian Gennadii Khazanov's memorable quip, "These guys of ours, they can't even stage a putsch correctly."

The first point: Yanaev's taking upon himself my responsibilities under the pretext of my illness, [my] inability to carry out my duties, represents a deception of the people, and for that reason cannot constitute anything but a coup d'état.

Second. This means that all subsequent actions are illegal and without legitimacy: neither the President nor the Congress of People's Deputies has given Yanaev such authority.

Third. I ask that it be conveyed to Lukianov that I demand an urgent convening of the USSR Supreme Soviet and the Congress of People's Deputies so that they might consider the present situation, for they alone have the right, after analyzing the situation, to pass a decision on necessary measures and the mechanism for their implementation.

Fourth. I demand that the activities of the State Committee for the State of Emergency be suspended immediately until such time as the aforementioned decisions are taken by the Supreme Soviet and the Congress of People's Deputies. The continuation of these activities and further escalation of the measures being taken by the Emergency Committee may result in tragedy for all peoples, exacerbate the situation still further, and perhaps wreck totally the coordinated efforts to bring the country out of the crisis that has been initiated by the center and the republics.

I demanded an answer. I was told: "Wait, you will get one." At first, there was no response at all. Then I was told: "The answer is coming." But I received nothing.

That was the situation.

Now the most important thing is that decisions have to be made. I have rescinded all the orders given by the Vice President, and the [Emergency] Committee, and the Cabinet over the past few days. With my authority as President, I removed them from office and dismissed them, and that which requires the decision of the Supreme Soviet has been submitted for its consideration. The USSR Prosecutor has informed me that he instituted criminal proceedings yesterday, and we have agreed that the investigative team will consist of USSR and Russian Federation investigators. [. . .]

2 | Proclamations, Decrees, and Appeals in Response to the Coup, August 19, 1991

Boris Yeltsin, the first freely elected President of the Russian Republic, issued the following "Appeal to the Citizens of Russia," on the morning of the first day of the coup. Yeltsin's proclamation was the first public response of any kind to the announcement of the State Committee on the State of Emergency. It was soon reproduced on photocopy machines and posted in metro stations and elsewhere throughout the city. Later that day, Yeltsin issued several decrees and appeals, some of which are reprinted below. Of special importance was his appeal to officers and soldiers to forsake the plotters and submit to the authority of the Russian government.

Document 1. Appeal to the Citizens of Russia
(issued at 9:00 A.M. on August 19, 1991)

Citizens of Russia:

On the night of August 18–19, 1991, the legally elected President of the country was removed from power.

Regardless of the reasons given for his removal, we are dealing with a rightist, reactionary, anticonstitutional coup. Despite all the difficulties and severe trials being experienced by the people, the democratic process in the country is acquiring an increasingly broad sweep and an irreversible character.

The peoples of Russia are becoming masters of their destiny. The uncontrolled powers of unconstitutional organs have been limited considerably, and this includes party organs.

The leadership of Russia has adopted a resolute position on the Union Treaty, striving for the unity of the Soviet Union and the unity of Russia. Our position on this issue permitted a considerable acceleration of the preparation of this treaty, coordination with all the republics, and the decision that the date for signing would be August 20. Tomorrow's signing has been canceled.

These developments gave rise to angry reactionary forces, and pushed them to irresponsible and adventurist attempts to solve the most complicated political and economic problems by methods of force. Attempts to realize a coup have been tried earlier.

We considered and consider that such methods of force are unacceptable. They discredit the Union in the eyes of the whole world, undermine our prestige in the world community, and return us to the cold war era along with the isolation of Soviet Union in the world community. All of this forces us to proclaim that the so-called committee's ascendancy to power is unlawful.

Accordingly, we proclaim all decisions and instructions of this committee to be unlawful.

We are confident that the organs of local power will unswervingly adhere to constitutional laws and decrees of the President of Russia.

We appeal to citizens of Russia to give a fitting rebuff to the putschists and demand a return to normal constitutional development.

Undoubtedly, it is essential to give the country's President, Gorbachev, an opportunity to address the people. Today he has been blockaded. I have been denied communications with him. We demand an immediate convocation of the Congress of People's Deputies of the Union. We are absolutely confident that our countrymen will not permit the sanctioning of the tyranny and lawlessness of the putschists, who have lost all shame and conscience. We address an appeal to servicemen to manifest lofty civic duty and not take part in the reactionary coup.

Until these demands are met, we appeal for an indefinite general strike. . . .

Yeltsin, President of Russia
Silaev, Chairman of the RSFSR Council of Ministers
Khasbulatov, Acting Chairman of the RSFSR Supreme Soviet

Document 2: Decree No. 59 of the President of the RSFSR
(issued at 1:44 P.M. on August 19, 1991)

In connection with the actions of a group of individuals who proclaimed themselves the State Committee for the State of Emergency, I order that:

1. The work of said Committee be deemed illegal and the actions of its organizers be regarded as constituting a coup d'état, which is none other than a crime against the state.

2. All decisions made in the name of this so-called Committee for the State of Emergency be regarded as illegal and carrying no force of law on the territory of the RSFSR. The territory of the RSFSR is governed by the lawfully elected government in the persons of the President, the Supreme Soviet, the Chairman of the Council of Ministers, and all state and local governing and administrative organs of the RSFSR.

3. Actions of government officials who carry out the orders of said Committee are subject to the Criminal Code of the RSFSR and are liable to criminal prosecution according to law.

The present decree becomes law at the time of its signing.

President of the RSFSR, B.Yeltsin

Document 3: Decree No. 61 of the President of the RSFSR
(issued at 4:47 P.M. on August 19, 1991)

An attempt to carry out a coup d'état has been made; the President of the USSR, who is the Supreme Commander of the USSR Armed Forces, has been removed from office; the Vice President of the USSR, the Prime Minister of the USSR, the Chairman of the Committee for State Security [KGB] of the USSR, and the USSR Ministers of Defense and of Internal Affairs have joined an unconstitutional organ and have thereby committed a crime against the state. As a result of these actions, the work of the lawfully elected executive branch of government of the Union of Soviet Socialist Republics has been paralyzed. In this extraordinary situation, I decree that:

1. Until the convening of the extraordinary Congress of the USSR People's Deputies, all organs of executive power of the USSR that

operate on the territory of the RSFSR, including the KGB of the USSR, the Ministry of Internal Affairs of the USSR, and the Ministry of Defense of the USSR, become subject to direct rule by the popularly elected President of the RSFSR.

2. The RSFSR Committee on State Security, the RSFSR Ministry of Internal Affairs, and the RSFSR State Committee for Defense temporarily carry out the functions of the corresponding Union government organs on the territory of the RSFSR. All regional and other organs of the USSR KGB and the USSR Ministries of Internal Affairs and Defense that operate on the territory of the RSFSR shall be subject to direct rule by the decrees and dispositions of the RSFSR President, the RSFSR Council of Ministers, the RSFSR KGB and Ministry of Internal Affairs, and the RSFSR State Committee for Defense.

3. All organs, officials, citizens of the RSFSR must take immediate action to prevent the implementation of any and all orders of the unconstitutional Committee for the State of Emergency. Officials who follow the orders of this Committee are removed from office in accordance with the Constitution of the RSFSR. Organs of the RSFSR Prosecutor's Office must take immediate measures to initiate criminal proceedings against the aforesaid persons.

President of the RSFSR, B.Yeltsin

Document 4: Appeal by Boris Yeltsin, President of the RSFSR, to the Soldiers and Officers of the USSR Armed Forces, the USSR Committee for State Security [KGB], and the USSR Ministry of Internal Affairs [MVD]

Servicemen!
Countrymen!

An attempt has been made to stage a coup d'état. The President of the country, the Commander-in-Chief of the Armed Forces of the USSR, has been removed from power. The Vice President, the Chairman of the KGB, and the First Deputy Chairman of the Defense Council [of the USSR] have formed an unconstitutional body, and have thereby committed the most serious crime against the state. The country is faced with the threat of terror. The "order" promised by the

A soldier reads Yeltsin's appeal to the armed forces

self-appointed saviors of the Fatherland will result in tragedy: wholesale repression of dissent, concentration camps, nighttime arrests. "A better life" will remain a propaganda lie. Soldiers and officers, at this tragic hour I appeal to you. Do not let yourselves be snared in the web of lies, promises, and demagogic arguments about the soldier's duty. Do not allow yourselves to become a blind weapon of the criminal will of a group of adventurers who have violated the Constitution and the laws of the USSR.

Soldiers! I appeal to you. Think about your loved ones, your friends, and your people. At this difficult hour of decision, remember that you have taken an oath of allegiance to your people, the people against whom you are being forced to turn your weapons.

A throne can be erected using bayonets, but it is not possible to sit on bayonets for long. The days of the conspirators are numbered.

Soldiers, officers, generals! An hour ago I appointed the head of the RSFSR Committee for Defense. He is your comrade-in-arms, Colonel General K.I. Kobets. I have issued a decree placing all the territorial and other organs of the Ministry of Internal Affairs, the KGB, and the Ministry of Defense [of the USSR] deployed on the territory of the RSFSR without delay under the command of the President of the Russian Federation, the Ministry of Internal Affairs of the Russian Federation, and the State Committee for Defense of the Russian Federation.

Dark clouds of terror and dictatorship have gathered over Russia. But they will not become an eternal night. Rule of law shall triumph in our land, and our long-suffering people will gain freedom. This time— for now and forever!

Soldiers, I trust that in this tragic hour you will make the right decision. The honor and the glory of Russian arms shall not turn crimson with the blood of the people.

> Boris Yeltsin, President of the Russian Federation
> 5:10 P.M.

3 | # Speech to the Russian Parliament, August 21, 1991

Boris Yeltsin came before the Russian parliament at 12:55 P.M. on Wednesday, August 21. By then, the plotters had been routed and were attempting to flee. Reprinted below is the complete text of Yeltsin's speech.

Distinguished people, deputies.

Russia and the country, as a whole, are living through a dramatic, perhaps tragic, period in its history.

In the history of our country there have been several attempts to stage a coup, at a time when it would have seemed that democracy was on the rise and gathering momentum. Right-wing forces have tried several times to stage a coup d'état, and they have at last succeeded.

You will recall that the first attempt took place at the beginning of the year, but at that time they were scared off by the statement made by the Minister of Foreign Affairs, Eduard Shevardnadze, and the corresponding reaction of public opinion in Russia, the country, and the world.

You all recall the session of the USSR Supreme Soviet, when the same people—Pavlov, Kriuchkov, Yazov—tried to extract for themselves some special powers at the expense of the authority of the President of the country, which virtually amounted to his removal from office, and so forth.

But this second attempt, too, failed: the Supreme Soviet gave them no support.

And finally, the third, this time successful, attempt came when the President was vacationing away from Moscow. Now he is no longer on vacation; he is forcibly isolated at his dacha in Foros, in the Crimea.

What happened is an unconstitutional coup d'état. It is unconstitutional because there have been no statements made by the President of the country, either in writing or orally on television or radio. There has been no medical examination, either by Soviet doctors or international experts, stating that he is unable to perform his functions. Information at our disposal speaks to the contrary. The President's personal physician saw him on the 19th but was subsequently disallowed contact with the President. [According to him,] the President was in good health, except for a minor arthritic condition, so there can be no question about his not being able to discharge his duties.

In circumstances when democracy in our country is on the rise, these actions are unprecedented and constitute an arrogant coup d'état. Let me point out that all of these people come from the political right. They were unable to find even a couple of individuals among the pseudo-democrats willing to join them, to give a little political variety to the membership of their Committee. They tried, we know, but failed to find anybody. The people they approached refused to cooperate with them, refused to take part in this unconstitutional plot.

Now what measures did we undertake on our part?

First, early in the morning of the 19th, we issued a statement to the people of Russia which was signed by myself and Comrades Silaev and Khasbulatov. Although the mass media of the Russian Federation have been placed under a virtual blackout, we have set up a powerful radio station right in this building, we have talked to people on the phone, and we have succeeded in broadcasting that statement, along with the subsequent Decree of the President of the Russian Federation, to other regions of the country.

During the first twenty-four hours a series of other decrees were broadcast in this manner, including a decree [no. 59] proclaiming their Committee unconstitutional; a decree setting up Russia's Committee for Defense; a decree giving Russia's President authority over all the executive branches of the USSR government situated on the territory of the Russian Federation, including the USSR KGB, the USSR Ministry of Internal Affairs, and the USSR Ministry of Defense.

In the absence of the Commander-in-Chief, and taking into account the fact that the Minister of Defense is a criminal, it was our duty to assume responsibility for the USSR armed forces stationed on the territory of the Russian Federation. Further, we issued a decree setting up a special group headed by the First Deputy Prime Minister of the

Russian Federation. This group was sent to the heartland of Russia and there began preparations for assuming power in case Russia's government had been seized and eliminated last night (and, who knows, this danger may still exist).

And now regarding the actions of Yanaev, Pavlov, and others, there was a decree on the armed forces. The President of the Russian Federation has assumed authority over the armed forces. The Taman and the Kantemirov divisions and the airborne Paratrooper Unit have gone over to the side of the Russian Federation, and they are acting on orders of the President of the Russian Federation.

What are the reasons for the failure of the attempts to isolate or, to use this junta's cynical phrase, to "intern" the leadership of the Russian Federation—the President, the Chairman of the Council of Ministers, and the Acting Chairman of the Supreme Soviet of the Russian Federation? The reasons are that the Tula Airborne Paratrooper Division, instead of storming and seizing the building of the Russian Federation's parliament, took it under their protection and guarded it from attack for twenty-four hours. We are grateful to this Division, its commanding officers, and its Commander, General Lebed. Of course, he is facing certain danger now, but according to my Presidential decree, and since General Lebed is now resident on the territory of the Russian Federation, I have placed him under the protection of the President of Russia, safeguarding him from possible prosecution on the part of the USSR organs of law and order.

I have also signed a decree on the operation of enterprises on the territory of the Russian Federation, a decree on the economic sovereignty of the Russian Federation. Let me elaborate on this.

Taking into account that the Union Treaty was to be signed on the 20th and that we had an agreement with the President of the Union that on the 21st and 22nd, he would be signing a decree transferring the property and the enterprises on the territory of the Russian Federation to the jurisdiction of the Russian Federation, we had prepared a decree placing those enterprises under the jurisdiction of the Russian Federation. But now that the Union Treaty was not signed yesterday, because of the actions taken by an unconstitutional group of rebels, and since the President is incommunicado, I have signed a decree providing for the economic sovereignty of the Russian Federation, stating that all property on the territory of the Russian Federation is placed under the jurisdiction of the Russian Federation.

In light of the curfew imposed in Moscow and Leningrad, I have removed the commanders of the Moscow and Leningrad military districts and I have appointed different persons who act on orders of appropriate authorities, and I have also appointed the Minister of Defense for the Russian Federation, Colonel General Konstantin Ivanovich Kobets.

I have also signed several appeals: to the citizens of Russia, to President Bush, to servicemen, and to his Holiness the Patriarch of Moscow and All Russia, Aleksii II. The last appeal was delivered by hand, by Vice President Rutskoi, and the Patriarch has supported us at this difficult period of time, and he said that the faithful would support us at this difficult time.

As Ruslan Imranovich [Khasbulatov] said earlier, we have formulated an ultimatum and discussed it with Lukianov. . . , though I must say that we cannot believe Lukianov when he says that he did not participate and did not even know that this group was planning an imminent coup.

Further, I have issued a directive to put the House of Soviets ["the White House"] under guard. This decision was fully justified, because there were plans to launch an attack on the parliament building, precise plans with everything worked out hour by hour and minute by minute. It is only thanks to our decisive actions and the actions of the people of Moscow who staged an all-day vigil at the building—we were inside the building and the people of Moscow were outside in the rain—it was largely thanks to them, when they stopped tanks and armored personnel carriers and the special forces that had been sent to storm the building and arrest the members of the Russian government. We must thank the people of Moscow, who deserve praise for such resolute actions.

The [RSFSR] Minister of Foreign Affairs, Kozyrev, has been sent to the United Nations to inform Peres de Cuellar and the United Nations about the unconstitutional developments in our country and what the Russian Federation plans to do about them.

I must say that Bush, Mitterrand, and others were firm in their denunciation of the coup d'état and the actions of this Committee for the State of Emergency. They do not acknowledge its decisions, but they support the actions of the Russian government, and therefore will see to it that the world community offers us support and expresses its opinion with regard to what has happened.

I asked them that they, for their part, demand to be put in touch with the President of the Union [Gorbachev]. But of course, communications with him are broken or, rather, blocked in Foros, in the Crimea, by the forces of the Union KGB, the Navy, and his own Presidential security detail, which is also KGB. So he has three rings around him.

My conversations over the telephone with Yanaev and Kriuchkov have shown that they are trying to justify their actions, saying that they have been acting constitutionally, that Gorbachev is unable to perform his functions, but this is not true.

Today, around three o'clock in the morning, Kriuchkov canceled, for the duration of this night, the actions directed at isolating and then taking by storm the House of Soviets [the White House]. He agreed to my proposal—that he and I together fly to Foros and bring back the President. But I need your permission for this.

[Voices of the deputies: "No, don't go!"]
Khasbulatov: Well, this is what I, too, have been telling the President.

In accordance with our request, Kriuchkov must come here at 13:00 hours.*

As to the idea of flying there, I don't think there is another way of finding out what the objective situation is. Needless to say, Kriuchkov must give his guarantees.

[Voices: "What kind of guarantees?"]

I repeat: this is the situation, but the decision is yours.

So this is the situation as of now. The leadership of the Russian Federation, the President and the leadership of the Supreme Soviet and the Council of Ministers, have been acting energetically; there is no panic, there is no despair, and we do hope that the days of the junta are numbered, and they must be removed from power. This Committee must be dissolved, and all of its eight members must be brought to justice.

---

*Kriuchkov never came.

4 Between Russia and the Soviet Union—With Notes on the USSR Council of Ministers Meeting of August 19, 1991

Nikolai Vorontsov, the USSR Minister of Environment and Natural Resources Management and a People's Deputy of the Russian Federation, was one of two cabinet ministers to object to the coup during the meeting of the USSR Council of Ministers on August 19, 1991. Because no official minutes were kept, Vorontsov took his own notes, which are to this day the only surviving record of the ministers' individual positions regarding the coup. The events of this particular meeting gained public notoriety at the session of Russia's Supreme Soviet held on August 23, 1991, which was attended by Gorbachev. After Gorbachev finished his address to the Russian parliament, Boris Yeltsin cajoled him into reading a transcript of the cabinet meeting based on Vorontsov's notes—a litany of betrayal by the ministers appointed to high office by Gorbachev himself. The transcript was published in Komsomolskaia pravda *on August 24, 1991.*

Vorontsov was interviewed by Gregory Freidin in Berkeley, California, in April 1993. Both this interview and Vorontsov's transcript of the cabinet meeting, including his parenthetical comments, are reproduced below.

Interview with Nikolai Vorontsov, April 1993

Vorontsov: For two weeks before the coup, I was on sick leave because of high blood pressure, and was living at the government sanatorium in the village of Uspenskoe. Needless to say, this was a working sick leave. Papers from my Ministry arrived every day, and a couple of times I went to Moscow to attend executive board meetings. That Monday, August 19, I was planning to come to Moscow, among other things, to attend the Congress of Compatriots to which I had been invited as a guest of honor. [. . .] At 9:30 that morning, there was to be a special mass at Uspenskii Cathedral in the Kremlin in honor of the congress. An event of this sort is both colorful and rare, and I would not miss it for anything.

My driver, Volodia, came to pick me up at 8:00 A.M. "Have you listened to the radio?" he asked me as soon as he greeted me.

"What happened?" I shot back, and he told me the whole story, that Gorbachev had taken ill and on and on. . . . I decided right away that my wife, Yelena Alekseevna Liapunova, and I should go to Moscow at once, straight to the Kremlin, to the Uspenskii Cathedral. The mass was to be attended by Boris Yeltsin, Gavriil Popov [Mayor of Moscow], Anatolii Sobchak [Mayor of Leningrad]—in other words, the leading democratic political figures. While on the way to Moscow, I called the Ministry and asked them whether there had been any communications from the Council of Ministers or other governmental organs. There was nothing. I told them where I was going and how to reach me. During the next few hours, I called them regularly to let them know where I was and to receive any important information. Only at 3:00 P.M., or even later, at 3:30, was I informed that the Union Council of Ministers had been scheduled to meet that evening at 6 o'clock.

We arrived at the Kremlin on time. The scene at the cathedral was quite confused; people did not know what was happening. Among them, there were many "compatriots"—second- or third-generation descendants of Russian émigrés, who had come to Russia for the first time in their life, and there, waiting for them, was this nice little surprise. I saw the Patriarch, I saw Mikhail Nikitich Tolstoi, a People's Deputy and the organizer of the Congress of the Compatriots, but none of the big-time politicians were in attendance. I asked my wife to keep in touch with me and left the cathedral for the White House. While on the way there, I telephoned the Ministry once again, and once again there was no communication from the Prime Minister's office or from the Emergency Committee, or, for that matter, anyone else.

I arrived at the White House at 9:50. Yeltsin was not there, and neither were Khasbulatov or Silaev. Nobody knew where they were. I dropped by the office of Gennadii Burbulis [Yeltsin's chief of staff]. There I ran into Academician Yurii Alekseevich Ryzhov, a USSR People's Deputy and Deputy of the USSR Supreme Soviet. I was very happy to see him there. As a rule he was the only member of the [USSR] Supreme Soviet Presidium to attend rallies organized by the democrats, just as I was there as the only member of the Union Council of Ministers. I also ran into Aleksei Vladimirovich Yablokov, who told me the previous week that he had been appointed by Yeltsin as his principal adviser on ecological matters.

The three of us, along with Burbulis, proceeded to the office of [Vice President Aleksandr] Rutskoi, who was the only top representative of the government in the White House. As we walked into his office, Rutskoi was drafting by hand the appeal by the Russian government, along lines that he had just discussed with Yeltsin and Khasbulatov. They had given him the main points over the telephone, and now he was drafting the final version of the text by hand.

At Rutskoi's, we learned that the meeting of the Presidium of Russia's Supreme Soviet had been scheduled for 10 o'clock in the morning, with the sole purpose of immediately convening an emergency session of the Supreme Soviet of the Russian Federation. The leadership—Yeltsin, Silaev, Khasbulatov—were still in Arkhangelskoe [at Yeltsin's dacha], and one must give credit to Rutskoi for his decisiveness and courage. He was ready to issue the famous appeal to the citizens of Russia on his own responsibility, if anything were to happen to the others on their way to the White House.

At around 10 or 10:15, we entered the meeting room of the Supreme Soviet Presidium. There were about fifteen members sitting around the table, one short of the quorum (sixteen out of the thirty members were needed). Rutskoi sat down in the Chairman's seat. Yablokov, Ryzhov, and I, too, sat ourselves at the table—just as an expression of solidarity. No sooner had we sat down than in walked Yeltsin, Silaev, and Khasbulatov. The doors remained opened, and the room was beginning to be filled by deputies of the Russian parliament as well as Union deputies—practically all of them members of the Interregional Group.*

---

*The Interregional Group, made up of about two hundred liberal-minded deputies, formed after the first free elections of the new USSR Congress of People's Deputies in 1989. The group was originally headed by Sakharov and Yeltsin.

Now, with Khasbulatov present, there was a quorum, and the decision of the Presidium could be binding. Khasbulatov chaired the meeting and did so, one must say, in the best and most dignified manner. He proposed the convening of an [emergency] session of Russia's Supreme Soviet. However, when Khasbulatov's motion was put to a vote, deputies Vladimir Isakov, Vice Chairman of Russia's parliament, and Boris Isaev, Chairman of the Council of Nationalities of the Russian parliament, voted to abstain.* The motion, consequently, could not be adopted (a majority of all the members of the Presidium was required for passage). Khasbulatov was undaunted and announced that he was nevertheless calling an emergency session of the Supreme Soviet on his own responsibility.

A press conference of the Russian leadership was scheduled for 11:00 A.M. By that time, we could already see out of the window that tanks were arriving from the direction of Kutuzovskii Prospect. Fearing that nobody would be able to attend the press conference because of possible cordons, we decided to invite foreign ambassadors to attend the press conference along with reporters. We thought that the presence of ambassadorial limousines, flags and all, would make it possible for the reporters to break through to the White House.

A few moments later, Yeltsin, Yablokov, Ryzhov, and I were marching to the Supreme Soviet hall where the press conference had already started. The person presiding over it, as we saw when we walked in, was Silaev. Let me point out that Silaev is a man without any political ambitions, just an honest and very capable administrator. Only extraordinary circumstances could have prompted him to take charge. He must have arrived some three minutes before Yeltsin did and, not knowing what might have happened to him, opened the press conference and began reading the text of the government appeal, the one signed by [Russia's] President, the Chairman of the Council of Ministers [Silaev himself], and the Chairman of the Supreme Soviet [Khasbulatov]. Silaev's voice projected such a remarkable force that, for a moment, Yeltsin was taken aback and paused in the doorway. But

---

*According to the Russian Information Agency, both Isakov and Isaev voted against Khasbulatov's motion. The person who abstained was Yurii Voronin, the head of the Parliamentary Committee on Budget, Taxes, and Prices. See *Putch: Khronika trevoznykh dnei*, with an introduction by A. Vinogradov and G. Pavlikovskii (Moscow: Progress, 1991), p. 59.

this lasted only a split second, and a moment later, we all took our seats on the podium—Yeltsin, Rutskoi, Khasbulatov, Silaev, Yablokov, Ryzhov, and I. Yeltsin read out the "Appeal to the Citizens of Russia," sharply worded and unequivocal. There were practically no questions, or, perhaps, we simply did not take any question, for obvious reasons. . . .

Freidin: Were there any ambassadors there?

Vorontsov: Yes. I remember the Italian ambassador and the ambassador from the Netherlands. I don't recall, though, whether [U.S. Ambassador] Matlock was there. I think those who learned about the press conference in time to attend did come, but events were unfolding at such a mad pace that some may have missed it through no fault of their own. There were, I recall, at least eight big ambassadorial limousines, with their country's flags, parked outside the White House.

After the press conference, the question was: what to do next? There was a meeting at the office of Sergei Nikolaevich Krasavchenko.* It was on the third floor, with a view of the embankment. I think Burbulis was there, too. The question was: what did we have in the White House? The answer: nothing. We had no autonomous communication system, no radio station, and there was no public address system that we could use to communicate with the outside. The list was long. It was an utterly dismal picture. In the meantime, some of the Supreme Soviet staff members and government officials began to leave the building. I even recall running into a vice premier of the Russian Government.

Freidin: What was his name?

Vorontsov: G.V. Kulik. I must say, though, that all the members of Russia's cabinet, including [Kulik], had voted to support their Prime Minister [Silaev]. And yet, during those days, neither Kulik nor Gavrilov was anywhere to be found. Prime Minister Silaev was highly visible, but the two vice premiers were unheard and unseen.

Back to Krasavchenko's office. The question was how to distribute the government appeal. It was clear that it would not be broadcast by the media.† The solution, of course, was to use the copying machines

---

*Chairman of the Russian Supreme Soviet's Committee for Economic Reform and member of the Presidium of the Supreme Soviet.

†The text of the appeals was published the following day, August 20, in *Izvestiia.*

of the Supreme Soviet. But who would be doing the copying? We did not want to compromise the members of the support staff—say, some woman clerk who was responsible for the copier—if the Emergency Committee really took over. To be asking the clerks to do this job, we decided, would be simply immoral. So we took a small copying machine from the reception room of Krasavchenko's office, and the two of us began copying the first appeals (five pages altogether) on a little Canon machine at the rate of no more than six copies a minute. We stapled them by hand and then, taking a stack (twenty-five or thirty copies), I marched out of the White House and distributed them there among the people. And people had already begun to arrive. They were practically tearing the sheets right out of my hands, but I tried to give them only to those who promised to make more copies and distribute them further. So some promised to make more copies on their office copiers, some on their typewriters, and some, simply by hand, "five copies using carbon paper." I kept going back and forth, making a total of four or five trips.

During one of these trips, I saw from the window that there was a commotion outside and a tank was being surrounded by a small crowd. I rushed downstairs. By the time I got there, I saw Boris Nikolaevich already standing on the tank. I elbowed my way to the tank and then I, too, clambered up on it. Who else was on it? Apart from Yeltsin and his bodyguards, there was People's Deputy Mikhail Grigorievich Arutiunov; Deputy V.P. Mironov; Viacheslav Bragin, who until recently chaired the Committee on the Press;* and USSR Deputy Yaroshenko, who was Minister of Economics in Silaev's government. When Yeltsin went to the United States for the first time, it was Yaroshenko who helped him to organize the planeload of disposable needles and medicines that Yeltsin had purchased with his speaking fees. Those were all the deputies who were on the tank.

After Yeltsin made his famous speech, I decided to make my own brief statement. I said that people assumed that the USSR government supported the Emergency Committee. "It is not that way at all," I said. "I am a member of the USSR government, and I can assure you that it's not that way at all."

---

*Bragin was subsequently appointed head of the State Committee for Television and Radio Broadcasting (formerly Gosteleradio).

You see, I had already had a similar experience back in March 1991 when there was an attempt to establish a state of emergency at a meeting of the Council of Ministers. At that time, three people—the Minister of Geology, G. Gabrieliants; Deputy Prime Minister for Fossil Fuels and Electrical Energy, L. Riabev; and I—managed to stop this attempt in its tracks. The only difference between that time and now was that in March 1991 Gorbachev was still sitting in the Kremlin.

Freidin: Who demanded the introduction of a state of emergency then?

Vorontsov: That whole story happened on the day of the opening of Russia's Congress of People's Deputies, when massive rallies were being held all over Moscow. The three figures who were pushing for a state of emergency were Pugo, Kriuchkov, and Yazov. Rather passively and vaguely, Pavlov, too, was in favor of it. I have my record of that meeting, and most of the ministers present said something like this: Yes, it is necessary to introduce a state of emergency, but. . . ."

I decided to speak out, but before my turn came, Gabrieliants got up and made a very good speech (during the putsch, he was in the Crimea). He said: "What are you doing? Do you want to go back to the old days?" I spoke after him, and the third to come to our side was Deputy Prime Minister Riabev. After the three of us had spoken, the attempt somehow did not go any further. This is what I was thinking of as I stood on the tank. If only the Council of Ministers had met, I thought, we would have been able to convince the members of the cabinet, as we had done in March, not to go along with the state of emergency.

On the tank, I began by introducing myself as a People's Deputy of Russia and the USSR Minister of Environment, a member of the Union cabinet. I said: "I want to inform you—officially—that there has been no meeting of the USSR Council of Ministers and as of now, none has been scheduled. So you must understand that if anyone speaks in the name of the USSR government [in support of the Emergency Committee], that person is lying. The Soviet government is a collegial body, and I assure you that it has not made any collective decision [on the state of emergency]." That was all. After me spoke Colonel General Kobets, Russia's Deputy and Minister of Defense. He made a good speech, invoking the soldier's honor, saying that our soldiers would never raise arms against the people. These were very important words and, like his other actions in those days, they played a major role in the defense of the White House. Look, here was this career officer, a general, who had made his choice, and that was very impressive and reassuring.

[. . .] Sometime around 3:30 P.M., when I called the Ministry again, I was told that the Emergency Committee's press conference was scheduled for 5:00 P.M. and that the Council of Ministers would be meeting at six. I was still with Ryzhov then, and both of us decided that we should try to find Eduard Shevardnadze. [After stopping at the Hotel Minsk], we found him finally at his newly renovated town house. When we drove up (by then we had been joined by A.P. Vladislavlev, Deputy Chairman of the Scientific-Industrial Union), we were surprised that access to the building was not blocked by anything or anyone. People could go in and out as they pleased. Inside, Shevardnadze, completely alone, was facing a group of foreign correspondents. There were no interpreters, and some of the reporters who knew Russian were doubling as translators. We were all very glad to see each other. He embraced every one of us and then introduced us to the reporters. They began to ask us questions, and first Vladislavlev, whose English was much better than mine, and then I made statements. I know newspapers reported on this impromptu press conference.

Soon it was time to go to the Council of Ministers meeting. As I was approaching the building on Pushkin Street a little after six, I had a strong feeling that I would soon be arrested. I had had plenty of exposure—the tank speech, the press conference with Shevardnadze. . . . There was more than enough for an arrest. To my surprise, nothing happened. One by one ministers were arriving, greeting each other as though nothing had happened.

I walked up to Vitalii Khuseinovich Doguzhiev, then First Deputy Prime Minister, and shook his hand for a long time and especially warmly. In March, he was simply Deputy Prime Minister, with a special responsibility for large-scale disasters. In that capacity, he was my immediate superior. Back in March, when there was that push for the state of emergency, I had had a meeting with Lukianov, who rudely rejected my entreaties, saying that there was nothing special going on and that I should mind my own business. After that I had gone to the Council of Ministers building and tried to get in touch with [Prime Minister] Pavlov. He was not there. The cabinet had met the day before, and a mass rally [in support of Yeltsin and Russia] was scheduled to take place the next day. I felt that since I was both a member of Russia's Parliament and a USSR Minister, I should try to serve as a channel of communication between the two antagonists and keep both sides talking. I saw Mikhail Sergeevich Shkabardnia, the chief aide of the outgoing government of [USSR] Prime Minister Ryzhkov who was then clearing his office. I said to him: "Listen, there might be bloodshed in the streets, we must do something."

"I cannot help you," he said, "I am clearing out of here."

Still, he offered the use of his special government phone line [with direct access to the members of the Cabinet]. With Shkabardnia's assistance, I got hold of Doguzhiev, which was a feat in itself, and pleaded with him to do something to help prevent bloodshed. He responded with proper concern, even thanked me for the information, and promised to do all he could to help diffuse the situation. Now I was hoping that my handshake would remind him of his position during the March days. [. . .]

The notes I took at the Council meeting have been published, and they tell the story of what happened there.

Notes on the USSR Council of Ministers Meeting of August 19, 1991

The extraordinary session of the Cabinet of Ministers began at 6:05 P.M. As usual, the Ministers of Defense, Foreign Affairs, and Internal Affairs, and the chairman of the KGB were absent [from the meeting].

V. Pavlov, Prime Minister: Are you prepared to work under emergency conditions? We had already come to an agreement with you in principle (he was alluding to special measures to bolster the economy). But today the situation is as follows: that which we had agreed upon, our decisions, are not carried out. As a result, there will come a point when production will simply come to a halt. This is not a political matter—we have no interest in political slogans.

Are you in agreement with the declaration of the Presidium of the USSR Cabinet of Ministers?

(This meeting of the Presidium had taken place late in the evening on Saturday, August 17. It was attended by the Prime Minister, the Deputy Prime Minister, the Minister of Finance, and heads of the Presidium apparat. At that meeting, there was dissatisfaction expressed—in my opinion justified—about the fact that the Cabinet of Ministers had not received the text of the Union Treaty; even the Prime Minister learned its text from the newspapers. In any case, we had not received the text of what the Presidium decided. And it is yet to be explained what relation this meeting had to the preparations for the putsch.)

K. Katushev, Minister of External Economic Affairs: An expanded meeting of our Ministry's executive board was held. We listened to the leadership's declaration and put it into operation. We are carrying out the tasks that have been assigned to us by the GKChP. We have also informed our trade representatives abroad.

V. Orlov, Minister of Finance: We are operating under a special security system to prevent the misappropriation of funds.

Sychev, State Board of Standards: No one has the right to refuse to follow the All-Union system of standards. . . . The state of emergency ought to have been introduced earlier.

Lev Ivanovich (head of one of the new ministries): We support you. Our society needs law and order. We have been waiting for this measure for a long time.

L. Davletova, Committee for Light Industry: Light industry is on the verge of collapse because of the sovereignty declarations by the republics. The directors of light industry are indignant over the fact that light industry was not included in the text of the Union Treaty.

V. Gusev, Chairman of the State Committee for Chemistry and Biotechnology: I contacted 100 enterprises. All of them support the appeals of the GKChP. But it would be foolish to think that everything's fine. I'm worried about the "Azot" factory in Kemerovo and the plants in Bashkiria, where strikes may break out.

On the question of politics: If we retreat an inch, we will lose our positions and our lives. We will not have another chance.

B. Paniukov, Minister of Civil Aviation: We were late in introducing the state of emergency. We must have law and order in the country.

An official from the Ministry of the Machine-Building Industry: All machine-building enterprises of the Soviet Union, the USSR Academy of Sciences, and the Engineering Academy are in favor of the state of emergency. We saw what took place out on Manezh Square—no more than 700 people showed up. We must push ahead decisively.

V. Pavlov, Prime Minister: But I am against tanks! Let people get out into the streets, let them talk. . . .

One of the ministers: Everything was fine in our industry before lunch. But after the lunch break, leaflets from the Russian government began to appear.

Sychev, State Board of Standards: Thank God for the State of Emergency.

V. Pavlov, Prime Minister: Yes, some troublemakers are strolling about on Manezh Square. But you cannot compare the ZIL factory and the "Uralmash" [factory complex] to Manezh Square. . . .

Deputy Minister of Power Supply: The mood is normal, there are no accidents, and the Moscow power stations have been secured—all without a hitch.

Deputy Minister of Agriculture and Food Supply: The situation in food supply will be difficult. We will have to inventory what we have. The West will give us nothing.

An official from the Ministry of Communications: Everything is under control in our industry.

A. Tiziakov, a member of the GKChP: Everyone wants order. . . . Democracy has brought us down to a state of . . . (several people interject: "Yea, enough already!").

N. Vorontsov, Minister of Environment and Natural Resources Management: Our executive board took measures to assure the continued functioning of the economic mechanism. Unified economic, including ecological, functioning, requires that the center work with the republics.

With regard to my position on what has transpired. I ask myself one question: in what situation do I find myself? I was nominated by the Supreme Soviet of the USSR and appointed to my position by President Gorbachev. All the ministers should ask themselves this question. I don't understand why we have been avoiding it.

The White House has issued a series of decrees that speak of the illegality of what has transpired. Since among the members of the central government I alone am a Deputy of the Russian parliament, I am prepared to provide communications, to serve as a shuttle between the White House and the Cabinet of Ministers, so that we can avoid a further deterioration of the situation.

(My services in this regard were never called upon.)

V. Shcherbakov, Deputy Prime Minister: The national economy must continue to operate no matter what. We will not be receiving credits in the next few hours or days. We will have to switch to the regime of operation under emergency conditions. With the exception of Moscow, we should not summon directors from their plants, or we risk disrupting the economy.

No one here came to work for a specific individual. The policy of the leaders of the GKChP is still not clear to me. I will continue to work honestly. As for my personal position I will determine it later. I am in favor of discipline, but without a return to the methods of 1929.

Yu. Masliukov, Deputy Prime Minister: We must have support from the personnel in industry and finance. Let's put an end to staff reductions.

(An argument between Masliukov and Pavlov ensues concerning various economic problems.)

L. Riabev, Deputy Prime Minister: We must move toward observing the Constitution as strictly as possible.

(Incidentally, it was the views of Riabev, Vorontsov, and Gabrieliants, the Minister of Geological Resources, at an earlier meeting that had prevented agreement on the use of force against the striking miners. Pugo, Yazov, and Kriuchkov had attended that session, in violation of the rules.)

V. Doguzhiev, First Deputy Prime Minister: I am in favor of the Union Treaty, though it requires some modification. As to the state of emergency, we have discussed the need for emergency measures many times over the years.

What has transpired does not signify a return to totalitarianism. The center must assume the function of guaranteeing human rights, including economic rights. Drastic economic measures are taken in capitalist countries, too. . . . We need to revise our approach to the 1992 plan and strengthen centralization.

N. Gubenko, Minister of Culture: My industry is not engaged in material production, but it does have a lot to do with moral and spiritual values. True, among the creative intelligentsia there are provocateurs who want to shed blood, but I am not speaking about them. At this point, all that has transpired is beyond the bounds of the law.

M. Shchadov, Minister of the Coal Industry: The situation in the country is very complex, and yet, some comrades are oversimplifying matters. The situation is changing by the hour. If a state of emergency is not introduced today in the Kuzbass and Vorkuta regions, then tomorrow the miners will strike and their blood will flow. The Kemerovo Region Soviet has decided to have the miners go on strike.

V. Pavlov, Prime Minister: Comrades! Why are we discussing political issues? There will be a Congress of People's Deputies (he has in mind the session of the Supreme Soviet), and it will decide everything.

We must support the Union Treaty, but amendments will be necessary. As professionals, we have views about the unified economic space, about the need to provide the country with bread and fuel. We have run out of corn: 5 percent of the cows and 10 percent of the total number of pigs have been slaughtered.

* * *

Note by G.V. Umnov of *Komsomolskaia pravda*: This was the only cabinet-level meeting held during the coup. In the course of those days, N. Vorontsov and the Minister of the Chemical and Oil Refining Industry, Salambek Khadzhiev, decided to transfer their ministries temporarily to Yeltsin's authority.

Vorontsov: "I decided to inform the cabinet of this decision, but Pavlov was gone and Doguzhiev was too busy. Another Deputy Prime Minister, the Academician Laverov, to this day maintains silence. Almost every minister is—to one degree or another—a real professional in his field, but if this is a professionalism totally devoid of civic and political convictions, we must fear such professionals."

Interview with Nikolai Vorontsov, April 1993

Freidin: There was at least one other version of your notes that circulated in those days.

Vorontsov: During the session of Russia's Supreme Soviet on August 22, I made a statement, saying that I had notes from the meeting of the USSR Council of Ministers on August 19 and that I would be happy to read them to anyone who would like to hear them. During a break in the session, I held an impromptu press conference and read my notes out loud to a group of reporters and deputies. This was how an unfortunate error crept in, and the Minister for Chemical Industry, Khadzhiev, became associated with the supporters of the putsch even though he was not present at the Council meeting and joined the Yeltsin forces as soon as he came back to Moscow on August 20. Some reporter must have confused him with the new Fuel Oil Minister whose name I could not recall then. It was this unfortunate transcript that made its way onto Yeltsin's desk.

Freidin: You mean the version that Yeltsin forced Gorbachev to read out loud before the session of Russia's Supreme Soviet?

Vorontsov: Yes. But even that unfortunate version gave one the sense of how much Gorbachev had been betrayed by his government. That was Yeltsin's point, and the transcript, even in a corrupt version, drove it home.

Freidin: Was Pavlov drunk during the Council meeting on the 19th?

Vorontsov: It is hard to say. His speech was slurred, he was clearly having difficulty speaking, but some drugs for hypertension have this effect, and my impression was that it was those drugs rather than alcohol. But I could be wrong.

Freidin: I recall that when I saw you that evening, you mentioned something about the reason Pavlov gave for the sudden introduction of the state of emergency, something about Stinger missiles and urban terrorists?

Vorontsov: It was rather incoherent, but, referring to Kriuchkov [head of the KGB] as his source, he said that a "left" coup d'état was imminent, that terrorists, armed to the teeth, even equipped with Stinger missiles, were lining up all along the Garden Ring Road, and that if it had not been for the state of emergency, the entire Soviet government would have been in danger. As I said, Pavlov was border-line incoherent when he was giving this preposterous information, and I did not take his words seriously.

Freidin: What happened after the Council meeting?

Vorontsov: I went briefly to the Congress of Compatriots and then home, where I was very glad to see my very worried wife, and you as well—this quite aside from any personal sympathies. I thought that you might be the last person from the outside world to see me alive, or free, the last link. I am glad those fears did not materialize. . . .

5 | Vladimir Shcherbakov Recounts His Role in the Coup

*Vladimir Ivanovich Shcherbakov, First Deputy Prime Minister of the
Soviet Union, explained his actions during the coup to an
extraordinary session of the Supreme Soviet on August 28, 1991. His
speech was broadcast on Moscow Central Television.*

I assert, quite unequivocally, that the Soviet government, the Soviet
Council of Ministers, as a collective body of government, as the executive power, did not take part in any secret conspiracies behind the back
of the President, the Supreme Soviet, and the people. And as a collective body, we did not commit any anticonstitutional actions.

Prime Minister Pavlov, who turned us into hostages of his
decision —the investigation will look into how this took place—and
the three Council ministers, Yazov, Pugo, and Kriuchkov, are another
matter. . . .

During the period of August 19–22, I confirm that we took no single
unconstitutional or illegal action. Moreover, we did not implement a
single decision of the State Emergency Committee. As of the 20th and
21st, we began refusing to implement these decisions officially. On the
20th, we reached agreement first with Comrade Vitalii Doguzhiev
[First Deputy Prime Minister of the USSR] and then at the Presidium
on the 21st, at 13:30—when the tanks, incidentally, were still on the
streets and nothing was clear as regards Gorbachev's health and what
was the matter with him. We refused to carry out the Emergency
Committee's instructions in the economic sphere: on lowering prices
for children's goods, on parity of prices between the city and countryside, on housing, and other such foolishness. We said that this was

adventurism, that it was yet another attempt to make the economy a hostage of political passions, and we refused to do this.

Second, we regarded the instructions of the Council of Ministers issued by Vice President Yanaev, on the introduction of censorship and on organizing the re-registration of the mass media, as unconstitutional, and refused to carry them out.

Third, we adopted a statement in which the following was laid down: We, the USSR government, state that under these circumstances we submit only to the Constitution and the laws of the USSR and we undertake strictly to carry them out, and are accountable only to President Gorbachev and the Supreme Soviet.

I regret that we removed the second phrase, but it was there. Further, it was written that under these circumstances, we refused to carry out the decisions of the Vice . . . of the Acting President, Yanaev, and of the Emergency Committee. It was made clear to us that we might not recognize the Acting President, but that under the Constitution we were bound to recognize the Vice President, and that if we adopted such a statement, it would be unconstitutional.

[Inaudible call from the hall; Shcherbakov pauses and sighs deeply.]

Further, what actually happened at the session [of the Council of Ministers] on August 19?

First, none of us knew; that morning, all of us learned of this from the radio and the television, each in his own way. In the morning, the Presidium met, and we phoned each other. No one knew anything, not a single minister knew anything. . . .

We went our separate ways, all trying to figure out what was going on. Some sort of additional information at least needed to be collected. We agreed to meet a little later.

At this time, I phoned Yanaev and put three questions to him. "Gennadii Ivanovich, I ask you to answer, quite clearly and comprehensibly, three questions. First, do you really have trustworthy information that President Gorbachev is ill and is not in a condition to carry out his duties?" He gave me not a word of proof, because it was clear that by that very evening the situation would be quite different. The second question: "Was the text of all these statements [of the State Emergency Committee] not distorted?" I never read them because it was all from the radio. But from what I had heard, it was clear to me that there was so much nonsense and so much of everything there that, again, it did not bode well. And the third: "You have adopted a statement, you the Soviet leadership. Three of you signed, but probably more of you got to discuss it." But at this point, I was no longer speaking. I knew, roughly, who had signed, and of course, if they sit down with a bottle, those kinds of people may sign anything you want. I asked him: "There were probably more of you people there—at least, tell me who was there. And in general, how is all this to be understood?"

He answered all three questions in the affirmative. I asked him: "Is Comrade Lukianov with you?" He said: "Yes, he is." "Does he support this?" "Yes, he does."

I asked him: "Then explain to me, Gennadii Ivanovich. Surely you know that you have steamrolled the state of emergency; nothing is left standing. How is all this to be understood? Lukianov could not have sanctioned this."

He said: "We reached agreement that we will explain everything at the session [of the USSR Supreme Soviet]. Anyway," he asked, "what are you planning to do?"

I said: "You know, in general, this is a dubious affair, and so, for the present, I don't know—I have no information. I will carry out my duties until the session [of the Supreme Soviet], but at present I will deal exclusively with the economy. The situation there is such that it will explode any moment now."

He said to me, "That's right. Okay, Pavlov will tell you the details. This is not for the telephone. . . ."

[Shcherbakov, Pavlov and other members of the Council of Ministers met on the evening of August 19. According to Shcherbakov's account, Pavlov began by asking Council members their attitude toward the text of the Union Treaty. Then, according to Shcherbakov, Pavlov asked the ministers to give their opinions about the introduction of the state of emergency. Shcherbakov describes Pavlov's report.]

Pavlov said that a critical situation had been brewing for a long time, but that of late, a military coup had been prepared. A large number of armed fighters had been concentrated within the Garden Ring Road. Their weapons were just hand-held grenade launchers for three battalions. He said a list of people [from the government and

Party leadership] to be removed in this situation had been seized from them—and that all of us, members of the sitting government, were on these lists, on different lists, but certainly on them. "But," Pavlov went on, "we have averted all this by introducing the state of emergency. Now, each of you, express your position. What is your attitude to this?" That is how the question was posed. . . .

I, of course, did not understand what was going on. My first thoughts were that this was a Khrushchev-model coup. So, on the first day, I was of course interested most of all in the health of Gorbachev, because this was a sort of hope for his return. Give all this, say, a week or two, and everything can be restored. I phoned a lot of people in the Russian Republic and tried somehow to understand. There was no information. And I came to the conclusion, after a conversation with Pavlov at night, when all members of the Presidium had left, that something had indeed happened to Gorbachev. After the full Council met, the Presidium continued the debate. We never reached agreement and decided to part for the day. Pavlov and I went down to his office, and he told me what had in fact happened. How he explained it I will discuss further.

[Pavlov] said to me that on August 18, he and his son—who had to fly off—were sitting and drinking. [Then, according to Pavlov]:

> "Kriuchkov called: 'Come urgently and immediately to the Kremlin—there is an emergency. An armed coup is being prepared. Members of the security forces have to make a decision on introducing a state of emergency.'
> "I asked him, 'Where is Lukianov?'
> "He said Lukianov was off to Valdai.
> " 'But how can such a matter be decided without Lukianov? Let's send a helicopter immediately.'
> "We gathered together. In came Baklanov, Shenin, Plekhanov, and, most important, Boldin. They said they had just gotten back from the Crimea. That they had waited in the President's reception room for an hour. They were unable to get in because there were doctors with him. That Raisa Maksimovna was also unwell, a most serious situation. They were let in for fifteen minutes. The President was in bed, was in effect not responding to words, in general was inactive. 'So we asked the doctors, "Is it a heart attack or a stroke or everything together?" They said, "We don't

know." But in general it became clear to us that it was not a minor matter, but that generally he would not be around for some time, and so we came back immediately. That, comrades, is what we report to you.' "

I still doubted that this was a military coup. I was thinking: they are not idiots, after all. They have set a date for a session [of the Supreme Soviet] and they understand that they cannot put the country on its knees in a week. Most important, if that is what they want, then why have they not arrested anyone?

All the same, on the 20th I started to understand. We maintained communication with all the presidents of the republics and, roughly at lunch time, I finally came to the conclusion that it was necessary to do something. The situation was so unclear and all of us—the USSR government—had become hostages in this situation. In political terms, we were unable to take a step either to the left or the right.

To begin, it was necessary to remove the Prime Minister [Pavlov] from the Emergency Committee, to untie his hands and to show him to everyone, because as long as the Prime Minister was included in the Emergency Committee, the whole world might think that we [the Council of Ministers] supported them [the Emergency Committee]. It was necessary for everyone to understand that we did not; nor did the head of state of the USSR government.

So I tried various routes. At first, I tried to reach an agreement simply that Pavlov was not being released from his home. That never worked. Then I went to him and we agreed that we would officially publish a statement on his illness and that his duties would be transferred to Comrade Doguzhiev. It was not that I was afraid; it was just that Doguzhiev was more experienced and stronger and knew how to govern, unlike myself.* In the government, our responsibilities are fairly clear. I deal with all kinds of analytical, economic, and social problems, and Doguzhiev deals with the rest. . . .

But the final thing: Coming out to this rostrum for the last time—I have spent a lot of time in this hall—I want to tell you what I think, not lecture you. The most difficult tasks still lie ahead, after all. An assessment of the plot has been given, yet we still do not grasp its cata-

---

*Shcherbakov is referring here to the fact that both he and Doguzhiev were first deputy prime ministers and that either might have replaced Pavlov.

strophic consequences. I do not absolve ourselves, the government, or myself personally, of the blame. In general, I think that our main fault, and our main tragedy, is that we did not understand what Gorbachev was doing. We did not understand it and had not evaluated it.

We understood that there was a build-up of forces under way on both sides. But we did not understand Gorbachev's efforts to achieve political stabilization through the Union Treaty, economic stabilization through a joint program, and international economic relations through the London accords. We were always grumbling in the government, "What is being agreed to behind our backs? Things are not right." We failed to put the collectives in the right frame of mind. This was our major mistake.

6 | The Coup and the Armed Forces

At the time of the August coup, Yevgenii Shaposhnikov commanded the Soviet Air Force. Following the coup, he was appointed Defense Minister of the USSR and Air Marshal. This interview was conducted by Soviet journalist Andrei Karaulov and was published in Nezavisimaia gazeta *on September 12, 1991.*

Nezavisimaia gazeta: Having worked for a long time alongside your predecessor, Marshal Yazov, were you surprised to see him among the members of the State Committee for the State of Emergency?

Shaposhnikov: Look at his date of birth: 1923. That means that Yazov was educated and grew up under Stalinism. Then came perestroika, democratization, and glasnost. And the further it went, the less he liked it. He was patient for a long time. But the Union was cracking, the armed forces were breaking apart and allying themselves with separate republics, and the economy was prey to chaos. So Yazov, the marshal, was seized by doubt. Yes, he would say to himself, we must live in a new way, speak in a new way, feel in a new way. . . . But what if this meant the destruction of all those things he has spent his whole life with? I think he was confused . . . I mean literally, confused, because he never, but never, went all the way. He would not have shot at people. I am convinced about that. Here are a few facts. On the morning of the 19th he convened the [Defense] Ministry's Collegium [of department heads]: a state of emergency was being introduced, as well as a higher level of preparedness for the armed forces throughout the Union; some cities, including Moscow, were to be occupied by military units. "Watch out," he added, "don't do stupid things. There are people who would throw themselves under tanks, or try to set them on fire; we don't want blood." Those were his words. That is why, I think, the soldiers did not receive that most serious order. All they were told was: Go in, and stay in such-and-such a place, and that's it. I understood already on the morning of the 19th that Yazov would not order the troops to shoot at civilians. In the final analysis, I think that is in his favor.

Nezavisimaia gazeta: But they had live shells in those tanks!
Shaposhnikov: Shells, yes, but as to shooting . . . Yazov was not capable of this. That is what I think.

Nezavisimaia gazeta: Were relations between you not the best?
Shaposhnikov: We were not close, personally. Our dealings were purely professional. Yazov always had his own viewpoint on everything; he thought he knew everything better than anyone else. On August 19, at the meeting of the Collegium, we were all in a state of shock, appalled, if that is the way to put it. There we were, sitting there, not knowing what to do or say. In fact, he did not give us any time to reflect; he spoke tersely, no more than ten to fifteen minutes. I noticed that he was not at all enthusiastic—rather, depressed, even a bit disoriented, I'd say. He marched in, told us that Gorbachev had taken ill, that the signing of the Union Treaty, scheduled for the following day, could not take place under the circumstances. But he did not say a kind word to put people at ease—something like, well, the state of emergency is being introduced, but we will continue our work, we'll hope. . . . Instead, he just said: "Armed Forces—upgrade status to battle ready, proceed!" He did not allow any questions, and in any case, to be honest, nobody showed any wish to ask. "That is all," he said, "Carry out your orders."

The atmosphere within the Collegium is far from friendly. That was the main problem. I think if the Collegium had a bit of a humane atmosphere in it, we would have shared our thoughts with each other. During my tenure, a relatively brief one to be sure, I cannot recall a single time when we would simply get together and speak with each other honestly about our worries. Not once. And not that time, either. We walked out. I was going down the stairs next to the Deputy Commander of the Navy. Among the armed forces, the Air Force and the Navy are considered to be the most democratically oriented services. I asked him: "Ivan Matveevich, what do you think? I feel really troubled by this. I feel it in my gut. It's some kind of foul play—looks like a coup d'état."

"I can't figure it out either," he said, "On the one hand they are from the Gorbachev team, and then, all of a sudden, they announce a state of emergency. . . ."

We left the building and each got into his own car. That was the end of our conversation. We were all afraid of one another—Stalin's legacy.

Let me tell you a story about Yazov. On August 20 the radio station Moscow Echo announced my arrest. [Leningrad Mayor] Sobchak said at a meeting in Leningrad that the whole of the Air Force had sided with Yeltsin. Foreign radio stations reported the same. At that time I was in my office. Suddenly the telephone rang. It was Yazov, summoning me.

Nezavisimaia gazeta: You risked never coming back . . .

Shaposhnikov: My attitude was this: They did not know exactly which side I was on. I had received some phone calls from the KGB: "We have heard reports of insinuations against you. You must issue a denial."

I played dumb. "I cannot deny something that I have not heard directly," I said.

"But according to Sobchak . . ."

"No," I said, "I don't know anything about it. Let's just hang up, both of us. There's no point in going on with this conversation." In other words, Yazov could not have had any evidence about me. So I went to the Ministry, waited there for almost an hour. Then I called him in his car.

"I'll be there soon; wait for me!" he replied.

So, for the first time in many years, I saw a Yazov with a human face. He came out to greet me: "Forgive me for being late, Yevgenii Ivanovich, but you understand the times are tough. Please sit down."

He sat down opposite me. None of this, I thought, boded well. He was simply planning to use a different approach with me. Instead, he tilted his head to the side, put his hand under his cheek and said: "What do you think I should do? Tell me honestly."

So I told him honestly. I told him that it was necessary to try to resolve the situation. How? With dignity, of course.

"Do you know a dignified way out?"

"Yes. Withdraw the troops from the city, cancel the state of emergency. . . ." I decided to go all the way: we were alone, after all.

"Suppose I do," he said, "What will happen to the Committee?"

"Dissolve the Committee and to hell with it. Declare it illegal. Transfer power to the Supreme Soviet. And bring Gorbachev back to Moscow. . . ."

No sooner had I spoken these words than three members of the Military Collegium entered the office. Yazov changed immediately, his face became entirely different. He asked the three to sit down and said to me: "Do you know why I asked you here?" I felt my blood run cold. It had been a mistake for me to speak to him openly. But he said to me: "There are too many democrats in the Air Force. You can expect anything from them at any time. Are you sure that you control these people?"

"Yes, I'm sure."

"So take the necessary measures and attend to your business."

Nezavisimaia gazeta: How do you explain this strange meeting?

Shaposhnikov: He had doubts. My impression is that when the three generals entered the office he wanted to defend me from them, to protect me. In fact I had the clear impression that he was looking for a way out.

After the meeting I returned to my office and summoned my senior aides.

"Well, men, what do you think of this? Let's put our heads together and forget for a moment about our epaulets." In the Air Force, people relate to one another in such a way that it is possible to look one another in the eye. "So what's to be done? What's your opinion?"

As I expected, the reply was unanimous: we've got to end this business.

"Very well," I replied, "it's all clear. Come what may, you will obey orders only from me and from nobody else, no matter who it is." The same order was issued to the troops.

As night approached on August 20, I heard that an attack was being planned on the White House. I called Colonel General Grachev. "What are you going to do?" I asked him.

"I've got the feeling that I'm holding the short end of the stick: these bastards want me to issue orders [to attack the White House]."

"And what will you do?"

"Well," said Grachev, "I'm going to resign."

"They won't accept your resignation—it's a state of emergency."

"Well, then to hell with it—I'll just shoot myself!"

"Grachev," I said to him, "hold your fire for the time being. I'd rather you and I make a visit to the White House. I've discussed it with my wife, though, and she thinks that if I were to go to the White House, Yazov might simply fire me, and I might lose all control over my troops. So the effect would be the opposite of what I intended.

"Grachev," I went on, "you've got such an incredible force on the ground. . . . Let's take the paratroopers and surround the Kremlin, or—better still—let's arrest the junta ourselves."

He said: "Yes, we've got enough power, but neither you nor I have enough of the other stuff."

"Like what?"

He said: "How many times have you been inside the Kremlin?"

"Three times, I think."

"And I," said Grachev, "have been there only once. So we'll send the paratroopers there, and the KGB security guys will take us off easily from around the corner. Don't you think they have done their prep work?"

I agreed with Grachev. He continued: "Let's just sit by the telephones and try to avert any stupid trouble. When the night is over, things will become clearer. If we move on the Kremlin, we may just get too entangled in this whole mess, risk the lives of a lot of people. . . . Let's just wait a little longer."

As soon as we finished, I got an idea of what to do. If they order the storming of the White House (regardless of who issues it—Yazov, Kriuchkov, Yanaev, it did not matter), I will go to them with an ultimatum: "Rescind the order or else; and if I do not get back to headquarters within ten minutes or if I do not call headquarters ten minutes from now, the bombers are going to take off and bomb you to kingdom come. This is the Air Force—no joke. What do you say to me now?"

We maintained continuous communication with the *Russians*, the White House. Once I said to [General Kobets's aide] Colonel Tsalko: "Aleksandr Valerianovich, please come to my office—I don't feel comfortable discussing this with you over the telephone."

He said he would come right away. Fifteen minutes later, he called and said: "Yevgenii Ivanovich, we have been surrounded by such care, such *watchful* care . . . , that I don't think I can leave the White House."

Then I had a conversation with Kedrov, one of Yeltsin's aides. I said to him: "I guarantee that neither the Air Force nor the Airborne Paratroopers will take a single step in your direction. Everything will be all right—there is nothing to fear."

He stuck the telephone receiver out of the window: "Do you hear what is going on outside?"

And I heard the crowd chanting: "Russia! Russia!"

On the 21st, early in the morning, I received a phone call: "You are ordered to attend a Collegium meeting with Minister Yazov at 9:00 A.M." Yazov took a long time to explain the situation, and the explanation itself was rather disjointed, which was something unusual for him. He spoke disparagingly about Yanaev and Pavlov, saying: "Oh those guys are bad; they are drunkards; they have dragged me into this without even knowing where they are going; and I have dragged you in, and you dragged in the soldiers, who are now sitting there in their tanks—the Army has been disgraced!" And he asked us to offer our opinions about what to do.

I got up and said: "According to the Russian Army tradition that the youngest should go first (I was the youngest among the members of the Collegium), I request permission to speak."

But Moiseev* intervened. "Wait, I have important information," he said and began to talk about something.

Suddenly Yazov interrupted him: "Mikhail Alekseevich, everybody knows that. Please let Yevgenii Ivanovich speak."

I began: "In the name of rescuing the reputation of the Armed Forces, we must give the order for the troops to leave Moscow." And then I repeated everything I had said to Yazov the previous day. Practically everyone in the Collegium supported my position.

"Well," said Yazov, "I understand your position. The Emergency Committee is meeting right now, but I decided not to attend. However, I will inform them about it. I will probably . . . give the order to withdraw the troops from Moscow. But I would like to tell you that I will remain a member of the Emergency Committee. I cannot be a traitor twice. This is my cross, and I will bear it to the end. . . ."

You see, Yazov could have switched sides, but he would not do it. We proposed then: "Dmitrii Timofeevich, we must announce your decision at once. The session of Russia's Supreme Soviet is to convene

---

*General M.A. Moiseev, the Chief of the General Staff, was retired from the service two days after the end of the putsch.

at 11:00 A.M. Let the deputies do their work in peace, in a normal environment."

It looked like he agreed, but then again something strange seemed to be going on. I returned to my office, I was waiting for the order, but no order was forthcoming. I called Rutskoi's secretary (the session had already begun) and dictated to him a note saying that the Army was withdrawing from Moscow and would no longer take part in this business. I saw Rutskoi read the note on television. It was, however, Bakatin who made the [public] announcement, saying that the Collegium of the Ministry of Defense had made this decision.

Nezavisimaia gazeta: So who stopped the putsch?

Shaposhnikov: I believe many things came together at the same time. In general—pardon me for saying something so banal—the times stopped the putsch.

Nezavisimaia gazeta: But was this really a putsch? This question is being asked with increasing frequency.

Shaposhnikov: Yes, it was. I see it this way: The action [of the Emergency Committee] had not been seriously thought out, whatever angle you approach it from. But some riddles remain, you are right. To be honest with you, I don't quite understand it either. This is one of the more enigmatic pages in this century's history. But sooner or later, people will solve this riddle.

[. . .]

Nezavisimaia gazeta: Do you think that some general or other—say, General Makashov*—could have had his divisions march into Moscow without an order?

Shaposhnikov: No. This is a different matter, though. All of us in the army are burdened with this one word: orders. And if someone violates his orders or, worse, decides to go into combat contrary to his orders, he will be stopped, which is not so hard to do. On the 22nd I saw Yeltsin in the Kremlin. He was leaving Gorbachev's office while I was standing in the reception room having a drink of water. I could

---

*General Makashev was known for his right-wing views and his association with the putschists.

hear Yeltsin say into the receiver: "Ruslan Imranovich [Khasbulatov], don't worry, I have the situation under control. If anything happens, I will go to the White House at once."

I asked him: "Would you like a drink of water, Boris Nikolaevich?"

He shook my hand and said: "You're a good man, you really did hang in there. But I don't have time to drink water. Three armored columns are moving toward the White House again."

I said: "Boris Nikolaevich, the Air Force is ready to carry out any order."

"All right, then do something about it."

I called Antoshkin, the Moscow District Commander of the Air Force: "Do you recognize my voice?"

"Yes, I do."

"Well, then listen to my order: The Air Force is to be brought to combat readiness at once. Fly your planes low, show force, show support for the White House. But hold the fire. If necessary, call Rutskoi."

That's how it was. Ten minutes later, I was called in to see Gorbachev. I entered his office, and there they were all sitting, all "nine plus one."* Gorbachev said to me in a rather restrained tone of voice: "Tell us what you were doing between the 19th and the 21st."

I gave a brief report.

"That's what we thought you were doing," said Gorbachev. "We offer you the post of Minister of Defense."

[. . .]

---

*The heads of the nine republics that had agreed to the Union Treaty, plus the USSR President, Gorbachev.

7 | From Dushanbe to Moscow

At the time of the coup, Davlat Khudonazarov, a native of Tajikistan, was Chairman of the USSR Union of Cinematographers. He was a member of the First Congress of People's Deputies in 1989 and then a Deputy to the Supreme Soviet of the USSR. In 1990, at the Twenty-eighth Party Congress, he was appointed a member of the Central Committee of the Communist Party of the Soviet Union as part of the so-called "Yakovlev list" of liberal deputies. He was interviewed by Gregory Freidin in April 1992 while visiting Hollywood, California.

Freidin: Tell me about the putsch. How did you first find out about it?

Khudonazarov: The morning of the 19th, in Dushanbe, I got a call from one of my friends telling me something had happened. "Oh stop kidding me," was my first response, but when I heard the news myself half an hour or so later, I fell into a sort of trance, as if my head was suddenly filled with cottonwool. I remained in this state for a couple of hours. I just did not want to believe that this was for real. I wanted to believe I was simply dreaming it all. But life went on around me, the sun was shining, and finally the reality of it sank in. Then I had to wait for a couple of hours until I could rouse out of bed my contacts in Moscow.

I telephoned Maria Zvereva and Andrei Razumovskii, my deputies at the Cinematographers' Union. "Listen, folks, please get together in the union, invite [Andrei] Smirnov [a former chairman of the Union of Cinematographers] and anyone Smirnov considers important."

They met, and soon afterward we agreed over the telephone that we all understood what kind of characters had seized power and that we must actively get involved in resistance. I also told them that I would be flying to Moscow and that they should expect me the next morning. So all was settled.

There was one detail, however. My family and I had the tickets to fly to the Pamir the next day.* But my wife said, "You know, Davlat, we'll fly to Moscow tomorrow with you."

This was very ironic. For the last three years I had been pressing her to come to Moscow with me and bring the children. So I said, "Why is it that you did not want to come with me then, when all was quiet in Moscow, but now you want to come?"

"Well," she said, "now there are tanks in the streets, and if anything happens to you, we want to be nearby."

To make a long story short, after a little family altercation, I said: "Okay, tomorrow I'm flying to the Pamir with you."

As soon as I said that, I dialed my secretary in Moscow again and told her, "Masha, I am canceling my Moscow trip tomorrow. I'll be flying to the Pamir instead."

After a long pause, she said slowly, "You know, Davlat, I think you have made the right choice—there are tanks all around here, it will be better in the mountains." I smiled to myself and hung up. So my wife calmed down.

While in Dushanbe on the 19th, I made several phone calls to Moscow. And during my third phone call there—I was talking to an official at the Cinematographers' Union—I heard him say: "Listen, there are tanks here, you know, perhaps we should be a little more cautious now."

When I heard that I simply blew my stack. "How can you say that? When we used to organize demonstrations and rallies we knew that even though we were criticizing Gorbachev, we were still under his protection. And now, when he is locked up somewhere, you are suggesting that we should keep quiet about those dirty bastards! . . ." I was saying this on the intercity phone line. "You are suggesting we hide! Under no circumstances. We must be completely open about our opposition."

When I hung up the phone, my wife said: "Listen, you have always been outspoken, but this time I think you have gone a little too far."

---

*Khudonazarov comes from Gornyi Badakhshan, a region of the Tajik Republic that is high in the Pamir Mountains, close to Afghanistan.

And one more detail. One of the Tajik Cinematographers' Union officials I was with on the 19th was Rubit Karimov, the Executive Secretary of the Union. This was in the morning shortly after I found out about the events and I was still feeling dumbfounded. Karimov (he is a man in his early forties) was riding with me in the car. He spoke to me softly, almost confidentially: "Davlat, as I recall, you, too, have spoken out against Gorbachev."

My mind was sort of wandering at that time, but all of a sudden I realized that he was throwing me a line, giving me the opportunity to change sides. I said: "What? Me? You mean have I ever spoken out against Gorbachev? I can't remember. . . ."

"Why yes," he was quick to remind me. "Last January you were organizing the protest, the letter of 196, you were accusing him [of responsibility for the bloodshed in Lithuania]."

"Don't you understand?" I said, "We were attacking from another side—the opposite side."

We were at the Tajik Film Studio that morning, and there, too, I noticed some people averting their eyes, pretending not to notice me—anything not to greet me, because then they would have had to say something. People did not want to be pinned down. And the atmosphere was strange. Instead of regular programming, the radio was repeating over and over again the melody that preceded important announcements. And from time to time, they would read the text of the Emergency Committee's or Lukianov's statement. That same evening, the Emergency Committee people went on television, and it became clear what kind people they truly were.

Twice I received calls from the editor of a small Tajik independent newspaper. "Master," he said, using a Tajik form of address, *ustot*, "we have reached the Supreme Soviet of Russia—Yeltsin is there." Later on, he called me and said that he had spoken with the Moscow City Soviet and that [Mayor] Gavriil Popov, too, was there. This editor was a wonderful fellow. He was sure that the coup would not work. Later, in the fall, when we lost the election,* he broke down crying at the press conference.

The next morning, on the 20th, I got up early, packed the bags, and by 6 o'clock we were at the airport. I passed my [five-year-old] son on to one of the passengers who was boarding the plane—this was a small

---

*Khudonazarov was an unsuccessful candidate for president of Tajikistan.

Yak–40—and he was soon seated; my [seventeen-year-old] daughter followed. It was my wife's turn now—we were the last to board. I said: "Please forgive me, but I've got to go to Moscow." Before she could even open her mouth, the flight attendant began to rush her to board the plane. So she had to get on board, and so we said good-bye.

I went to the ticket office to try and get a ticket to Moscow. It was about 6:15 in the morning by then (3:15 A.M. in Moscow). The flight for Moscow was to depart soon. The plane was already on the tarmac. There was a lot of agitation around the boarding gate, which clearly meant that the big bosses were flying to Moscow.

I had made up my mind, of course, that I should try to be as inconspicuous as possible, so I avoided the special reservations office for Deputies and VIPs (they might report my whereabouts). My plan had been to get off the plane in Moscow unnoticed and get to the city by the suburban train and subway, instead of hiring a taxi. Alas, there were no tickets for ordinary folks.

In the meantime, I saw that the airport was filling up with very important people—Secretaries of the Tajik Communist Party Central Committee and people like that. They were standing in a small crowd talking to each other, laughing heartily, making a lot of noise. They were clearly euphoric about something. I took aside one of their sidekicks who was weaving in and out of the crowd, and asked him what the commotion was all about. "They are all going to the [CPSU] Central Committee Plenum in Moscow," he replied.

On the spur of the moment, I walked up to one of the Second Secretaries of the Central Committee and said to him: "What's going on? You are going to the Plenum in Moscow and you have not even informed me?"

"Well," he looked at me with some mixture of surprise and condescension, "we didn't even know that you were here."

Needless to say, they had no desire to have people like me attend the Plenum, and since I did not represent the republic's Communist Party organization, they were not obligated to include me in their delegation.

"Get me a ticket," I said, "help me." He began to hem and haw, but I noticed that he was looking at me in a rather strange way. The eyes were saying something like: "You may be still hustling, Davlat, but soon you'll be a dead man." For them, I was already a corpse, really.

Suddenly I noticed a limousine drive up to the entrance, and out of it stepped the head of the Committee for State Security and, with him, Kakham Makkhamov, First Secretary of the Tajik Communist Party and the President of the Republic. So I turned to him: "Kakham Makkhamovich, no one has informed me about the Plenum, and now I can't even get on the plane—there are no more seats left."

He, too, was all excited, even euphoric. "Don't worry—I can yield my seat to you."

"Thank you," I said, "but I'd rather you keep your own seat and help me get mine." Then he turned to someone else.

I waited but nobody volunteered to assist me. The place was teaming with VIP aides, who under any other circumstances would have fallen all over themselves to get a ticket for a member of the Central Committee of the CPSU and Deputy of the USSR Supreme Soviet. But nobody made a move. They knew who was standing before them.

Fortunately, a good colleague of mine, Bozaruli Safarov, a member of the Supreme Soviet and formerly a functionary in Aeroflot, saw what was happening and came to my aid. He took my papers, disappeared, and a few moments later brought me back a ticket. That's how I boarded the plane.

We were airborne. I was sitting in an empty row. All of a sudden, Makkhamov got up from his seat and came and sat down right next to me. Then, the head of his security detail got up and took a seat next to him. Strangely, he proceeded to go to sleep. Soon, though, the food was brought in, and after we finished eating, I asked him: "Kakham Makkhamovich, what do those guys think they are doing? I think it's real adventurism. I hope there is going to be a meeting of the Politburo before the Plenum. I think it would be a good idea to draw the line between them and the Party."

He hemmed and hawed: "Well, yes, I think things have been going more or less all right, but the Treaty—the change in the country's name is very unfortunate.* It's very hard to take." And so on. It was clear he was not too eager to answer my questions, so he got up and excused himself to go have a smoke in the pilot's cabin. He did not come out until the plane landed in Moscow an hour and forty minutes later. In the meantime, I was having a chat with his security man, and he agreed with me completely, calling the coup leaders "adventurists

_____

*This is a reference to the proposed change in the name of the country to the "Union of Sovereign Republics."

and idiots." He was an officer in the KGB! I can't remember his name, but he was a man in his mid-thirties.

After we arrived at the airport in Moscow, I ran into the group of people who were going to serve as Russia's provisional government in case Moscow was lost. Aleksei Yablokov was there, and a few other people—I can't recall their names. With them was a group of military men of various ranks and ages. I walked up to them and asked: "Are we hanging in there, fellows?" "Sure," they said, "we're going to kick them out of here"—they meant the putschists. About thirty or forty of them were there, counting both the civilians and the military. They demanded a plane but got no response for a few hours. Finally they were given a plane and flew off to Sverdlovsk.

There was a lot of traffic on the road, and it took us a long time to get to Moscow from the airport. When I finally reached my hotel, my secretary at the Cinematographers' Union informed me that heads of the creative arts unions were gathering at [Minister of Culture] Gubenko's office.

I rushed there at once. What they were trying to do was to coordinate the position of the creative intelligentsia. Gubenko addressed me first. I responded: "These are putschists and usurpers—that's what our position should be." I remember using these very words. Gubenko asked my opinion; I responded unambiguously and sharply.

"Well," he said, "I wonder if this sort of opinion is shared by everybody." Other people spoke, including the Chairman of the Architects' Union, Platonov. He essentially expressed the same sentiments, if in rather more delicate terms.

Finally, Gubenko spoke. "I feel closer to Platonov's opinion. I am for a softer approach. It is inappropriate to be unequivocal like Khudonazarov. Everything is much more complicated. As I was made to understand, there is nothing simple about this." He went on in this vein, making things sound more and more ambiguous.

As soon as I realized that he was going to befuddle the issue, I broke in saying, "I have a document here with me." By that time I already had an official statement of the Cinematographers' Union. So I said: "Here is my union's position. Would you like to join us in condemning the putsch?" I did not get either "yes" or "no" then.

Later on, Platonov and I kept in touch and tried to coordinate our actions. We even convinced Tikhon Khrennikov [Chairman of the Composers' Union] to sign an appeal, and he thanked me later for the opportunity.

The meeting with Gubenko was at around noon. After leaving Gubenko, I went to the Cinematographers' Union to make phone calls. I called Sobchak and asked him how things were in Petersburg. He reassured me that everything was quiet. I asked him to get hold of Lavrov, the theater union chairman, whose signature I needed for the appeal. He told me that he thought it was important to have as many people around the White House as possible.

At some point, I found out that the Central Committee Plenum was not going to take place for a variety of reasons. It had been in preparation, though. The main reason it never convened was that Gorbachev could have run the risk of being removed from his post of General Secretary. For that reason, Gorbachev's supporters were not very eager to see it convene. My position was different. I was an advocate of the split. Even if only a small group had split from the Party, I still felt that it would have been important for it to make its statement against the coup.

I called the Central Committee Secretaries over and over again, beginning with Ivashko [Gorbachev's Deputy Party Secretary]. Their aides would pick up the phone and tell me that they were in a meeting or away from their offices. This went on till the evening. I, a member of the Central Committee, could not make contact with the organization. In the evening, Platonov joined me for a fifth round of phone calls. All in vain. Finally, it occurred to me that we could use a fax. I called the Central Committee again and asked them for their fax number. They said: "What fax? We don't have any fax around here." I called another Central Committee Secretary's office. They didn't have a fax either. I called another, still another. The answer was the same.

Finally, I figured it out: the Secretary in charge of International Affairs, Falin, must have a fax machine. So Platonov and I sent our protest statement care of Falin. But the aide on duty there, the one who gave me the fax number, said: "You know, there is nobody there right now to receive your fax."

"How come?" I said.

"It's after five o'clock—the workday is over."

"I hope they switch it to automatic," I said to him and hung up, chuckling to myself: "There is a coup d'état, but they've done their nine to five and gone home. What a wonderful life they have!" The fax had been switched to automatic, and the next day I did learn from Ivashko's aides that the statement Platonov and I had sent him was put on his desk in the morning [of the 21st]. But I could not reach Ivashko himself. He was in a meeting, probably discussing our statement together with other similar documents (I was sure Latsis had sent them his own).*

That day, the 20th, I also called a few people at the Central Committee, including Andrei Grachev, who would later become Gorbachev's press secretary, and Vladimir Yegorov, who was Gorbachev's adviser for cultural affairs. In other words, I tried to reach the decent people I knew there and offer them some support in a human sort of way, so that they would not lose heart in that dead zone.

On the evening of the 20th, I went to the White House and stayed there until 2:30 in the morning, leaving after it became clear that nothing untoward was going to happen. I was there in a group with other deputies; Vladimir Volkov decided to stay till the end.

I will not go into the atmosphere at the White House that night—it is all too well known. A lot of people there looked rather operatic. Some clutched submachine guns and had terribly serious faces. At one point, I noticed a row of bottles filled with light-colored liquid. I thought it was white wine, but it turned out to be incendiary liquid.

Aleksandr Gelman has wonderful stories. He was in Burbulis's office at night and they had quite a few drinks there. So at one point they asked Kobets† to call his buddies at the [Union] Ministry of Defense and ask them whether they were going to attack the White House or not. He called. They told him that they wanted to attack but could not because their scouts had told them that there were too many people around the White House.

You should ask Gelman, although, I don't know, perhaps he would be too embarrassed to write this up for publication. But his story is that after they had finished one bottle, they started looking for more, asking around to see whether anyone had anything stashed away somewhere. General Kobets owned up to it and brought one from his office. Lots of funny stories. But I was not there myself.

After I left the White House, I walked to my hotel [the Hotel Moskva] in the drizzle, in the middle of the curfew, but, of course, nobody stopped me. The streets were absolutely empty.

---

*Otto Latsis, a liberal reformer and an editor of the journal *Kommunist*.

†Colonel General Kobets was Russia's Chief Military Liaison with the Union Defense Ministry.

The next day, or, rather, a few hours later, I was back in the White House where Vorontsov and I tried to organize the temporary transfer of Union government structures to Russian jurisdiction. We convinced the Minister of the Chemical and Oil Refining Industry, Khadzhiev, to join with Vorontsov's Ministry [of Environment] and my [Cinematographers'] union in this venture. We were trying to convince Gubenko to do the same, but he refused to join us, saying that he was going to do things his own way.

* * *

And now, a few thoughts on what happened after the putsch. Right away there appeared lists of heroes. At one point, in the union, I was given a piece of paper with names. "What is this?" I asked.

"These are the names of the *activists*."

"What kind of activists?"

"These are the people who took part in the events."

"So what," I said. "What shall we do with them? Does this mean that other people did not take part, or that these are true revolutionaries and that others, who are not on the list, were counter-revolutionaries? Let's agree once and for all that I have not seen this list and that you did not prepare it."

I know that later some people were given days off and bonuses at work for having defended the White House. It's ludicrous! As if that were why people decided to resist!

8 | Breakthrough: The Coup in St. Petersburg

Anatolii Sobchak, a well-known lawyer and public figure, was the Mayor of Leningrad (now St. Petersburg) and one of the most prominent members of the Supreme Soviet of the USSR when the coup took place. He was interviewed on August 26, 1991, by A. Golovkova and A. Chernova for Moskovskie novosti.

The night of August 18–19 I spent in my Moscow official apartment.*

Early on Monday morning I was awakened by a telephone call. It was my friends from Kazakhstan calling to inform me about the military coup (thanks to the difference in time zones!).

My first move was to look out the window to see whether the building was surrounded. It was not. Otherwise, I would have had to go to my neighbors. The official building in Krylatskoe was filled with members of the USSR Supreme Soviet. I telephoned for the car and my bodyguard. Oleg was on duty that day (I will not divulge his last name for understandable reasons), but the actual guarding was being done by the boys on Yeltsin's team.

I found out that Yeltsin was expecting me at his dacha in Usovo, which is beyond Arkhangelskoe.

Tanks were rolling along the Outer Ring Road. What a pitiful sight. Right there on the highway shoulder, a tank was burning. No, nobody had set it on fire. It was burning by itself. Far more unpleasant: I ran into a group of paratroopers as I turned off the Outer Ring Road. But they did not stop me.

*Many members of the USSR Supreme Soviet who were not permanent residents of Moscow had special apartments in the capital for official use.

Yeltsin's dacha was being guarded by no more than six or eight men with machine guns. I entered—and froze in surprise. The whole Russian leadership was in the room. One platoon of special forces would have been enough to deal with our Russian statehood.

Yeltsin asked what I could suggest.

I said: "We must call a session of Russia's parliament. And the session should last around the clock."

Yeltsin: "We have already decided to do just that. Any moment now, they will bring the text of the Appeal to the Citizens of Russia. After that, we'll decide whether to stay here or leave."

Opinions were divided. Either alternative was dangerous.

Khasbulatov: "I'm leaving as soon as I get the text. You decide for yourself."

The text was brought in. The head of the Russian Supreme Soviet [Khasbulatov] left for the White House. He was using a private car, it seems. He did not want to be recognized.

I began to insist: "We should break through after Khasbulatov. Is there another road? I am very worried about the special forces guys at the Outer Ring Road turnoff."

They said there was no other way out, except by foot.

I: "After all, this is the presidential entourage. . . . Let's fly the flag and off we go. The sooner the better."

They put a bulletproof vest on Boris Nikolaevich. His daughter said: "Papa, don't worry. Now everything depends on you alone."

By the way, no one displayed any visible signs of agitation. Not even the President's wife, Naina Iosifovna.

I asked Yeltsin whether I was needed in the White House or could I go back to Leningrad. He said, "You may go."

I made myself clear: "I will follow you all the way to Kutuzovskii Prospect, and from there on, I'll decide depending on the situation. If we slip through, I'll double back to the Outer Ring Road and ride to the Sheremetevo Airport."

Thank God, the special forces were already gone. Either they had gone to catch us but missed, or another group charged with arresting us arrived too late at the dacha in Usovo. (As we found out later, it was the latter: they arrived ten minutes too late.)

We were driving fast. In front of us was the Traffic Police car, so others let us pass. Ditto the tanks and the armored personnel carriers

(APCs). Yeltsin's guards were covering both sides of his limousine. We whipped through the Ring Road in ten minutes. Rublev Highway was next. The road is narrow, and it was full of tanks and APCs, but seeing our flag, they, too, moved to the shoulder. Fortunately, there weren't many of them.

We had broken through! Now, I had to turn off for Sheremetevo. Once there, I learned that the next plane to Petersburg would leave in two and a half hours.

Later on I found out that an order to arrest me had in fact been issued. But they did not bother to send a special forces unit after me. The order was issued to the airport KGB agents. They agreed—in word only. When I was sitting in the deputies' VIP lounge, three men came in. The concierge asked them to show their identification. They showed their papers.

I said to Oleg, "Get ready."

He said to me, "I know one of these guys."

The three passed into the cafeteria. Oleg followed them. They came back together, said that they were from the special unit fighting currency speculation, and that they intended to guard me all the way until I got on the tarmac. Now I had four bodyguards. Three of them had machine guns.

In order not to waste time, I got on the line to Petersburg and gave instructions to the OMON [special police] to protect the building of the Leningrad Television Station. I tried to assess the situation. In a live broadcast, the Commander of the Leningrad Military District, General Samsonov, had already declared that he was taking all power in the city in his own hands. As for the rest, it seemed quiet; there were no troops in the city itself.

Later I discovered that they also had a plan to arrest me at the Pulkovo Airport [in Leningrad]. But, on his own initiative, the chief of the Leningrad Police, Arkadii Kramarev, had already sent a car for me with OMON troops. My assistants from the Mayor's Office came to meet me at the airport as well.

I dove into the car and went straight to the headquarters of the Leningrad Military District. My guards stayed downstairs. Later they told me how one of Gidaspov's guards, who was hanging out in the hallway of the headquarters, beamed with joy and from behind my back stuck his tongue out at them.

The office of the Commander-in-Chief is on the second floor. The door was not locked, the room was empty. I yelled at the top of my voice so that the whole building could hear: "What kind of crap is this? Why isn't there anybody guarding the office of the District Commander!"

A frightened lieutenant colonel ran out of some place or other. Under a different set of circumstances, he would not have let me in, but now he was standing at attention. I went on: "Take me to the Commander-in-Chief!"

"Yes, sir. They are meeting right in there, sir. . . ."

"Take me there at once!"

We went down to the ground floor. They were all sitting there, the little dears: Samsonov, Kurkov (head of the KGB), Savin (Interior Forces), Viktorov (head of the Northwestern Military District), and, of course, Gidaspov, the first Communist of the region. And finally, the loyal democrat and our benefactor, Arkadii Kramarev. He was the only one of *us*.

I noticed that they were surprised by my sudden appearance, and I did not let them open their mouths. Right away, I gave them a whole speech, reminded them about General Shaposhnikov, who had refused to shoot the people in Novocherkassk in 1962.* I explained to them that, from a legal standpoint, they were all conspirators, and that if they moved so much as a finger, they would be tried—just like the Nazis at Nuremberg.

I reproached Samsonov: "Well, General, remember Tbilisi.† . . . On April 9, 1989, you were just about the only one there who behaved rationally. You avoided carrying out illegal orders, you remained in the shadow. . . . What's happening with you now? Have you decided to join that criminal gang? . . . That Emergency Committee is illegal!"

Samsonov: And why is it illegal? I have an order . . .

[*Sobchak*]: You know very well that I am one of the people who drafted the Law on the State of Emergency. There are only four situations in which it may be imposed on a specified territory, namely:

---

*Sobchak is referring to the bloody suppression of a strike and mass protests triggered by longstanding grievances in the southern, largely Cossack city of Novocherkassk. The story of these events was aired and debated during the early glasnost period.

†Unarmed demonstrators in the Georgian capital were massacred by Soviet troops in the spring of 1989.

human epidemics, cattle epidemics, earthquakes, and mass disorders. Which one of these is taking place?

Samsonov: But we are introducing the state of emergency just in case. I have an order. There is a coded telegram. . . .

[*Sobchak*]: Show it to me.

Samsonov: I can't. It's secret.

[*Sobchak*]: Then answer, does it contain the following words: "Introduce martial law in the city of Leningrad"?

Samsonov: No, there are no words like that. . . .

[*Sobchak*]: I know there aren't. And you'd better remember General Rodionov* during the First Congress of People's Deputies. On April 9th he, too, overstepped his orders. All he was ordered to do was protect military installations, but instead he threw in his troops against the people. Are you taking the same path?

Gidaspov: Why are you raising your voice at us?

[*Sobchak*]: And *you* would be better off not speaking at all. Don't you understand that by your very presence you are destroying your own party? Instead of sitting here now you ought to be running through the streets yelling that the CPSU has nothing to do with this.

Gidaspov: But we have an economic collapse, industrial production is falling. . . .

[*Sobchak*]: That's a lie. In the first six months of this year Leningrad's industry overfulfilled the quota.

I turned to Samsonov: "Viktor Nikolaevich, I ask you to do everything in your power to prevent the army from entering the city."

He said: "All right, I'll do it."

I went to the Mariinskii Palace, the City Hall. There I learned that our Vice Mayor, Rear Admiral Viacheslav Shcherbakov, was returning from his trip. I held a meeting with the Chairman of the Leningrad City Soviet, Aleksandr Beliaev. I said, "We should call a session of the Soviet." He said, "We already have, and the deputies have been informed."

I made arrangements with the television station to make a live appearance on the program "Fact." My appearance was scheduled for 7:20 P.M.

I showed up at the studio five minutes before the broadcast, accom-

---

*General Rodionov was in charge of the troops at Tbilisi.

panied by Viacheslav Shcherbakov and Yurii Yarov, the Chairman of the Regional Soviet; the putschists had included both of them in their Emergency Committee without ever asking them. The president of Leningrad TV, Boris Petrov, even secured a satellite connection, so viewers far beyond the Leningrad city limit watched us.

I had the idea of referring to the Moscow putschists as "ex" (ex–Vice President, ex–Minister of Defense, and so forth), and then also, of prefacing their names with the title "Citizen," as if they had already taken their seats in the dock.*

If until that evening there had been no sign of popular resistance to the putsch (the session of the Leningrad Soviet had not yet taken place), the joint appearance of the Mayor, the Vice Mayor, and the Chairman of the Regional Soviet dispelled the suffocating atmosphere and disorientation all the more effectively.

After the television broadcast we called in additional OMON forces. Here too, Kramarev showed that he was more than equal to his task. Shcherbakov was shuttling between the Mariinskii Palace and the Military District Headquarters. . . .

Samsonov all the while was under tremendous pressure from Moscow. Hysterical, the putschists were screaming at him over the phone, accusing him of selling out to the democrats.

In the meantime, two columns of armored vehicles were moving toward the city from the south. Their movements were closely monitored by the Traffic Police, who remained loyal to democracy. Barricades had to be erected, but we did not have enough time. The tanks were expected within an hour. We figured out that we could block the approaches with the heavy earth-moving equipment based at the airport. But after the tanks had passed the town of Gatchina, Samsonov gave me his officer's word of honor that he would not let the armored vehicles into the city. He ordered the column to move from Gatchina toward Siverskaia. There, in the birthplace of Pushkin's ancestors and his nanny, on the grounds of the military airport, those tanks would remain stationed for three full days.

How, and with what arguments, did Shcherbakov and I succeed in persuading Samsonov? I don't know, but I think it was common sense.

---

*"Comrade" was the usual form of official address in the Soviet Union. Ironically, only people whose rights were suspended—because they were suspected of breaking or had broken the law—were addressed officially as "Citizen."

We said to him: "Don't you see, General, what nonentities these people are? Even if they take power, they will not be able to hold on to it."

The tension had eased somewhat. I got on the line with Yeltsin. Then I took a nap for an hour on the little couch in my office. And at six o'clock in the morning, I went to the Putilov factory. I managed to arrive before the shift started. There, at the factory gate, a car with a megaphone was already waiting. We held a rally. After that, I went to the management office in order to ensure that everyone who wanted to join the rally in the city could receive a pass. As I was leaving, a large group of the Putilov workers, three or four thousand, was already marching down Stachechnyi Prospect [literally, the Avenue of Strikes]. I myself should have been leading those people all the way to Palace Square, but my security people told me that, given the information at their disposal, I ought not.

The whole city was on Palace Square at 10:00 A.M. Whole columns of people had to be turned away even before they could reach the square. However broad the square, the human sea had turned out to be even broader. We decided that people should go back to their places of work by 1:00 P.M. That was exactly what happened. There were no no-shows.

They told me later that even prisoners asked to go to the barricades, promising they would turn themselves in afterward.

One of the speakers was Dmitrii Sergeevich Likhachev, the most senior scholar and a patriot, a member of the Academy [of Sciences], and now a popular hero as well.

It was clear that putschists would not succeed in Petersburg.

Toward the evening, I had a heaven-sent idea. Our problems could be solved if Yeltsin appointed Shcherbakov to be the Military Commandant of the City of Leningrad and the Leningrad Region, and also making him the personal representative of both the Russian President and the Defense Committee of the Russian Federation.*

What kind of a team does Yeltsin have there? A fax arrived with a decree appointing Shcherbakov head of the Leningrad Military District [General Samsonov's position]. That was almost a catastrophe: now Samsonov would really go out of bounds. . . . Besides, such an ap-

---

*At that time the Russian Federation had not yet established a Ministry of Defense, and the relevant functions were carried out by a Committee for Defense.

pointment did not solve any problems, since in addition to the Military District we also had a naval base and a Border Military District. . . .

I was right. . . . Samsonov called me: "What are you plotting behind my back?"

I reassured him: there was a mistake, we'll correct it immediately. But the radio was already transmitting the news of this—for us—fatal appointment. I explained over the phone several times what kind of text we needed. Finally, the necessary document arrived from Moscow.

At three in the morning, still more news arrived. A unit of the Military District's special forces was being deployed along Kaliaev Street and was moving in the direction of City Hall. Previously the unit's mission was to recapture airplanes hijacked by terrorists.

Shcherbakov said: "The whole of the OMON and your police force will be no obstacle to those guys. They'll take care of them in five minutes."

We decided to go separate ways. I went to the Putilov factory, called out the director, explained the situation.

Thank God there was no need to rouse the Putilov workers . . . .

9 | Our Children Were on the Barricades

Aleksandr N. Yakovlev, along with Mikhail Gorbachev and Eduard Shevardnadze, was one of the founding fathers of perestroika and glasnost. A close associate of Gorbachev's, he became a full member of the Party Politburo in 1987 and soon earned a reputation as the most outspoken advocate of radical change. Increasingly frustrated with the conservative Party apparat, he resigned from the Politburo at the Twenty-eighth Party Congress in the summer of 1990, remaining a prominent, though at times distant and critical, member of Gorbachev's circle of advisers. Four days before the coup, he was expelled from the Party. The following interview was conducted by A. Shcherbakov, reporter for the magazine Ogonëk, *where it appeared in the issue for August 31–September 7, 1991. During a visit to Berkeley and Stanford in February 1993, Yakovlev added some details to his account of the coup in an interview with Gregory Freidin. Excerpts from that conversation have been interpolated into the* Ogonëk *interview.*

Yakovlev: I was awakened at 4:30 in the morning by the former general of the KGB, Oleg Kalugin, who told me the news of the coup d'état. I said to him: "Oleg, are you in your right mind?" "Sane as sane can be" was his answer. I got out of bed and looked out of the window: on both sides of the street, there were unmarked cars filled with the "boys." I called Boris Nikolaevich Yeltsin. He ordered Viktor Barannikov, Russia's Minister of Internal Affairs, to take the necessary steps, and before long, a unit of Russia's security forces arrived at my door.

[A few of them rushed into my apartment and told me that the place was now under their control and that I had nothing to worry about. "I can defend myself, too," I said to them, "just give me one of your machine guns." "That's against our rules," their chief replied, "If you are armed, we won't be able to protect you."]

Soon, the "boys" who had had me under surveillance earlier turned around and sped away. And then the reporters came, some of them offering help take me into hiding. I received many such offers, more than twenty, as I recall, some coming from people I was not even acquainted with.

Ogonëk: Why did you decide not to attempt to escape from what was a probable strike against you?

Yakovlev: I had to work.

Ogonëk: But you could have continued with your work in a more secure place than your Moscow apartment.

Yakovlev: In circumstances of this sort, you must work in public view, so that people can see you, so that they can understand you are not hiding. This makes it easier for them to believe in their eventual victory. Few things are as significant as making a speech at the Moscow Soviet—before a huge crowd of people, just a few hours after the putsch, to say to people something that might inspire them.* The other side had tanks and weapons at its disposal, and all our side had was enthusiasm and faith that we were in the right.

Ogonëk: I heard over Moscow Echo that someone had spotted you in the White House with a pistol in one hand and a radio in the other.

Yakovlev: Well, that was a small episode, and not a very important one either.

Ogonëk: Do you believe that the putsch, or attempted putsch, was inevitable—was predetermined, as it were, by the logic of events?

Yakovlev: This is one possible explanation for what happened. But I prefer to look at things from a different perspective. The split in our society—in terms of the ideology, politics, psychology, structure—began to be felt in 1985.

---

*This is exactly what Yakovlev did on the afternoon of the August 19.

Roughly, two main trends emerged. One was objective: it expressed the desire for change on the part of the people and their realization that it was not possible to live the old way any longer. The other trend was reactionary through and through: to sabotage perestroika and change. This reactionary trend became especially strong when the issue of free elections began to be debated in earnest and when people began to demand the removal of the Party from the structures of state power. It was then that the Party became the main engine of resistance to perestroika.

In this regard, I was very much taken aback by the effort of President Gorbachev (I guess in this case, he was acting as the General Secretary of the Party) to whitewash the Party's leadership—people who did not utter a single word in public against the coup d'état, against the seizure of the President, against the murder of the three individuals. As he presents it, members of the Party leadership were locked in an inner struggle.

I, for my part, couldn't care less where and how they were arguing among themselves. I now hear that so-and-so had inner objections against the putsch. But what does that mean—*inner objections*? My son, who is the father of three children, spent the fateful night on the barricades. And so did my daughter and her husband. But the high-ranking leadership had *inner objections!* In my opinion, this is no way to take a stand.

Ogonëk: Would it be fair to summarize your position as follows: Totalitarianism in our country will not be vanquished as long as a party that believes in the idea of violence as the main political force— namely the Communist Party of the Soviet Union—is alive and well?

Yakovlev: I agree.

Ogonëk: One of the key questions debated among the democrats even before the putsch was the question of what kind of political organizations we are going to promote: whether it would be preferable to have a strongly disciplined organization, possibly with a narrow base, or a looser, more broadly based movement. How does the putsch affect your thinking on this issue?

Yakovlev: I can only give you my own opinion. Before the putsch, I was slightly more inclined (say, 51 to 49) toward a broadly based movement. And now I have reversed my position. I am inclined to think that we need a well-organized force that might serve as a guarantor against things like the putsch. Let me tell you, though, that the overwhelming majority of the leadership of the Movement for Democratic Reform* proved themselves to be capable of taking a strong and unequivocal stand. There were exceptions, but they were insignificant.

I was in constant communication with Gavriil Popov, Yeltsin, Shevardnadze, and Laptev [Deputy Chairman of the USSR Supreme Soviet]. It was Laptev who continuously informed us about the situation in the Kremlin. I was in touch with one official (I did not know him personally) who informed me of what was going on in the Emergency Committee, what their plans were. This was vital information.

[I had another old friend in the Kremlin, a technical worker, who kept me informed about what he could see from his window—whether the limousines were coming in or out, how many, and so forth. One time he called me and said that the limousines were moving in a strange way: a cortège of them would start moving in one direction and then, all of a sudden, would turn back. . . . I remember his words: "Aleksandr Nikolaevich, they are like eels on a hot griddle." That, too, was important information, because it gave you some sense of the mood inside the Kremlin, and the mood was one of confusion.]

One of my old friends from the Central Committee kept calling me on the phone and telling me what was happening there and how and in what way the leadership was planning to offer support to the Emergency Committee.

Ogonëk: Let's talk about the individuals from the other camp. Were there any surprises for you when you learned about the composition of the Emergency Committee?

Yakovlev: No surprises, except for one. I was both shocked and offended to find Yazov among them. He is a World War II veteran who fought in the trenches, a soldier, a unit commander. He and I were neighbors at the front. He is a real soldier, and this was always apparent in his attitudes and actions. How this man could have done what he did is still a psychological riddle for me. It is possible that he was influenced by the military, who are used to measuring the might of a

---

*Reference is to a loose political movement that Aleksandr Yakovlev, along with former USSR Foreign Minister Eduard Shevardnadze and Moscow Mayor Gavriil Popov, began to organize in the spring of 1991.

nation by counting rockets and bombs. The more shells, guns, rifles, and rockets you have, the more influential is the voice of your country. In their opinion, the Soviet Union under Stalin—a totalitarian country practicing mass repression and re-enserfment of the peasantry—was an "influential" power. But as soon as we embarked on the road to disarmament, tried to break out of our isolation and join the civilized world, we became, in their opinion, a second-rate power. . . . Do you comprehend the meaning of this base propaganda?

Ogonëk: The putschists' game was a gangsters' game—without rules. Why, then, did they, to put it simply, make a mess of things? Why didn't they clamp down on the leaders of the democratic movement, who are so popular among the people?

Yakovlev: First of all, I believe they were frightened by the possible reaction to such a move. Further, I suspect that these very mediocre individuals—who, moreover, had lost touch with the people—thought that, given the stresses of our socioeconomic crisis, all they needed to do was to make the first move and that after that, everybody would simply sigh a sigh of relief and say: at last, we'll have order, we'll have food. As enemies of democracy and freedom, they could not comprehend—they did not possess the mentality necessary to understand—the reality of our own day, the fact that the sense of being free and living in a democracy is more important for our people.

After all, how could they have expected that so many would ignore the instructions issued by the commandants, ignore the ban on demonstrations and strikes? . . .

[Early on, Gavriil Popov got in touch with the directors of several of Moscow's major factories and the city's transportation departments, including the Moscow metro, and elicited from them an agreement to go on strike at a moment's notice, pending a signal from the Mayor's Office. The Emergency Committee was duly informed of this arrangement. The quid pro quo with the Military Commandant was that the city would continue to function normally as long as the security forces did not interfere with the demonstrators.]

They could not even begin to imagine that people in Moscow would begin building barricades. And they certainly did not suppose that during the first hours of the coup d'état, some military units would refuse to shoot at people and that some of them would even join the democratic forces.

Now, every one of the putschists must bear his responsibility for what took place. But this should be done with strict adherence to law! We must not stoop to revenge, to a settling of accounts, to summary justice. . . . Since we are for the rule of law, we must follow it to the letter.

Ogonëk: I think that some of the democrats, carried away by their zeal to restore justice, may cross the bounds of democracy and law.

Yakovlev: The word *democrat* does not fit such individuals. You can't be a democrat and advocate smashing, crushing, bashing. . . .

Ogonëk: Some people even today believe that the putsch was a game, orchestrated from behind the scenes by Gorbachev and the leftists. . . .

Yakovlev: By the left? This is fantastic. . . . How could the left have done it? Do you mean to say they could have gone to Pugo or Kriuchkov and said, "Hey, fellows, let's organize a junta"? This is pure nonsense. As to the second possibility . . . I do not think that Gorbachev had anything to do with this conspiracy. I do not want to think otherwise!

IV

Defending the White House

Almost from the inception, the White House became the strategic center of confrontation during the August coup. The democratic resistance, led by Boris Yeltsin, was concentrated at the White House. From there, they communicated with the rest of the country and the world via telephone, fax, and radio broadcasts. It soon became apparent that control of the country could not be secured without taking over the building that housed the Russian government—a government that had become virtually synonymous with opposition to the putsch. In this section, we concentrate on events in and around the White House, with special attention to the early hours of Wednesday, August 21, when thousands of Muscovites prepared to defend the building against what they believed to be an imminent attack.

THERESA SABONIS-CHAFEE

1 | Reflections from the Barricades

*Theresa Sabonis-Chafee, then a graduate student in International
Relations at the Woodrow Wilson School of Public Policy at Princeton
University, was in Moscow when the coup took place in August 1991.
She had arrived there in January 1991 to work at the World
Laboratory, an international science policy organization.*

It occurred to me on the metro at 12:15 A.M. that I did not really know
what I was doing, that I was likely to be deported, and that my
Russian-language skills (which had been nonexistent seven months
earlier) could charitably be described as "poor," but I resolved not to
think about it too much. I am a student of international relations, a
teacher of Soviet history, and a tax-paying resident of Moscow, I reminded myself. How could I do anything else? As my train sped toward the center of town, closer to the home of the government, I
reflected on the day's events so far.

I had awakened early and traveled nearly two hours to my Russian
teacher's summer home, as I had done several times a week for the
past few months. The village was still and nervous, and radios could be
heard from every front yard. I noticed it was not the usual program, but
was unaware of the Soviet tradition of playing solemn classics when a
head of state or important official has died. I was later told that the
music usually continues for hours or even days before it is supple-
mented with information. This time, however, the information had
been released promptly. My teacher, Natalia, was startled to see me.
"Oh, Terry," she said, "you didn't listen to the news this morning."
Then, as she prepared breakfast, she slowly explained what had happened. We ate a tense meal, listening to the radio announcer. In a
funereal voice, he was reading the same brief statement that had been

repeated since 6:00 A.M.: The President is ill. A provisional government will run the country. The announcement was repeated regularly
for the next few hours, interspersed with movements from *Swan Lake*.
Tchaikovsky is one of the few great artists to be accepted as politically
correct by every Russian administration, and so, although the provisional government did not once mention the word "socialism," their
style was unmistakable. The past had seized power.

Natalia decided to return to Moscow to assess the situation and to
wait for instructions from her office. While the family packed, neighbors arrived with their office telephone numbers. They asked Natalia
to phone and inquire when they would be called out to help with the
harvest. I sat outside, staring at the snapdragons, wondering whether
the notorious patience of the Russian people would allow for even this.
Radios could be heard from all the neighboring yards, and *Swan Lake*
contributed to the surrealism of the morning. War or state oppression,
which would it be? Which was better? How could there be civil war in
a city of nine million? What would that look like? I thought about the
overthrow of Khrushchev and his reforms. Although it seemed incon-
ceivable, maybe perestroika and glasnost could be reversed.

At a demonstration during the hungry winter months, I had seen a
woman carrying a sign that proclaimed, "I would trade this government for a kilogram of macaroni." How many people would be content
to trade this struggling democracy for a government that was more in
control? Could the new government feed the people—and if it could,
would that be enough?

Natalia and I traveled together into Moscow, where we parted at the
river port. I went to the embassy to try to get some news. At every
metro station and in many metro train cars, young people were dili-
gently posting an announcement from Yeltsin denouncing the coup and
calling for resistance. Crowds of subdued people strained to read the
document in all the places where it was posted, but I saw no signs of
real resistance. At the embassy there was little news. Americans were
not yet being advised to evacuate, but they were requested to file their
whereabouts immediately. Many American citizens were there filling
out registrations, last-minute documents for marriage to Soviet citizens, and official invitations for Soviet friends to visit them in the
United States.

I went to my office building and looked for my friend Zhenia, who
worked in the office next door. Raised on banned books and American

movies in the Brezhnev years, Zhenia is a communications engineer who also translates technical manuals and is involved in many international cooperation projects. I had often sought his advice on what we called "the Soviet soul." I felt badly in need of reassurance, but he was not around.

In my own office, I found my friend Tania in the room we share. She was relieved to find me, afraid that I had gone off on my own. We decided to depart together for Red Square to learn what was happening. On the tram, an older man heard us speaking in English. "Someone shut up the American monkey," he shouted. "We don't need her kind here anymore." The passengers stared at me in mute embarrassment. No one said anything to him. After we stepped off the tram, Tania said to me, "You see, some people are pleased. Today they feel that no one can touch them."

The square was surrounded by tanks and personnel carriers, and the large exhibition hall containing an exhibit about the Afghan War was being used to house troops and equipment. It too was heavily surrounded, but people crowded around the young soldiers, calling them "child" and asking them "Do you really intend to kill your own people?" I suddenly realized that the low rumble I was hearing was the sound of tanks in motion. It vibrated the street slightly, and left the same echo in my stomach as fireworks displays. In Manezh Square, people crowded to hear the announcements being shouted from bullhorns. Organizers of the resistance were standing on abandoned cars, urging everyone to go to the White House, the official building of the Russian Federation government, to help protect Yeltsin and the deputies who were inside.

We walked slowly, arriving at the White House at sunset, and watched the chaotic process of assembling barricades. A nearby construction site had been cannibalized, city buses strategically abandoned, and trolleybuses derailed. Crowds of people lurched frantically after the leaflets that were occasionally dropped from the upstairs floors. When it began to grow dark, Tania insisted that we leave, and we picked our way through the barricades toward the metro. As we left, I listened to an announcement asking people to return in shifts. A man stopped us on our way, inquiring about the situation at the White House. As Tania described the barricades, he said proudly, "Our trucks have been there all day." He was from the Mosfilm studio, one of many agencies that decided immediately where their loyalties lay in this crisis and just as quickly donated their share of state resources.

At home I cooked dinner while Tania called her parents in Leningrad. Tania's father, a retired military officer of high rank, had been pleased when the coup leaders seized control. "Father was always in charge," she said by way of apology. "He never felt what it was to be a cog in a machine—he always commanded the machine." We watched the news, which was followed by a press conference called by the eight leaders of the coup, and Tania translated their stock answers with a mixture of humor and rage. "This show is from a time we thought was behind us," she said. The press conference was followed by a ballet production of *Swan Lake*. Tania left my apartment before 11:00 P.M.

At midnight, I caught the metro train, just in time to make one transfer before the system closed. I had decided to go alone, with no one to worry about me. The train and all the stations were empty. I wondered if the line that connected with the White House would be closed for the curfew. I was relieved to find the October Station still open, but was immediately surrounded by a slightly drunk group of teenage boys, so-called Moscow hooligans. They realized I was foreign, and as they crowded around me making rude suggestions, I wondered what I expected to do for the resistance if I could not even effectively chase off teenagers.

By the time I arrived at the connecting platform, they were circled around me, dancing and shouting. Seeing my plight, an older and very severe looking man invited me to sit next to him. There was something familiar about his spare, intense look and manner, but I could not place it exactly. The hooligan boys seemed to afford him immediate respect, and after exchanging quiet words with him they rushed to make apologies to me.

He asked where I was headed.

"To the meeting," I said, and he was pleased.

"Let's go together. You are an American? But you speak Russian?"

"Yes, some," I replied, hoping I knew enough to maintain a conversation. I did not want to lose sight of him now that I had found someone confident.

He recognized my surname as Lithuanian, and introduced himself as Leonid Konstantinovich, a journalist who had covered the struggle in Lithuania. He showed me his latest work in *Literaturnaia gazeta*, one of the many newspapers that had been shut down that morning. Together with the now-subdued hooligans, we exited at the metro station closest to the White House. Ironically, the name of the station was Barrikadnaia, or "Place of the Barricades." It was an area where important battles had been fought during the Revolution of 1905. I remembered a memorial on the nearby 1905 Street which bears the words, "Cobblestones are the weapons of the proletariat."

As we approached the White House, I could see that the proletariat of 1991 was better armed. A construction crane had been commandeered and the barricades were now much higher than they had been, a tangle of concrete traffic barriers, metal scrap, and vehicles. People were milling about, building fires for warmth. "They won't help much," Leonid said, referring to the barricades and gesturing at a few small tanks trying maneuvers, "but they are vital for the spirit." Once we climbed the barricades, the boys went off in their own direction, and Leonid asked me what my plans were. I admitted that I had none, just that I wanted "to have stood with Russia."

August is already fall in Moscow, and the night was chilly. It was raining lightly. Leonid astonished me by inviting me into the building. "I don't know if we can do it, but let's try," he said.

We were still awaiting approval for entrance at 3:00 A.M. when we saw Yeltsin rush into the building. The crowd responded enthusiastically. The guards let us in shortly after Yeltsin. I had no press credentials, but Leonid kept saying to the guards, "She's not a journalist, she's a historian. Don't you think this is history?" He later confessed that "when I met you at the metro I understood how I would get into the building." His own credentials, from the Lithuanian parliament building, would not have been enough without a foreigner to give him the proper air of authority.

In the press room, an article about Leonid was passed around, and I then understood what had commanded the sudden respect of the young hooligans. Russians say that anyone who has served time in political prison is easily recognizable, that a certain look grows on a man if he "sits" for a long time. Leonid Konstantinovich wore that look proudly, and had even maintained a prison-style haircut. I am certain now that this unspoken credential, not my passport, had gained us access to the seat of the now-besieged government.

We toured the building with four members of the foreign press. People from many newspapers that had been shut down were camped out in the building, preparing one-page photocopies with their mastheads and news that they had gleaned from the foreign press. Radio Russia, closed by the putsch government, had moved into the building and was preparing its broadcasts for the morning. A young boy who spoke some English and who looked all of seventeen was managing the foreign press. I asked him why he was there. "I work here." He admitted humbly, "I always handle the press. It's just more interesting today than usual." He took us to the top floor to survey the crowd below, and apologized to the photographers that he could not permit them to open the windows.

Leonid interviewed the head of security for the building. At that time two agencies were providing their services—Aleks and Kolokol Security. Both were private security agencies, with a staff largely comprised of Afghan War veterans. They were busy with strategy, and paused only briefly to answer his questions. Then we made the acquaintance of People's Deputy Mostovoi, a member of the Human Rights Committee of the Supreme Soviet of the Russian Republic.

Deputy Mostovoi, who had come to the building as soon as he heard about the coup, did not want to discuss the putsch government or speculate about the future, but he seemed pleased to have an audience. While other deputies napped on their desks, he maintained a steady several-hour-long monologue for us, reviewing his life, his family, the history of perestroika, and how much hope he had for Yeltsin. He seemed to be trying to recall how he had come to this point in history.

I struggled to understand all his conversation, and wondered why he had the time to bother with us. It slowly dawned on me that the deputies, including Mostovoi, had plenty of time—all of them were virtual prisoners, with no way to leave safely. We had simply found a deputy with insomnia.

After a few hours Mostovoi was ordered by a stern secretary to get some rest, so Leonid and I went to the dining hall for a smoke. It was there I learned that Leonid had been imprisoned in 1986 for some articles he had written about political repression. He had served three years and two months in a political prison. He was released just in time to begin covering the early events in Lithuania. We discussed our plans for the morning. He suggested that, since the metro would open soon, I should go home for a while, then meet him back at Building Entrance No. 8, at either two, three, or four o'clock in the afternoon.

At 6:00 A.M. sharp, Radio Russia began blaring the little news they had over the building's loudspeakers, punctuated by the songs of the late Vladimir Vysotskii, a much-loved Dylan-style Russian folk singer. His whiskey-ruined, desperate voice was rousing the staff back to their tasks when I left.

At home, I was barraged with phone calls from the States, from Moscow friends, and from a friend who was on vacation in the Altai region. Everyone wanted to know what was going on. So did I. I slept for two hours and then went to British Air to change my airline tickets. I was scheduled to depart in four days for Japan and Hawaii, but I could not imagine leaving now. At the embassy I had heard an estimate that the situation would be resolved one way or another in two weeks. It was rather arbitrary, but it sounded right, so I canceled my tickets, planning to reschedule them in September. I wondered what I would be leaving behind when I returned to the university. The ticket agent was glad to have a seat freed up: Americans had not been ordered to evacuate, but most were in a hurry to leave.

Then I made my way back to the White House. One stop away from Barrikadnaia, I went to buy some food and cigarettes for Leonid. Here, people were behaving as if it were a normal day. The ubiquitous commercial kiosks were all open, selling everything from imported underwear and tennis shoes to crystal and ice cream. As usual, the line for underwear was short, the line for ice cream long. I wondered whether the city understood that it was under siege by the past. Then I spotted clusters of people reading the one-page notices that had been prepared by the Russian press-in-exile the night before. It gave me a little hope, but I could not understand why so few people were joining in the general strike called for by Yeltsin.

I got back to the White House at 3:15 P.M. A large crowd was departing. Yeltsin had just given his first public speech. One look made it clear that the situation had somehow become more serious. The crowd was much larger, security tighter, and the people more frenzied as they lunged for news flyers. I doubted that I would be able to get back into the building, but Leonid met me as promised and swept me past the guards. I asked him what he thought would happen that night. "Do you play chess?" he asked suddenly. I was taken aback, and stammered, "Not well." He went on : "But you understand. If you are a good player, and I play against you, Tereza, and I am also good, I can anticipate your moves. But if you begin to invent your own rules, then I'm a fool if I think I can anticipate anything: it isn't my game. And this isn't our game. We only wait."

Just before a scheduled 6:00 P.M. press conference, Vysotskii's singing was interrupted by a sudden order to evacuate all the women from
the building and for men to claim their gas masks from the second
floor. I stood in the entryway, undecided for several minutes. Many of
the secretaries were weeping as they left. Leonid offered little advice.
"It's dangerous, of course, and you should go, but if you want to stay
we can try to find a small gas mask." I wanted to stay, but when I
imagined trying to understand everything in an emergency with no
interpreter, I reluctantly left with most of the other women, and joined
the crowd outside.

After I left, Leonid tried to defend the rights of the handful of
women who insisted on staying, but he was soon evicted along with
them. After waiting several hours he finally succeeded in re-entering
the building to help Radio Russia with their broadcasts.

I wandered among the crowd, debating the merits of shouting,
"Comrades, I need an interpreter," but decided I would rather be
treated as a Russian among Russians. I saw an elderly man standing in
the rain with his Orthodox prayer beads. I wanted to send up a desperate prayer too, but it came out instead as an odd, silent, appeal to the
crowd—"Okay everybody, let's make God proud." Security forces
around the building were trying to bring everything quickly to order.
They created cordons of people with their arms linked, one immediately around the building, then a second to help with crowd control. The first cordon was men only, until they realized that there were
not enough large gas masks. Then women who could fit into the small-
est size gas masks also joined the first cordon. I ended up in the second
cordon, controlling access to a drive-in entrance. We were to prevent
people from entering unless they had one of four credentials: proper
documents, a badge identifying them as a People's Deputy, a military
uniform from Russia, or a weapons delivery. I felt a little hypocritical,
preventing entrance to a building where I had myself spent the night
with dubious credentials, but I wanted to contribute somehow, and this
was the task I had been assigned. The tension of this evening seemed
quite different from the incredulity of the night before. Crowd control
and security had become much more important.

My arms were linked with those of a full-bearded man named Aleksii (who recognized my accent and was greatly pleased to meet an
American) and an older woman who never introduced herself. Instead
she held my arm firmly and solemnly dedicated her attention to in-

specting documents. She was the classic model of a Russian grandmother, short and solid, applying all her considerable zeal to preventing people from entering. I have encountered many of her caste here in Moscow, but it was fascinating to witness a *babushka* applying those energies to the defense of Yeltsin. Sometime around 9:00 P.M. she disappeared into the crowd.

The number of people present was variously estimated as somewhere between 30,000 and 50,000. The security forces began recruiting men to join the Russian Army, and the crowd applauded as each new group of volunteers jogged by. They were of all ages, and some who had arrived at the White House directly from work were now jogging by in business suits, taking military instructions from the security guards and Afghan War veterans. As I dutifully inspected documents, I wondered what we would accomplish.

* * *

It rained intermittently, and as the sun set on the White House the sense of unease grew. Bolsheviks, so the Russians say, prefer to shoot at night. Two of the famous skyscrapers constructed by German prisoners of war stood over our shoulders like the ghost of Stalin. The barricades around the building had been improved, and the statue of triumphant Soviet youth that stood in the square had also been improved by the addition of a tricolor flag, symbol of the democratic opposition. Someone said that the U.S. Embassy, which was a block away, was also flying the tricolor flag. We could not see it from where we stood, but I hoped it was true. I had still not heard the official U.S. position on what was happening , and was terribly afraid that they were waffling. I thought about Tiananmen Square, and tried to summon all the reasons why this should be different. I wondered what I would do if a person standing near me was shot. For some reason, it seemed more frightening than the prospect that I might be shot.

The crowd would fall silent for each announcement, but there was little information. An aged colonel general (three-star general), veteran of the Great Patriotic War (World War II), assumed command of the newly assembled troops, and stood by himself in a cordoned area, splendidly attired in his full uniform and chest of medals, awaiting the tanks—expecting, perhaps, to order them to leave. Young soldiers defecting from the Soviet forces were admitted to meet with

Russian officers who had come over to Yeltsin's side. Cases of guns and ammunition—I never learned where they came from—streamed in through our entrance. People not standing in the cordons were clustered around small radios. As I waved another case of ammunition through the entrance, I suddenly realized that this was not going to be a slaughter of innocent protesters, but a war—perhaps a hopeless one, but a war.

I was a child during Martin Luther King's marches, and was raised with a profound respect for nonviolent protest. It would be easier for me to join a nonviolent protest, however doomed. I thought again about the question that had troubled me all morning, about civil war. I had to decide, for myself, whether I could "stand with Russia" even if it meant this. I decided to stand.

There was not much nobility in it, just a slow, deep and very Russian anger. All my connections to the USSR had been in the context of the reforms. It was because of them that I had changed my career and organized a student exchange to Soviet Georgia. When my students were invited, in 1988, to help destroy a decommissioned SAM missile outside Tbilisi for national TV, I had dearly hoped that it was not an empty gesture. Back in the States, I had gone on to graduate school and had begun to study Soviet politics.

And then I had come here, and somewhere amid the long lines, the "war of laws," and often incoherent change, two things had happened. I had really learned how fragile, yet how dear, were the hope and the freedom brought by the reforms; and this had become my home. It was my city: my friends who had risked their careers and lives in service of those dreams, my students who were studying to meet the challenges of their new world—and the putsch government dared to proclaim the death of all our hopes, the dreams on which we had all survived through the winter.

Three uniformed KGB officials arrived at our gate and we all fell nervously silent until they announced themselves "For Russia." The murmur "They're ours" rippled immediately through the crowd (to the Soviet mind, it was unimaginable that they would lie about such a thing). After a brief interrogation, our gate commander escorted them into the building. At around 11:00 P.M. we heard an announcement that Yazov, the Minister of Defense, had defected to Russia. A roar of cheering went up in the crowd. Even though the news later proved to be erroneous, it lifted everyone's spirits immensely. We all took a break, and *babushkas* appeared from all directions with *bliny,* bread with meat slices, tea and coffee. Cartons of cigarettes were passed around.

An American film crew was searching for someone who spoke English. Aleksii shouted to our organizers that I was an "Amerikanka." The young commander of our group was astonished. He summoned the film crew, who asked me what the news about Yazov meant. I speculated that a government that is trying to rule by force cannot survive if it loses its military commanders. My Russian comrades asked me to repeat what I had said, in Russian. "If Yazov is ours, it will be our Russia," I told them.

Some of us, myself included, thought it was all over then. Our commander, Igor, was anxious to take good care of the foreign "guest." He suggested that I have a rest in one of the many buses that were parked against the building. Soaked and exhausted, I agreed, and he promised to wake me when there was news.

I slept until 1:00 A.M., and awoke to the Radio Russia broadcast. But something was clearly wrong outside. The cordons had been reformed to keep people out of the roadway, and the loudspeakers were booming instructions. I came running out of the bus, and Igor found me. "The tanks are coming," he said. I was confused. "If Yazov is for us, why are the tanks still coming?" I asked. He looked grim. "Anarchy" was all he said. I wondered what it would feel like to be a nineteen-year-old in one of those tanks, "just following orders" to crash the barricades and come upon thousands of my own countrymen with their arms linked and their hearts resolved. I hoped it would be enough.

Defenses of the building were rearranged. Gauze and cotton makeshift gas masks were distributed. As groups of Afghan veterans took over securing the entrances, the whole crowd—no longer just those who were helping with crowd control—linked arms. Former Foreign Minister Eduard Shevardnadze hurried through, greeting the troops. Then we waited, and the rain drummed down. Five or six times an hour we would be called again into formation. The announcements said that one tank was coming, then that four were coming, maybe more; that they were thirty meters away. We heard the tank locations. I was expecting to hear the unmistakable sound I had learned to recognize the day before, the sound of tanks at close range. I knew that if we heard it here, all of our lives would be changed forever.

Ira, a bilingual employee of an international exhibition hall, was standing near me. I asked her what she had done on Monday. "I cried," she said. "Then I cleaned my apartment. My friends reminded me that it was the first time in seven years that my home was likely to be searched, so I came here instead."

I noticed many young people, and thought of my former student, Arkhil. His parents were at a conference in Italy, and he was supposed to be staying at his grandmother's house near the center of town, in an area now surrounded by tanks. I knew he had led a sheltered, privileged life. Was he all right? What did he think of this situation? I later learned he had spent the night standing not far from me. Arkhil bears the same name as his grandfather, a famous Soviet hero of World War II. He had taken his grandfather's antique rifle to the White House and stood on the barricades with the volunteer army. Arkhil is sixteen.

For a while I talked with a young Uzbek named Lyosha. An agricultural engineer, he had worked in Moscow for six years. His company holds several seats on the new Moscow stock exchange. Most of his colleagues were at the White House, discussing in quiet moments what effects the coup had on the world stock market. Lyosha was telling us about his two-month visit to the United States when he suddenly turned to me. "I don't understand you," he said in English. "Why are you here? It could be dangerous and these are not your problems." I disagreed. "I am a teacher of Soviet history and a student of international relations—of course these are my problems. If this can happen, it is problem for the whole world. It is a problem of civilization." "Yes, I see," he replied. But he seemed unconvinced, and all night, as we received new announcements of conflicting information, Lyosha would call to me from his place in line: "Are you afraid yet, Tereza?" We all were. We wondered what was happening in the rest of Moscow. From where we stood, we could not hear the shooting.

We stood until 5:30 A.M. As the sun rose over our soggy, exhausted crowd, everyone relaxed. In daylight, the threat seemed less plausible. Many of us would not know until much later how close the tanks had come: one was stranded on the barricades just outside the White House. At 5:30 A.M. Yeltsin announced that the danger had passed and that we could go home, although he encouraged us to observe the general strike and not go to work. No one was sure that victory had been won. Many people remained on the barricades for another full day. Arkhil remained on guard with his grandfather's gun for three days—until Yeltsin's team departed for the Crimea.

* * *

Those of us who left the White House early in the morning struggled to get information from the still-exiled press or from foreign news services. We discovered that Yazov had not defected to Russia, as we had heard, and that the coup leaders were still in power. We began trying to locate friends who had been lost in the past few days. When I found my teacher Natalia again, her coffee table was piled high with new books: Solzhenitsyn, Bulgakov, and all the great literary-political writers. Of the books she had selected, she said, "I never bought them, because they were expensive, and I could read them in the library. But now I have bought all the writers I love who will be banned again."

Katia, who had lived with me a few months before, found me as soon as I walked into my apartment. She begged me to find someone to smuggle to America some video film and photos taken during the previous night. "They have to understand what this is," she said. She believed that the resistance would be crushed by the putsch government. She explained that her film crew, which usually produces commercials and rock videos, had been filming since the coup began. A scriptwriter and production assistant, Katia had interviewed soldiers in their tanks, passersby, protesters at the barricades. Some time in the afternoon of the first day, their video equipment was seized. The crew managed to preserve some of the earlier film, and continued recording events using a photo camera.

On the second night, with only a photo camera, they had gone to the barricades on the Garden Ring Road, not far from the White House. Katia says the soldiers began shooting just after the flash from a crew member's camera managed to capture a photo of one tank aiming at the crowd. A boy who was standing next to her and the photographer and jeering at the tanks was shot. Katia was sick, and the crew rushed to pull her away. They all fought down their own hysteria and together the crew continued photographing all night. I promised to try and find someone to smuggle their film.

I spent the day trying to find a smuggler. Late in the afternoon, I stopped in at my office and finally found Zhenia, who had been searching for me for two days. From him, I learned that the putsch government had fled. I collapsed into a chair, laughing, crying, and confused. With part of our attention still on the radio, listening for further news, we compared stories of the past few days. "Why did you, of all people," he asked, smiling as he quoted from a favorite American Western, "try to save this miserable town?"

* * *

In Soviet tradition, even numbers of flowers are for sad occasions, odd numbers for celebration. People brought flowers in even numbers to the site where the young men died, and in both even and odd numbers to the barricades. The rest of the week was a celebration. Although it seemed to me that people of all ages had been at the White House, the city officials said that most of the defenders had been young. In their honor, there were fireworks and endless rock concerts. At the funeral for the three boys who died, I met an elderly woman. "I am so proud of our youth," she said. "I am a teacher, and I do not understand our boys today. But all of them, the good boys, the bad boys, the hooligans—they were there."

On the way to Moscow's international airport with Zhenia a week later, I spotted a famous monument depicting stylized fragments from an antitank barricade. It had been erected to commemorate the nearest point to the city that the Nazis had occupied in the Great Patriotic War. It is chillingly near, but I was stunned to think of how much closer the putsch government had come to occupying the capital city. Was it possible that they could have succeeded?

I shuddered, remembering that we had all believed it was possible. The personnel director of Zhenia's office had been so confident of a putsch victory that he had prepared a formal document denouncing many of our colleagues, including (I was told) Zhenia. One poll, taken before the outcome of the coup was certain, had indicated 56 percent support for the putsch government. Fearful of the temporary "attendance rules" instituted in offices, few people in Moscow had joined the general strike. Even Igor, the commander of my group at the White House, was careful to arrive at work on time, going directly from the White House defense groups to his construction-site job.

I asked Zhenia one last time about the state of the Soviet soul. "This gives us hope, of course," he said in reference to recent events. "But we are not finished. We have to continue. As Chekhov said, 'Every day I squeeze the slave out of myself, drop by drop.' A slave knows how to be a slave, and he can imagine how to be a master. But to learn to be a free man—that is the hardest lesson. It takes some time."

2 | Concerning the Defenders of the White House

Russian writer Aleksandr Prokhanov was one of the authors of "A Word to the People," a hard-line Communist-Nationalist manifesto that was published in Sovetskaia Rossiia *on the eve of the coup calling for strong measures to arrest the disintegration of the Soviet Union. He was interviewed by the newspaper* Komsomolskaia pravda *on September 3, 1991. Some months earlier, he had become the editor-in-chief of the premier ultranationalist, violently chauvinist newspaper,* Den.

Aleksandr Prokhanov told *Komsomolskaia pravda* that a state of emergency was still needed in order to curb the political and economic chaos that continued to engulf the Soviet Union. During the Emergency Committee's brief reign, Prokhanov had visited the White House, if only to observe. The biggest problem with the Emergency Committee—some of whose members he knew personally as great leaders and men of action—was its inability to act decisively and competently. A "circus" was how he qualified their activity, declaring it to be not the work of a few highly placed conspirators, but an impersonal "provocation staged by history itself"—an event inevitably attending the disintegration of a large empire. A real coup d'état, in his informed opinion (and he had just finished a book on the coup d'état in Afghanistan), "ought to have been carried out in a single night, with all the potential opponents rounded up and jailed and all the channels of communication cut." "Only after that," continued Prokhanov, "should the coup leaders have brought out into the streets the military hardware—in order to depress still further a population already

Defenders of the White House, Tuesday night

shocked and disoriented" by what had transpired during the night.
He went on:

"What has taken place is incomprehensible to me. It is beyond comprehension in general. Nobody stormed the Palace [the White House], special forces were taking a rest, and at the same time, orders were given to drag all the military hardware into the streets, which made people all excited, just as the bees get excited when a bear sticks his paw into a hive. And the people, who at first were frightened by this sight but soon found out that the soldiers did not have any ammunition, took a seat on the tanks, stuck flowers into the empty gun barrels, began to spoonfeed the soldiers, and within about four hours the army had completely lost its capacity to act. . . .

"I repeat: What has transpired appears to me as some sort of a satanic circus. Indeed, look what happened as a result of this quasi-conspiracy, under the tank treads of which three people perished: the movement for strengthening the state is completely routed. That is why I do not want to talk about this conspiracy. The courts will pass their judgment on that. What I want to talk about is the real coup d'état that was carried out under the cover of the quasi-conspiracy. . . . I am convinced that if the people involved had actually set out to do what they are being accused of, they would have completed the job. I still think that the general scheme according to which events unfolded did not include the use of violence. . . . The coup may have fizzled out even before the Committee's press conference. I suspect that something happened when General Varennikov and others flew to Foros [on the eve of the coup]—and *that something* does not fit into the scenario that is being fed to us right now."

Turning to the scene at the White House, Prokhanov divided the defenders into four categories.

"When I got there (though I was not planning to defend the White House), the first thing that struck me was the 'pop culture' atmosphere —some kind of a youth or rock revolution. It was the protest culture: students, hippies. It was Paris in 1968, with Sartre and Marcuse, the existentialists. And it seems to me that they were defending the romance of the situation: 'Tanks in the city, tanks in the city. . . .' The 'rock prophecy,' it seemed, was coming true.

"The second category was the people defending their own way of life. The 'perestroika segment,' as they are called, but actually the bourgeoisie, who had something to defend. If the Emergency Committee had triumphed, a number of cooperatives would, of course, have been destroyed; there might even have been expropriations. These were people threatened with eradication as a social class: people involved in joint ventures, members of cooperatives, and so forth. It was with great pleasure that I drank a bottle of Bavarian beer at the barricades and smoked a Camel cigarette, a treat from a defender of the White House who was standing next to me.

"Third, of course, there were a large number of women and girls there. Oh, that remarkable Muscovite femininity! Strange as it may be, even the women close to me, who know my hard-line views, made runs to the barricades with food for the little soldiers. That was the women's movement—in shock, struck with horror. But they were not those women of the barricades, the genie of the revolution, from Delacroix's paintings. They were the kind of women who were crying out, 'Thou shalt not kill! Stop! May the Lord protect you!'

"And the fourth, very active, segment: professional politicians who marched to the microphone, shift after shift, and directed the entire procedure."

3 | **Death on the Streets**

This account appeared in the Guardian, *a weekly newspaper for Moscow's foreign community, in an issue dated August 23, 1991. The author, Michael Hetzer, was editor-in-chief of the* Guardian.

I was standing atop a bus about 200 yards from the advancing tanks when the pop-pop of gunfire erupted in the early minutes of Wednesday morning. I thought someone was throwing firecrackers.

My miscalculation was a symptom of the prevailing mood. The entire rain-soaked night seemed unreal. Surreal.

I had already been at the building since 5:30 P.M. Tuesday. In the streets surrounding the Russian parliament building until the first shots were fired, women walked dogs, lovers strolled in tight embrace, groups of men passed vodka bottles while others munched on food from well-stocked picnic baskets. Under a steady rain, people huddled beneath umbrellas and clustered around radios tuned to the resistance's station, Radio Liberty. Young and old cheered when the news came that Prime Minister Valentin Pavlov was ill. They cheered when they heard that General Dmitrii Yazov also was ill. They cheered for every scrap of metal that was piled on their barricades, every call for unity in the speeches, and every rack of black bread that was carried into the parliament.

So when, at 12:05 A.M., I heard gunfire yet did not immediately dive for cover away from my vulnerable position, it was not out of bravery, but out of serious misreading of the situation.

Shortly after the first shots, word spread like a brushfire through the crowd of some 15,000 that tanks were on the Garden Ring Road and had already killed several people.

"They're expected to circle around and approach from along the embankment," said one of the organizers from his perch atop a rag-tag barricade near the Kutuzovskii Bridge, directly in front of the parliament building. "If you're here out of simple curiosity, now is the time to leave. All men should take up positions."

Thus began a systematic formation of row upon row of human chains. A disquieting hush fell over the people. They whispered to those around them. You could hear the scuffle of feet on the pavement and the hiss of rain drops splashing into the puddles.

At 12:10 A.M. more shots could be heard over the hill on the Ring Road. This time the sound, fast and regular, was unmistakably automatic gunfire.

"They're coming!" one woman cried. "The bastards are coming." Later there was another burst of gunfire and then several terrific explosions.

People held their positions, hand in hand, their eyes glued to the horizon. Would the tanks come across the bridge? Would they come along the embankment? Would they approach from Barrikadnaia metro station or along Kutuzov Prospect? Everyone expected the column of tanks to appear at any moment.

As it happened, the assault never came. The six tanks that provoked the violence hardly represented a serious attempt to take over the Russian parliament building. Rather, they were an example of the kind of spontaneous violence that can erupt any time so much weaponry is on the city streets.

Within a half-hour of the final gunshots I ventured up to the Garden Ring Road in the direction of the shots and witnessed the aftermath: a bloody spot on the asphalt where a demonstrator was crushed, a makeshift cross erected over the site, and a heated argument raging in an underpass between demonstrators and soldiers of four captured tanks about the terms of surrender.

According to eyewitness accounts, the six tanks had approached a line of demonstrators who had taken up positions along the Garden Ring Road near the U.S. Embassy. Two tanks advanced on the crowd, crushing two people. Angry demonstrators threw Molotov cocktails at the remaining tanks, whose drivers halted rather than killing more people. Fires burned atop the lead tank.

Finally, one driver opened his hatch and peeked out his head. A demonstrator who had climbed onto the tank tried to wrest the driver from the tank but was himself pulled inside. The soldiers opened fire.

The man inside the tank was killed, despite attempts by others to rescue him.

The rest of the evening stretched like an epilogue to these events. But for a few moments around 4:45 A.M., fifteen minutes before the end of the curfew, it seemed the feared main assault was coming. Suddenly, every streetlight along the Garden Ring Road went out and the roar of approaching tanks could be heard. Such a timed advance seemed to signal a serious assault. Demonstrators took up positions to block the vehicles.

Four armored personnel carriers approached the demonstrators and then halted. They idled a few moments and then turned and fled. A victory cry rose from the demonstrators.

The carriers had only been patrolling. And the extinguishing of the street lights was not part of an assault plan; it marked the coming of dawn. Somewhere along Moscow's Garden Ring Road an unseen electric eye had detected the first hint of coming daylight.

The long night was over.

4 | A Man in the Crowd

This account appeared in the popular weekly Ogonëk *(October 5–12, 1991). The name of the author was withheld by the magazine.*

On the morning of August 22 a young man came to our editorial offices with a stack of photographs and began to tell us about where he was during the coup and what he photographed. Unfortunately, the photographs were of poor quality, but his story seemed interesting to us—not as that of a fully objective witness of these tragic events (it is too personal for that, and indeed how could anyone *be* objective back then?)—but as an interesting example of the awakening of the civic consciousness in a man who was, in all respects, well adjusted.

—Alla Tsenina and Sergei Filippov

On Monday the 19th I walked over the bridge from the Hotel Ukraina to the White House. Everything there was unsteady somehow. There were not many people. Appeals were posted about. People were erecting barricades. It was evident that they were there of their own volition, without orders. Some vehicles were being deployed. On the bridge there was a column of troops, and people were speaking to the soldiers. Then I realized that they had convinced the soldiers, won them over. The column turned around and began to depart toward Kutuzovskii Prospect. And what can I do? I wondered.

There were four tanks over to the right, on the incline of the embankment. The first tank was No. 104. There was a major standing on top of it. His name was Sergei Vladimirovich Yevdokimov. He said that he was part of the Taman Division. We struck up a friendship. We shared the same first name and patronymic. I spent four hours with him. At times I would depart for a short while, but I always returned. And each time our conversation began with my asking him how he could go against the President of Russia, who in all our history had been the only one elected by universal suffrage. "I am not against the President, but I have my orders," he would reply. "I promise you that we will neither shoot nor mow down the Russian people. I do not even have live ammunition. But I cannot leave. Orders are orders."

"Sergei, you're taking a big risk," I responded. "Think about it: they'll take away your stripes. You see, history is happening right before our eyes . . . it's being created. You'll be a part of it. You can either go down with all of *them*—or go out a hero." He agreed. I then ran over to the White House and yelled out that there were some tanks that were ready to defect to our side. We had to back them up. Then a Deputy walked by—I don't remember his name. I quickly photographed him.

"How are you preparing to defend us?" I asked.

"The people of Moscow are preparing to defend themselves," he responded. "Look, there are some militia men over here with machine guns, and over there some boys from 'Aleks' [a security firm] are setting up defenses."

"But this is really not serious," I shot back. "They have no hardware."

"What do you propose?" he asked.

"If you give me permission," I said, "then I will bring some tanks over here right now." He liked my proposal but said that it needed to be discussed. He brought me over to Lieutenant Colonel Sergei Yushenkov, who is also a Deputy. I explained my idea to him. He, too, liked it very much. We then went to Rutskoi. Ultimately, Major Yevdokimov received a personal authorization from Yeltsin, and the tanks came over to the White House.

Soon the President began to issue mandates to the deputies, granting them special powers. These mandates were signed by Yeltsin personally and stamped with an official seal.

I approached a deputy. "Do you need help?" I asked.

"Yes," he replied, "do you have a group?"

"Yes, there are thousands of people right there outside."

"I don't need thousands, but I do need about fifty to go over to Moscow Echo. The radio station has gone off the air."

I went outside and ran into a group of Chechens who had come to defend Khasbulatov—well, Yeltsin too. (Before, I had not gotten along with them very well, but now I found them to be very agreeable.) I drafted fifty of them. "Wait here, I'll be right back," I told them. Then I joined the Deputy—whose name I don't remember but whose photograph I took—and together we brought the group over to the area where the zoo is, Krasnaia Presnia.

The deputy was a bit overwhelmed. "How are we going to get there?" he asked.

"Look," I told him, "you have a mandate signed by the President. Don't worry. Just give us orders and we'll take care of the rest."

The Deputy laughed. "Okay, I order you to secure some means of transportation!"

We blocked the road and stopped a city bus. The deputy presented the mandate to the driver. The driver wasn't impressed. "I'm at work," he said, "so go and . . . yourself."

This goes to show that we have ignorant people in our country. Perhaps he was not against us, but for whatever reason he failed to grasp the urgency of the situation. "I order you to obey!" shouted the Deputy. We then grabbed the driver by the arms and legs and carried him out of the bus. The driver grabbed his bag from the storage compartment and ran away.

I sat down at the steering wheel. We drove off. Over the microphone I made an announcement: "Attention, I've driven a bus only once before."

At the Moscow City Soviet we hooked up with some more deputies. I turned off the lights inside the bus, and no one even stopped us, even though we drove onto Red Square itself. However, we were not allowed to enter the radio station right away. First, we had to knock down the door. The militiamen who were guarding Moscow Echo resisted at first, but they backed down as soon as they saw the mandate signed by Yeltsin. We took up posts in the hall where the watchman has his station. Meanwhile, the deputies got in touch with the Minister of Communications and thirty minutes later received authorization to put the radio station back on the air. After that I returned to the White House.

By now everything was organized over at the White House. Groups of volunteers had been set up. Copying machines were spewing out leaflets. I joined others in distributing these from the balcony when I suddenly remembered that my car was still parked at the Hotel

Ukraina. "Let me take these leaflets and distribute them to the closest military units," I said.

I grabbed a large stack and left. I spoke with commanders everywhere and explained the situation. And still I had an entire stack of leaflets left over. Then I began to post them along the street, but I was arrested by the militia. I explained everything to them. They let me go, but said: "Don't post any more of those leaflets, or else you'll be arrested again—and next time you might not be released."

That night I was unable to sleep very much—maybe two or three hours.

The next day I again went to the White House, but now I could not get in, since a stringent security system had already been set up. Okay, I figured, I'll go do something out on the street. I stood there thinking for a while and then got a small group together. Valerii Borisovich Pinaev, Yurii Dmitrievich Zubkov, and some others joined me. We were together for almost the whole day. At about seven o'clock on the evening of the 20th we made a large flanking motion to inspect the approaches to the White House. Giant barricades were already being set up.

Valerii spoke up when we were near the U.S. Embassy in front of the tunnel on the Garden Ring Road. "Look, Sergei. There are no barricades here, but only some black Volgas that are blocking traffic. If tanks come through here now, these cars will separate and let them through." Recognizing the danger, we sped back to the White House. I explained the situation to some people. Soon everyone began to shout, and after gathering together a couple hundred people, we went over to the Garden Ring Road to build barricades. It started to rain heavily and we got soaked to the bone. The Garden Ring Road is wide, and we did not have many people. By now all the black Volgas had disappeared without a trace. We worked so fast we had not noticed anything. I remember that at one point a bread truck zoomed up and the driver told us that tanks were coming toward us from the direction of the Paveletskii Train Station. Several people ran back to the White House to get reinforcements. Our hands were already shaking from work—we were afraid we would not finish. So we began simply to flag down trucks that were passing by.

Drivers who refused to cooperate were forcibly removed from their vehicles, which were then incorporated into the barricade. We deployed a KamAZ truck, two Intourist "Icarus" tour buses, and a ZIL stretch limousine. A column of street-cleaning trucks approached. They pulled over to the side. Some moments later, the tanks appeared.

[The incident that follows took place soon after midnight on Wednesday, August 21.]

Two or three thousand people linked their arms together. Everybody was lined up in a row that stretched across the width of the Garden Ring Road. The row was not single-file—rather, it was quite deep. The tanks approached in a column. They came right up to the crowd and halted. Some women ran up to them and shouted: "Stop!" Suddenly, machine guns started to fire. My memory is a bit foggy, but at this point there was some kind of surge in the crowd as about 150 people threw themselves in front of the tanks. "What the hell are you doing?!" someone shouted. I don't remember what I did exactly, except that I was swearing a lot, and I grabbed at the machine gun of the tank driver, who climbed up to the turret. But once he shot from under my armpit, I quickly came to my senses. I immediately jumped back, and off the tank. The crowd, too, was dispersing. "Everyone form lines!" someone shouted. The soldiers on the tanks kept firing into the air. But we were already drawing back into formation and linking arms. Then, once again, the tanks descended upon us.

It was a miracle that so many of us managed to get out from under the tracks of the tanks. We stood our ground until the end, hoping that they would stop. In single file, pushing relentlessly forward, the column of tanks pounded away at our defenses like a battering ram—and then moved on forward into the underpass to shatter our barricade of trolleybuses. Boy, I thought, if only we could stop them there. At this point the drivers of the ZIL street-cleaning trucks—which were parked on the other side—drove their vehicles over to the tunnel and blocked the exit. The small tanks were already ramming the trolleybuses, whose wheel-bases were lowered. A tank rammed one trolleybus, started to crush it, and almost made it over the top—but in the end could not move it out of the way. Two vehicles went over to the side; one of them tried to break through the barrier from the left, but got trapped. People immediately ran in that direction from left and right. At the same time, one of the armored vehicles cut through one or two trolleybuses and got stuck in the center. The armored personnel carrier—it was No. 536—had hardly run over one of the trolleybuses, however, when it began to descend upon some people, leaving victims in its wake. But we had already figured out that they were shooting into the air and not directly at the people, and so a bunch of hotheads jumped down [from the sides of the underpass] onto the tanks. I was really impressed by a man who was carrying a megaphone; he was about forty-five years old. It was purely on his account that two of the small tanks came to a halt. While everyone else was hiding, he stood on the underpass wall, directly under the barrels of the machine guns, screaming: "Shoot me, I have children just like you, but shoot, I'm not afraid, all of us are unarmed out here."

Just then vehicle No. 536 destroyed a trolleybus, fired shots, and descended upon some people. One of the boys opened a back door and tried to get to the crew for negotiations—for which he received a bullet in the forehead. The tank dragged him back and forth for five minutes. Someone eventually tried to pull the body out and stick a beam or a bar in the track of the vehicle. This person also got trapped and crushed, I think. On the other side, a woman screamed: from the other side she must have gotten crushed, too. [This last conjecture proved to be incorrect.]

I was also really impressed by the driver of the MAZ crane truck. He was a very brave man: with a single motion he cut through to the trolleybus that the tank had moved aside and turned it around, shoving it back in place and blocking the passage. He did this several times. The people below, in the underpass, were getting mad: they were being killed, and there was nothing they could do about it. Of course, the guys began to react—they threw stones, branches, and Molotov cocktails. Naturally, they aimed especially at No. 536—which burst into flames and continued to thrash about. The men threw a tarpaulin over it and one guy even sat down on it. The kid who sat down on the tarpaulin perished, I think.

I recall that there was an army major who was running around and worrying about what might happen to people. When the tank caught fire, he yelled out that there might be live ammunition that could explode, in which case a lot of people could die. It turned out that he was right. There was a complete set of ammunition in the vehicle. A shell had been loaded into the breach. The crew members jumped out and then fought the fire on their tank. We then extinguished the fire. At this point their officer, a major, a very strong man, snatched a machine gun from a soldier, released a few rounds into the air, pushed his way through the crowd, and ran off somewhere in the direction of the Kremlin.

The tanks that had suddenly halted went in reverse and moved back into the underpass tunnel to protect themselves from the stones and Molotov cocktails. The soldiers stood ready with their machine guns. They understood they had done something terrible and stood there like cornered wolf cubs. And if the people had moved any closer—many of them saw the casualties and were shouting "Death to them!"—there would have been many more victims. At this point the major who had warned us earlier about the explosives started talking and calming everyone down. Then some deputies showed up. Negotiations for surrender began. Finally, the soldiers came out of the armored vehicles wearing their [special forces] berets, medals, and decorations. They departed in formation. And they were not that young, either; they were twenty or more years of age.

I don't remember how the night ended. At seven in the morning I went to bed and around noon I was back at the White House. Again someone was making a speech about something. And I sensed that victory was ours.

5 | **On the Barricades**

Dr. Aleksei Kozhevnikov of the Institute for the History of Science and Technology in Moscow wrote the following account—in English—to a friend in Berkeley, California, on August 22. He sent it by electronic mail and it was published in the Daily Californian.

The general situation is the following. Muscovites are defending the huge building of the Russian parliament right near the American Embassy. There are many politicians inside who organize the opposition, including Yeltsin, members of two parliaments—Soviet and Russian—and others. The first night there were about 10,000 people around the building. Yesterday noon there was a large rally with maybe 300,000 people if not more. And last night probably more than 50,000 were constantly staying in defense. Half of them were highly organized: they were divided into detachments and stood in lines close to each other around the walls and on the nearest barricades. Another half were sitting or moving around. There are many armored vehicles in various parts of Moscow. They move in complicated ways and no one, at least outside the building, understands clearly the military situation.

The radio announcements and rumors are contradictory and not very reliable. Soldiers, when spoken to, do not express readiness to fight with people. Most probably, some troops refused to fight and left the city, but new ones are coming. Two small detachments of tanks and armored vehicles came to the building to help in defense. Besides these places with troops—some blocks in the center of the city and around the parliament building—the rest of the city is quiet and ordinary life goes on. Although a curfew was proclaimed, it is not respected at all.

I stayed in the defense line the first night. The second night I went around carrying a placard with a call to soldiers for fraternization. The idea was to meet possible troops earlier and speak to them—everybody was expecting a confrontation this night—even before they reached the major defenses. It turned out that this night [Tuesday, August 20] there were relatively few troops in Moscow, since many left the city in the evening.

I guess that the small battle that took place happened unintentionally at about 1:00 A.M. A small detachment of armored vehicles most probably was not trying to storm the building, but was passing by via Tchaikovsky Street (the one with the American Embassy), about 300 meters from the parliament building. There were barricades on this street at the two entrances of the tunnel. Some vehicles were stopped peacefully (I saw two, maybe there were a few more). Five of them decided to pass through and they got into the tunnel rather easily. I did not watch this, but reportedly there was some shooting into the air. The second barricade was larger. There were some trolleys across the tunnel entrance, and finally the vehicles could not make a hole in it and they were blocked inside. They stopped at a place, about a hundred meters long, with the tunnel entrance at one end, the barricade at the other, and walls (one to five meters high) on their left and right sides.

About three hundred people, including myself, rushed to the place where they heard shooting. When I came close, five vehicles were near the barricade and about two dozen people came down close to them. The soldiers were not very aggressive. In three vehicles they opened the hatches and looked out from them so that the people could speak to them. The defenders who came to the barricades were not an organized detachment but a kind of crowd. Some people behaved peacefully. I too came down to the vehicles with my placard and spoke to the soldiers. Some others (mostly teenagers) were excited and psychologically ready to fight, and their words and gestures may have looked aggressive and unpleasant to the soldiers.

Things quickly became more dangerous when one of the vehicles with closed hatches began to move, actively trying to throw off a man or two who stood on its armored top. A dozen boys were running around it, evading its wheels and attacking its armor, although the most serious weapons they had were iron and wooden sticks.

I climbed up on the wall. Probably a minute after this one of the boys was shot. He was attacking (probably without any weapon) the vehicle from its rear; he came in contact with it, its door opened (probably from inside), and someone shot him to death at point blank range. He fell so that half of the body was inside the vehicle and the feet dragged on the ground. The vehicle continued moving back and forth, people were still attacking it, and those standing on the walls started screaming "Murderers!"

After a minute the boys picked up the body, which had fallen out. The vehicle was hitting the barricade, trying to make a hole in it; a trolley was crashed, but still it could not make a hole large enough to escape. Some reported later that it crushed two more people. I could not see this from where I stood, but there was a great danger and a real possibility for this.

Other vehicles stayed quiet, but there was general hysteria. A soldier from one of them ran out and raised his hands, appealing to the people and apologizing. From the walls people threw stones and sticks at the aggressive vehicles; then they took some gas from a car on the street and started throwing bottles of it. The vehicle began to burn on its top. It was shooting from the machine gun into the air. I could do nothing more with my placard and left the place when the vehicle began to burn.

Finally, two vehicles went back into the tunnel, where the people could not attack them from the walls above. Soldiers from three other vehicles surrendered with them and left their vehicles in the hands of the boys. Probably there were no more victims. When I visited that place an hour later, several members of parliament and a general who organized the defense of the building were there and they were negotiating with the soldiers. The situation had cooled down a bit, and even the excited teenagers were helping to introduce some order.

But we were still expecting the general attack on the building, first at 2:00 A.M., then at 4:00 A.M., and I moved back closer to the major defense lines. The night came to an end quietly, although several times there were announcements about approaching troops. At 6:00 A.M. I returned home.

The present situation is unclear. The military made some more dangerous announcements on the official radio station. There are also rumors that the situation has improved greatly and that the plotters either escaped or were arrested. Anyway, there will be reason for me to go to the [parliament] building this evening. It is 4:00 P.M. now, the rain has stopped, and I am finishing this letter and going out.

P.S. I was informed that your letter to me of August 20 arrived. I have not read it yet. We—at least those who take an active interest in the events—have much information, including the leaflets, orders (both official and oppositional), free radio service (irregular), and free newspapers in the form of leaflets. The strangest thing is how easily and naturally people find themselves feeling and acting in the historical situation. As if it is ordinary life.

6 | **In and Around the White House**

*Viktor Sheinis was a Deputy of the Supreme Soviet of the Russian
Federation and a key member of its Constitutional Oversight
Committee. He serves on the Council of Representatives of the
Democratic Russia Movement. Before entering politics during
perestroika, Sheinis had a career in academic research in the area of
economics and political economy. Alla Nazimova is a well-known
labor sociologist. Like her husband, she is an active member of
Democratic Russia. Nazimova and Sheinis were interviewed by
Gregory Freidin in Berkeley, California, in January 1992.*

Freidin: When did you first hear about the coup and what was your
initial reaction?

Sheinis: I received a call from a young man who worked, among
other places, for *Nezavisimaia gazeta* and Radio Liberty, Misha
Sokolov. He woke me up. It was about 7:00 A.M. He asked me if I was
aware of the latest news. There had been plenty of news lately, and I
try to keep up, so I said cautiously: "Yes, I know the latest news."

"And what is your reaction?" he asked.

"Could you more specific?" I parried. And that is when he told me
what had actually happened that morning.

Right away, we turned on the radio and television, and also tried to
listen to the foreign broadcasts. We heard the official announcements.
Then we tried to tune in our favorite radio station, Moscow Echo, but
by that time it had already been forced off the air.

Freidin: What was your schedule on Monday? Whom did you
see, what did you do, what actions did you try to undertake? Let's

start with the schedule. When did you begin to act?

Sheinis: Naturally, the events made a complete mess of my schedule. If I recall correctly, some Supreme Soviet committee on which I had the honor of serving was scheduled to meet at the White House that morning at 11:00. What other plans I had I can't recall, but naturally, the events canceled them all, and I made my way to the White House with all possible haste. I arrived there close to 9:00 A.M.

Freidin: What was the mood of the people around you? Your own reaction?

Sheinis: I must say that I was in my worst mood from about 7:00 A.M., when I found out about it, until about 11:00 A.M., when the Presidium of the Supreme Soviet went into session. There I saw that we were prepared to resist. We took a rather uncompromising stand. From that point on and throughout the crisis, I don't think I experienced again any depression or sense of catastrophe.

Freidin: Could you be more precise about the sense of foreboding— or, as you put it, catastrophe—that you had before that session of the Presidium? What was your greatest worry?

Sheinis: The greatest worries had to do with our historical experience, especially the invasion of Czechoslovakia in 1968, Poland in 1981. I knew what happened there very well. I was afraid that the next step would be the dissolution of Russia's parliament; Russia's government would cease to function, and the people associated with the democratic movement, including Yeltsin, would be interned. I suspected we were dealing with rather conservative people who tend to follow the tried and true methods of the past. In my mind then, the most likely outcome was the Polish scenario of 1981.*

Freidin: Did you think about the outbreak of violence on a large scale, the possibility of civil war? That was my biggest worry that morning.

Sheinis: No, I was not thinking about civil war. My question was: will we be capable of organizing passive resistance on a large enough scale? In Poland, they failed to organize something really effective, even though in the first days of martial law there, it seemed that the

---

*That is, introduction of martial law.

government might be willing to make concessions. I was almost sure that the democratic leadership would be neutralized. That was a matter of common sense. From that point on the question would be: would the society, deprived of its democratic leadership, be capable of acting on its own?

Freidin: Do you know anything about the reaction of your neighbors?
Sheinis: No. At that time, I did not yet have an opportunity to discuss the events with neighbors.

Freidin: What about your family?
Nazimova: In the political sense, we represent a typical *politicized* family. We saw eye to eye as far as the events were concerned and did not have much of a discussion. I had to feed my husband, see him off, and rush to my office. At that time, I was in the middle of my brief stint at the Union of Journalists, on the Committee for the Defense of Freedom of Speech. That's where I was going then. But first, I'd like to tell you about the reaction of our neighbors.

I must say that, living in a huge apartment building like ours, one does not know one's neighbors. I don't even know all the neighbors who live on our floor. Quite unexpectedly, right after the latest news on the radio, our doorbell began to ring. Apparently, our neighbors knew more about us than we did about them. Right away we had three neighbors at our door, offering their telephone numbers and other co-ordinates, saying: "If you have any trouble, please come to us. You can stay with us for as long as you need, and if there is anything we can help you with, all you need to do is say the word." They also came in the evening—just to check that we were all right. I was really struck by this, because before we might have said hello to each other and that was all. That's the kind of life we lead—too busy.

Freidin: What kind of people were they? Professionals? Academics?
Nazimova: Not really. One was a kind of rank-and-file engineer. The other was a single mother raising two teenage daughters, with great difficulties. But the third—true—was an old friend and colleague of ours. The first two were a real surprise for me.

Freidin: They were all women?
Nazimova: Yes, these were women. But I think the reason was that

their men, by that time, may have already gone to work. Besides, women are much more social, it's easier for them to make contact.

Now what happened at my work. It was 9:00 A.M. or so. I met my colleagues, and all of us had pretty much the same reaction. We were very upset. But soon I learned crucial information, namely that Yeltsin, Khasbulatov, Rutskoi, and Silaev had already prepared a public statement, that this statement was absolutely uncompromising, that they were on their way to the White House, and that they had been able to escape detention and were about to arrive at the White House. The mood changed as soon as we received this information.

Freidin: But what were people saying before that? Was there any cynicism?

Sheinis: No, absolutely not. But, of course, I was surrounded by the deputies who were close to me in spirit and in political outlook. Broadly speaking, the mood was to resist.

Freidin: Were there any specific plans to mount resistance?

Sheinis: Specific plans? No, we had none—nothing concrete. To my knowledge, some plans appeared only toward the end of the day on the 19.

Nazimova: When I arrived at the Journalists' Union, I started calling the Supreme Soviet to find out the latest news. When I first got there, Sasha Gutiontov—you know the columnist from *Izvestiia* and also the chairman of my committee—ran into my office and told me that Yeltsin's press conference had been scheduled for ten o'clock. He rushed there. Viktor called me right after the Yeltsin press conference and dictated to me the text of Yeltsin's statement. I typed it up and called my former employer, the Institute for the Study of the International Labor Movement. My old colleague copied it right away and pasted copies on walls. There was sort of a sense of a shared resolve, an unwillingness to return to what we had had before [before perestroika]. Perhaps the reason for this is that most employees of the Institute were pretty much of the same generation, people in their forties and fifties. We all remembered very well the times when we had to live under the iron heel, so to speak. Nobody wanted to return to those times.

Now a few words about the director of the institute, Timofeev. He submitted to the instructions issued by the Academy of Sciences to have all employees report to their offices and rigorously to check attendance in order to prevent people from going to the White House. So the bosses turned out to be real scoundrels.

Freidin: I have this question. Both of you are quite well-known public figures; your address is known. I am sure your names were on the list of those to be arrested. . . .

Nazimova: Yes. Viktor was number thirty.

Freidin: If I were in your shoes, I would have left home immediately —even before breakfast. Why didn't you? Was it resignation before the inevitable?

Nazimova: I understood that this might happen to Viktor. That's why I felt I had to feed him a good breakfast. Of course we understood that the risk was there. When we left home, we tried to figure out if we were being followed.

Sheinis: I don't know how to explain it. But I had no sensation of fear or imminent personal danger during those three days.

Freidin: But you said earlier that you felt real despair when you first heard the news.

Nazimova: Yes, at first, there was the sense of defeat; we felt defeated and vulnerable. The sense was: it's all over.

Freidin: You felt exposed?

Sheinis: I was thinking to myself: Damn it! We're not prepared— just like the leaders of Solidarity, or like Alexander Dubcek and company!

Nazimova: Let me add something. Before the events, we often said —especially after what happened in Vilnius—that we must have all the addresses and telephone numbers, especially the addresses, because phones might be cut. And I remember my first thought, too, was: Damn it. I don't even have any addresses where I can get help, except for two or three friends! We were just never organized enough to do this. Unfortunately, Democratic Russia does not have a regular procedure for this sort of thing.

As for the tanks, here's a story for you. The Committee for the Defense of Free Speech, where I worked, is situated on the Garden Ring Road, next to the Press Center. And that complex of buildings was surrounded by tanks. Besides, the Garden Ring Road is the biggest parkway in the center of the city, so there were columns and columns of them moving in front of our building. I was looking out a third-floor window at a huge armored turtle parked below. The soldiers were getting out of the hatches very cautiously and apprehensively, almost furtively. All of us, myself and my coworkers, were simply glued to the windows—this sight was so unusual for us.

Freidin: Can you say something about the coordination of activity among the demonstrators who surrounded the White House? Did the White House have a hand in it? Let me elaborate on my question. When I drove by the White House at 10:30 that morning, the perimeter of the building was empty—I asked the cab driver to drive around it. Then we drove on to the Minsk Highway, and that is where we met a column of tanks. I remember I counted over 150 tanks and armored vehicles, then gave up. I was en route to Peredelkino at the time. When I returned to the White House at around two o'clock or so, I noticed that some people from the White House were giving some kind of instructions to the demonstrators.

Sheinis: I don't know whether there were instructions or not. But I can attest to the fact that Aleksandr Vladimirovich Rutskoi had a personal role in the goings on around the White House. I could see him coming out of the White House into the inner courtyard and also to the outside. I could see that he was giving instructions to individuals, speaking to people. I myself walked out of the White House on a few occasions to talk to the Muscovites who gathered there.

Freidin: When, approximately?

Sheinis: Later in the afternoon of the first day. I remember it was drizzling, and people were holding umbrellas over me, asking questions. They were asking me about what was going on in the White House. People would say: "How come we don't have copies of the government statements?" They meant the first statement by Yeltsin and the appeals signed by Yeltsin, Khasbulatov, and Silaev. I went back to the White House then and knocked on all the doors, asking people to turn on all the photocopy machines in the White House to make more copies. Later on, I myself took stacks of those copies outside, and people would snap them up in a matter of seconds.

Nazimova: And they would circulate them widely. . . .

Freidin: I'm sorry I did not bring my own copy of the leaflet for your autograph. But you were going to say something about what was happening earlier.

Sheinis: Actually, it was about the session of the Presidium of the Supreme Soviet, which began at 11:00 A.M. The committee meeting I was supposed to participate in that morning—I recall now that it was the Committee on the Union Treaty—did not take place, understandably.

The session of the Presidium lasted for about an hour and a half. At a certain point, we began to discuss the text of the statement to be issued by the Presidium. The draft was composed by Volodia Lukin.* The discussion dragged on and on, and I was beginning to get irritated at the growing number of amendments and reformulations and so on. It was not the time to be indulging in niceties. I took the floor and said: "Respected citizens, we are sitting here and discussing fine points, but the situation may change any moment and we will have to declare, following Mirabeau, that we are here because of the will of the people and we will surrender only at the point of the bayonet." I cannot say that my appeal impressed my colleagues that much. What I was suggesting specifically was that it was incumbent on us to think about the measures we would undertake if the forces of the new order took the White House by storm. I understood that to discuss these matters at the session of the Presidium, attended by a lot of people, might not have been altogether appropriate. But we were losing time, valuable time! And I felt that we did not have the luxury to be arguing about the style of the statement.

As soon as the session was over, I called Alla and dictated the statement to her, and then I called my own institute, IMEMO [Institute of Foreign Economies and International Relations]. I called the director —his name is Martynov—with whom I had had a number of disagreements. Nevertheless, Martynov was a liberal, a man who unambiguously followed Gorbachev's course. This is why, incidentally, he was elected to the Communist Party Central Committee at the [Twenty-eighth] Congress, which you yourself attended. And although I did not think he was a man of great influence, I still tried to use our association to find common language between the Russian government and the segment of the Central Committee that was faithful to Gorbachev and was unlikely to support the putschists.

---

*Vladimir Lukin, later named Russia's Ambassador to the United States.

I got his secretary first and after some delay she connected me to Martynov. The conversation was rather brief. There is a psychological story here. For the first time in my life, and perhaps for the last time, I was speaking with a man who was so shaken, so disoriented, so helpless, so discombobulated by what was going on. . . . Naturally, he did not support the coup. I gave him the most essential information about the session of the Presidium. My criterion for selecting the pertinent information was the Hradczany Congress of 1968.* So I said to him: "The session of the Supreme Soviet [of the Russian Federation] is called for the day after tomorrow."

He responded: "But they will not let you hold it."

At the end of our conversation I promised that I would come to the Institute as soon as I found the time and consult with my colleagues on the course of further action.† This is one of a very small number of my promises that I have not been able to keep, and to this day, I regret breaking it.

Freidin: You left the White House on several occasions. Could you tell me what the people in the White House thought about the people around the building.

Sheinis: I can't speak for everybody. I am sure—in fact, I know—that very early on certain security measures were taken and a security force was established. Military school cadets were invited to join the security forces, and so were the more reliable elements of the Ministry of the Internal Affairs. Soon General Kobets took command and was able to activate his wide network of colleagues in the military. But this was on the periphery of my vision, at least, during the first few hours. I was then preoccupied—together with other members of the Constitutional Committee who were present—with drafting the document prepared by Valerii Zorkin. Now he is the chairman of our Constitutional Court, but at that time he was merely a Soviet professor serving as an expert for our committee. In juridical terms, the text was very powerful, demonstrating that the actions of the putschists were unconstitutional. As soon as the text was ready, we all signed it and had it copied and distributed at once.

---

*Reference is to an underground congress of the Czechoslovak Communist Party after the country was invaded by the Warsaw Pact armies.

†Sheinis had been nominated by his Institute for a seat in Russia's parliament.

Freidin: Let me reformulate my question. Did you feel inspired by what was going on outside the White House, all that public support?

Sheinis: You know this is a crucial, if not *the* crucial, question. I think I would be exaggerating if I were to say that what was going on outside in any way influenced what was going on inside the White House. We had very little information. One thing I can say is that it was decided at one point to send [delegations of deputies] to the factories. But there was no follow-up and nothing was appropriately organized. Toward the evening, another decision was made: to send deputies to the army regiments to discuss what was going on with the military. And that evening, the deputies I know well, those associated with the Constitutional Committee, all went to the regiments.

Freidin: You were already visiting the garrison on Monday night?
Sheinis: Yes.

Freidin: I thought that was happening on Tuesday.
Sheinis: I did it on Tuesday as well. On Tuesday, actually, I spent most of the day going from one regiment to another.

Freidin: Can you tell me a little about the call for a mass rally for Tuesday as well as the call for a general strike, which I remember was issued at a certain point on Monday. Did you have anything to do with these decisions?
Sheinis: It became clear already on Monday night that there was no general strike.

Freidin: I was outside the White House while the issue of the general strike was being debated inside. From time to time, someone would come out of the White House to tell the crowd who was taking what position.
Sheinis: If you have in mind the session of the Presidium, it took place in the morning, beginning at 11:00 A.M.

Freidin: I was there outside the White House by early afternoon, and I remember distinctly people coming out of the White House and announcing that so-and-so took such-and-such a position regarding the general strike. I think that even some form of minutes, too, was being distributed. I think this was around 2:00 P.M. on Monday.

Sheinis: You are right, but it was not the Presidium session. Deputies were meeting regularly throughout the day. This was taking place in the Circular Hall, which is not the largest auditorium, and as I recall, it was not filled to capacity. There were about one hundred to two hundred people sitting there at any one time. People were coming and going. Not all of them were deputies—some were assistants, experts, and so on. There, it is true, issues were debated nonstop. That was also the place where important information was being made public as it was arriving in the White House. The person who played perhaps the most important role in the collection and distribution of information was Sergei Filatov, now the First Deputy Chairman of the Supreme Soviet, who was at that time the Secretary of the Supreme Soviet Presidium.

Nazimova: I must interject here. It has to be admitted that communication between the White House and Moscow public was very poor. The radio station Moscow Echo was not broadcasting properly. People did not know what they should be doing. When on Monday evening I came home after all my daily labors, I had no idea what needed to be done. I called Viktor at the Supreme Soviet. The phone was answered by Viktor's colleague, Volkov, who said, "Everyone should come to the White House, because there is a chance that the building will be stormed."

Freidin: When was that?

Nazimova: Between 7:00 and 8:00 P.M. I called everybody I could. I knew a lot of people. At my former Institute, I was the chief organizer of the Democratic Russia Movement. I had a list of all the telephone numbers, so I called a lot of people. Many came, and we all spent the night outside the White House.

Freidin: Were there any delegations sent to the factories after the call for a general strike was issued?

Sheinis: I don't know whether anything was done or not, but if it was, the numbers were not very significant.

Freidin: Did you participate in the discussion of the question of general strike? What were the arguments pro and con?

Sheinis: If there were any, I did not participate in them. What I can remember as far as the issue of the strike is concerned was the feeling of deep disappointment that the general strike was simply not working out. Of course, we were getting reports that at one factory or another outside Moscow people went on strike or put up demands, and that miners struck somewhere. I had no opportunity to verify these reports subsequently, but I believe that many of them would not have checked out. But the fact that Moscow was not striking was completely clear to me by the evening of the 19th. The call for a general strike was unanswered, had no effect.

Freidin: Why was it that it had no effect?
Sheinis: There are profound reasons for this.

Freidin: But let us limit ourselves to those days. What did you think then?
Sheinis: First of all, it had no effect because we had no organization at the factories. Democratic Russia learned to do two things: to mobilize huge masses of people to take part in a demonstration, and to campaign for candidates in elections.
Nazimova: In fact, it was one and the same organization—the people in charge of election campaigns were the same people who mobilized for the demonstrations. Our organizations, the voter clubs, were set up in the election precincts, around residential areas, not at places of work.

Freidin: Very interesting. There were a few hotheads in the crowd outside the White House calling on people to arm themselves, and I had a feeling that the audience was not entirely unreceptive. My impression then was that at a certain point, after the White House had made a decision not to use violence (if indeed such a decision was made), those hotheads disappeared.
Nazimova: Well, I can answer this question, because I was making my rounds outside the White House on Monday evening. Young men in their mid-twenties were walking around in the crowd asking people to give up their stashes of Molotov cocktails to have them stored in a safe place—to avoid a possible provocation. I even remember the place they used to collect that stuff—at the right wing of the White House.
Sheinis: I, too, was appealing to people with the same request, but I have a very soft voice and, lacking a bullhorn, I don't think I was heard by more than a hundred people.

Freidin: I recall that even the White House did not have a public address system.

Nazimova: True. They got one set up only late on Tuesday evening.

Freidin: Did you hear or watch the press conference of the Emergency Committee?

Sheinis: First, I heard about it. I was on my way to the regiments at that time. But I watched it early on Tuesday morning when it was being rebroadcast.

Freidin: Could you tell me what was taking place in the regiments? I am especially interested in, first, the mood among the officer corps, and second, how they explained to themselves what they were doing. And who were the deputies who went with you?

Sheinis: I don't remember exactly, but, say, on Tuesday, at one time, I was with Bella Denisenko, at another, with Aleksei Surkov, then with Sergei Yushenkov, and then with Nelazov, a teacher. There were also some deputies from the Moscow Soviet. I just don't remember their names now.

Freidin: What regiments did you visit on Monday?

Sheinis: On Monday, late in the evening, I went to the Supreme Soviet Military Academy.

Freidin: What kind of an academy is that?

Sheinis: That's just the name. It is situated somewhere close to the Outer Ring Road. Then, following that, in the early hours of the morning, I went to the Ostankino TV Tower where a regiment surrounded the Television Center.

A small detail. In the evening, when we left the White House by car, the building was already pretty much surrounded by the barricades, and cars had real trouble getting out of there. On Tuesday, one could no longer drive out of the White House. Cars were parked outside the Krasnopresnenskaia metro station.

Freidin: How did the officers explain to themselves what they were doing? Say, those around the Ostankino TV Tower?

Sheinis: Let me start with the Military Academy. There I encountered the same kind of feeling of disorientation that I had earlier seen in Director Martynov. Except that the military understood even less. The officers we spoke to had been taken completely by surprise. In general (with one exception about which later), their mood can be summarized as follows: We don't want to participate in any of this— whether on one side or the other. At the same time, it was clear that their loyalty to the Soviet Union had the upper hand. They would say: "We have taken an oath of loyalty to Soviet power. We have to carry out the orders. The orders violate the law. But it is your business to sort this all out, and if the orders are indeed illegal, then it is up to you to rescind them. The army should not be deciding which orders it will carry out and which it will not."

The conversations lasted a long time—an hour, two hours. By the way, as a rule, we were not allowed to enter regimental territory. So the conversations were taking place in the vicinity of the guard house. We talked about all sorts of things, about Nuremberg . . .

Freidin: Yes, the Nuremberg trials—that was the only thing that I could say to the tankers who surrounded the White House on Monday.

Sheinis: They would tell us that they were following Yazov's orders. We would tell them that Gorbachev was the only one authorized to issue such orders. They would parry that they had been told that Gorbachev was ill. And so it went. We would discuss the political situation. They were in favor of retaining the Union, they were critical of the policy of the Russian government, and on and on. There was not really any order to these conversations. But I want to say one thing: we were never prevented from distributing the statements and decrees of the Russian government among the soldiers. This was true even when the officers were clearly ill-disposed toward us.

We had quite a volume of these official statements, Yeltsin's first decrees and so on. On Tuesday we even had the ultimatum of the Russian government addressed to Lukianov [Chairman of the USSR Supreme Soviet].

Freidin: Tell me about the hostile officer.

Sheinis: That was on Tuesday in the daytime. We received information that in the vicinity of the Leningrad Highway there was a concentration of the military forces that were likely to be used in attacking the White House. And so we got into a car—Bella Denisenko, myself, and two other male deputies (I can't remember their names). We were always traveling in groups of four, not counting the driver. So there we were, driving along the Leningrad Highway looking for the troops. It took us a long time. At a certain point we were following some sort of military vehicle. Later it turned out that it was a regiment meant to guard prisons. We talked to them, probably wasting our time, because that regiment was unlikely to participate in any action against the White House. Finally, we were driving back, and all of a sudden we saw a group of tanks flying the flag of Russia, and driving in the opposite direction. Those were the tanks that had gone over to the Russian side late on Monday (there were about twelve of them). We wondered what they were doing there and why they had left the White House. After a while, we caught up with them. When we asked them why they had left the defense of the White House, a lieutenant colonel—I think his name was Kobyzev, as he informed me later—told us in a rather energetic fashion that we must leave the territory of the regiment. We told him that as deputies we had the right to enter the territory of any military regiment. He would not budge. So I produced a document, signed by Khasbulatov, saying that Sheinis is allowed to conduct discussions in military regiments in order to explain the position of the Russian government. The man took this document, looked at it, and said, "Very interesting." Then he put it in his pocket and resumed pushing us out. We asked for permission to take leaflets to the soldiers. He said he would do it for us. We refused.

They were very rude to Denisenko, who was not too passive herself. He threatened her, saying that he would order his boys to kick us out of there. She responded by turning to the "boys" and saying to them, "Look I have sons your age, how can you behave like this toward me?!"

Finally, after it was clear that we were not getting anywhere with him and we decided to leave, I asked him to return Khasbulatov's letter. "Oh, don't worry," he said to me, "Khasbulatov will write you another one." Which, actually, was not that far from the truth. The fact is that they had been photocopied, and I had lots of them. In conclusion, he took the paper out of his pocket, tore it in half and gave it back to me in that form. I recounted this story at the session of the Supreme Soviet, which opened the next day.

Freidin: Were there any conversations about going underground on Monday?

Sheinis: No. Deputies talked among themselves, acknowledging that we were unprepared, but these were, so to speak, private conversations. And when we got together for meetings, all we did was receive and exchange information about what was going on where, what cables had been received, and what the plan of action was. Those of the deputy corps with whom I was in constant contact were in full agreement that our main business was to visit as many military garrisons as possible.

Nazimova: Here is an interesting story for you. This was Monday night—or rather, the early hours of Tuesday morning. I was standing near the little bridge outside the White House, helping with the building of the barricade there, when I noticed Sergei Yushenkov walking in a sort of steadfast manner—with a column of tanks moving behind him. I knew Yushenkov personally. So I began cheering right away: "Here are *our* tanks, *our* tanks are coming!" There was a woman standing next to me. She turned to me and said: "How *can* you be cheering tanks!" She did not understand that those tanks had crossed over to our side, and when I explained it to her, she, too, started cheering, without even pausing.

Another interesting episode. I was going home at around six or seven on Wednesday morning [after spending the night outside the White House]. I was in a tram car and sitting across the way from me was a young man, apparently also going home after spending the night outside the White House. Somehow, we could recognize each other very quickly—we all had wet clothes, drawn faces, exhausted looks, dirty shoes (it was raining). I turned to him and said: "It's all over now, everything will be all right." He looked at me, figured out quickly the difference in our generation and said: "Only middle-aged people like you were afraid that we would not succeed. We young people we didn't have any doubts that we would win."

Freidin: Of course, how old could he have been—twenty?
Nazimova: He was a sophomore or a junior in college.

Freidin: In 1985, when Gorbachev took over, he was fourteen or so.
Nazimova: He grew up in a world different from ours.

Freidin: What kind of people were around you on Tuesday night and Wednesday morning?

Nazimova: I was really surprised to encounter there some of my Institute colleagues—I won't name names—whom I had always thought of as being, if not apolitical, then extremely cautious. It was clear that their sympathies were on the side of democracy, but they would not allow themselves to make any public statement about it. As a rule, they never joined demonstrations or attended rallies. I never saw them participate in meetings when I was organizing our chapter of Democratic Russia. But on the second night of our vigil outside the White House, I found myself standing right next to one of those, shall I say, utterly respectable men. He, too, was ready [to sacrifice himself]. It was clear that we would be swept off our feet by the crowd if either a tank or some other military vehicle came close to the perimeter. We were standing between a tall fence and the wall of the White House. There was no escape there.

Another detail, indicative of the kind of solidarity people were experiencing. It was raining rather heavily. A very young man, a boy really, came up to me and asked whether I had anything to protect myself against gases. We were all afraid of gas at some point. I said I did not. He then produced a piece of gauze, folded it into a few layers, and then dipped it right into a puddle. "Take this," he said. "We'll yell if there is a gas attack, and then you'll have to breathe through this thing." People really cared about each other. It was very, very touching.

Freidin: I can very well imagine that, perhaps, after we are no longer alive, revisionist historians will be arguing about this event until they are blue in the face. Nobody will be able to understand why Yeltsin and company were not arrested, why the government did not cut off all the communications from the White House, and so on. Too many miracles.

Nazimova: I agree. They could have taken care of the whole thing in one day.

Freidin: For a nonparticipant, none of this looks like a serious game.

Nazimova: There is one explanation that must be taken into account. The leaders of the coup were all people of the old school. They were used to the idea that if someone at the top gives an order, that order is obeyed below.

Freidin: They were of the old school also with regard to competence and efficiency. They did not plan things well and they bungled it.

Nazimova: Nor did they have unanimity among themselves, each suspecting the other as a potential betrayer. Who would be the first to betray whom? Who would be the first to go to Gorbachev and beg forgiveness? That was the question.

Freidin: Here is my story of Monday night. Right before the putsch, I had made a date to meet Nikolai Nikolaevich Vorontsov [USSR Minister for Environment and Natural Resource Management] and his wife, Yelena Alekseevna Liapunova, at the Congress of Compatriots on Monday night. Vorontsov was supposed to make an opening statement there. I had spent all afternoon outside the White House and from there went straight to the Tchaikovsky Concert Hall, where the opening ceremonies were to be held, arriving there quite wet from the rain and disheveled. Armored vehicles were parked all along the entrance to the Concert Hall, and right there in the middle of Mayakovsky Square, a team of workers was trying to launch a hot-air balloon with a big sign: "Welcome, Compatriots!" The sign was soggy, and the balloon had gotten water-logged. It lifted up a little, hovered, and then collapsed. How symbolic, I said to myself.

Once in the concert hall, I could not find Vorontsov, but I did meet Yelena Alekseevna. She was very worried. She knew that her husband had climbed onto the tank with Yeltsin that morning, and she had not heard from him since. The scene in the foyer was very strange: a group of female dancers in Russian peasant dress were stepping out through the crowd, accompanied by three accordion-playing men outfitted in some fake traditional garb. You didn't know whether to laugh or cry at this sight, or both. After the bell rang, Liapunova and I took our seats in the orchestra, to the right of the stage. There was a man sitting across the aisle from us, a conceptual artist from Leningrad who had emigrated to the United States. I remembered his *nom de plume*: Smorchevskii-Butterbrod. After the opening speeches had been made, he asked to speak, and to my surprise, Mikhail Tolstoi, the master of ceremonies of the Congress, gave him permission. Smorchevskii did not mount the stage, but took a microphone and positioned himself right in front of it. Most people could see him. Both the way he spoke and what he said were very moving. He invited the hall to stand up for a moment in honor of President Gorbachev, who, he said, "may have already been assassinated." Another man shouted something from the balcony, but I could not hear him well. The audience, most of it at least, got up to their feet. Some remained seated, including a few Russian Orthodox priests sitting across the hall from us. I wondered then whether it was a political statement on their part, or perhaps they were afraid they might violate the dignity of the Orthodox priesthood. I still don't know.

Liapunova and I left soon after the opening speeches. We just could not continue sitting there watching all sorts of performances when we did not know whether Vorontsov had been arrested, or worse. We got up to leave, and as we were walking out, I stopped to shake Smorchevskii's hand and to thank him for his speech. He and I were approximately the same age, middle forties. Both of us had lived through the invasion of Czechoslovakia, and now once again we were reliving the days of our youth. Suddenly I heard somebody behind me say in a loud whisper: "We'll break your fucking neck if you keep on doing what you are doing." Dumbfounded, I turned around: there were two tall athletic-looking guys standing behind me. My blood ran cold, just like the old days. I said goodbye to Smorchevskii and followed Liapunova out of the hall. We were not followed.

I offered to accompany her home. Outside, automobiles were parked side by side with armored personnel carriers. I wanted to take a cab, but Liapunova insisted that we go by metro. Only later did I realize why: she wanted to be around people, just in case. The train was half empty (it was 8:30 or so). A youngish bespectacled man walked silently through our car, holding a pathetic handmade placard with the announcement of the big rally at the White House on Tuesday in condemnation of the putsch. Passengers, poker-faced, looked at him in silence. There were no gestures of encouragement, or, for that matter, hostility. At the next stop the man walked out of the car and entered the next one.

Soon after we arrived at the Vorontsovs, we saw the replay of the famous press conference, and a few minutes later Nikolai came home. We watched the news together and he told us about the Cabinet meeting earlier in the day and about some arrests. It was time for me to go home. They walked me out and saw me get into a cab, and asked me to make sure to call them as soon as I got home. I did, and they were relieved to hear that I had gotten home safely.

Nazimova: Here is another episode I would like to share with you. On Tuesday Viktor had to attend a reception at the Hungarian Embassy; he had to present a paper or some information or documents. I drove him there in our car. Later he came home for a nap—it was not possible to take a nap in the White House. That evening, we got a call from Sasha Gutiontov, who told us that a curfew had been declared. "How are you going to get to the White House?" he asked, trying unsuccessfully to persuade us to stay home. "You'll be arrested right away." Well, I dropped our car off at the garage near our house, and from there Viktor and I walked to the metro and from the metro to the White House. The streets were absolutely deserted, but there were no patrols and no one tried to stop us. In the metro, the closer we got to the Barrikadnaia station, the more crowded the train became.

Sheinis: It was absolutely clear that people were going to the White House.

Nazimova: There were so many people there that it was difficult to break through the crowd, and Viktor had trouble getting into the White House. Finally, someone recognized him—"This is Deputy Sheinis!"—and the crowd parted to let him through.

V

Getting the News In and Out

One of the plotters' first moves when they seized power was to take control of the country's mass media: the press, television, and radio. Their actions were designed to control the flow of information and to ensure that it flowed in the proper direction, just as their predecessors had done for so many decades before the introduction of glasnost. The accounts that follow, by both Soviet and foreign journalists, show how professional journalists coped with the crisis and managed, even under highly adverse conditions, to get the news in and out.

IAIN ELLIOT

1 | Three Days in August: On-the-Spot Impressions

Iain Elliott served for many years as an editorial and feature writer for The Times *of London and an editor of* Soviet Analyst. *In 1988 he moved to Munich as Associate Director of Radio Liberty. It was in this capacity that he witnessed the events of August 1991 in Moscow. His account appeared in* Report on the USSR, *a publication of the Radio Free Europe and Radio Liberty Research Institute, in September 1991.*

In the steady rain of Monday afternoon on August 19, I watched the indignant crowds on Kalinin Bridge and the Smolensk embankment building barricades and thrusting leaflets into the hands of young, confused tank crewmen. Workers dragged concrete blocks into place with their trucks. Young lads carried up stretches of railings. Middle-aged academics, briefcase in one hand, scaffolding pole in the other, delayed their return home to add their contribution to the defense of the White House and their elected representatives. The first barriers of trolley-buses with slashed tires grew stronger by the minute. Building sites were ransacked, and a vast supply of long steel rods for ferroconcrete construction gave the barricades the appearance of some ancient phalanx of spears. A veteran of the Afghan War said that such rods were the most effective defense available against the tanks. At five o'clock a familiar sound caught my attention: the news from Radio Liberty emerged loud and clear from the center of a large cluster of umbrellas at the end of the bridge.

At 5:15 P.M., troop transport vehicles, which were trying to force their way through to the makeshift barrier on the bridge, abandoned the attempt, and in a dangerous operation, turned around amid the crowds before disappearing in the direction of the Hotel Ukraina. Some frustrated soldier inside one of the transporters fired a few rounds into the air to frighten the crowds into clearing a path. Later, a column of several dozen light tanks came charging recklessly around a corner at the Smolensk metro station. The tank officers were desperately waving passersby out of the way, but were clearly determined not to relax speed for fear of finding themselves pinned down like so many others by leaflet-waving youngsters. Nonetheless, someone had managed to scrawl with a piece of chalk on tank No. 073, "Freedom, not tanks!"

Outside the Marx Prospect metro station people were clustered around Boris Yeltsin's "Appeal to the Citizens of Russia," posted on a wall opposite the Bolshoi Theater. In front of the nearby Moscow Hotel a large crowd was cheering the speeches of young deputies. A general strike was spreading, there was widespread support for Yeltsin, and Russians were no longer prepared to give way to totalitarianism. The young deputy Dmitrii Chegodaev, a "Democratic Russia" leader, was particularly effective with his megaphone, summoning the crowds to an all-night vigil outside the White House. I was to speak to him again under happier circumstances an epoch later, on Thursday night. Still with his megaphone, he was persuading laughing but determined Muscovites to stand clear so that two powerful Krupp cranes could remove "Iron Feliks"* from his high pedestal before the KGB headquarters. For several hours in the late afternoon, agile young people scrambled all over the towering statue, placing steel cables around his neck, and linking them to an ancient yellow bus. They were convinced by Sergei Stankevich and other spokesmen for Yeltsin and [Mayor] Gavriil Popov that this day of victory should not be marred by further casualties, and waited patiently until almost midnight, when the hated symbol of KGB repression was eventually laid low in a safe, well-organized operation.

That tense Monday evening, however, I heard from one of the deputies at the White House that Radio Russia and Moscow Echo had been suppressed. I had visited Sergei Korzun, chief editor of the popular Moscow Echo radio station in its cramped quarters just that morning, shortly after KGB officers had told him to close down. He said then

---

*Feliks Dzerzhinskii, the founder of the Soviet secret police (the *Cheka*), whose gigantic statue stood in Lubianka Square.

that he had no intention of obeying them since he did not recognize their authority, and it therefore seemed probable that he had been arrested. This turned out not to be so, and Moscow Echo was soon back on air, although its broadcasts were interrupted more than once in the grim hours that followed. I spoke that week with several journalists, print and radio; their experiences varied greatly, as did their fascinating accounts of how they had somehow succeeded in defying the incompetent junta's attempts to suppress their activities. But they shared with the young men who stood unarmed before the tanks a courageous determination to do everything in their power to ensure the collapse of the coup.

Suddenly a dozen tanks roared past the Metropol Hotel and Sverdlov statue, heading for Manezh Square, scattering those who, like me, were strolling away from the speakers toward the line of tough OMON paramilitary police blocking off Red Square. Three tanks sped past and on through Manezh Square, but the fourth ground to a halt so abruptly I thought for a moment that it had hit one of the passersby. It was a relief to realize that nothing more dramatic than engine failure had occurred. Within seconds the snorting tanks with flak-jacketed soldiers on top clutching their Kalashnikovs were surrounded by people from the meeting determined to educate the soldiers about how they were being misled. Leaflets fluttered from the windows of the deputies' offices in the Hotel Moskva, but possibly even more effective were the plump, motherly Russian women who gave the undernourished soldiers everything they had in their baskets, from bunches of grapes to a very large jar of stewed fruit, which an officer demanded be promptly returned. "And they make our children take part in this!" shouted one irate woman.

Confused and unhappy, the soldiers and tank crews listened to a range of hecklers, from lecturers on the nature of democracy to the only drunk I was to see among hundreds of thousands of demonstrators against the junta. Ripping open his shirt and thrusting his naked chest against the muzzle of a Kalashnikov in the hands of a nervous teenager, he shouted: "You won't shoot us, will you? After all, we're Russian, and you're Russian." At last the rain stopped and the setting sun made the red bricks of the Lenin Museum glow. Tank crewmen helped some pretty girls climb up beside them to decorate their tank with flowers. An angry officer chased the girls off, but agreed to withdraw the remaining tanks the way they had come, if only the crowd would step back enough to allow them to maneuver around. And so the tanks left, ignominiously towing backwards the one broken down, the triumphant cheers of the crowd resounding across Manezh Square while the OMON looked on impassively.

Monday set the scene for the defeat of the bungling junta. The politically aware among the population realized their strength, and I saw little evidence of doubt among those on the barricades whether democracy would prevail. Of course all too many Muscovites kept their heads down, waiting to see which way the wind was blowing before voicing any opinion about events. And there were several in buses and the subway who even argued in favor of the junta, hoping for a return to the Brezhnev stagnation when at least there was something to buy in the shops.

On Tuesday, August 20, meetings were taking place all over Moscow as the staffs of newspapers, factories, and other institutions decided where they stood. Some simply went about their business as usual. Others were divided, and opted to sit on the fence until it became clearer onto which side it would be in their own best interests to jump. For people in the media this was not really an option; those who did not immediately go public with a statement opposing the coup were denounced by their more courageous colleagues as compromisers. But some newspapers that immediately decided to defy the junta's ban found that they lacked the means to publish a normal issue—and not, in most cases that I heard about, because there were tanks barring the way to the printing presses. More often it was simply that the responsible official for the formerly Party-controlled newspapers refused to provide the keys; and since access to copy machines was still severely restricted, it was not always a simple matter to run off several thousand leaflets or brief "emergency" issues of a newspaper. Even obtaining supplies of xerox paper required considerable initiative.

Under the leadership of Irma Mameladze, Alla Latynina, and Yurii Shekochikhin (who is also an elected deputy), *Literaturnaia gazeta* journalists held a meeting at their editorial offices in Kostianskii Lane to protest the actions of the junta and arrange for joint action by the democratic media. The weekly is printed courtesy of the *Pravda* presses, and since they lacked the facilities to produce an immediate "emergency" issue themselves, they decided to pile into their bus and join the demonstration of solidarity at the Russian parliament. They were not impressed by the attitude of their editor Fedor Burlatskii, who stayed in the Crimean sunshine and provided no leadership for their protest. It was not until Wednesday, August 21, that he phoned in his protest over the closure of his newspaper, in time for the front page of that week's delayed issue.

Vitalii Tretiakov, editor of *Nezavisimaia gazeta*, produced a special issue of his newspaper by fax despite the ban, and quickly organized underground distribution of it and the following issues. When I called at his offices on the first floor of the "Voskhod" factory off Miasnits-kaia Street (temporarily called Kirov Street under Communist rule), he paid tribute to all those who had helped provide paper and copy facilities. He expressed particular gratitude to the Library of Foreign Literature; as an article in the Saturday issue pointed out, while some printing houses made the impossible demand of an official letter of permission from Minister Poltoranin before taking the risk of printing the liberal newspaper, the director of the library, Viacheslav Ivanov, simply said "Come." It was late when they arrived. "But no tasks are hopeless where Deputy Director Yekaterina Genieva is concerned. If not already aware of her energy and determination one would have been astonished to see how necessary but difficult-to-find people appeared; how doors, the keys to which it was impossible to find, were opened; and so on." The newspaper published a list of library staff who had shown particular dedication.

Among the most active in producing and distributing leaflets were young members of the Memorial Society, who took paper from every office they could find and produced thousands of leaflets on their overworked copy machines. "Suppressed" newspapers and press agencies provided them information by fax, which they sent to the West via Prague and Bratislava, since they were unable to fax direct. One lad had an uneasy moment when two policemen approached as he was distributing leaflets to tank crews. But all they asked was, "Have you got any more for us?" On Tuesday Aleksandr Daniel* had a bad moment when a truck pulled up outside [the Memorial Society's makeshift headquarters] and a KGB officer rang the bell. They talked, and then he said, "It's all right, we won't shoot you."

Outside the White House on Tuesday there was a steady flow of speakers to inspire the thousands of supporters who had gathered to

---

*Aleksandr Daniel, historian and human rights activist, is the son of the late writer Yulii Daniel.

prevent the storming of the Russian parliament. Yeltsin, Eduard She-vardnadze, and Yelena Bonner were enthusiastically received; the poet Yevgenii Yevtushenko less warmly, although he did succeed in capturing the atmosphere in his poem "19 August," which he proclaimed to the crowds:

> *This August day will be remembered in song and saga.*
> *Today we are a people, no longer idiots deceived.*
> *And today Sakharov, shyly wiping his cracked*
> *spectacles, is coming to the aid of our parliament.*
> *Beside the tanks the conscience awakens.*
> *Yeltsin climbs on a tank. And beside him*
> *Not the ghosts of former Kremlin leaders,*
> *but the skilled men of Russia, not yet vanished,*
> *And tired women, victims of long queuing.*
>
> *No! Russia will not again fall on her knees for interminable years.*
> *With us are Pushkin, Tolstoi.*
> *With us stands the whole awakened people.*
> *And the Russian parliament, like a wounded marble swan of*
> *freedom, defended by the people, swims into immortality.*

Former KGB General Oleg Kalugin introduced a KGB lieutenant colonel who appealed to his boss "Volodia Kriuchkov" to abandon the junta, because it was "about to collapse" anyway. He said that most of his brother officers had declared for Yeltsin. (The same message was received by a BBC correspondent who phoned the KGB public relations office in the Lubianka. "We're all for Yeltsin here!" he was told.)

At first it was announced that Yeltsin could not speak to his supporters outside the White House "because he had a great many matters to attend to," but when he did in fact appear on the long balcony, it was clear that there were other concerns also. He was surrounded by police shields, and at one point an armed policeman jumped up on the wall in front of his president, pointing at what might have been a sniper high in a nearby building. There were several false alarms about the impending storming of the White House, and instructions were given on what to do in a tear gas attack. As usual, Russians rose to the occasion with a stream of anecdotes: "Why are these people cheering when we know that a column of fifty tanks is coming to crush us? They've probably heard that it's not fifty but only forty-nine!" Matched only by the enthusiastic reception given to Yeltsin were the cheers that greeted the appearance of the popular comedian Gennadii Khazanov, who mimicked Gorbachev and caused shouts of laughter with his sharp comments about would-be dictators with shaking hands. There were other, less repeatable jokes about "Yanasha" [Yanaev] on the walls of transportable toilets provided for the defenders of the Russian parliament.

The first reports from the Tchaikovsky Street underpass on the night of August 20–21 were inaccurate, with as many as ten said to be killed and dozens wounded. Katia Genieva, deputy director of the State Library for Foreign Literature, who, despite the curfew and the tanks in the streets, was working through the night to arrange for the printing of thousands of copies of an "emergency" issue of *Nezavisimaia gazeta*, found time to worry about my wife and me. She thought that we should catch the first plane home: "It's going to be nasty in Russia now; they'll arrest all of us; I'll help in any way I can." My wife Elizabeth, in Moscow for the BBC Russian Service, thought it much too interesting to leave. Two trucks stopping immediately opposite [the library building] in the dark small hours to allow armed soldiers to jump out made me wonder whether it was not getting too interesting to stay. A dozen heavy tanks in camouflage paint, which made them seem even more outrageous in the center of a city, roared along the embankment toward the White House.

By the time I reached Tchaikovsky Street, however, it was quiet. Grim but determined "afgantsy" [Afghan War veterans] talked about their experiences as they stood in the persistent drizzle beside a burned-out trolleybus. Girls were placing flowers to cover bloodstains. There were several makeshift shrines of broken planks. Just a few yards from the reconstructed barricade I noticed a wall covered with leaflets. One was headed "Radio Liberty Informs" and a typed page gave a dozen items with world reactions to the coup. Yaroslav Leontiev, the duty editor for Radio Russia that night, had compiled a fairly comprehensive chronology of the tragic events from the flood of phone calls received. He told me that only information confirmed by independent sources was included. Although an attempt was made by the junta to remove Radio Russia from the air, its frequencies were defiantly stuck up on walls around the city and, being on medium waves, appeared to have most listeners on the radios I heard around the barricades.

Radio Liberty also contributed significantly to defeating the junta's attempt to impose censorship, as Gorbachev, Yeltsin, Yelena Bonner, and others have since confirmed. Everyone I talked to, on the barricades, at the White House, or in newspaper offices and institutes, had warm words for Radio Liberty and for the work of our freelance correspondents in particular. Sergei Markov, a young politics professor at Moscow University, told me how he had recorded from a broadcast Yeltsin's first decree opposing the junta. Markov cycled through the rain to the local soviet at Dubna and had the satisfaction of watching the executive committee put Yeltsin's instructions immediately into effect after they had listened to the recording. Markov, who is leader of the Russian Social Democratic Party, spent the long night of August 20–21 in the White House with Radio Liberty providing a steady stream of information from Russia and abroad. On Saturday, at the memorial meeting on Manezh Square for the three victims of the coup, I could see over the shoulder of the man in front reading his copy of *Vecherniaia Moskva*. "According to Radio Liberty," it read. Yeltsin himself heard evidence enough of the value of Radio Liberty broadcasting in the fraught days of the putsch, when Radio freelancers were broadcasting direct from the tenth floor of the White House. On August 27 he issued a decree providing Radio Liberty with a Moscow bureau and full accreditation for its correspondents in the RSFSR.

Three indispensable human factors for building a solid foundation for democracy in Russia were very much in evidence in those exhilarating August days. There were elected representatives of the people who provided the right leadership at the right time. There was a politically conscious section of the population—probably not the majority, but sufficiently numerous to prevail—that was prepared to stand up for democratic principles despite very real dangers. And there were enough journalists with the initiative and courage to ensure that the democratic politicians and their supporters could communicate with each other quickly and effectively to organize the defeat of the reactionary forces.

Among the politicians, Yeltsin of course played a decisive role: he appeared to be the right person in the right place at the right time. When there was a very real fear of snipers, he was prepared to take the risk of speaking to the crowds from the top of a tank—a risk that proved justified, since even the "Vremia" television news carried the image around the country with at least some indication of the contents of his inspiring "Appeal to the Citizens of Russia." I wondered if Yeltsin too was reminded of the statue at the Finland Station in Leningrad, with a triumphant Lenin atop an armored car. Yeltsin epitomized the fledgling Russian democracy in a way that no other politician could. Shevardnadze, Khasbulatov, Burbulis, and several leading deputies showed similar courage and dedication to defeating the junta. On August 20, Deputy Valerii Borshchev of the Moscow City Soviet on Tverskaia Street described to me how their building, like the White House, had become a center of resistance, defying the tanks gathered outside. Shevardnadze had spoken to the crowds there too.

I met several of the leaders of new Russian parties—some numerically more significant than others and with a wide range of policies, but all convinced of the benefits of a multiparty system. At a press conference on Thursday morning, August 22, Nikolai Travkin of the Democratic Party of Russia, Viktor Aksiuchits of the Russian Christian Democrats, Sergei Markov of the Social Democrats, and Vladimir Filin of the Republican Party of Russia debated issues such as privatization, social services, and policies on national minorities in the RSFSR and ethnic Russians in the other republics. Their views varied greatly, of course, but they agreed on the need to put their policies into practice only through the electoral process and parliamentary debate, and all had proved by their actions in the preceding days that they were united in their determination to defend democratic government. The Kadets (Constitutional Democrats) with their green flag embossed with a white swan were present at most street demonstrations, although they told me they had only a few hundred members. They stand for the same policies that won their party strong support among middle-class voters for the Constituent Assembly of 1918.

Many a true word is spoken in jest, and it was widely claimed in the streets of Moscow that since the democratic forces had failed to prepare themselves to deal with the hard-line putsch that everyone expected, gratitude for its failure was owed more to the bungling of the junta than to the competence of the democratic leadership. Deputy Telman Gdlian joked that Dmitrii Yazov should be shown leniency because by threatening students with military service he had increased their determination to oppose a military takeover. Others pointed out that when Boris Pugo branded as "traitors" the OMON officers who pledged their loyalty to Yeltsin, he merely strengthened their resolve to fight to the end in defense of the White House. Certainly their failure to win the obedience of army, KGB, and MVD units at least sufficiently to remove quickly the RSFSR leadership; their failure to cut telephone communications, jam radio broadcasts, and suppress the free press; their complete inability to inspire either trust or terror—rather than contempt—in the broad masses who watched their feeble television performances all meant that they deserved to lose every bit as much as the RSFSR leadership earned its victory. Without doubt the strong line taken by President Bush, Prime Minister John Major, Chancellor Kohl, and other Western leaders heartened the democrats and further demoralized the junta.

All of this became known to those who manned the barricades only thanks to the democratic media. In addition to the ones mentioned above, I saw many "emergency" issues of the democratic newspapers pasted on walls and even on tanks; they certainly reached the troops and had the desired effect. Aleksandr Kabakov, political commentator of *Moskovskie novosti* and author of "The Defector," a screenplay predicting the disintegration of the USSR and armed clashes in the Moscow streets, was tired and unshaven but triumphant after the defeat of the putsch. He told me that the film of "The Defector" had received an unplanned premiere immediately after Sobchak's defiant speech on Leningrad television. He also passed on four issues of the "emergency" version of *Moskovskie novosti* (A3-size photocopy) that had been distributed at the height of the crisis. Issue no. 3 included an appeal by the indomitable and ubiquitous Yelena Bonner for half a million Muscovites to demonstrate their support for the Russian parliament "to show that we are worthy of the title of citizens of the capital and of the state, rather than just a crowd, interested only in sausage."

Most of the newspapers that appeared with the permission of the junta were opposed by some of their staff. In addition to the "putschist" *Moskovskaia pravda*, there was an "illegal" *Moskovskaia pravda* appearing as an A4-size leaflet, appealing to readers to ignore the normal-size "legal" issue. *Moskovskii komsomolets* managed to produce five "emergency" issues in the form of A3-size photocopies. *Rossiia*, the White House–based newspaper of the presidium of the RSFSR Supreme Soviet, produced a series of A3-size leaflet issues with appeals to pass them on and reproduce them as much as possible. This activity was complemented by the radio stations ineffectively banned by the junta: Radio Russia, Moscow Echo, and Radio 3-Anna, which gave its air waves to Radio Russia correspondents Liubimov and Politkovskii, broadcasting from inside the White House. Its frequencies could be seen posted on the walls of Moscow streets.

The Western radio stations broadcasting in Russian and other languages of the former USSR spread this information further. Even Mikhail Gorbachev, isolated in the Crimea, was able to follow events in Moscow and elsewhere thanks, as he acknowledged, to the BBC, Radio Liberty, and the Voice of America. It was gratifying to see so many tributes in the liberal Russian press to the work of the international broadcasters. A random survey of the newspapers I managed to buy, beg, or scrimmage for in the course of that week found information attributed to Radio Liberty in *Vecherniaia Moskva* (August 22), *Literaturnaia gazeta* (August 21), and *Moskovskie novosti* (August 24)—where Aleksandr Kabakov wrote of how he had listened to Andrei Babitskii and Mikhail Sokolov reporting for Radio Liberty from the White House. *Rossiiskaia gazeta* (August 23) wrote that on the morning of August 21 the barricades damaged by the APC attacks were being restored when, "to relieve the pickets who had lived through those heavy hours, Muscovites began to arrive on the first metro trains, having spent the night at their receivers, listening on Radio Liberty to information about the attack that had begun."

But for me as an observer of these events, the lasting impression is of the youth of the majority of those who defended democracy on the barricades and distributed leaflets, and of their conviction that they had no alternative. As Yeltsin said in his victory speech at the rally on August 22: "It has again been shown how great are the powers of the people. The political course of Russia, and the honor and virtue of its highest bodies of authority, its leadership, were defended by unarmed, peaceful citizens. It is symbolic that among those who became the defense of the Constitution, the law, and human worth, there were a great many young people. This means that the future course of this reform is ensured."

Many Western specialists dismissed the dissidents of the Brezhnev era as too small in number to have any significant impact on political reform. But the self-sacrifice of those few courageous individuals who in the 1960s and 1970s placed their civic duty and the defense of human rights above their own well-being was not wasted. Through samizdat and Western radio broadcasts, their example reached the post-1968 generation, and it was not lost.

On Saturday evening Elizabeth and I visited Misha and Flara

Litvinov, parents of Pavel Litvinov, one of the few who demonstrated for some minutes on Red Square against the invasion of Czechoslovakia before being arrested. Among those squeezed into their hospitable kitchen to watch the amazing scenes on Russian television were Kronid Liubarskii and his wife, Larissa Bogoraz, who had played their part in the events of that week in a worthy culmination of their distinguished lifetime work in defense of human rights. One could not avoid the conviction that it was they and their small circle that had planted the seeds that flowered this August in Moscow. I remembered Lev Timofeev, Gleb Yakunin, Mstislav Rostropovich at the White House, but it was the words of Yelena Bonner among the representatives of that tiny band of dissidents that came to mind. When she spoke on August 20 she called on Muscovites no longer to act like *bydlo* (cattle) but, avoiding bloodshed, to stand for a free, democratic Russia against the junta: "They cannot stand over us. We are above them, we are better than they, more honest, and we are many!"

2 | Getting the News on "Vremia"

Sergei Medvedev was a journalist for the central television news program "Vremia" when the coup began. His film report, shown on "Vremia" on Monday, August 19, gave national coverage to the resistance movement mobilized by Yeltsin against the junta. From Medvedev's report, millions of Soviet citizens learned for the first time about Yeltsin's "Appeal to the Citizens of Russia," and they saw film clips of Yeltsin standing courageously atop a tank. The report also included pictures of the construction of barricades around the White House. Although Medvedev was dismissed from his job after the airing of his report, he was reinstated on Wednesday, August 21, and on Thursday he became the anchorman for "Vremia." He was interviewed by Bill Keller, Moscow Bureau Chief for the New York Times, *on September 25, 1991.*

Medvedev: My wife learned from the radio that a coup had taken place. Then we turned on the television, and our program "Morning," which starts at 6:30 A.M., was not on. Announcers were sitting there and reading the statements of the GKChP. Of course we were very upset. I was particularly upset, because on that day I was supposed to anchor the program "Vremia."

By nine o'clock I was at work. All the bosses of "Vremia" were already sitting in their places. Our chief editor, Olvar Kakuchaia, said they got him up at two in the morning. They gave Kravchenko* almost no chance to sleep; they had found him at home. He called our chief editor. Then, in the middle of the night, just as it was getting on toward

---

*Leonid Kravchenko was head of USSR Gosteleradio, later renamed State Company for Television and Radio Broadcasting.

dawn, they began to surround the building with military vehicles and paratroopers, judging by their clothing. All of this was visible from the windows of the building. There was almost nothing being broadcast. Some programs were closed, and others, like our news program, were given a packet of documents that had been adopted by the putschists.

Our main source of information on TV was CNN. [. . .]

At around 11:00 A.M.—I'm afraid to say precisely, maybe it was 11:40 A.M.—I saw on CNN that tanks had entered Moscow. But I did not see tanks when I was going around the city. I was especially on the lookout in the morning, but didn't see anything. There was no one on the streets, no special brigades of police. Moscow was quiet.

When the tanks arrived, my colleagues and I began to count them. We counted forty. We understood that this was very serious business. The tanks went through the center of Moscow. They came down Kalinin Prospect. Then CNN began to show the first spontaneous meetings. We tried to go out on the street. But it turned out that, starting that morning, taking cameras out for filming was controlled.

Representatives of the State Emergency Committee, KGB employees, sat at Gosteleradio. They forbade anyone to leave. Then, in the middle of the day it became possible to leave to film with a permission signed by the chief editor—no one lower than that, not a deputy, no one but the chief editor. The chief editor signed such a statement for me. It was interesting that no one else was making such requests. Everyone sat in the studio. Everyone sat in place. [. . .]

Kakuchaia signed the statement for me to go film, saying, "Be very careful. You shouldn't go out because of the tanks."

I said: "All the same, we'll go."

We left. We went to the other building because the cameras and the operators are there. It's in the other direction, across the street. At first they wouldn't let us in one entrance; we got in through another one. We were lucky to carry out a camera, and we went out through the exit without the signature of the KGB chief who was sitting with us in the building. I think we managed to do this because there was some confusion there about who had allowed us to pass. They weren't sure what kind of signatures were needed. These paratroopers didn't know whose signature was valid and whose was not.

Therefore we left quietly, got in the car, and drove off. First, we went to Manezh Square. On Manezh Square, a meeting had already ended, but meetings kept occurring spontaneously, one after another.

Several rows of trolleybuses were at the entrances. We did manage to get to the square. Police were all around. I said, we are news people, from television, and we are authorized by some kind of authority—I didn't say by whom—to film everything. The police were busy with the trolleybuses, trying to pull them away with tow trucks. And when they had cleared a passage, we managed to get through it.

We passed through three or four cordons and entered Manezh Square. Military vehicles were already there. People sat on the armor. We recorded all this, talked with people. We saw that there was no particulai confrontation between the people and the army. They were talking with each other.

Then the square began to empty out, and it was explained that for more than an hour people had been going to the White House.

[Medvedev says that he then decided to go to the White House with his film crew.]

We drove in the car almost to the first barricades. When I saw the barricades, honestly speaking, I rejoiced, because I understood that there would be resistance, not just in words, as often happens in Moscow—noise, shouting, but things don't go further than that.

We began to film all of this. We began to film meetings with people who were building the barricades, then how the leaflets were being thrown out of the building; orators were speaking. We were there for quite a long time. It was already almost 8:00 P.M. when we returned to the studio. We returned, and I was 100 percent convinced that in the studio nobody had any need for what we had filmed. And unexpectedly, the first deputy, Valentin Lazutkin, deputy to Kravchenko, said, "Get the material ready about what is going on today in Moscow." We sat down very quickly and began to edit. He said: "Later I'll look to see what you have."

About five minutes before 9:00 P.M., as the information program was about to begin, we didn't have anything ready. At that time, he entered and said, "Let's have a look."

I said: "Valentin Valentinovich, we're not ready yet. We've only done half of it. We can show you what we have, but without sound." I read to him from the script. There was no sound yet.

We showed him the first part of our report. There was the big statement from Yeltsin, with an appeal to the people. This appeal was about four minutes long. Lazutkin looked at all this and said: "What comes next?"

I said: "Well, we'll show the barricades and the people there."

He said: "You must shorten Yeltsin." He didn't say take it out completely, but it had to be shortened to the minimum. Out of four minutes, maybe forty seconds were left, maybe a minute.

I said: "The rest of what [Yeltsin] said I will try to put in my script."

He said: "Okay."

After this I ran to the editing room. We finished the report, with interviews, with the barricades. In general everything was there.

Then, when the report was broadcast, it was as though the ceiling crashed in on my head. All the telephones began to explode. Yurii Prokofiev, the Secretary of the Moscow Party Committee, phoned. Aleksandr Dzasokhov phoned—he's a Central Committee Secretary. Boris Pugo phoned. I don't remember who else for sure, because I didn't talk with them. Lazutkin talked with them. Kravchenko phoned —Lazutkin later told me about this—Kravchenko phoned and said this report was a direct appeal to come to the barricades; it was instigating material. But judging by everything, he was repeating someone else's words, because Lazutkin said it appeared [Kravchenko] had not seen the material.

I didn't wait around to see how everything would come out, although before I left, one of the deputy editors began to shout at me: "How could you deceive us? You gave an interview to people in the opposition." He blamed me for a phrase at the end of the report: "If we have the chance, we will give you additional information later about what is happening in Moscow." Everyone blamed me for this phrase.

Later, I learned that many who defended the White House found out where to go and what to do precisely from this report. But at that time, I didn't know any of this. I just went home. I didn't want to wait. I just slammed the door and went home to my wife and child. We put our daughter to bed, and I said to my wife: "Let's go to the White House."

She said: "It's terrible to leave the child." She was sleeping on the balcony. Usually she sleeps very soundly, so we put her to bed and left.

We left the car at the Hotel Ukraina [across from the White House], and we were going along, and the first person I saw was my friend Paul Hofheinz from *Fortune* magazine, who should have been in Italy on vacation. We greeted each other. We went around together.

People came up and congratulated me, slapped me on the shoulders. I understood that they would protect me. I felt reassured.

The next morning, a big meeting took place of the leaders of television, where they considered, among other things, the question of what to do with me. Kravchenko ordered our chief editor to demote me from the position of commentator to senior editor. In monetary terms, the salary is half as much. And I was deprived of the right to appear on the air. Then the chief editor said to me, "Listen, Seryozha, you have to go hide somewhere, because I don't know what will happen next. Go take a vacation immediately."

I didn't say anything against it. I got my papers all in order for a vacation leave. But the next day I took a camera and we went out again to film. I don't know why they gave it to us. It was simply a coincidence, and we went to the White House again and shot everything.

But of course when we returned, they said to me, "You're still here? Surely you can't make a report."

The next day, we went again to the White House, this time inside the building. We talked with many people, met many friends. Meetings were going on. It was already clear that events were developing in the other direction now.

On August 22, according to the schedule, I should have been the anchor on "Vremia." Although I was on vacation, there was still a schedule. I phoned Lazutkin at home and asked, "Am I working, or not?"

He said, "What? You don't know that I tore up Kravchenko's order in front of your bosses?"

I said, "Can I come and anchor 'Vremia'?"

He said, "Yes, you can."

I arrived at the office, took what I had filmed, which had not been broadcast, edited it and put it on the air on the 22nd. It was very emotional. It was the first "free" program since the 19th.

Keller: Why didn't the putschists get tougher?

Medvedev: Today, there are very many versions about this. Things really were unclear for us, at least. We waited all the time for someone to come to the office and explain what was to be broadcast and what was not. But no one came, although they closed some of the newspapers. But I don't think they were incompetent, because among the top leaders was Kriuchkov. His office knows what to do. So it could not have been the incompetence. I think that there might be two versions. The first is that they did not feel confidence in themselves. They tried [to carry out the coup] more or less in a democratic way, to create a facade of democracy.

This explanation is plausible because the next day Prokofiev called again about my report and said "It was nothing terrible." No one understood the meaning of his phone call. We objectively showed what was going on in Moscow. I think this might be the explanation for the fact that they didn't apply censorship.

Keller: Maybe they were used to the fact that the leaders of Gosteleradio were always obedient.

Medvedev: Yes, never before had there been a situation where someone gave a command and TV did not fulfill it. I don't remember such a case ever. At least not consciously.

Keller: Did you feel that among the leaders at Gosteleradio there was a wish to get correct information on the air?

Medvedev: Yes, there was such a desire, and there was uncertainty, this I observed. Some kind of paralysis affected people. There were all kinds of reactions from different people—fear, uncertainty, readiness to fight back.

Keller: After the putsch, do you feel the atmosphere here is really free?

Medvedev: It's a very complicated situation, because a new leadership, Yegor Yakovlev, has arrived. Eduard Sagalaev* is back. Obviously so far there is no worry. "Give people the chance to work. Please. Give them what they need." But now there is a struggle of those who worked here earlier—for twenty, twenty-five years—with those who have just arrived, because they feel that the new leadership would like to get rid of them. This feeling of concern about one's fate, one's situation at work, has united people. This is unusual for any TV operation, because there's always lots of jealousy.

Keller: Would you compare the psychology of the older and younger generations?

Medvedev: I think the main difference is that the veterans—those who have worked here a long time—they feel an internal censor. It

---

*Eduard Sagalaev ran "Vremia" during the heyday of perestroika.

interferes in what they say and show, that which might have been done. Something inside just says "no, that won't fly," even if he wants to do it. All the same, it won't work out. I speak this way because I also work in this system. I began under Brezhnev. I worked for seven years in radio, and I, too, have this feeling.

I was born in the former city of Königsberg [now Kaliningrad], which in 1946 went from East Prussia to Russia, to the Soviet Union. I was born there in 1958. My parents went there from Leningrad after they graduated. My mother is a teacher. My father used to work in television; he was director of a TV studio, then he became the chairman of the television and radio committee of Kaliningrad. Now he's retired. I graduated from Moscow State University, the journalism faculty. After graduation in 1981, I worked at Gosteleradio. Until 1987 I worked on radio, and since 1987 on "Vremia." I worked, for a few months only, on a newspaper in Kaliningrad. I love radio and television a lot.

Keller: Was there a period during the coup when you thought it was the end of freedom?

Medvedev: There was a moment in the morning, when I heard the radio and turned on the TV. But the further events developed, the more certain I became that it would not last long, especially when I learned that a portion of troops had gone over to the side of Yeltsin and machines and tanks that supported Yeltsin had moved in around the White House. Then I was absolutely convinced that it would be really hard for the putschists, and they would not be victorious.

3 | The Foreign Press and the Coup

Ann Cooper reported from Moscow for National Public Radio from 1986 through 1991.

"Boy, have I got bad news," announced my husband, Bill Keller, when I answered his phone call from Moscow. It was early morning, August 19, 1991, and I was still in my room at the Hotel Lietuva in Vilnius.

For Moscow correspondents, August was normally a welcome respite from the crush of political news. Kremlin leaders went off to their Black Sea beach resorts, and foreign correspondents could safely leave for their own vacations—or for business trips, like the one I was on to gather material for a retrospective piece about Lithuania's independence campaign.

Bill quickly described the announcement of Gorbachev's phony illness and the membership of the ominous State of Emergency Committee.

"This is not a joke," he concluded, knowing that I might need a little convincing after living through several years of rumors and false alarms about conservative plots to oust Mikhail Gorbachev.

We talked briefly about the crudeness of the scheme. The goal was obvious: Gennadii Yanaev and his fellow thugs, relics of the Soviet past, wanted to reverse the breathtaking transformations of the Gorbachev era and preserve their own cozy world of power. Their use of the absurd "Gorbachev is sick" story, and their appeals to a false Soviet patriotism, indicated how thoroughly out of touch they were. The lies of the past were no longer calmly accepted by an obedient society; indeed, it seemed to us that the *putchisty*, as the coup plotters came to be known in Russian, would need an unthinkable amount of force to impose their will on a public now accustomed to speaking its own mind.

Lithuania had already shown us that tanks and bullets were not always enough to trample a budding democracy. Seven months earlier, Bill and I had watched in horror as the Soviet military shot its way through a peaceful crowd of unarmed protesters to seize the Vilnius television tower. The military easily grabbed control of the tower and the republic's main broadcasting studios, but in the wake of the attacks, more protesters than ever poured into the streets. Lithuania was not vanquished. The January violence in Vilnius had struck many as a dress rehearsal for a grander scheme. No more dress rehearsals now. This was the real thing.

I ran down the hall to tell my National Public Radio colleague, Ben Roe, and we set to work, begging for new plane tickets back to Moscow, canceling our interviews and phoning friends in Vilnius, where the news was just beginning to spread. Our friend Gintas picked us up right away, and we sped off toward the Lithuanian parliament building, stronghold of the republic's democratically elected government. The route to parliament was already littered with metal beams and concrete blocks designed to thwart tanks; after January, the Lithuanians had become master builders of the instant barricade.

Inside the parliament building I felt as though I was wandering through a rerun of January. Local militia loyal to Lithuania's pro-independence government jammed into a lobby area, counting out bullets for their rifles. Legislative workers rushed out of the building carrying electronic equipment—no doubt for storage in safer hideaways. Parliamentarians and journalists swapped scraps of information in the hallways. Rita Dapkus, the indefatigable Lithuanian-American who ran the parliament press office, settled in for the expected siege with a wry smile. "At least this time we've got company," she said, noting that Moscow, and not Vilnius, appeared to be the first target of the putschists.

Later, on the way to the Vilnius airport, Gintas asked shyly whether, when the dust settled a bit, I could check the status of his application to emigrate to the United States. Gintas actually had a good chance of getting out of the Soviet Union, because his wife's family lived in California. The coup gave his application a new urgency, and his request for help brought me close to tears. How many people like Gintas had we met—people who flourished when given new freedom to speak and write, to travel abroad, to create private businesses, to form political parties or publish anti-Communist newspapers. At a minimum, a return to dictatorship would reverse their achievements and destroy their dreams. It was these personal anxieties, rather than the larger threat to international order, that preoccupied me in the first hours of the coup.

What, for example, might become of our loyal driver Volodia, who picked me up at the airport when I landed in Moscow early Monday afternoon? As usual, Volodia was bursting with news—the latest radio announcements, how many tanks he had counted on his way out of the city. I wondered how the new regime might reward Volodia's enthusiastic assistance to a foreign journalist. Two of the putschists, Prime Minister Valentin Pavlov and KGB chief Vladimir Kriuchkov, had made hysterical anti-Western statements in recent months, and a new round of antiforeigner propaganda seemed certain if they succeeded in bringing the country under their control.

I saw the first tanks shortly after Volodia turned onto Leningrad Highway. We were still in Moscow's suburbs, and the convoys we passed were parked along the roadside, apparently awaiting further orders. Most of the soldiers who lounged atop the armor appeared to be from Central Asia, a worrisome sign because central Asians seemed far more likely than Slavic soldiers to obey any orders aimed at subduing Russian civilians. Later, though, I saw that most troops deployed in Moscow—particularly around Manezh Square—were Slavic. They looked like raw recruits, uncertain what they were doing there and extremely uncomfortable when civilians caught their eye and asked point blank: "You wouldn't shoot at us, would you?"

The putschists had called a press conference for 5:00 P.M. Monday. When I arrived at the Foreign Ministry's press center at 4:00 P.M., it was bedlam. For some reason, guards at the door were favoring foreign correspondents, and I managed to fight my way into the building in time to get through the security check and find a seat.

As I waited for the beginning of this surreal event, I wondered how one should address questions to the leaders of a coup.

Should they be simple and straightforward? Carroll Bogert of *Newsweek* apparently thought so. She was recognized first and asked: "Where is Mikhail Sergeevich Gorbachev? What is he sick with?"

Or should one load the question with all the contempt one felt for the men on the stage?

"Bearing in mind the wording of your communique, did you ask for advice from General Pinochet?" demanded an Italian correspondent.

His impudence won a round of applause from his colleagues, but no satisfactory response from the putschists.

In the end, it was a journalist from the scrappiest of the new Soviet newspapers who found what struck me as precisely the right balance of contempt and courage, delivered in a voice with only the thinnest veneer of civility: "Could you please say whether or not you understand that last night you carried out a coup d'état?" asked twenty-four-year-old Tatiana Malkina of *Nezavisimaia gazeta*.

Malkina's impertinence did more than confront the putschists with the "coup" label. It was a warning of sorts, from an entire generation that came of age in the perestroika years, a generation that had never known the fears and subservience of its parents and was not about to meekly surrender its future to a bunch of old Communist fossils. It was an ominous sign for the putschists.

Our apartment was complete pandemonium that night. Irina, our beloved teacher and translator, monitored radio and TV while I juggled the constant jangle of phone calls—from editors in Washington and from Russian friends and acquaintances in Perm, Sverdlovsk, Izhevsk, and other provincial cities Bill or I had visited.

"This is Igor from Izhevsk. Do you remember me?"

"Yes," I lied.

"We have no information here. Can you tell me what's happening in Moscow?"

Of course I could, because even though I only later remembered precisely who Igor was, I was certain he had helped me generously when I was in Izhevsk. Provincial hospitality was one of the great joys of travel in the Soviet Union; it more than made up for the nightmare of Aeroflot flights and the discomforts of provincial hotels.

Irina and I took turns fielding these calls, swapping our news about Boris Yeltsin's defiant stand at the Russian parliament for information about the scene in the provinces. It seemed that outside of Moscow and Leningrad there were no protests in Russia, but neither were there tanks. And so far, the putsch's information blackout had succeeded in censoring Yeltsin's protests.

That was about to change, though. At 9:00 P.M., "Vremia," the main television news program, opened with yet another reading of the statements and decrees of the GKChP, the country's ostensible new rulers. And then, suddenly, amazingly, there was Boris Yeltsin's burly figure standing on an unfriendly tank outside his parliament building, spitting out an eloquent denunciation of the coup. Yeltsin's audacious act would later become the most stirring symbol of resistance to the coup. Now, inexplicably, the putsch-controlled airwaves were transmitting this symbol to the entire country, along with a daring narration by Sergei Medvedev, a young reporter for central television.

Medvedev informed his viewers about Yeltsin's call for a nation-wide strike. When Yeltsin's image faded, there was Medvedev at the barricades around the Russian White House, describing the barrier-building and interviewing a series of calmly determined Muscovites who had come to defend the building.

Medvedev's report sent an electrifying message around the country: although the putschists had deployed tanks on the perimeter of central TV headquarters, they were not in full control of what went out on the air. Psychologically, that bit of information was as important to the resistance as was the powerful image of its leader, Boris Yeltsin.

After "Vremia," we had fewer callers from the provinces. Now people knew; Yeltsin had drawn his line and urged the public to stand behind him. What would the people do?

On Tuesday morning, as we drove around Moscow, it seemed at first that the people would acquiesce rather than rebel. The city looked dismayingly normal. Shops were open, offices functioned, factories produced. When I stopped people on the streets, most said they opposed the coup, but few were ready to respond to Yeltsin's strike appeal.

"We'll see how things develop further," one woman told me.

I asked what developments she was waiting for. She said she and her coworkers simply hadn't yet gotten around to talking about Yeltsin's appeal.

When might they talk about it, I asked. "After lunch," she said, looking like she hoped I would go away. I expressed amazement that more than twenty-four hours after it began, she felt no sense of urgency about the coup—even though she claimed to sympathize with Yeltsin. Nothing strange about it, said the woman, explaining that the construction office where she worked was subordinate to the national government.

"What difference does that make?" I asked, mystified by what seemed to me a non sequitur. Irina guessed that the woman worked in a secret, defense-related office and was simply unable to cope with the notion of questioning anyone in authority—even men who had illegally seized power.

By early Tuesday morning all routes to the Russian White House were mazes of barricades. These made strong symbols of resistance, but they were rather pitiful defenses against a possible tank assault. The buses, cars, bricks, and metal strewn across the roadways would prove no more effective than the barricades of Vilnius or Tiananmen Square, should the military decide to attack.

The closer we got to the White House, though, the more buoyant the mood became. Several armored vehicles had come over to Yeltsin's side during the night. Unlike the troops on guard a couple of miles away, down by the Kremlin, the soldiers on these rebel tanks were smiling and chatting with demonstrators. They were happy to talk with a reporter.

"The people elected Boris Yeltsin, and the army is with the people," said one paratrooper when I asked why his unit had switched loyalties. Other soldiers responded with similar slogans. It was nice rhetoric, but no one was willing to tell me the details of how the group decided to defect to Yeltsin.

Even so, the paratrooper's explanation offered a reminder of the legitimacy Yeltsin had attained when Russian voters elected him as their President two months earlier. Russians had never before been given the chance to choose a leader democratically. Yeltsin's decisive mandate now put him on the moral high ground as he battled a gang of men with no legitimate claim on power.

The coup was one of life's rare moments of absolute clarity, when many are called upon to choose sides, and there is no gray area for retreat. As I picked through the campfires and debris around the White House early Tuesday morning, it seemed to me that very few had chosen Yeltsin's side; in a city of nine million, only a few thousand remained after Monday's all-night vigil. Even later that day, when the few thousand grew to a rally of tens of thousands, the crowd looked puny compared with the unbelievable masses I had seen at anti-Soviet rallies in the Baltic republics.

"It's not enough people," I thought as I watched the hourly expansions and contractions of the White House crowd. But what constituted "enough"? A military attack launched when the crowd had dwindled to only a few thousand could still easily become a massacre. Perhaps it was this nightmarish vision that kept the tanks away.

NPR's two weekday news programs are on the air nine hours a day, and during a fast-breaking event like the coup, a correspondent has to be reachable by phone throughout that broadcast time. In Moscow that meant sitting tight by the telephone, at home. This was enormously frustrating when I worked alone, as I usually did. But with Ben Roe in town, one of us could be on the streets, calling in information, while the other pulled phone duty.

Our broadcast link was an ordinary phone line like those available to Soviet citizens. International calls had to be booked in advance—perhaps one or two days ahead, to get through to America. For several months, though, I had taken advantage of a little-known fluke in the phone system that allowed me to bypass Soviet operators altogether. Although I could not direct dial to America from my phone, I could dial a call to Finland. Thus, I could easily reach the AT&T "USA Direct" number in Finland and immediately be connected with any telephone in the United States.

Now I worried that the putschists might shut down our only viable connection to NPR. Ironically, I should have worried about AT&T instead. Ma Bell apparently was not aware of its illicit Moscow-to-Finland traffic until the coup caused a huge jump in its use. By September the Finland route was blocked—apparently at AT&T's request, though no AT&T operator could ever give me a plausible explanation for this decision.

Fortunately the phones never went down during the coup itself. In fact, if the putschists did have any kind of blueprint for curtailing the work of foreign correspondents, they never carried it out. Our reports were not blocked, and we had considerable access to information—at least about the resistance.

The hard part, of course, was reporting on the putschists themselves, who did not appear again in public after the Monday night press conference. Their whereabouts and intentions became the subject of dozens of rumors over the next two days. But the only authoritative information about them came from TASS, the government news agency whose bosses had put up little resistance to the dictates of the coup leaders.

TASS's main rival was the independent news service Interfax, which managed to keep functioning throughout the coup, sending fact and rumor several times a day to its fax clients. Interfax had a nationwide network of aggressive reporters; Western reporters considered its reports uneven, but indispensable. During the coup, two of Gorbachev's more moderate aides used Interfax to issue a statement demanding the withdrawal of tanks and insisting that the President was not sick at all. The most poignant Interfax report was a rambling statement from former Foreign Minister Eduard Shevardnadze, who months earlier had stunned the world with his resignation and chilling prediction of an impending coup.

"I am aware that this may be a cry in the dark," began Shevardnadze, in his Interfax appeal for peaceful resistance. "I would like you to interpret my message correctly. May it not be regarded as a plea of despair. It is first and foremost an expression of hope and confidence in this country."

Fax machines were crucial to Yeltsin's strategy for challenging the coup leaders. Using his authority as Russian President, he issued a series of decrees, essentially taking control of the Russian Republic. Yeltsin aides transmitted these decrees by fax to newspapers all over the country. A couple of weeks later, in the southern Russian city of Krasnodar, I could see the impact this had had in the provinces. During the coup, with other information sources silenced, Krasnodar's local youth newspaper ran all of Yeltsin's decrees verbatim; as a result, readers many hundreds of miles from Moscow had the impression of a President busy grabbing control from the coup leaders.

Krasnodar's Communist Party paper did not run Yeltsin's decrees—only the bulletins approved by the putschists and put out by TASS. An editor at the Communist paper gave me this absurd explanation: while he did receive the Yeltsin faxes, he did not know whether they were authentic, so he ran TASS instead. Little wonder that the Yeltsin-appointed reformers who took over in post-coup Krasnodar were trying to confiscate the Party paper and all of its property.

The putschists had better luck controlling the electronic media, although there was an important exception in Moscow. Moscow Echo was a tiny independent station that had kept Muscovites well informed during the January siege in Lithuania, when most other media were muzzled. Several times during the August coup security thugs pulled the plug on Moscow Echo, only to have it reappear a few hours later from some other clandestine site. The cat and mouse game gave the Muscovites a morale boost every time the station came back on the air.

The reporting, though, turned out to be less than reliable.

On Tuesday night, with Ben on the streets for us at the White House, Irina and I had Moscow Echo tuned in during the single violent clash of the coup. A breathless reporter came on the air, describing a line of tanks, lots of shooting and a death toll of around ten. A few minutes later, Moscow Echo's transmissions went dead in mid-sentence. And a few minutes after that I had to be on the air with NPR, giving a live update of what was going on. Needless to say, my report was full of gloom. Only a bit later, when Ben managed to call me, did I realize that there was no tank assault on the White House. The clashes that did occur were a few blocks away. Fortunately, Ben's eyewitness description replaced my misleading report when the "All Things Considered" broadcast was repeated that night.

By Wednesday morning Volodia had become an expert navigator of the White House barricades, which extended for blocks beyond the actual Russian parliament building. After picking up Irina and me, he maneuvered through seemingly impassable routes, depositing us at the Hotel Ukraina across the river from the White House. Ben and some other reporters had managed to grab an hour or two of sleep at the Hotel Ukraina, and Irina and I brought them cookies and soft drinks for breakfast. These were the non-nutritional, high-energy mainstay of my diet during much of my five frantic years covering the Soviet Union.

After yet another cookie breakfast I waded through the crowds to the emergency session of the Russian parliament called by Yeltsin. In the lobby I mingled with parliamentarians and journalists. "We have won," said a smiling Lev Timofeev, a gentle writer who spent years in prison for the intellectual honesty of his essays on Soviet economics. Others told me essentially the same thing—that, having made it through a crucial night with no attack, it now appeared the military was in rebellion and would not come after Yeltsin.

I remained unconvinced as I went into the parliamentary chamber. Before the session got under way someone had a seizure; the man's desperate gasps seemed to me a horrible metaphor for Russia's struggle against the putschists.

Russia's top leaders took the stage—Yeltsin, Prime Minister Ivan Silaev, vice president Aleksandr Rutskoi, and the parliamentary chairman Ruslan Khasbulatov. These four men presented an incredible profile in courage throughout the coup; it remains incomprehensible to me that their alliance collapsed soon afterward—that Rutskoi and Khasbulatov later became the bitterest of Yeltsin's enemies.

After the dramatic speeches in parliament I rushed home to file for "Morning Edition." On the Garden Ring Road I noticed that the tanks parked outside the Foreign Ministry press center had disappeared. What could it mean? The press center was hardly a major strategic target, yet it was one of the few buildings where tanks had been stationed. I needed to find out what was happening at Red Square, but traffic in central Moscow made it impossible to go check and still make my Morning Edition deadline. Volodia dropped me at home, then dashed off with Ben to inspect Red Square.

Unlike most of my colleagues, who lived in foreigners' compounds, I rented a tiny Soviet apartment. An elderly neighbor got on the elevator with me, sorting through her mail.

"Our newspapers are very sad today," she told me. "Everything is very sad today."

"Maybe it will all turn out all right," I said, not stopping to explain why I felt a sudden burst of optimism.

Half an hour or so later my optimism was confirmed. Ben called to say that he and Volodia arrived in time to witness the parade of tanks leaving Red Square. Soon after that I went on NPR with the first concrete news indicating the coup was ending.

The rest of the day was a wild parade of rumors. Some putschists had committed suicide. No, they all boarded a plane to seek asylum in Central Asia. No, they were drunk in the Kremlin. No, they had been arrested. No, they were headed down to see Gorbachev, to beg his forgiveness. . . .

As the hosts of NPR badgered us for confirmation of each story, I recall finally going on one broadcast, running through every rumor I had heard in the past couple of hours, and ending by advising the host to "take your pick."

"Who's in control, who's running the country?" the hosts persisted, until about 4:00 A.M. on Thursday, when "All Things Considered" was heading into its final hour. Damned if I knew. All I could say with certainty was that the putschists were gone, Muscovites had deliriously celebrated their departure at the White House, and Mikhail Gorbachev was back in Moscow. An NPR host wanted to know what Gorbachev's return meant for the future of the Union Treaty, a document defining new relationships among Soviet republics. I pointed out that since dawn was just approaching, and democracy seemed out of danger for the moment, most of Moscow was getting some well-deserved sleep; the fate of the Soviet Union could be resolved later, after everyone woke up.

4 | The August 19 Press Conference

The mass-circulation magazine Ogonëk *(October 5–12, 1991) published this interview with Tatiana Malkina, a twenty-four-year-old journalist for the newspaper* Nezavisimaia gazeta. *Tatiana Malkina rose to fame at the August 19 press conference of the Emergency Committee when she alone dared to pose the unequivocal question: "Could you please say whether or not you understand that last night you carried out a coup d'état?" The following account weaves interview material with commentary by the journalist Asya Kolodizhner.*

Malkina: The 19th of August is my birthday. Mom got up at six in order to prepare a lot of food for me to take to the office for a birthday celebration. All departments of *Nezavisimaia gazeta* are in a single large stable, a section of the former "Voskhod" factory. At work we're all crazy about one another and so I decided at once to treat everyone. Suddenly my mother woke me up: "Get up, Tania, they're saying something on the radio. . . ." Half asleep, I responded grumpily: "Come on, Mom, can't you let me sleep once a year." My mother then turned up the radio all the way. And imagine, there I was, the angelic birthday girl, lying in bed and swearing horribly. Mom's used to that. Now I had to wake up my colleagues and argue over who was going to wake up the chief. . . .

But of course no one canceled the refreshments. Tania's excited coworkers greeted the victuals with a thunderous ovation. At the office, Tania first of all set about calling Yanaev's secretary.

Malkina: During the previous two months at *Nezavisimaia gazeta* we frequently discussed a similar version of the coup. We imagined and tried to figure out who would do what to whom. I am a big fan of odious figures. And those of us in our department agreed early on that [in case of a coup] Gennadii Ivanovich Yanaev was mine. . . .

> For most of the summer Tania aggressively sought meetings with the Vice President, whose secretary, Vladimir Nikolaevich, was politeness personified, and who promised that if Gennadii Ivanovich was going to grant an interview to anybody, then of course it would be to *Nezavisimaia gazeta*. . . . Then he confidentially informed her that Yanaev just couldn't see her right now. You see, the Vice President had some ambassadors to see . . . from Mauritania, Tanzania. . . . The list of Gennadii Ivanovich's state duties was endless (maybe he was getting ready for the coup?). Tania punctually rang Vladimir Nikolaevich twice a week, and he soon got to know her.

Malkina: Every now and then I got angry and said, "Listen, it's not that the press takes such a lively interest in Gennadii Ivanovich. Could it be really difficult to find time for a thirty-minute interview?"

"Now Tania," responded the secretary, "a half hour is not nearly enough for your newspaper. We need to find time for a serious discussion."

Eventually, my boss told me: "Just forget about him. Who cares about this Gennadii anyway?" And then the Emergency Committee came along.

On the 19th I placed my call. "Vladimir Nikolaevich, you owe me one. Everything has changed completely, everything has become s-o-o-o interesting. Gennadii Ivanovich is our President now, just about. . . ."

Vladimir Nikolaevich responded gently, playing along as it were, that Yanaev was terribly busy and had pressing business affairs. He asked me to call back in an hour. When I did so, he was very severe with me. He said that there would be no interview today, but that there was going to be a press conference at five o'clock. But he said nothing about the special one-time pass for the press conference or about the fact that it would be hopeless trying to attend it.

> Tania went to the press conference with a colleague. At the entrance to the building there was a huge crowd, some guards, and admission for "pool" reporters only. Journalists are used to sur-

prises, and after a long altercation with the guards, Tania's colleague got inside and handed some sort of pass to her behind the back of one of the guards.

Malkina: There was a second checkpoint right in front of the entrance to the auditorium, where you again had to show a pass. Once more we had to dodge and enter together as a single "pool." The officer who frisked us almost got hold of my mace cartridge, which I covered with a handkerchief. Luckily, however, he didn't realize what it was. Oh, you know, I said to him, those are my personal items, feminine things, and I nervously began to enumerate all kinds of cosmetic items. In short, we slipped through.

During the press conference I wanted to stand up, pull a stupid face, and pronounce in a serious tone: "Gennadii Ivanovich! You know today's my birthday. Now in 1968 at this time you were sending troops into Czechoslovakia, but I was only a year old, and now today you've offered me this present. A classy present! Thank you!" Then I would shed a few tears. . . .

We were almost late, and we entered simultaneously with the . . . leaders. Suddenly, my mood turned ugly. Oh, what asses! It was not just that they were scoundrels and criminals, no, it was simply a panopticon. . . . "Good heavens," I thought, they are far outside the bounds of reason, they are irrational and the irrationality can set in for good." You know, they made me experience such a feeling of rage that I simply wanted to strangle them. . . . And yet the journalists were still asking such flabby questions. When it comes to poor Ignatenko [Gorbachev's press secretary], they hack at him as hard as they can, but now these same handsome things can't even open their mouths . . . not a word. . . . All the foreigners were sleeping or something. . . . The only serious question came from the journalist from *La Stampa*. But questions like this are not for these rulers manqués.

After the press conference people began to recognize Tania on the street and in the subway. The reactions were diverse. A female TV viewer called the editorial offices, insisted on speaking to the editor-in-chief, and vented her anger about Tania's behavior at the press conference. For some reason, she above all did not like Tania's dress. Then a young man sent in some verses . . . which also contained a few words about her dress.

Tania's mother wore this dress in her youth. It was considered to be a holiday outfit, and Tania would wear it if on a given night she said to herself, "Tomorrow I'll be a lady." And on the 19th she was wearing it; it was her birthday, after all. . . . Her usual form of dress is a pair of jeans and a sweater.

Malkina: I do not want to be remembered by my fellow citizens as a heroine because of that one question. Any journalist from the *Nezavisimaia gazeta* would have asked a similar question. The press conference was a purely emotional moment, and indeed we realized even that morning that the whole thing was a soap opera and that the strings were being pulled from backstage. . . .

There were many young journalists among those who did not allow the news blackout to develop. The majority of workers at the newspaper *Rossiia* are under thirty. They all stayed at the White House during the coup and released over forty leaflets. Tania Voloshina, who is twenty-seven and the mother of four-year-old Sasha, and Lena Moskaleva, who is twenty-two with two children, led the editorial team of *Rossiia* on the fifth floor of the White House for three days and three nights. . . . Moscow Echo did not stop its work for an hour, even after it was taken off the air. Democratic publications put out the *"Obshchaia gazeta."**

Any of the young people who are accustomed to using Aesopian language or to concealing their gestures of defiance could have asked a question like Tania's. They do not find it necessary to struggle against self-censorship, like their older colleagues. They are also unaware, it would seem, of Glavlit [the USSR censor]. These journalists were not educated by Prague 1968, but by the Baltics. . . .

A truly independent press is on its way.

---

*This was the name of the joint newspaper put out during the coup by eleven newspapers banned by the Emergency Committee.

5 | A Russian Reporter Remembers the Coup

Valerii Kucher is a journalist from Magnitogorsk. In 1983 he became the editor of Magnitogorskii rabochii, *a local newspaper he helped transform into a radical mouthpiece of glasnost during the Gorbachev years. Kucher's outspoken journalism won him a seat in the USSR Congress of People's Deputies in March 1989. He was elected to the new Soviet parliament as a representative of the Journalists' Union. At the time of the coup he was the editor of* Rossiiskie vesti, *the weekly newspaper of the government of the Russian Federation. He was interviewed in Moscow in March 1992 by Irina Mikhaleva, who works for the Moscow Bureau of National Public Radio.*

We were awakened by a call from Magnitogorsk. It was a little after 6:00 A.M. in Moscow. It was my daughter. The time difference is two hours. "Do you have a coup d'état there?" We did not understand what she was talking about. "Turn on your radio—you have a coup d'état." So we turned on the radio at six in the morning and we heard the announcement.

I drove to the White House at once. On my way there, I passed by several tanks. The first person I saw at the White House was General Kobets. We actually ran into each other as we were entering the White House. He was very agitated and kept repeating: "Damn it, damn it, we must organize something, we must do something, we must organize something."

"But what happened? What are we to do?" I asked him and followed him to his office. I tried to find out what was happening.

"I have just come back from Yeltsin's dacha," he said. "We have decided we must organize the defense of the White House. The situation is dangerous—it's a putsch. Anything could happen now."

It was hard to understand what was really going on at that point, because there was nobody from the top leadership around.

Mikhaleva: What was your emotional state at that moment?

Kucher: I felt agitated and disoriented. I should tell you, though, that I was not vacillating, was not trying to make up my mind what side I was on. No, it was completely clear to me. I was not even conscious of any decision. Just as you aren't conscious of your heartbeat, so I was not conscious of the decision. It came naturally, it went without saying. . . . But I did feel anxious, agitated, because there was no information about anything. I called the editorial office of the newspaper [*Rossiiskie vesti*], told them where I was, and asked them to stay put and wait for me. That's how I reacted at the beginning. I tried to stay in close touch with the people in the leadership.

Mikhaleva: What was the scene at the White House?

Kucher: I went to the Information Center. Phones were ringing nonstop. After a little while, newspeople began to gather. The first news I heard when I got there was that arrests had commenced. It was close to 9:00 A.M. I was told that arrests had begun, that some individuals had been already arrested, that the Emergency Committee had already launched the policy of repression. Soon afterward, the leadership, including Silaev and Yeltsin, had a meeting with the deputies in order to make the first announcement. I was present at that meeting, and it was right there and then that Yeltsin spoke about the events as a "putsch." He did not equivocate, and this decisiveness and clarity in the use of words struck me then and etched itself deeply in my memory. These were precise terms. "It is a putsch," he said, "it is a conspiracy." The impression he conveyed was that of great possible, probable danger, and also that the situation was grasped with all the precision and clarity of which our language is capable. This sharp decisiveness and absence of any equivocation on the part of Yeltsin and his close aides somehow gave a more manageable shape to my personal anxiety, straightened it out, so to speak. The situation became clear in my own mind, too.

I decided to convey this sense of clarity, this analysis of the events to my colleagues, the news staff of *Magnitogorskii rabochii*. I did not think that I was courting possible danger, that people would be divided into those who supported or did not support the putsch. What was important for me was to share my sense of the events with the people of Magnitogorsk, to make sure that they heard my voice. So I arranged to be interviewed over the phone. The interview came out on August 20. In a way, I was infected by Yeltsin's clarity and decisiveness, and in the interview I, too, called a spade a spade: "It is a conspiracy, a putsch, an attempt at a revanche." The guys at the newspaper—you have to understand this is a provincial newspaper—were very worried. They took the whole night to put the issue together and print it. The workers who had a democratic orientation guarded the paper throughout the night. I have been told also that not a single person left the editorial office until they finished printing the issue. In the morning, even before the trams began going, they had hand-delivered stacks of the paper at the factory gates. So in part, thanks to my interview, which was published in the issue, people were informed about what kind of an event was taking place in Moscow. While I was dictating the interview, I was looking out of the window of the White House. I was trying to convey my state of mind, my feelings.

I had the sense then that the headquarters of resistance were formed very quickly, that self-defense teams were organized almost at once, as people began to gather around the White House.

Mikhaleva: Did you have a sense on that first day that people at the White House were being organized according to some plan?

Kucher: I understand what you are asking. The answer is no. The sense I had then was that I was witnessing some sort of a spontaneous organization, that it was self-generated, that people were forming into groups and undertaking actions as they went along. Things were organized on the fly. I had the feeling then that I was completely, but completely alone. You were on your own completely, with no one standing over you, and you could do practically anything. If you wanted, you could stay at home, or you could participate. It was up to you. Those were the days of real choice, political, civic, individual choice. As the events were unfolding, I almost had the sense of a cloud cover lifting, of fog dissipating, of things becoming clear and lucid. It was only then that I understood what a horrifying country we had been living in, what danger had been stalking us, what kind of organization the CPSU really was, what a monster that system of partocracy was! It was only then that I fully understood those ideas that I had been voicing before the putsch—whether in my conversations with friends, newspaper reports, or speaking at public rallies. Those three days gave me the opportunity to gain a real understanding of the political choices. I used to teach Russian grammar to little kids. In those days I was not quite sure about the rules myself, and I remember that I would finally understand this or that rule only in the course of my explaining it to them. Only then would I be able to find my own words to explain to them why there should or should not be a comma here. Likewise, during those three days I acquired a system of my own convictions and my own arguments in support. I had held the same convictions before, but only during the putsch did they permeate my whole being and become truly my own.

Mikhaleva: What were the most memorable events for you?

Kucher: I remember well, first, how we were growing more and more agitated; two, how fear inside the White House was growing toward the evening of the 21st; three, how we experienced the sense of growing clarity about our position: on the one hand, you felt growing fear, on the other, growing resolve. There you were, with fear and resolve seesawing inside you and outside you. All of a sudden you felt terribly frightened and then, out of nowhere, you would begin to feel great resolve.

I saw the center of danger, which was inside the White House. But then, I would leave the White House and practically a few hundred yards away, life was as normal as ever, and people were going about their business as though nothing had happened. I saw people leaving the White House. Those were government officials, each carrying his briefcase, hastening to leave the area after the announcement of an impending attack had been made. A little later, when the danger had passed, some of them would come back. Among them were even government ministers who would come in and ask for firearms. After the danger was over, they liked the idea of parading about the place with a pistol. What I am saying is that some people were enjoying the play-acting, some were practically posing, reminding me of Grushnitskii, the poseur character from Lermontov's *Hero of Our Time.*

That first day, I was trying to be close to Yeltsin. That is why I was able to see how he would come out to share his decision with the people. I was not there when those decisions were being discussed and formulated, but I saw him come out with his new decision and announce it to us. I was there with him on the White House balcony as he spoke to the people, protected by those large shields that his bodyguards held on both sides of him. He was always very swift when he was in public, almost dashing. There was that sense of certitude about him. He first demonstrated it when he climbed that tank with his megaphone. That happened after Yeltsin's meeting with the deputies. Silaev spoke first, then Yeltsin appeared, followed by Burbulis and other leaders. Yeltsin made his speech then and left. He was followed by General Kobets, and people listened to him no less attentively than to Yeltsin. I recorded Kobets's speech. He, too, was very clear, but unlike Yeltsin, he did not offer any analysis of the events. He did say that the army would never shoot at its people, but he never called the GKChP conspirators or putschists. He was very measured. There were also questions from the deputies. I remember one repeating the question of some woman in the crowd when Yeltsin said to the soldiers: "You won't shoot at your President, will you?" And that woman said: "It's all very well that they won't shoot at the President, but what about me, will they shoot at me?" So one of the deputies asked the same questions.

Then I arrived at our editorial office, gathered everybody and said to them: "Folks, we've got to take a position. Our position should be firm, We are for democracy, we are against the putschists. We must do something." We had a small group of people with computers. This had been a very recent development with us, we had just then gotten the computer equipment. So, we put together leaflets and printed them. By the evening we had a lot, and all of us, including the women working in the accounting office, were distributing them by hand.

Mikhaleva: Hadn't your newspaper been shut down by then?

Kucher: Yes, of course. We had actually talked to the printers, but without much success. Our paper, from the very beginning, was conceived as an alternative to the Party's central press. We were a *Russian* paper. But our printer was the printing house of *Moskovskaia pravda*. They gave us the runaround at first, and toward the end of the day they simply said that they could not print our paper. I had hoped they would print us. So, we decided to go it alone. By ten that night, we had already produced a large stack of leaflets with Yeltsin's first decrees. And that's what we did every day. In the three-day period, we issued six leaflets, if I remember correctly.

Mikhaleva: How many copies did you produce?

Kucher: Not that many—all that our equipment could produce. I remember taking a stack with me to Kalinin Prospect, and people simply tore them out of my hands. I believe the reason few people got hold of these leaflets is that they would quite literally tear them apart, trying to yank them out of one another's hands. This was an explosion of glasnost: people believed every word they read in them. We would post them where we could—in the subways, on lampposts, and so on.

Mikhaleva: When did you get the sense that the putsch was failing?

Kucher: I was afraid that the White House would be attacked, I had a strong feeling that would happen. As to the ultimate failure of the putsch, I had no doubts about that almost from the very beginning, before everybody else understood it. The reason is that I received a phone call from the United States from my friend Professor Steve Kotkin, an American Sovietologist. He called me on the evening of the 19th and asked me how I was doing, what was happening. I tried to inform him the best I could. He said, "Listen, Valerii, my prediction is that it will all end very soon, two to three days at the most, and then it'll be all over. So, don't worry." That's the kind of conversation I had with my friend Stephen Kotkin. I knew that he understood the situation here pretty well, I was sure that his prediction would come true. Jokes aside, I did not think the putschists would succeed, but I was pretty sure they would try to attack the White House.

On the 19th, we had printed our leaflets, distributed them, and then in the early hours of the morning, I left the White House and went home. A few hours later, I was back there. I saw it as my function to collect the decrees and all other information there and pass them on as soon as possible to the editorial offices, so that they could quickly print them. Nobody gave me this assignment—it all happened spontaneously.

Speaking of interesting moments, I remember that first evening, I came out of the White House to see what was going on around it, and there on the barricades, I saw the Japanese ambassador. It was the 20th. He drove up to the barricades in his embassy car. I was very intrigued by his presence there. I walked up to him, greeted him, and asked for an interview. He agreed. After this interview, we became friends. It was clear that he wanted to make a statement. The Japanese leadership had a rather strange, reserved reaction to the putsch, but he wanted to show where he stood, and it was very important for him that an editor saw him there and even interviewed him right on the barricades. For me it was important to clarify for my readers the Japanese government's attitude to the events. He was very judicious in his remarks, as you can understand.

I had frequent meetings with General Kobets during those days, talked to him, interviewed him, saw how the security regime in the White House was growing tighter and tighter. At a certain point, a security detail took a position on the roof, and at a certain point, they began distributing bullet-proof vests. By the evening of the 20th, the internal White House radio station began its broadcasts. I have a tape of Sergei Stankevich's report about Gorbachev in Foros. All these reports were eagerly awaited and were quickly snatched up by reporters and passed on to editorial offices. I always tried to pass on this information to my old colleagues in Magnitogorsk as well as my Moscow paper.

On the evening of the 20th, the situation was very grave. We were expecting the attack at any moment, and there were constant rumors about the "appointed hour" of the attack. Around ten in the evening, I went home to pick up my wife. I wanted her to see the White House and what was happening around there. Despite all the barriers, etc., we managed to get right into the thick of it, almost right up to the very White House. We took a walk around the barricades. I wanted to show her what was going on, because she was just holed up in our apartment on the Rublev Highway, frightened to death that something might happen to me. People were sitting around bonfires under the drizzle. . . . A few days later, I found out that the head of the Moscow Weather Bureau sent an official letter to Ivan Silaev denying the rumors that he was in cahoots with the junta and that it was he who used some means to bring about the rain over the White House on the 20th. It was an official letter, really, in which he denied his complicity in and ability to produce localized rainfall and asked Silaev to dispel all such suspicions. That kind of absurdity also took place then. Suddenly, many government officials began to fear that they might be suspected of cooperating with the junta.

Mikhaleva: Was there a Press Office at the White House?

Kucher: Yes. It was Sergei Stankevich, for the most part, who played the role of the Press Secretary. The important information was the decrees and official decisions, and as soon as I received them, I would pass them on to the editorial office.

On the evening of the 20th (it could have been early the next morning—I can't recall now), I ran into Poltoranin, the Press Minister [Chairman of Russia's State Committee on the Press], in Yeltsin's waiting room. I said to him: "Mikhail Nikiforovich, look, we've started publishing a newspaper, we print it ourselves and then post it all over the city. You know, the junta banned us, but we couldn't just sit still, so we found a way to print the most important things."

He said that they were discussing the idea of an opposition press and publishing a joint newspaper to tell people what happened. "Get on the phone to Yegor Yakovlev," he said. "Use the government line and call him—he's waiting to hear from people. Send him your representative."

This idea of publishing a joint newspaper was floating around then. I remember discussing it quite spontaneously with our correspondent, Nikolai Vishnevskii. It was he who said to me during our planning meeting at the editorial office that it would be a good idea to publish a joint newspaper with all the other banned papers. By the time we had gotten hold of the telephone numbers of the editors-in-chief, the idea, as it turned out, had already surfaced elsewhere.

After my conversation with Poltoranin, I called Yegor Yakovlev and asked him what my newspaper's contribution should be, what we should be writing now. He said: "Call *Kommersant*, send your own reporter there, and then you'll decide what you should cover. But for the time being, we'll just publish a joint newspaper containing all the official decrees of the Russian government, and if you don't mind, we'll put your name down, too, as a cofounder of the issue."

Of course, I agreed. But we did not have the time to bring out a second issue of the joint paper—the putsch was over. The idea, though, was to have one liaison person from every paper, somehow to coordinate the coverage, and to publish it under a single roof, so to speak. I liked this idea so much that I decided to set up a Club of Eleven Editors, associated with my paper, and later on, sometime after the putsch, we produced the second issue of this joint newspaper. This then was the opinion of every one of these editors about the situation in the country. Actually, we put out two issues after the putsch. That's how the idea of the joint newspaper was realized. Of course, it had no real future: even the two issues that I put together after the putsch were a rather artificial creation. My impulse was to preserve that feeling of solidarity we all had then, but under normal circumstances, there was neither a need for it nor an inclination. We simply do not have that kind of cause today, a powerful cause to bring everybody together.

Mikhaleva: What do think about the radio reporting in those days?

Kucher: Of course, those days were ideally suited for the radio. Moscow Echo was superb, unique. I tuned in as often as I could. They did an excellent job.

Mikhaleva: My own impression is that, for the most part, in the country as a whole, people reacted rather impassively, with indifference. Only a small number took an active part in the events. The rest appeared indifferent. What do you think? What caused this attitude?

Kucher: I explain it by the fact that people had been lied to so much and for such a long time that they simply could not understand what was going on. Only now, perhaps, are they capable of more or less sober analysis. Indeed, only now is it beginning to sink in what would have happened had the putschists won. Finally, the events developed so fast that people simply did not have the time to make judgments, to form an opinion. They could not appreciate the enormity of what had happened, that the entire social system had changed.

Mikhaleva: And you yourself, did you understand that the putsch meant the end of communism, that communism would come to an end in these three days, that the whole system would collapse? Did you really think that on, say, Wednesday the 21st?

Kucher: No, of course not. I'll be frank with you—I could not foresee the rapidity with which the events actually unfolded. And I was very surprised that things moved so fast. But I knew, I sensed it with my whole body, that if the junta took the upper hand, democracy in Russia would be doomed. But I did not understand that this huge machine, this enormous edifice, had such spindly legs, was so easy to knock down. As we wrote in that first issue of the joint newspaper after the putsch, democracy had won because a free people and a free press took their stand together. It turned out that people's inner mood, inner feeling, was so much opposed to the CPSU and its system, so much opposed to all they stood for, that the collapse of communism did not take that much effort. But it is true there wasn't any exuberant reaction on the part of the people in those three days. They did not respond in one big outburst, with fireworks and so forth, but slowly and in different ways. They have been responding ever since. It takes time to absorb freedom, to become comfortable with it—that's my opinion.

Mikhaleva: What about now? If a putsch were to happen now, would it succeed?

Kucher: I know there is talk like that and some regret that the putsch failed. But let us look at those who came to defend the White House. They were younger people, for the most part. The veterans of the CPSU, the Komsomol, the war veterans did not man the barricades. Young people came, and there were many young women. It was a very good-looking crowd, good faces. . . . Perhaps, for the young people, it was an opportunity to put themselves to a test as a social force. And of course, in defending the White House, these people did not have any specific political or social program in mind, they did not think that, for example, we must take strong measures to stabilize the ruble, to carry out a radical land reform and so forth. Those were not the slogans that moved them in those three days. What did they feel? My sense is that people simply could not stand the idea of having those Party martinets remain in power. Nobody wanted all those Lukianovs, Ryzhkovs, all those monsters, those Party bosses to continue governing the country.

Mikhaleva: What was Gorbachev's role in all of this, in your opinion? I know it is a complex question, but I would like your own personal opinion.

Kucher: In my reporting, I once came across an interesting document —I have written about it in my newspaper. It was a transcript of Lukianov's talk with a delegation of Russia's deputies. It was not intended for publication. Among them were Silaev and a few other members of the government. In this talk, Lukianov used threats, saying that if Russia continued to refuse to abide by the Union laws, there would be unpleasant consequences. He spoke with authority, as one of the key members of the Union government; he spoke as the master of the situation. And in that conversation, he said that Gorbachev was aware of the measures that might be undertaken against Russia's government. Later on, he changed his tune. But the transcript prompted me to write a note to Lukianov. Then, some military people have told me that they intercepted Gorbachev's communications with the Kremlin on the eve of the coup. I asked them if I could listen to the tape. They promised to give it to me, but I never received it. When I reminded them of the promise sometime later, they told me that they had lost it. It is hard to say what actually transpired. However, during the putsch, many in the White House were saying that Gorbachev knew about the plans to stage a coup.

Mikhaleva: Tell me more about what people were thinking about Gorbachev in the White House in those days?

Kucher: People associated with the apparat of the Council of Ministers —I emphasize, the apparat—tried hard to raise suspicions about Gorbachev; some in the military did too. Again I emphasize that these were the officials of the apparat, not elected officials; they were officials who are no longer there. They tried to present Gorbachev as a virtual accomplice of the putschists, if not the actual leader. Those people, I would say, were simply scoundrels. As to the elected officials of the Supreme Soviet, the democratic leadership, they had a clear position: "What happened to the President? If he is sick, give us the opinion of medical experts. Tell us where he is. Give us precise and clear information. Demand to speak to the President." Those were two distinct attitudes. It was clear that one segment, the apparat, wanted to count him with the traitors, to implicate him, to compromise him. Indeed, how else can one interpret that incident when I was told that they had the tape of an intercepted communication and then was told that the tape had been lost? Why did they approach a reporter with this sort of information? It's a question, isn't it? Perhaps someday I will name that person. Moreover, that person said to me: "We'll use the tape when the time is right."

So, to sum up what I think about Gorbachev, I believe that he could not have been among those who were prepared to use violence and terror against their own people. That is my personal conviction. As to the rest, I have no idea. When they talked to Gorbachev previously about the necessity to introduce a state of emergency, he may have said something to them that they interpreted as tacit approval. He could have meant one thing and they understood it in their own way. Perhaps there is some truth to those who say that his equivocations were so ambiguous that one could interpret them any way one wished. And surely he had doubts about his course, about his methods; surely, he considered all sorts of options in trying to find a way out of an impossible situation, agonized over them. But I do not believe that he was capable of those methods, of that role, of that massive lie. It is unthinkable for me. Of course, there are also some people now who want to present the putsch as a kind of comic opera. But the danger was real. And it wasn't just the tanks that posed this danger, not the immediate threat of violence. The question was the course the country would take: toward democracy or toward partocracy. That was the fork in the road.

Mikhaleva: But why would people who had already been invested with power, why would those people stage a coup? In order to prove that they actually had power? After all, Kriuchkov and Yazov had plenty of power, they pretty much controlled the situation. So why would the people who had real power decide to stage a coup?

Kucher: You know what? They did not have power over the people. It was a strange situation. For this is a real mystery: what is the relationship between the people and the rulers? Even today, I do not understand what it should be. But I know that in one way or another, the people give the rulers their consent, which allows the government to carry out its policy. What the putschists did not have was that consent, they did not have influence among the people, they could not gain a sure footing. For that reason, they decided to destroy those who had and continued to gain influence among the people. Take our problems today [early 1992]. If it had been Pavlov who decontrolled prices, people would have torn him to shreds. It is a question of trust, and because people trust this government, they are not in revolt. That is why they are still tolerating both Yeltsin and [Yegor] Gaidar.

That is what the putschists did not have, that is what they had lost. Even though they had the opportunity to issue orders, to use all the trappings of this enormous state, they understood that people had an aversion to them. They were *outside* the people. How did this come about? I think that people had become so sick of this Party, sick of the corruption around them, sick of this small clique presiding over their lives, their apparent incompetence. People had grown to hate them so much that it was imperative for the Party bosses to do something. To throw tanks against the people? That, obviously, could not achieve the desired effect. So what they set out to do was to destroy a few democrats. They could have been effective had they carried out large-scale repression, had they managed to destroy physically the people who were on their list. But they failed. What they did not understand is that they would have had to destroy hundreds of millions in order to re-instill fear in people. People had lost fear.

Mikhaleva: Why?

Kucher: It was not the kind of army that could do that. I remember talking to one of the first tankers who arrived at the White House. I asked him: "Who are you?"

"We are Soviet," he said.

"What the hell is Soviet?" I replied, "and what the hell did you come here for?"

Later on, I realized that this was not the right approach for talking to those people. They were frightened or something, they looked confused. For a soldier, to attack you had to be sure of yourself, and that is what they lost, they were not sure of themselves any more. This confusion created a vacuum, a split: they were not yet citizens of Russia, but they were no longer the soldiers of that old system. An army in such a psychological state is not capable of violence against the people. It is, in this sense, part of the people.

Mikhaleva: Returning to those three days at the White House, who were the people who impressed you most? What was the most memorable event?

Kucher: Government officials fleeing the White House looked to me like cartoon bureaucrats with briefcases. For the first time in my life, I was able to see what the *apparat* was really all about. They all looked alike, all carried similar-looking briefcases. The apparat was leaving the White House. In droves. That was the first, most memorable picture.

Second, I saw and felt—experienced for the first time—what it meant to make a real choice. I saw this in simple people. I saw this in militiamen, armed and wearing flack jackets. They were the first line of defense, and they would have been mowed down in the first few seconds of the attack. But they would not have turned back. People were facing possible death, just simple people, and they were standing firm—unlike the bureaucrats. I still carry this picture vividly in mind: some are fleeing, and some are standing firm.

And here is another impression that cuts deep into my memory. At moments of great stress, some people think only about themselves, about the opportunity to glorify themselves, to promote themselves. I saw in those days some individuals placed high in the government who, after the main danger had already passed, were asking for personal weapons. And they would sling those over the shoulder. It was clear that this was all make-believe. The same could be said about all those orators who suddenly appeared out of nowhere and began making fiery speeches after the coup had failed.

Mikhaleva: What about the situation inside the White House?

Kucher: To my surprise, the White House for a long time *smelled of the people.* It became democratic, totally democratic to the point that things were strewn around all over the place, canned food, heaps of bread loaves, cigarette butts on the floor, masses of people sleeping on the floor, including reporters. It was some kind of a revolutionary flophouse. Everything was simple, primitive even—not like today. Today you need a pass to get in, and you cannot even get into the cafeteria at Staraia Square.* The danger, the mortal danger people faced then, made you feel absolutely democratic. You felt like the other guy, it gave you a sense of solidarity, a great sensation of democracy. Nobody cared about rank or other distinctions—just people. Doors were open: feel free to come into any office. Everything there was in motion. But there was a time when the White House was practically empty, with only a few individuals staying put. It was when orders were issued for everybody to leave the White House by five in the afternoon. The attack was expected. So there were ten, maybe twenty minutes, the most tragic twenty minutes, when the entire building was empty while outside a sea of people was lapping at the White House walls. In those moments, the White House was quiet and empty—like a bomb shelter, with a few security people armed to the teeth (originally, there was little weaponry around).

Mikhaleva: Was it true that merchants came to the barricades with loads of food and cigarettes to distribute free of charge to the defenders of the White House?

Kucher: Yes, that was true, there were mountains of sausage at the White House, mountains of bread, cigarettes, tea, and so on. Indeed, the White House reeked of smoked sausage and baked bread for weeks

---

*Now the executive headquarters of the Russian government, the buildings on Staraia (Old) Square formerly belonged to the Central Committee of the CPSU.

afterward. Businessmen were not the only ones who were responsible for this cornucopia; the White House supply staff had done a lot also. I recall when General Kobets was only beginning to think about organizing the defense of the White House, practically the first thing he thought about was finding portable toilets. And he did find some. There was also a lot of intelligence gathering, tracking of the putschists' moves: for example, the headquarters at the White House were aware of every airplane takeoff and landing on the territory of the Soviet Union; they knew about every movement of troops. They were receiving confidential information from the General Staff, of course. Then, deputies were sent to meet with the troops on the Garden Ring Road. . . .

But let me tell you that some people were making money on it, too. One guy approached me and offered me something for money. He was speculating. I mean that even amid these tragic events, some members of the intelligentsia elite were seeking to promote themselves, some of the common folk were looking for opportunity to make a profit. That, too, was part of the picture, as it always happens when really big events take place—the good was side by side with the bad, the tragic, side by side with the ridiculous.

Chronology of Events of
August 19, 20, 21, 1991

In compiling this Chronology of Events, the editors relied on several published chronologies; documents such as the decrees issued by the Emergency Committee and by the government of Russia; their own memories of events; and—because there are many inconsistencies among all the above—a good deal of common sense.* Accordingly, the chronology should be used with caution. Note also that times given for some of the events refer to the moment of their being reported by a news service and not necessarily the moment when they took place.

The world found out about the conspiracy on Monday, August 19, 1991, but the coup d'état as such had commenced on the previous day.

On Sunday, August 18, in the Presidential vacation home in Foros, in the Crimea, Mikhail S. Gorbachev was at work on his speech for the signing of the Union Treaty (the signing was scheduled for August 20). At 4:00 P.M., he discussed his speech on the telephone with his aide, Georgii Shakhnazarov, who was staying at a nearby resort. At 4:50 P.M., Gorbachev was informed that a delegation, headed by his chief of

---

*The following sources have been used: *Khronika putcha: chas za chasom. Sobytiia 19–22 avgusta 1991 v svodkakh Rossiiskogo Informatsionnogo Agenstva* (Leningrad, 1991); *Putsch: The Diary* (Oakville–New York–London: Mosaic Press, 1992); *Current Digest of the Soviet Press*, vol. 43, nos. 33 and 34 (1991); *Komsomolskaia pravda*, August 22, 1991; . . . *Deviatnadtsatoe, dvadtsatoe, dvadtsat pervoe* . . . (Moscow, 1991); Valentin Stepankov and Yevgenii Lisov's *Kremlevskii zagovor: versiia sledstviia*, (Moscow, 1992); and General Aleksandr Lebed's memoir *Spektakl nazyvalsia putch*, published in Tiraspol in 1993, the first installment of which was reprinted in *Literaturnaia Rossiia*, September 24, 1993.

staff, Valerii Boldin, and including the Chief of the Security Directorate of the KGB, Yurii Plekhanov, had arrived—uninvited—and was
requesting a meeting with him. Reaching for the telephone to find out
the reason for this surprise visit, Gorbachev discovered that all of his
lines of communication with the outside world had been cut. After a
brief family council, Gorbachev met the visitors, who, speaking in the
name of the Emergency Committee, offered him an ultimatum: sign
the declaration of the state of emergency and transfer presidential powers to Vice President Yanaev, or resign. Gorbachev refused to do either. The delegation returned to Moscow empty-handed, and the
machinery of the coup d'état, much of it slapped together at the last
moment, went into motion.

August 19, 1991

1:00 A.M. Gennadii Shishkin, First Deputy Director of TASS, is awakened by a
phone call from Leonid Kravchenko, the Director of Gosteleradio, and asked
to come to the Central Committee headquarters.

4:00 A.M. The Sevastopol Regiment of the KGB surrounds Gorbachev's dacha at
Foros in the Crimea. The runway at the airstrip where the presidential plane
and helicopter sit is blocked on the order of Commander of the Air Defense
Forces, Colonel General Maltsev.

4:30 A.M. A coded cable, signed by the Minister of Defense, Dmitrii Yazov, is
sent to the Commander of the Far East Forces; the Commander of the Airborne
Paratrooper Forces; commanders of army groups, military districts and fleets;
and heads of the chief and central directorates of the Ministry of Defense,
ordering them to upgrade the readiness status of the forces under their command to battle-ready.

6:00 A.M. Central television and radio are taken over by the State Committee for
the State of Emergency, consisting of eight government officials: Vice President
Gennadii Yanaev; KGB head Vladimir Kriuchkov; Defense Minister Dmitrii
Yazov; Minister of Internal Affairs Boris Pugo; Prime Minister Valentin
Pavlov; First Deputy Chairman of the National Defense Council and leader of
the military industrial complex Oleg Baklanov; chairman of Peasants' Union
Vasilii Starodubtsev; and the President of the Association of State Enterprises
and Industrial Groups in Production, Construction, Transportation, and Com-
munications, Aleksandr Tiziakov. Only one nationwide channel is broadcast-
ing. Each hour, the following items are read: Decree of Vice President Yanaev;
Declaration of the Soviet Leadership; Appeal to the Soviet People; Appeal to
[Foreign] States and Governments and the Secretary General of the United
Nations; Resolution No. 1 of the Emergency Committee; and a declaration

criticizing the Union Treaty by Anatolii Lukianov, Chairman of the USSR Supreme Soviet. All of these statements, except for Lukianov's declaration, pronounce Gorbachev to be "no longer capable of performing his duties due to the state of his health." Lukianov's declaration is dated August 16, 1991; the others, August 18, 1991.

Minister of Defense Dmitrii Yazov, a member of the Emergency Committee, convenes a meeting of the commanders of the country's military districts. His instructions: maintain order and increase security at military installations.

7:40 A.M. KGB personnel enter the offices of the Moscow Echo radio station, shut it down, and seal the premises.

8:25–9:00 A.M. In Lithuania, the Radio and Television Center is taken over by Soviet Army troops. Broadcasts are interrupted, but radio transmission continues in the capital, Vilnius.

One of the first steps by the conspirators is to limit the press to nine central and Moscow newspapers.

8:30 A.M. Viktor Urazhtsev, People's Deputy of the RSFSR and the chairman of Shield, a veterans' association, is arrested outside the RSFSR Supreme Soviet Building (hereafter, the White House).

9:00 A.M. Telman Gdlian, a USSR People's Deputy famous for his struggle against official corruption, is arrested in his apartment by agents of the KGB. He is held under guard with two other RSFSR deputies, Mikhail Kamchatov and Nikolai Proselkov, at a military base outside Moscow.

The "Appeal to the Citizens of Russia" is signed by the President of Russia, Boris Yeltsin; Ivan Silaev, Prime Minister of Russia; and Ruslan Khasbulatov, Acting Chairman of the Supreme Soviet of Russia. The appeal declares the State Committee for the State of Emergency along with its decrees and orders to be illegal and unconstitutional; orders local authorities to observe strictly constitutional laws and presidential decrees; demands that Gorbachev be allowed to address the country; convenes an Extraordinary Session of the Congress of People's Deputies of the USSR; and calls for a general strike in support of these demands.

The Moscow City Soviet sets up headquarters to deal with the emergency situation.

9:20 A.M. Yeltsin signs Decree No. 59, declaring that (1) the Emergency Committee is unconstitutional and its actions a coup d'état; (2) decisions of the Emergency Committee have no legal force on RSFSR territory; and (3) officials following the orders of the Emergency Committee are in violation of the RSFSR Criminal Code and subject to prosecution.

9:30 A.M. In Moscow, movements of military columns begin, including army trucks, tanks, and armored personnel carriers (APCs). Broadcasting over the Russian television channel of Russian Federation broadcasting is interrupted.

10:00 A.M. The Press Service of the Foreign Ministry of the Russian Federation announces that foreign correspondents are invited to a press conference to be held at 11:00 A.M. in the House of Soviets of the Russian Federation (hereafter the White House). Yeltsin is expected to conduct the press conference.

The Leningrad Military District Commander, General Viktor Samsonov, announces on local radio and television the formation of the State Committee for the State of Emergency and the introduction of emergency measures affecting the workplace, public transport, the media, and communications. Strikes and public meetings are prohibited.

The Presidium of the Supreme Soviet of the RSFSR decides to convene an emergency session of the Supreme Soviet on August 21, 1991.

APCs surround *Komsomolskaia pravda*'s editorial offices.

10:30 A.M. Prime Minister Pavlov, a coup leader, suffers an attack of hypertension.

11:00 A.M. A large tank column advances into Moscow along the Minsk Highway.

11:30 A.M. Members of the USSR Committee on Constitutional Oversight sign a statement declaring the formation of the Emergency Committee to be without legal foundation. The statement, heavily distorted by the head of the official news agency TASS, Lev Spiridonov, is published in the Tuesday papers.

11:45 A.M. Demonstrators begin arriving at Manezh Square bearing banners of protest. No measures are taken to disperse the crowd. Vladimir Zhirinovskii, leader of the Liberal-Democratic Party, is chased from the square by protesters.

11:54 A.M. An army captain interviewed outside the building of the news agency TASS asserts that his unit would use its weapons against the civilian population if so ordered.

12:19 P.M. A spontaneous gathering takes place on Manezh Square and across from the Moscow City Soviet. Ten armored vehicles arrive from Maiakovskii Square but are blocked by the crowd on Tverskaia Street. The White House is reportedly surrounded by tanks.

12:30 P.M. Armored transport vehicles moving toward the center of Moscow are stopped by the crowd in front of the Moscow City Soviet. Demonstrators mount the vehicles and the vehicles turn back. The Russian tricolor flag appears in the window of the city soviet. Yeltsin is expected to speak.

The spontaneous gathering on Manezh Square now numbers several thousand people and continues to grow. Yeltsin's address "To the Citizens of Russia" is read and word about Yeltsin's call for a general strike spreads on Manezh Square. Demonstrators block Tverskaia Street near the Hotel National with two trolley cars.

Tanks have been positioned at all bridges in Moscow. According to Moscow Echo, the Commander of the Moscow Military District, Colonel General Nikolai Kalinin, newly appointed by Yanaev, announces that a state of emergency has been introduced in Moscow.

Chairman of the USSR Supreme Soviet Anatolii Lukianov has announced his intention to convene an emergency session of the USSR Supreme Soviet on August 26 and suggests that committees of the Supreme Soviet begin to consider the decrees of the Emergency Committee.

1:00 P.M. Yeltsin has emerged from the White House and mounted Tank No. 110 of the Taman Division, from which he appeals to Muscovites and all the citizens of Russia to give a worthy response to those involved in the putsch and to demand the return of the nation to normal constitutional development. Standing next to Yeltsin, Nikolai Vorontsov and General Konstantin Kobets also address the small crowd.

1:30 P.M. Military vehicles continue to mass around Manezh and Theater Squares. A motorized rifle unit is posted at the Bolshoi Theater. Buses with special assault troops are parked near the Historical Museum. Demonstrators again stop armored carriers between Manezh Square and Alexander Garden. Army Major Viktor Gogolev publicly announces that there are no orders to shoot. A Moscow City Soviet Deputy announces to the crowd that two factories are out on strike [unconfirmed] and People's Deputy Telman Gdlian has been arrested.

A group of demonstrators leaves for the White House. A large concentration of military personnel is observed in the vicinity of the White House.

Ruslan Khasbulatov has announced that the Presidium of the Supreme Soviet has resolved to convene an emergency session of the Supreme Soviet of the Russian Federation to be held on August 21. One issue will be on the agenda: "The political situation in the republic owing to the coup d'état."

1:35 P.M. Major General Aleksandr Lebed arrives at the White House on the orders of the Commander of the Airborne Paratrooper Forces (APF), Colonel General Pavel Grachev, to take command of the defense of the White House with the Second Battalion of the Riazan Regiment of the APF. The mission is accomplished that night.

2:00 P.M. The Central Telegraph in Moscow, now controlled by a troop of military personnel from the Taman Division, has terminated intercity and international communications.

People's Deputies of the Russian Federation have called on the Muscovites to come to the White House to defend it from possible attack.

2:37 P.M. In Leningrad, Nina Andreeva, an outspoken conservative, expresses full support for the coup and the expectation that a majority of the Soviet population will support it, with the exception of Moscow and Leningrad.

2:43 P.M. In Leningrad, an emergency session of the Leningrad Soviet is to be convened at 4:00 P.M. A crowd of about 1,000 people gathers outside the building.

3:10 P.M. The Commander of the Air Defense Forces, Colonel General Maltsev, has issued the following order over the telephone: "There have been attempts on the part of people close to Gorbachev to break through to Gorbachev. If such attempts are repeated, I order you to arrest all involved and hand them over to the KGB." This information is publicized by Sergei Stankevich on August 20 over the White House intercom system.

3:28 P.M. According to the Russian Information Agency, Gorbachev is under house arrest at his dacha in the Crimea.

The Memorial Society issues a statement condemning the coup.

3:30 P.M. At the White House, barricades are erected out of stones and bricks to prevent the storming of the building which, as rumor has it, will begin at 4:00 P.M. In the White House, a staff for the defense of the building is organized under Colonel General Konstantin Kobets, designated Chairman of the State Committee of the Russian Federation for Defense. [The decree confirming the appointment is signed on August 20.]

4:00 P.M. The air space over and the sea and approaches to Gorbachev's residence in Foros have been declared off limits by the Emergency Committee.

4:47 P.M. Yeltsin has issued Decree No. 61 transferring all executive organs, including the KGB, the MVD, and the Defense Ministry at the All-Union level, to his authority within the Russian Federation.

4:57 P.M. The Council of Ministers of the Russian Federation issues the resolution "On the Illegal Introduction of the State of Emergency" supporting Yeltsin's "Appeal to the Citizens of Russia" and Decree No. 61. The Leningrad City Soviet issues a similar statement.

5:00 P.M. In Moscow, Russian Prime Minister Ivan Silaev holds a meeting near the White House and reads the two presidential decrees and the resolution of the Council of Ministers of the Russian Federation. He calls upon Muscovites and Russians to oppose the unconstitutional coup d'état. He states that the whereabouts of Gorbachev are unknown to the Russian leadership.

Armored carriers clear all approaches to Manezh Square. The trolleycars over-turned by demonstrators across from Tverskaia Street are removed and ar-mored vehicles placed along all streets leading to the square. An officer requests that the gathering disperse, but the crowd is now growing again. Copies of the presidential address and decree shower down onto Tverskaia Street from windows in the Moscow City Soviet.

Meanwhile, Yanaev, Pugo, Baklanov, Starodubtsev, and Tiziakov are holding a press conference at the USSR Ministry of Foreign Affairs Press Center. Yanaev states that Gorbachev "is resting and undergoing medical treatment in the Crimea." He explains that the state of emergency has been declared "in a very difficult period for the country in order to avoid excesses of any sort."

5:10 P.M. Yeltsin issues his Appeal of the President of Russia to Soldiers and Officers of the USSR Armed Forces, the KGB, and the Ministry of Internal Affairs [MVD]. Characterizing the actions of the Emergency Committee, he says: "The 'order' promised us by the self-appointed saviors of the Fatherland will end in wholesale suppression of dissent, concentration camps, and night-time arrests."

In Moscow, tanks and military vehicles attempting to cross Borodin Bridge toward the city center were stopped by demonstrators who have blocked the route with buses and trolleycars. The military forces turn back, with one offi-cer firing his automatic rifle into the air.

5:15 P.M. The barricades around the White House have been reinforced with concrete blocks and dumpsters, but there has been no attempt to storm the building. Several thousand Muscovites have formed a human chain around the building complex in order to defend it.

5:30 P.M. Yeltsin has issued Presidential Decree No. 62 creating "a government in exile," including Vice Premier Oleg Lobov; member of the Presidium of the RSFSR Supreme Soviet, Sergei Krasavchenko; and member of the State Coun-cil, Aleksei Yablokov. They leave Moscow for Sverdlovsk (Yekaterinburg) and establish temporary headquarters in a special bunker 70 kilometers outside the city.

The USSR Central Bank has announced that it is terminating the sale of hard currency to citizens going abroad on personal business.

5:55 P.M. At the emergency session of the Leningrad Soviet, the deputies oppose the introduction of a state of emergency in the city. Sobchak has flown to Leningrad from Moscow. All approaches and entries to the Leningrad Soviet have been blocked by trucks.

6:00 P.M. A meeting of the USSR Council of Ministers is convened by Valentin Pavlov to discuss the operation of the economy under the state of emergency. Among the ministers present at the meeting, only Minister of Culture Nikolai

Gubenko and Minister of Environment and Natural Resources Management Nikolai Vorontsov express their loyalty to President Gorbachev. Vorontsov offers to serve as an intermediary between the Emergency Committee and the Russian leadership in the White House.

A scheduled plenary session of the CPSU Central Committee is postponed until the USSR Supreme Soviet has been convened to discuss the introduction of the state of emergency.

6:38 P.M. Yeltsin has issued his Appeal of the President of Russia to the Patriarch of All Russia.

7:00 P.M. The Congress of Compatriots opens in Moscow. Yeltsin is now not expected to officially open the congress as planned for 7:00 P.M. Participants in the congress issue no statement regarding the unfolding events in the country.

7:20 P.M. Leningrad Mayor Anatolii Sobchak appears on Leningrad television's program "Fakt" along with Deputy Mayor Viacheslav Shcherbakov and the head of the Leningrad Regional Soviet, Yurii Yarov. Sobchak calls for a political strike and a rally to take place the following day on St. Isaac's Square. Earlier in the day, Sobchak reported at an emergency session of the Leningrad City Soviet that President Gorbachev had been asked to resign but had refused and demanded to be allowed to make a televised appearance. Sobchak's speech at the session of the city soviet was broadcast live by radio to St. Isaac's Square where a protest rally was taking place. The work of erecting barricades has continued outside the city soviet.

8:08 P.M. The press center of the Leningrad KGB acknowledges that the introduction of the state of emergency came as a surprise to many KGB officers. It appears that support for the State Emergency Committee within the KGB is far from unanimous.

8:52 P.M. The Russian Information Agency reports that Yeltsin has addressed several thousand people gathered outside the White House. He announced that the Russian government would remain in the White House around the clock.

9:00 P.M. The USSR television news program "Vremia" goes on the air according to its regular schedule. In addition to the reading of the Emergency Committee decrees, the program contains sensational reports from Moscow and Leningrad showing—in a sympathetic light—mass resistance to the coup.

9:40 P.M. The "Vremia" studio receives irate phone calls from, among others, Boris Pugo, CPSU Politburo member Aleksandr Dzasokhov, and the head of the Moscow Party organization, Yurii Prokofiev, who are outraged by the report from Moscow. Finally, Yanaev calls and says that "it was a good, balanced report."

10:00 P.M. An announcement is made on the newly created Radio of the Supreme Soviet of the Russian Federation—Radio Russia—broadcasting from the White

House to clear away the barricades to make way for a tank unit from the Taman Division which will guard the White House during the storming that is now expected to come during the night. Shortly thereafter the tank unit, commanded by Major Sergei Yevdokimov, takes up its guard post.

Eight armored scout vehicles flying the Russian tricolor arrive at the White House under the command of Major General Aleksandr Lebed. Lebed reportedly announces that he and airborne troops from the Tula Division have arrived to protect the legal Russian authorities on orders from the APF commander, Colonel General Pavel Grachev.

10:20 P.M. Human rights activist Yelena Bonner calls upon Muscovites to "defend freedom."

10:30 P.M. Yeltsin signs a decree (No. 63) naming and condemning the leaders of the coup for their criminal acts. He appeals to all organs of state to uphold the Constitution and offers legal protection to officials disobeying the orders of the Emergency Committee. This is the last decree issued during the first day of the coup.

According to a press release of the Emergency Committee, the Ministry of Internal Affairs of the Russian Federation has ordered that cadets from the academies of the USSR Ministry of Internal Affairs be transferred, fully armed, to Moscow no later than August 21. Acting on orders from the Emergency Committee, the USSR Minister of Internal Affairs has voided the orders of Russia's Ministry of Internal Affairs.

11:30 P.M. The independent news agencies Interfax and Postfactum as well as the Russian Information Agency are still operating. Copies of the underground editions of *Nezavisimaia gazeta* and *Kuranty* are circulated.

Moscow Mayor Gavriil Popov returns to Moscow and addresses the crowd outside the White House.

August 20, 1991

12:00 A.M. Five of thirteen mines in Vorkuta go on strike. By noon three more mines have joined the protest. It is expected that the remaining five will go on strike as well. Miners in the Kuzbass also prepare for strikes.

Personnel of the radio station Moscow Echo have been informed that the Sklifosovskii Emergency Medicine Institute, which has the largest facility for emergency treatment in Moscow, is preparing to receive large numbers of wounded.

12:15 A.M. The Russian Information Agency reports that the leadership of the army, the MVD, and the KGB as well as members of the Emergency Committee itself are vacillating in their support of the coup.

In Leningrad, Mayor Sobchak holds a press conference and predicts the defeat of the coup. He states that all the deputies favor convening an Extraordinary Session of the Congress of People's Deputies of the USSR. He also says that General Samsonov has given his word of honor that military forces will not be moved into the city. Nonetheless, there are reports of troops and tank columns moving toward Leningrad. Meanwhile, the mayoral offices have been barricaded and Molotov cocktails readied. A guard for the building is assembled out of officers of the OMON and Afghan war veterans.

1:00 A.M. Half the telephones in Ivan Silaev's office have been disconnected, complicating his communications with government officials in other parts of Russia.

Nearly 10,000 people have assembled outside the White House. Self-defense units are being formed.

2:00–3:00 A.M. There is a report that Yeltsin tried to contact Yanaev, unsuccessfully. Later, Yeltsin reaches Yanaev, who tells him that Gorbachev is not yet capable of performing his duties owing to the state of his health.

3:11 A.M. There is an unconfirmed report that Gorbachev flew out of Simferopol the evening of August 19, his destination was unknown. Witnesses report that he appeared to be in good health.

4:00 A.M. Demonstrators believe that the storming of the White House is imminent. The people who spent the night defending the building appeal to Muscovites to relieve them so that they can go home and rest. According to the independent news agency Interfax, Ivan Silaev appealed to the defenders of the White House not to disperse "until people come to relieve you."

4:52 A.M. A column of armored transport vehicles approaching Leningrad is sighted 52 kilometers outside the city. According to official orders, these units should have arrived at midnight. By 5:00 A.M., KGB and Army divisions have joined the column near Gatchina outside Leningrad.

5:00 A.M. A deputy of the Leningrad Soviet reports that close to 150 military vehicles, tanks, and APCs are moving toward Leningrad. Self-defense units are being formed outside the building of the Leningrad Soviet.

6:07 A.M. In Moscow, Silaev gives a radio address at the White House. He thanks the demonstrators.

6:54 A.M. In Moscow, the citywide protest against the introduction of the state of emergency in the USSR, planned for noon, is moved from Manezh Square to the White House due to fears that tear-gas may be used against demonstrators. Manezh Square is completely filled with armored vehicles and troops.

8:02 A.M. According to the Russian Information Agency, Colonel General Pavel Grachev, has been put under arrest [this report proved to be incorrect]. Highly placed officials of the Russian government report that the Airborne Assault Division which arrived from Tula to protect the White House was acting on Grachev's orders.

9:00 A.M. The White House Radio announces Yeltsin's decree calling for a political general strike.

9:31 A.M. Outside Leningrad, the column of armored vehicles stops its advance and retreats farther from the city.

A meeting is in progress on the square at the Kirov Factory in Leningrad. The number of protesters on the square is estimated at 10,000.

10:00 A.M. In Leningrad, the protest meeting planned for Palace Square begins. It lasts until 1:00 P.M. with an estimated 130,000 to 300,000 participants. The meeting issues a unanimous declaration in support of the decrees of the Russian parliament, the Leningrad Soviet, and Leningrad's mayor. After the meeting, groups of protesters proceed to the Leningrad Soviet to guard the building.

In Moscow, Russian Vice President Aleksandr Rutskoi, Silaev, and Khasbulatov have reportedly left the Kremlin by car to present Anatolii Lukianov with an ultimatum.

Thousands of people continue to arrive in the vicinity of the White House. The building of barricades continues.

Yanaev has issued a decree, dated August 20, overruling Yeltsin's decrees nos. 59, 61, 62, and 63 of August 19 on the grounds that they are "at variance with the laws and the Constitution of the USSR."

The Emergency Committee issues its Resolution No. 3, establishing tight controls over the electronic media, closing down Russia's Television and Radio as well as Moscow Echo, and ordering the KGB and MVD "to take additional measures in order to ensure that the decree is carried out."

10:36 A.M. A memorandum, signed by Yeltsin, Rutskoi, Silaev, and Khasbulatov, is presented to the Chairman of the Supreme Soviet of the USSR (Lukianov), requesting, among other things, an urgent meeting with Gorbachev, the lifting of the state of emergency for the duration of the session of the RSFSR Supreme Soviet, the lifting of censorship, and the disbanding of the Emergency Committee.

11:00 A.M.–12:00 noon. Major General Lebed withdraws his battalions from the vicinity of the White House on orders from Colonel General Grachev.

11:00 A.M. The head of the Governing Board of the USSR Central State Bank, Viktor Gerashchenko, sends a cable to the heads of the Central Bank Branches and the National Banks in the republics demanding that they carry out their duties as outlined in Resolution No. 1 of the Emergency Committee or face dismissal.

The RSFSR Press and Information Ministry registers *Obshchaia gazeta* (Joint Newspaper), a publication formed by a consortium of eleven independent papers banned by the Emergency Committee.

According to the press service of the CPSU Central Committee, the Deputy General Secretary of the CPSU, Vladimir Ivashko, has been hospitalized for a minor operation. According to the same source, no plenary session of the Central Committee is expected in the next two days.

11:15 A.M. The leadership of the USSR Cinematographers' Union issues a statement protesting the introduction of the state of emergency and declaring the actions of the Emergency Committee illegitimate.

11:30 A.M. Rutskoi, Silaev, and Khasbulatov return to the White House from their visit to Lukianov. They are greeted by an enthusiastic crowd when they arrive at the White House.

11:31 A.M. The Presidium of the RSFSR Supreme Soviet has resolved that an emergency session of the Supreme Soviet is to be convened at 11:00 A.M. the following morning (August 21).

11:54 A.M. There is an unconfirmed report that Gorbachev arrived outside Moscow by plane the previous evening. Rumor has it that he is being held under KGB guard at a residence outside Moscow. There are unconfirmed reports that Air Force General Yevgenii Shaposhnikov has been placed under arrest on Yazov's orders. [These reports proved to be incorrect.]

12:00 noon. Outside the parliament, a rally begins under the slogan "The Defense of Legality and the Rule of Law." The estimates of the size of the rally vary from 70,000 to over 150,000.

There are now four different radio stations broadcasting from inside the Russian parliament building.

At the rally, Russian Vice President Rutskoi explains that the putsch leaders have been given 24 hours to meet the Russian authorities' demands. He reports that Lukianov himself admits the illegality of the State Emergency Committee's actions. Yeltsin also addresses the rally and reaffirms the position of the Russian leadership.

Meanwhile, outside the Moscow City Soviet, Aleksandr Yakovlev, Gavriil Popov, Eduard Shevardnadze, and Sergei Stankevich address a rally of thousands. They call the coup plotters "state criminals." At the conclusion of the rally, the demonstrators march to the White House carrying a giant tricolor flag which is to adorn the balcony of the White House.

A meeting of the heads of the "creative" unions is held at the office of the USSR Minister of Culture, Nikolai Gubenko, to discuss a common response to the introduction of the state of emergency.

The Central Committee of the USSR Komsomol has issued a strong condemnation of the Emergency Committee.

12:17 P.M. It is reported that the Emergency Committee is preparing a decree to remove Yeltsin from his post as President of Russia and prosecute both Yeltsin and General Kobets.

Units of the USSR Ministry of Internal Affairs in Krasnoiarsk hold a gathering in support of Yeltsin.

12:30 P.M. Colonel Ivanov of the staff headquarters of the Leningrad Military District Emergency Committee states, in reply to a reporter's question, that the attitude of troops toward the addresses issued by Yeltsin and the Leningrad Soviet is "positive."

An emergency meeting of the Congress of Russian Business Circles issues a strong condemnation of the Emergency Committee and appeals to the business community abroad for support.

12:34 P.M. The Presidium of the Moscow Soviet appeals to the military to avoid civil war and not to open fire on citizens.

1:00 A.M. Mstislav Rostropovich has arrived in Moscow from Paris and proceeded directly to the White House.

1:40 P.M. Russian Vice President Aleksandr Rutskoi has briefed reporters about his meeting with the Chairman of the Supreme Soviet Lukianov (see 10:36 above). According to Rutskoi, Lukianov said that he would convene a meeting of the Presidium to consider the legal status of the State Emergency Committee's decrees and would insist that Gorbachev be permitted to attend. Lukianov hoped to contact the President, who was reported to be alive and well. Rutskoi believed that Gorbachev was still under guard by a special unit of KGB troops at a dacha in the Crimea, and not in Moscow as some have reported.

Colonel Qaddafi of Libya has sent a congratulatory telegram to Yanaev.

Moscow Echo radio station is back on the air.

2:50 P.M. According to the Russian Information Agency, the Emergency Committee has issued arrest warrants for the USSR People's Deputies Sergei Belozerstev and Oleg Kalugin.

3:00 P.M. General Kobets sends the Supreme Commander of Russia's Cossack Forces, Mikhail Nesmachnyi, to the Mounted Regiment of the Mosfilm Film

Studios to take possession of horses and weapons needed by the Cossacks for the protection of the legitimate government of Russia.

USSR Minister of Environment and Natural Resources Management Vorontsov and USSR Minister of Chemical and Oil Refining Industry Khadzhiev sign orders transferring their respective ministries to the jurisdiction of the President of the RSFSR "temporarily, until power is restored to the President of the USSR."

3:09 P.M. The Ministry of Foreign Affairs of the Russian Federation issues a diplomatic note disclaiming responsibility for any acts by the Emergency Committee and requests foreign governments to freeze gold and currency reserves and cargo until an extraordinary Congress of People's Deputies of the USSR convenes.

3:15 P.M. President Bush calls Yeltsin and asks him about the steps taken by the Russian leadership to restore order. Bush expresses unqualified support for Gorbachev and Yeltsin on the part of G7 nations and praises Yeltsin for his courage.

3:26 P.M. Inside the International Section of the CPSU Central Committee, instructions are circulated on preparing secret documents and internal memos for destruction.

4:00 P.M. In Moscow, the rally outside the White House ends and the movement of military units intensifies. The Moscow Soviet receives a report that the storming of its building is scheduled for 8:00 P.M. The mayor and city soviet call upon Muscovites to go there and stand witness to any bloodshed.

The formation of self-defense units outside the White House continues.

4:02 P.M. Editors of banned newspapers jointly prepare a sixteen-page issue of *Obshchaia gazeta*.

4:11 P.M. It is raining in Moscow. The Russian Information Agency reports that troops loyal to the Emergency Committee will attempt to storm and seize the White House this evening. A part of these military forces are reportedly near the center of Moscow and are armed with sniper rifles equipped with night vision scopes.

4:28 P.M. Moscow Mayor Gavriil Popov holds a meeting to warn all Muscovites about the criminal penalties for those who attempt to create alternative organs of power on the basis of orders of the Emergency Committee.

4:39 P.M. Former USSR Foreign Minister Eduard Shevardnadze, speaking at a meeting outside the White House, says that "the dictatorship will not succeed."

4:51 P.M. Sergei Stankevich announces on the radio of the Russian parliament—Radio Russia—that the storming of the building may be imminent. He calls for full readiness and requests all women to leave the building.

4:55 P.M. Boris Yeltsin meets with Eduard Shevardnadze to discuss joint efforts to restore law and order in the country.

5:00 P.M. Prime Minister John Major of Great Britain telephones Yeltsin to inform him that his government is not even considering the question of recognizing the Emergency Committee. In response to Yeltsin's words about the planned attack on the White House, Major assures Yeltsin that were this to happen, the world community would act most decisively against the putschists.

The Japanese government has announced the suspension of trade and economic cooperation with the USSR.

A column of a hundred tanks enters Tallinn, the capital of Estonia, and proceeds to a neighborhood where the Russian-speaking population is concentrated.

5:19 P.M. The President of the Republic of Moldova, Mircea Snegur, has issued a decree declaring the Emergency Committee illegitimate and its acts illegal.

5:25 P.M. According to the Russian Information Agency, a snap poll of Muscovites has been taken on August 20. Out of 1,500 polled, 10 percent supported the introduction of a state of emergency and 79.4 percent were opposed. Only 3.9 percent expressed confidence in Yanaev as Acting President; 2.3 percent in Prime Minister Pavlov. In addition: 53 percent believed that Gorbachev must resume his duties as USSR President; 82 percent supported Yeltsin; 72 percent wanted order in the country restored; 64 percent believed this should be done within the constitutional framework; and 59 percent believed the actions of the Emergency Committee would exacerbate chaos and disorder.

5:28 P.M. According to news reports, the defense of the White House is to be reinforced with six battalions from the Leningrad region as soon as air transport can be arranged.

At the meeting of the Presidium of the Supreme Soviet of Russia, the storming of the White House was judged to be highly likely.

5:44 P.M. Yeltsin has addressed the crowd outside the White House. He says the junta will stop at nothing to hold on to power because they have everything to lose. He notes the state of emergency has only been introduced in those places where supporters of democracy hold power. He calls for calm and asks people to refrain from any acts of provocation against the military.

5:48 P.M. Yeltsin assumes the responsibilities of Commander-in-Chief of all the armed forces on the territory of the Russian Republic until Gorbachev resumes his duties as President of the USSR.

12:00–6:00 P.M. A meeting is being held at the office of the USSR Deputy Minister of Defense Vladislav Achalov for the purpose of preparing operational plans for attacking the White House. Among those present are: Vladislav

Achalov; Pavel Grachev, Commander of the Airborne Paratrooper Forces; Boris Gromov, Deputy Minister of Internal Affairs; Genii Ageev, First Deputy Chairman of the KGB; General Viktor Karpukhin, the Commander of the "Alpha" unit; and General Boris Beskov, the Commander of the KGB unit "B." They are joined later by General Aleksandr Lebed and Dmitrii Yazov. The attack plan, code-named "Thunder," was to be carried out at 3:00 A.M.

6:00 P.M. Speaking over the White House intercom system, Yeltsin adviser Sergei Stankevich reports that, according to reliable sources, Gorbachev and his family are being held at the presidential dacha in Foros in the Crimea.

There are two divisions in Moscow: an armored and a motorized infantry division. Two special police units are also stationed in the city. The troops are grouped at Kuntsevo, the city center, the Kirov metro station, and on Leningrad Prospect. Oleg Poptsov, the head of the Russian Republic Television and deputy of the RSFSR Supreme Soviet, calls on the residents of Moscow and officials of transport enterprises to block the advance of these troops by forming a ring around the White House.

Volunteers outside the White House are being instructed in self-defense, including the use of gas masks and Molotov cocktails. The defenders are asked to form into units of ten. Women have been asked to fraternize with soldiers. Some women carry signs saying "Soldiers, do not fire at mothers."

Leningrad's deputy mayor, Rear Admiral Viacheslav Shcherbakov, has been appointed by Yeltsin to be Commander of the Leningrad Military District.

6:25 P.M. Lukianov informs Yeltsin's aides that he has spoken with Yazov and Kriuchkov and both denied plans to storm the Russian parliament.

According to Yeltsin's Press Office, Yanaev telephoned Yeltsin soon thereafter. Yeltsin: "What are you planning—to seize the White House by force? Do you realize the consequences of this action for you both in this country and abroad?" Yanaev: "I know nothing about such an order. I will make inquiries, and if there is such an order, I shall rescind it."

7:00 P.M. In Moscow, 40 tanks move from the direction of Kalinin Prospect. In addition to the KGB troops stationed at the Hotel Rossiia, there are reports about the movements of an armored tank division and airborne combat troops. Meanwhile, radio broadcasts continue from the White House.

Inside the White House, an order goes out not to turn lights on: snipers have been spotted on the roof of the Hotel Ukraina across the river from the building.

7:35 P.M. Yeltsin has appointed Colonel General Konstantin Kobets Defense Minister of the Russian Republic.

8:00 P.M. Yeltsin declares: "I don't believe that Anatolii Lukianov did not know about the impending coup."

A meeting of the Emergency Committee is convened, chaired by Yanaev and attended by a several top government officials not members of the Committee. Yanaev reads his statement denouncing the rumors that the Emergency Committee is planning to attack the White House and suggests that it be made public. His suggestion is met with silence.

Later, after the Emergency Committee went into a closed session, a decision was made to arrest Yeltsin "for a certain period of time."

The Commander of the Moscow Military District, Colonel General Nikolai Kalinin, announces a curfew in the city of Moscow from 11:00 P.M. to 5:00 A.M. He also indicates that a withdrawal of heavy military equipment from the capital will begin at around 11:00 P.M.

Among the defenders of the White House are personnel of the RSFSR Ministry of Internal Affairs armed with Kalashnikov rifles. Employees of the private security firm "Aleks," wearing black stockings on their heads to conceal their identity, are guarding the White House.

Russian Foreign Minister Andrei Kozyrev announces at a press conference in Paris that the possibility of setting up a Russian government in exile has not been ruled out if the situation further deteriorates in the Soviet Union.

There are mass rallies taking place in the cities of Saratov and Samara in support of Yeltsin.

8:10 P.M. The Supreme Soviet of Lithuania condemns the actions of the Emergency Committee as illegal.

8:37 P.M. The President of Tatarstan, Mintimir Shaimiev, supports the Emergency Committee. A public rally protesting the introduction of the state of emergency, held in Kazan on August 20, was dispersed by Special Forces troops.

9:20 P.M. The news program "Vremia" announces new decisions by the Emergency Committee, including the curfew in Moscow.

9:33 P.M. Leningrad Mayor Sobchak and Deputy Mayor Viacheslav Shcherbakov appear on Leningrad Television. The latter appeals to servicemen in the Leningrad region to make a choice in favor of the people and fulfill the decrees of the Russian President. The emergency sessions of the Leningrad City and Regional Soviets continue.

9:38 P.M. Yeltsin offers legal protection to those in the ranks of state organs who immediately fulfill the decrees and orders of the President, Council of Ministers, and other agencies of the Russian Republic.

9:43 P.M. The Russian leadership has issued an Appeal of the RSFSR Government to the Organs of Law and Order and the People's Militia.

9:47 P.M. Rumors [subsequently proved false] circulate that USSR Defense Minister Yazov has resigned and repudiated the army's involvement in the coup. Chief of the General Staff Mikhail Moiseev is said to have replaced him. The Defense Ministry's press service denies this report.

9:59 P.M. In Leningrad, artillery officers make several demands for Gorbachev's release and in support of Yeltsin's call to bring the conspirators to justice.

10:00 P.M. Tanks with numbers painted over are seen moving away from Manezh Square in the direction of the White House.

All police stations in Moscow have been shut down. The military has taken over.

10:37 P.M. Russian Defense Minister Kobets issues Order No. 1 commanding all military forces on Russian territory to disregard all orders of the Emergency Committee, to prevent the use of force against the civilian population or elected government, and to return to their normal stations.

10:43 P.M. In anticipation of the expected storming of the White House, Russian Defense Minister Kobets issues Order No. 2 rescinding the curfew order. He calls on all involved in defending the White House to remain at their posts on alert.

The Moscow metro announces that trains will stop running at 11:00 P.M.

10:50 P.M. Yeltsin has issued an Appeal to the Troops of the Taman and Dzerzhinskii Motorized Infantry Divisions and the Kantemir Tank Division. He urges them to come over to the side of the elected government of Russia in defense of democracy: "My dear sons! I hope that you will make the right choice. I hope that you will take the side of legitimate authority, the President of the RSFSR."

11:00 P.M. Russian Defense Minister Kobets addresses the People's Deputies of the Russian Republic in front of the White House. Members of the Russian government are issued weapons. He announces that the building will be protected by nearly 2,000 organized defenders, including 300 armed professionals. The professionals include militia of the Russian Republic. Kobets also expects reinforcements from Minsk. In addition, there are thousands of people surrounding the building who are prepared to block the path of military vehicles. There are sixteen barricades around the White House. Lights inside the White House are extinguished. Gas masks are issued to everyone inside the building. The head of security for the Russian parliament receives a report that the assault on the building has been set for 2:00 A.M.

Throughout the evening, groups of deputies of the RSFSR Parliament leave the White House to meet with commanders of military detachments in Moscow and its vicinity.

11:02 P.M. The President of the Georgian Republic, Zviad Gamsakhurdia, appeals to the governments of Western nations to recognize the independence of the USSR constituent republics in light of the coup d'état in Moscow. At the same time, he qualifies the event as "either a backroom deal or a public spectacle staged so that certain politicians could collect political dividends that they have been counting on."

11:08 P.M. The Supreme Soviets of Estonia and Latvia have declared the actions of the Emergency Committee unconstitutional.

11:11 P.M. Moscow Mayor Popov issues local instructions "On the Activity of Public Organizations and the Suspension of the Activity of the Moscow Organizations of Veterans of War and Labor" (which had declared their support for the Emergency Committee).

August 21, 1991

12:00 midnight. The White House volunteers form groups of 100; bulldozers and tractors are repositioned to face in the direction of the anticipated attack.

Gennadii Burbulis asks the volunteers not to sacrifice themselves but to allow the attacking vehicles to go through: "We must win a moral victory."

If they are to arrive at the White House for the attack, the paratroopers under the command of General Pavel Grachev must begin to move at midnight, but Grachev has refused to give the order.

12:06 A.M. Bursts of automatic gunfire are heard from the direction of the U.S. Embassy.

Shots ring out in the vicinity of the White House.

12:10 A.M. More shots are heard from near the White House.

12:20 A.M. People's Deputies meet briefly in the White House to discuss which routes to take to meet military formations massing in the area around the building. The Krymskii Val by the river and Kalinin Prospect, a broad avenue that leads straight to the White House, are especially dangerous places to be at this time.

12:31 A.M. In the area of the barricades erected near Smolensk Square, single shots ring out. A detachment of five armored vehicles attempts to pass through a tunnel running along Tchaikovsky Street between the U.S. Embassy and Smolensk Square. The head vehicle is trying to ram a trolleybus but it fails to make an opening in the barricade.

A 23-year-old Afghan veteran, Dmitrii Komar, jumps onto APC No. 536 and tries to "blind" the vehicle with a tarpaulin. He is thrown off, gets up, and jumps into the open hatch of the APC. The APC lurches, and Komar is thrown out of and dragged alongside the APC. Vladimir Usov, who is running to help Komar, is shot dead. Another defender, Igor Krichevskii, throws a stone at the APC. As he begins to move in the direction of the vehicle, he is shot in the head. All three men are dead.

The Russian Information Agency reporters at the scene are approached by an army major who does not give his name but identifies himself as officer of the 27th Brigade. He tells the reporters that the storming of the White House is scheduled for this night, that the attack is to be launched by thirty tanks and up to forty APCs, and that close to one thousand soldiers are to participate in the operation.

12:35 A.M. The transmitter of Moscow Echo, whose reporters have been broadcasting live from the White House, ceases functioning.

12:37 A.M. According to the Russian Information Agency, a poll conducted in Voronezh disclosed that 49 percent of the 724 polled residents of the city consider the Emergency Committee illegitimate; 28 percent consider it legitimate; 23 percent are not sure.

12:45 A.M. The chairman of the Control Commission of the RSFSR Communist Party telephones Chairman of the USSR Supreme Soviet Lukianov, asking him to do everything possible to avoid bloodshed. Lukianov replies that he cannot do anything and that it was Yeltsin who had provoked the situation in the first place ("Where did his weapons come from?" Lukianov wondered).

12:57 A.M. The City of Samara supports the President of Russia.

1:03 A.M. Russian Vice President Rutskoi warns those gathered in the White House about a possible assault by KGB agents dressed in civilian clothes. He orders the security force to open fire without warning in case of such an attack.

Defense organizers at the White House ask citizens gathered outside to form a human chain.

1:30 A.M. There is an unconfirmed report that a military group with tanks is storming the building of the Moscow City Soviet.

The Moscow Military District Headquarters reports that the Kantemir and Taman Divisions are being withdrawn as unreliable. Only KGB and special-forces units will remain in Moscow.

1:35 A.M. People's Deputy Urazhtsev reports that he was arrested by the State Emergency Committee earlier in the day and urged to join the coup. Later he was released. He says, "I think they do not believe they can win. They're demoralized."

1:40 A.M. Kazakhstan President Nazarbaev calls Yeltsin and tells him that he has spoken with Yanaev who "promised not to use force."

1:45 A.M. Some 30 deputies go out onto the street to try to prevent bloodshed.

1:49 A.M. The Patriarch of All Russia, Aleksii II, issues an appeal for peace, saying that "who raises arms against unarmed people commits a grave sin which excommunicates them from the Church and from God."

1:00–2:00 A.M. Colonel General Vladislav Achalov, USSR Deputy Minister of Defense for Emergency Situations, reports to Yazov about the first fatalities and the rapidly growing numbers of defenders around the White House. He warns Yazov that the planned attack will result in massive bloodshed. Yazov calls off the attack.

2:00–2:30 A.M. The estimated number of people surrounding the White House varies from 10,000 to 50,000. Reportedly thousands more block distant approaches to the Krasnopresnenskaia Embankment where the White House is situated.

Eduard Shevardnadze arrives and enters the parliament building. It is announced by megaphone that soldiers from one military unit assured the People's Deputies they would not fire on the people.

The APC involved in the fatal incident was attacked by a Molotov cocktail and is burning near the tunnel under Kalinin Prospect. The human chains defending the parliament are shifting in response to reports about movements of the attacking troops.

The OMON troops that have guarded the Moscow Soviet Building leave for an unknown destination.

2:30 A.M. Members of a Moscow motorcyclist club (*rokery*) return from Kutuzov Prospect and report that no troops are there. Rumors circulate that additional forces have landed outside Moscow and are moving in. The White House defense headquarters is unable to confirm this.

There has been no attempt to storm the Moscow Soviet. Columns of military vehicles leave in the direction of Pushkin Square.

2:43 A.M. River transport crews bring their vessels to the Krasnapresnenskaia Embankment of the Moscow River and declare their support for Yeltsin.

3:04 A.M. Colonel General Vladislav Achalov, USSR Deputy Minister of Defense for Emergency Situations, has given assurances to a USSR People's Deputy that the military command has no plans to storm the White House.

3:08 A.M. Over the previous two hours, the Russian leadership has been in contact with Yanaev, Moiseev (Chief of the General Staff), Kalinin (Commander of the Moscow Military District), and USSR Supreme Soviet Chairman Lukianov. All of them—except Kriuchkov, who could not be found—swore that they would stop the troops. Although it is quiet near the White House, it is not known whether the coup leaders will keep their word about not attacking the White House..

3:15 A.M. The troops involved in the assault operation are leaving Moscow in a chaotic manner. The State Traffic Patrol reports that tanks have been crossing the Garden Ring Road for several hours—in the outgoing direction.

3:16 A.M. Moscow Echo is back on the air.

3:24 A.M. Deputy Minister of Internal Affairs Colonel General Boris Gromov, representatives of the KGB, as well as the Moscow Military District Headquarters deny that the military vehicle burning near the White House belongs to them. It is supposed that there were casualties among the crews.

3:30 A.M. The Taman Tank Division has already withdrawn from the city and the withdrawal of the Kantemir Division is in progress. The retreat from Moscow is proceeding at full speed, though in an apparently disorganized manner.

3:40 A.M. Rutskoi has spoken with Lukianov: Gorbachev's health is fine. Members of Gorbachev's Security Council, Vadim Bakatin and Yevgenii Primakov, have also confirmed this information.

4:15 A.M. An Air Force official says that "zero hour" has already passed, so everyone can sleep easily now. He asserts that there is not even one airborne unit in Moscow. He adds that "the rumors about Yazov's resignation are greatly exaggerated; the Minister of Defense is in command and leading the army."

4:20 A.M. The City of Moscow Military Commandant, Lieutenant General Smirnov, expresses regret for the victims and believes that no military commanders issued orders to storm the parliament. He states that no troops will attempt to seize the White House either tomorrow or the following day: the rumors about the arrival of additional paratrooper forces at the Kubinka base near Moscow are unfounded.

4:30 A.M. The State Emergency Committee headed by Yanaev meets at the Hotel Oktiabrskaia.

An aide to General Kobets reports that units of the Vitebsk KGB Division have halted at the entrance to Moscow.

5:00 A.M. The cadets of the Briansk Police Academy are heading toward Moscow to aid in the defense of the White House. Pugo has ordered the Moscow police to disarm the cadets.

5:16 A.M. Troops have occupied the first two floors of the television center in Tallinn, Estonia.

5:25 A.M. Yeltsin's aide State Secretary Gennadii Burbulis has contacted Kriuchkov several times during the night about possible movements of KGB troops and has warned the KGB chief about the dire consequences of any storming of the White House. Two KGB brigades in Moscow have just been turned back after Burbulis called Kriuchkov. In Burbulis's opinion, "a turning point has been passed."

The top leadership of the KGB is meeting through the night. Heads of departments either refuse to follow orders or maintain neutrality.

5:30 A.M. Kobets's headquarters learns that the majority of KGB units from the Vitebsk Division never entered Moscow. White House radio announces that the Briansk, Orel, and Vladimir police academies went over to the side of the Russian Supreme Soviet.

5:50 A.M. The leaderships of several republics of the USSR are preparing an ultimatum to the Emergency Committee. The Russian Supreme Soviet will consider it at 11:00 A.M. The central demand: the coup must be ended today.

Early morning. Yanaev calls Burbulis and explains: "I only wanted to improve the country economically, not knowing what consequences this would have."

6:07 A.M. The Russian Information Agency reports that, thanks to the intervention by People's Deputies Gleb Yakunin, Vladimir Kriuchkov [not the KGB Chairman], Sergei Yushenkov, and others, the six APCs trapped in the underpass and blocked by an irate crowd of protesters were able to leave in peace. Part of the retreating Kantemir Division, they were mistakenly thought to be on their way to attack the White House.

8:00 A.M. The defense staff of the Russian parliament reports that the danger of an attack has not passed and calls upon the defenders to remain.

A meeting of the executive collegium of the USSR Ministry of Defense is convened.

9:00 A.M. Defense Minister Dmitrii Yazov signs the order for the troops to begin returning to their permanent bases immediately.

9:25 A.M. Defense Minister Yazov resigns.

10:18 A.M. Moscow Echo goes off the air, again, on the order of a unit of paratroopers. The unit was sent to the studio on the orders of the Moscow Commandant. The explanation: an unknown radio station calling itself Moscow Echo was broadcasting from 1:19 A.M. to 3:47 A.M., sharply exaggerating the number of victims and spreading other misinformation.

10:43 A.M. The Moscow City and Regional Soviets call on people to come to the defense of the White House in the evening and to report the movements of military units in the area by telephone.

11:00 A.M. The emergency session of Russia's Supreme Soviet begins, as planned, with a single item on the agenda, "On the Political Situation in RSFSR Obtaining as a Result of a Coup d'État." The session is televised live on the USSR TV channel.

Ruslan Khasbulatov opens the session of Russia's Supreme Soviet with praise for those who opposed the coup and defended the Russian leadership. He says the response to the events by the leaders of Kazakhstan, Ukraine, Moldova, and the republics in the Caucasus was somewhat late in coming. He thanks the leaders of countries in the West and Eastern Europe for their strong support against the coup attempt.

The armored vehicles that have been posted outside the Novosti Information Agency for two days are being withdrawn.

11:09 A.M. Presidential Decree No. 65 "On Insuring the Functioning of Enterprises and Organizations in the Russian Republic" is circulated. The decree is dated August 20.

11:56 A.M. The Moscow city government declares the curfew introduced the previous day to be illegal and demands the immediate withdrawal of troops beyond the city limits. Soon after, the Commander of the Moscow Region Military District, Colonel General Nikolai Kalinin, makes the following statement: "Respected Muscovites! The past twenty-four hours have demonstrated the unsuitability of continuing the curfew in the capital city. Taking into account the sociopolitical situation in Moscow, I have decided to discontinue the curfew beginning August 21."

11:00–12:00 Members of the Emergency Committee arrive at the Ministry of Defense to convince Yazov to rescind his order to withdraw the troops from Moscow. Yazov refuses and suggests that they all go to see Gorbachev in the Crimea.

12:00 noon. Yeltsin's Press Secretary, Pavel Voshchanov, reports that an agreement has been reached with Kriuchkov that the Russian Republic leadership will go to Foros to meet with Gorbachev.

Deputy General Secretary of the CPSU Ivashko tries to contact Yanaev to learn the whereabouts of the CPSU General Secretary Gorbachev.

12:30 P.M. Russian Defense Minister Kobets has confirmed to a reporter that Kriuchkov's order to attack the White House does indeed exist.

12:55 P.M. Yeltsin announces at the emergency session of the Russian Supreme Soviet that KGB chief Kriuchkov should be arriving there at one o'clock. He again calls the coup unconstitutional and refers to two previous attempts at a coup from the right. He requests that Western leaders attempt to contact Gorbachev who is still being held in the Crimea.

1:20 P.M. In his speech to the emergency session of the RSFSR Supreme Soviet, Khasbulatov outlines the reasons for the coup, the chief among them, the desire of the "reactionary forces to torpedo the Union Treaty." He expresses indignation about the coverage of events provided by the newspapers *Pravda* and *Sovetskaia Rossiia* and Soviet TV. He recommends the immediate transfer of these media organs to the authority of the RSFSR government.

1:31 P.M. The Russian Supreme Soviet authorizes Russian Prime Minister Silaev and Russian Vice President Rutskoi to accompany KGB chief Kriuchkov and medical experts to reach Gorbachev and confirm that he is both alive and in good health.

The session takes a recess during which time it is learned that Kriuchkov who, it is suspected, gave the orders to storm the White House, will not be appearing.

1:53 P.M. Yeltsin has announced that the members of the Emergency Committee are headed toward Vnukovo Airport in Moscow. He recommends the authorization of their detention at the airport.

2:00 P.M. Kazakhstan President Nursultan Nazarbaev resigns from the CPSU Central Committee Politburo, stating as his reason the fact that the Central Committee Secretariat supported the coup by attempting to force regional Party organizations to collaborate with the Emergency Committee.

2:12 P.M. Ruslan Khasbulatov reports that two officials of the KGB came to the White House and requested that the live TV broadcast of the Russian Supreme Soviet session be terminated. The broadcast continues uninterrupted.

2:18 P.M. The plane carrying several members of the Emergency Committee (Kriuchkov, Baklanov, Tiziakov and Yazov), along with Lukianov, Ivashko and the commander of the presidential guard, Plekhanov, takes off for the Crimea from the Vnukovo–2 Airport before a unit of Russia's MVD forces arrives there to arrest them.

2:20 P.M. Officials of the Moscow city government and the military conclude negotiations on the removal of troops from the city.

2:30 P.M. Radio Russia resumes broadcasting from its regular studios.

2:55 P.M. Commander of the Moscow Military District Colonel General Nikolai Kalinin announces that earlier in the morning the Defense Ministry Collegium met, in the absence of Dmitrii Yazov, and decided to rescind the curfew in Moscow and to withdraw the troops from the capital and return them to their permanent bases.

3:12 P.M. Sources at the Scientific-Industrial Union report that Arkadii Volskii spoke with President Gorbachev by phone today and that the President was in good health. [Gorbachev's communications lines were not restored until after 4:15 P.M.]

3:15 P.M. According to the Russian Information Agency, the Chairman of Ukraine's Supreme Soviet, Leonid Kravchuk, informed Lukianov in a telephone conversation that if the state of emergency were to be introduced in Ukraine, mass protests and disturbances would be likely and that he, Kravchuk, would not try to dissuade people from taking part in them.

4:00 P.M. The evening edition of *Izvestiia* goes on sale with a banner headline, "Reaction Has Failed."

4:08 P.M. The presidential plane carrying members of the Emergency Committee, Lukianov, Ivashko, and others lands at the Belbek Military Airport in the Crimea. Two government limousines whisk the passengers off to Gorbachev's dacha in Foros. As soon as they arrive, Gorbachev's personal guard puts them under arrest. Gorbachev refuses to see them until his communications are restored; after they are restored, he refuses to see them until the arrival of the RSFSR government delegation.

Gorbachev's first phone call is to Yeltsin, followed by calls to the leaders of other republics, Chief of the General Staff Moiseev, and the Kremlin Commandant.

4:14 P.M. Seven members of the State Emergency Committee are reported to be under arrest. Rumors circulate that the USSR Defense Minister Yazov has committed suicide [this proves incorrect].

4:30 P.M. Aleksandr Dzasokhov, member of the CPSU Politburo and a Secretary of the Central Committee, holds a press conference and declares that "the use of emergency powers by whatever political force is inadmissible.

4:52 P.M. A plane carrying Ivan Silaev, Aleksandr Rutskoi, two members of Gorbachev's Security Council, Vadim Bakatin, Yevgenii Primakov, ten People's Deputies of the RSFSR, and 36 militia officers, armed with submachine guns, takes off from Vnukovo–2 Airport for Foros.

4:56 P.M. Khasbulatov reports that the plane carrying members of the State Emergency Committee has landed in the Crimea. The plane carrying Silaev, Rutskoi, and others is en route.

A meeting between Yeltsin and the Chief of the General Staff of the USSR Armed Forces Moiseev has been scheduled for the evening.

A resolution is adopted by the Presidium of the USSR Supreme Soviet calling the coup unconstitutional.

5:05 P.M. The collegium of the USSR Ministry of Defense indicates that all troops have been withdrawn from Moscow.

5:12 P.M. According to the poll conducted on August 20 by the All-Union Center for the Study of Public Opinion, out of the 4,567 people surveyed from different regions of the USSR, 20 percent supported the Emergency Committee and 62 percent considered its actions illegal. In Russia and Kazakhstan, the figures were 23 and 57 percent, respectively; in Ukraine, 14 percent were for the Emergency Committee and 72 percent against.

5:30 P.M. An avalanche of press conferences begins with state officials and other representatives hastening to declare their respect for the elected authorities and to repudiate the actions of the coup leaders. At his press conference, the USSR Minister of Foreign Affairs Aleksandr Bessmertnykh explains that he was ill until today.

5:36 P.M. An emergency session of the Moscow City Soviet is scheduled for 10:00 A.M. Thursday morning to discuss the political situation in Moscow.

5:53 P.M. President Nazarbaev of Kazakhstan reports that he has just had a telephone conversation with Gorbachev. The Soviet President is still under the protection of his thirty KGB guards. Members of the Emergency Committee are at the dacha in Foros seeking an audience with the President. Nazarbaev urged Gorbachev not to negotiate with the coup leaders and to await the delegation arriving from Moscow.

6:08 P.M. The Presidium of the Moscow City Soviet proclaims the funeral day of those killed to be an official day of mourning. In addition to the three fatalities, there were four others wounded by gunfire.

6:22 P.M. A presidential aide, Georgii Shakhnazarov, reports that it is not known when Gorbachev will return to Moscow to resume his duties, but that members of the State Emergency Committee will be removed from their posts. He refuses to say whether they will be prosecuted.

6:30 P.M. The landing strip at the Belbek Military Airport near Gorbachev's dacha in the Crimea is blocked off, reportedly on Kriuchkov's order. The plane carrying the RSFSR delegation may have to land in Simferopol, which is five hours' drive from Gorbachev dacha in Foros.

6:36 P.M. Departments of the USSR Ministry of Internal Affairs and the KGB in charge of Moscow and the Moscow region have been transferred to Russia's jurisdiction.

6:45 P.M. After contacting by telephone the plane carrying the RSFSR delegation, Gorbachev orders the Chief of the USSR General Staff Moiseev to clear the landing strip at Belbek. The order is carried out at once.

7:02 P.M. Troops leave the radio and television centers occupied earlier in the day in Lithuania and the telephone communications center seized in Vilnius two days earlier.

7:14 P.M. Arkadii Volskii (member of CPSU Central Committee) has called on the Central Committee to condemn the coup in order to free the Party from any suspicion concerning its involvement in the events.

7:16 P.M. The plane carrying the RSFSR government delegation lands at Belbek, and the passengers, including Silaev, Rutskoi, Primakov, and Bakatin, are soon greeted by the Gorbachevs. Rutskoi recalled: "It was clear from the looks of Gorbachev and Raisa Maksimovna that what had taken place was not a show, that they had indeed been isolated and psychologically were ready for any eventuality."

Before leaving for Moscow, Gorbachev meets with Lukianov and Ivashko. He calls Lukianov "traitor!"

8:00 P.M. President Gorbachev is expected to be arriving in Moscow from Simferopol later tonight.

8:11 P.M. Russian Defense Minister Kobets issues an address to Muscovites praising their efforts and calls for calm to expedite the removal of troops from Moscow.

8:26 P.M. The Russian parliament is now in recess until the following day. A crowd of people still remains gathered outside the White House and several thousand decide to spend the night there, keeping vigil. The barricades are being cleared away but one remains as a symbolic reminder of Moscow's determination.

Debris has been cleared from Smolensk Square where people were crushed by tanks, but the overturned trolleycars still block traffic. The withdrawal of troops continues.

9:05 P.M. The evening news program "Vremia" broadcasts a brief statement issued by Soviet President Gorbachev. He stresses that he is fully in command of the situation. He will return to Moscow in a few hours.

9:30 P.M. Yeltsin issues "Demands of the President of the RSFSR to the Organizers of the Anti-Constitutional Putsch" calling for an end to all anticonstitutional actions by 10:00 P.M. It is addressed to Yanaev, Baklanov, Kriuchkov, Pavlov, Pugo, Starodubtsev, Tiziakov, and Yazov.

10:00 P.M. Yeltsin has issued Presidential Decree No. 69 "On the Mass Media in the Russian Republic," affirming press freedom and transferring Gosteleradio installations on Russia's territory to Russia's jurisdiction.

Yeltsin has issued Presidential Decree No. 70 removing a number of chairmen from their posts on the executive committees of Soviets of People's Deputies in the Russian Republic because of their collaboration with the Emergency Committee.

10:39 P.M. Gorbachev is expected to arrive in Moscow from the Crimea around midnight. He may hold a press conference after his arrival.

10:49 P.M. At a press conference (held earlier in the day), First Deputy Prime Minister of the USSR Vladimir Shcherbakov attempts to explain the inactivity of the Council of Ministers during the coup. He states that the Presidium of the Council of Ministers, which met earlier, has discussed the issue of the Cabinet's resignation but decided against it. He also reports that Valentin Pavlov's condition is poor and that the Soviet Prime Minister knew nothing ahead of time about the plans for the coup.

11:00–12:00 In Leningrad, the City Soviet decides to work through the night and keep security forces posted around the building.

12:00 Midnight. The presidential plane carrying the Gorbachevs, the members of the RSFSR government delegation, and Kriuchkov (the other members of the Emergency Committee are on a separate plane) takes off from the Belbek Military Airport for Moscow.

At around 2 A.M., the TU–134 presidential plane lands in Moscow.

Index of Personal Names

About the Editors

Victoria E. Bonnell, Professor of Sociology at the University of California at Berkeley, has written about Russian history, society, and politics. Her books include a study of Russia's prerevolutionary labor and revolutionary movements, an edited volume on Russian workers under the tsarist regime, and a forthcoming work on political iconography in Soviet propaganda art. She has visited Russia many times over the past twenty-three years and has been a close observer of the Russian scene.

Ann Cooper worked as a journalist in Moscow from December 1986 through September 1991. She opened National Public Radio's bureau in the Soviet capital in 1987 and served as NPR bureau chief for the next four and a half years. She also contributed articles to the *New York Times* on politics and change in the Soviet Union. Ms. Cooper worked previously for *National Journal, The Baltimore Sun, Congressional Quarterly*, and *The Louisville Courier-Journal*. She is currently NPR's correspondent in South Africa.

Gregory Freidin, Professor of Russian Literature and the Humanities at Stanford University, is a writer and commentator on Russian culture and politics. The author of a critical biography of Osip Mandelstam, he is completing a book about Isaac Babel and his reception in Russia and the United States. His articles on contemporary Russian politics and cultural life have appeared in many journals. He returns frequently to Moscow, where he lived before emigrating to the United States in 1971.